Selected Papers of David Wechsler

DAVID WECHSLER

SELECTED PAPERS
OF DAVID WECHSLER

With Introductory Material by

ALLEN J. EDWARDS

Department of Psychology
Southwest Missouri State University
Springfield, Missouri

ACADEMIC PRESS   *1974*   *New York and London*
A Subsidiary of Harcourt Brace Jovanovich, Publishers

ACADEMIC PRESS, INC.
111 Fifth Avenue, New York, New York 10003

United Kingdom Edition published by
ACADEMIC PRESS, INC. (LONDON) LTD.
24/28 Oval Road, London NW1

Library of Congress Cataloging in Publication Data

Wechsler, David, Date
        The collected papers of David Wechsler.

        1.   Intellect—Addresses, essays, lectures.
2.   Mental tests—Addresses, essays, lectures.
3.   Emotions—Addresses, essays, lectures.   I.   Edwards,
Allen Jack, Date   II.   Title.
BF431.W348   153'.08   73-9450
ISBN 0-12-741250-6

Contents

PART III

PART IV

Contents

PART VII

PART VIII

PART IX

PART X

PART XI

PART I

INTRODUCTION

Psychology is concerned with many aspects of human behavior. This is apparent from the large number of divisions within the American Psychological Association. No one individual has the energy, time, or competence to be equally informed and to contribute to all of these. Interests dictate that most psychologists select an area, or at best a few related ones, and make their contributions of whatever type and degree. Within each of these, there are some who establish a justified reputation as leader—their work serves as impetus to many others.

At the same time, there is the total field of psychology, and the few who serve with such distinction in various areas that they are recognized by members in the field. More important than this, though, are those psychologists who influence society by their works, and who reflect a major concern for man and mankind.

If one were to choose the one area of psychology which is most representative of concerted effort and practical meaning, surely the measurement of intelligence and its implications would be foremost. The names of contributors—Binet, Terman, Thorndike, Spearman, Thurstone—"hang together" in their diversity in a fashion unlike that of any other area. In our generation, their peer is found in David Wechsler.

But the contributions of Wechsler are not merely recent. He has involved himself wholeheartedly in the field of psychology since World War I, and in the area of mental measurement almost as long. His energies and devotion are most commonly recognized in the scales bearing his name. The utility and importance of these works are obvious. Underlying these are the assumptions, speculations, hypotheses, and theories which reflect the man's mental depth. These may be even more important since they may be used for future developments and direction by others. Tests, in one sense, are dated and obsolete at the time of publication, no matter how useful for immediate, practical problems. Ideas are only as dated as the mental depth of the individual.

Publication is an important criterion by which an academician and scientist may be judged. It is here that he exposes himself most concretely and definitely. In the fixed world of print, there is no refuge. Every person who can read may be judge, critic, and interpreter. The major figures in psychology have earned their positions both by what they write and the extent. Frequently, they show productive careers over many years and in a diversity of topics. In this sense, David Wechsler must be awarded a foremost place in the field of psychology to accord with his distinctive place in mental measurement.

The fullest measure of a man is his social responsibility. When a man brings his mind to bear on social problems and devotes his energies to their understanding and amelioration, he has contributed a great measure to society and his own self-actualization. Even here, David Wechsler assumes his place. There is the obvious concern and dedication of his years at Bellevue Psychiatric Hospital. There is the acknowledged utility of his scales which offer psychometric support for decisions on type and extent of psychological problems. Consequently, these may suggest elements of treatment. Yet, really, "Chief Psychologist" may only represent a job, and test scores are no more than statistical expressions. More definitive measures of social responsibility are needed, subtle though they may be. The writings included in this book help serve such a purpose. In addition to picturing the development of Wechsler as psychometrician on the one hand and psychologist on the other, they also afford glimpses into the humanity of the man.

Perhaps the single best instance of this is in the address "Intelligence in a Changing World." Previously unpublished, this paper synthesizes views that are not new. Indeed, one could read the various editions of *The Measurement of Adult Intelligence* and find much that makes the ideas in this address predictable. In the same way, excerpts could be cited from several published papers included here. In the first presentation concerned with the range of human capacities published in *Scientific Monthly* in 1930, Wechsler presents not facts alone, but implications. In part, he says:

> Perhaps an even more vital implication is the one that bears on the current beliefs as regards racial differences. Scattered studies, especially in this country, have given rise to the belief in the existence of varying degrees of superiority and inferiority among different national groups. What these studies have revealed are certain measurable trait or capacity differences, but those who have made use of them have almost altogether failed to appraise the significance of these differences. For certain purposes it may be useful to know that one group attains an average intelligence quotient of 87 and another of 92, but from a social point of view, even more important is it to evaluate what such differences mean. It is important, for instance, when you are grading school children, but practically negligible when you are comparing human beings. . . .

Or, in another view, summarizing his ideas on artificial intelligence or machine thinking, Wechsler says:

> It is probable that as time goes on the machines will progressively take over much of the "mental" work now done by human beings. This, in my opinion, is to be regretted not so much because it may throw people out of jobs (new ones can and undoubtedly will be created for them), but more important because it will condemn most human beings to kinds of work that have little human dignity.

The citations could continue, but perhaps are better left for the reader to discover.

In discussing the varied definitions of intelligence, Wechsler ("Intelligence in a Changing World") points to the common denominator: ". . . the relative ability of the individual to perceive, to understand and to deal with the world around him." In this context, he goes on to say:

> . . . The really crucial term is the word understand, understand in the sense of not only an awareness of the logic of a situation, but of related moral and social values as well. . . .

This book presents selected writings of an intelligent man.

The first quarter of this century in the United States was a period of developmental activity for the field of psychology and for the mental test movement in particular. Influences from England and Germany were most heavy, but the French psychologists exerted a continuing weight as well. It was during this time that David Wechsler received a Masters Degree at Columbia University where his major advisor was R. S. Woodworth. During this period, he was also privileged to study with J. McKeen Cattell, E. L. Thorndike, and Thomas Hunt Morgan. Primary emphasis in his training was on experimental psychology, an interest followed in research after graduation. His doctoral dissertation in 1925 also was based in experimental psychology. Later, in several instances, he designed necessary "hardware" to derive data to test hypotheses generated by the problem studied. This background assumes importance for it imbues Wechsler with an attitude not often found in the clinician.

His interest in clinical conditions was aroused during his master's program and was reflected in his master's thesis. The principal subject matter of the thesis dealt with the prosaic and conventional matter of retention, but it was applied to Korsakoff's psychosis. The study was original and important enough so that it was published in *Psychiatric Bulletin* in 1917, was recognized as a basic study in the field for a number of years, and is still referred to in the literature.

Wechsler entered the army a few months after graduation from Columbia and was assigned as a psychologist at the Army Military School and at Camp Logan, Texas. This experience gave him contact with various mental examinations, both of a group and individual nature. He was personally involved in the administration of the Army Alpha and Beta tests, the Stanford–Binet 1916 Revision, the Yerkes Point Scale, and the Army Performance Test. A number of inductees had shown the ability to make adequate adjustment in their civilian lives, holding jobs and being accepted by their peers as competent, normal individuals. These same men, upon induction into the military, repeatedly failed on the kinds of standardized tests used to test intellectual ability. This divergence in test performance as compared with environmental coping suggested to Wechsler that there must be some limitation in the commonly accepted definitions of intelligence of that day with consequent effects on measures devised. His experience during that time and in years following suggested that a broader definition was needed, and that measures which relied upon intellectual abilities as the total assessment of intelligence were limiting and limited.

Further opportunities for exposure to the leading psychologists of the day were provided Wechsler while still in the Army. He was assigned to the University of London as an Army student, and there worked with both Spearman and Karl Pearson. Each of these men had influence on his development, sharpening his ideas and offering new possibilities for incorporation into his psychological perceptions. Spearman was influential in terms of his concept of intelligence, particularly with the idea of G. Later, Wechsler decided that Spearman's bi-factor theory was not a sufficient explanation of intelligence, largely because of the influence of Truman Kelley and L. L. Thurstone. Yet the concept of G has remained a central feature of his position. With further clinical experience, Wechsler eventually concluded that intelligence must be some effect and not a cause. The central role of personality, of which intelligence is a part, is the eventual resolution accepted by him.

Pearson brought to Wechsler's attention the procedures of correlational methods, and he realized their potential application in the field of mental measurement. Such techniques allowed the analysis and interpretation of data in a fashion which had been impossible before. Relationships among variables could now be assessed with some attention to relative roles of each.

In the two-year period between the ages of twenty-one and twenty-three, David Wechsler completed and published a master's thesis, and had the benefit of exposure to Cattell, Thorndike, and Morgan, as well as Woodworth, at Columbia. He had previous extensive exposure to and training with the then-developing intelligence tests, both group and individual. He also had the privilege of association and study with both Carl Spearman and Karl Pearson. From such a beginning, one might expect great developments. The only question remaining is which directions will be taken and what will be the overall effects on the future development of the man.

David Wechsler was discharged from the U. S. Army in August, 1919. He was immediately offered a fellowship to a French university of his choice, provided by the Society of American Fellowships and French Universities. The honor and opportunity were too great not to accept, and he attended the University of Paris during the course of the next two years. Part of his work was done under Henri Piéron at the Écoles des Hautes Études. At the same time, he had the opportunity to work with Louis Lapique at the Sorbonne in his physiology laboratory. Research was conducted on the psychogalvanic reflex, the basis for his Ph.D. dissertation at Columbia. This dissertation was published under the title "Measurement of Emotional Reactions" in this country in 1925. As with his master's thesis on retention in persons showing Korsakoff's psychosis, the doctoral work on the psychogalvanic reflex was unique in this country and served as a source for investigators for a number of years. Wechsler conducted further research on his own, including "On the Specificity of Emotional Reactions" published in 1925. As a result of his research in this area, he concluded that emotional reactions were primarily specific in nature, a conclusion which has been supported and documented by other researchers. Wechsler has drawn the same conclusion about the nature of creativity. Thus, he accepts the position that there is no general capacity that influences creative effort, that it is more specific to areas of accomplishment. Wechsler identifies himself more with Poincaré, the French philosopher and mathematician in this regard. In his position on the psychogalvanic reflex and emotional reactions, Wechsler demonstrates some early evidence for the presence of nonintellective factors which may influence intellectual effort, which are a part of the global concept of personality, and yet are not a part of intelligence. His position on creativity suggests somewhat the same role for talents as they may be expressed.

Wechsler returned to this country in 1922, and despite the promise already demonstrated, found the jobs available to be minuscule. Cattell had founded the Psychological Corporation by this time, and Wechsler visited his former mentor. Cattell expressed the belief that psychology as a profession needed an outlet such as the Psychological Corporation in order to develop more fully. The principal motive was not to acquire profit, but to offer a professional service. Being "at large" at the moment, Wechsler was allowed to try his hand at consultation and sales, on a share and share alike basis. He was visited one day by a reporter from the New York *World*. The reporter brought with him a burning question. Is there a difference in the intelligence of men and women? With unusual business acumen, at least according to Wechsler himself, he asked the reporter why not attempt to find out. The editor of the Sunday *World* agreed to finance the project and, for the next two weeks or so, psychologist and reporter cooperated in a data collection endeavor.

At the time, Ziegfeld's shows were most popular, with their emphasis on glorification of the American woman. It was to this group that Wechsler took the reporter, and to whom he administered some of the subtests of the Army Alpha. One must realize that many of the women in Ziegfeld's shows were college students and graduates rather than the chorus girl level generally associated with burlesque houses. As a result, Wechsler had chosen a biased sample, though he was aware of that fact. Indeed, the results were sensational and led to publication in the *World* that probably would not have occurred if a different group had been selected.

As one might expect, the women tested by Wechsler showed Army Alpha scores equal to or better than Columbia freshmen. The reporter found this grist for his mill indeed, the article was published, and both Wechsler and the Psychological Corporation received a small but welcomed remuneration.

It was also at this time that Wechsler devised the series of tests for the Yellow Cab Company in Pittsburg published in 1926 in the *Journal of Personnnel Research* under the title "Tests for Taxi Cab Drivers." Items designed to measure mental alertness and general intelligence were included as written examinations, but Wechsler also devised some mechanical measures for reaction time, alertness of attention, and a carefulness factor. These devices were his own creation.

For a man who had found himself in a state of indecision and had used that experience as the basis for an article ("Quelques Remarques sur la Psychopathologie de L'Indécision," 1922) decisive actions in this country had occurred indeed. Given a task, he accepted the challenge with initiative and verve, traits which continue throughout his life.

Before long, Wechsler was offered and accepted the position as Psychologist in the newly created Bureau of Child Guidance in New York. This bureau was one of a demonstration type which had been financed by the Commonwealth Foundation to serve as a model. Local communities in which these bureaus were established, were later to assume the financial burden for their continuation if they proved successful. Wechsler prepared himself for the responsibilities of this new position by working with H. L. Wells at the Psychopathic Hospital in Boston and attending a series of conferences offered by Healy and Bronner. He was privileged to have as his director of the New York Bureau of Child Guidance a most eminent psychiatrist, Dr. Bernard Glueck. Glueck was committed to the concept of the team approach in diagnosis and evaluation. As a result, each staffing included reports not only from psychiatrists but from psychologists and social workers as well. In this setting, Wechsler was responsible for administration of standardized intelligence, personality, and educational achievement tests. This experience, and the conclusions and implications which might be drawn from the data, proved very useful for his work later as Chief Psychologist at Bellevue Psychiatric Hospital. It was during this period that he conducted the study which resulted in the publication "On the Influence of Education on Intelligence as Measured by the Binet–Simon Tests" (1926). His interest in experimental psychology remained, however, for during the same year he published "An Apparatus for Measuring Reaction Time without a Chronoscope" as well as the article dealing with tests for taxi cab drivers.

From 1925 until 1932, Wechsler entered private practice as a clinical psychologist. Other positions were held by him during this time as well, including his efforts as Acting Secretary of the Psychological Corporation. He published, with Harold Jones, two articles in the *American Journal of Psychology* in 1928. The first of these was "A Study of Emotional Specificity" and the second "Galvanometric Techniques in Studies of Association." In the following year, he joined with R. G. Freeman, Jr., in the publication of a series of studies on chronaxie in children. This threshold measure of muscle nerve responsiveness to electrical stimulation had begun for Wechsler while studying with Lapique, and excited considerable interest in this country for several years. A followup article was published with Freeman in 1932 (''Note on the Correlation between Chronaxie and Reaction Time''). Wechsler's continuing interest in the psychogalvanic reflex and galvanometric technique found expression in an article published with Crabbs and Freeman, entitled ''Galvanic Responses of Preschool Children,'' published in 1930 in the *Journal of Genetic Psychology*.

In the almost 15 years since completing his master's degree at Columbia and 5 years since receiving his doctorate, most of Wechsler's efforts may be viewed as those of the experimentalist. Certainly, there had been the publication of ''On the Influence of Education on Intelligence as Measured by the Binet–Simon Tests'' and the central feature of emotionality in several studies, but the primary emphasis even here was on experimental methodology and reporting. The picture is of David Wechsler as experimental psychologist, and though this picture remains directly to some extent in several future publications and subtly in all his work, he publishes an article in 1930 that widens the scope of his interests and influences the nature of future contributions to the field of psychology. This article was entitled ''The Range of Human Capacities.''

The central theme of this article deals with the comparative similarities among men even with all our diversities. Of course, there are the few rare exceptions which are so outstanding as to bring our attention to their novelty. Wechsler cites specifically the instances of Einstein, Pasteur, and Shakespeare. But he also points out that Cattell had observed earlier that the range of mental abilities, at least as measured at that time, were restricted roughly to a ratio of one to two. This fact became the basis for the study published in the *Scientific Monthly* in 1930 and followed by a statistical rationale for analysis published in *Psychological Review* in 1932 and entitled ''On the Limits of Human Variability.'' Indeed, the issues seemed of such central importance and interest to Wechsler that he persued the topic and published in 1935 a book that he considers his major work: *The Range of Human Capacities*. This book was the source in which he pulled together available data on human traits and abilities for which quantitative data existed. His analysis disclosed that the range of very nearly all traits, including the intellectual ones, was fairly small. Interestingly, he concluded that there is a point in age at which maximum contributions may be made, a statement preceding the work of Lehman by several years. An updated version of Wechsler's book was published in 1952, in an edition which was reissued in 1971.

One might wonder why Wechsler would consider this particular work his major contribution in the face of experimental contributions of pronounced significance in his earlier professional life, the development of the scales bearing his name, the publications revolving around clinical uses of tests, and the various editions of *The Measurement of Adult Intelligence*. Yet a close examination of *The Range of Human Capacities* indicates that it may indeed be the single most significant contribution. For one thing, it is a more comprehensive work than any other by Wechsler, allowing the inclusion of a variety of traits of human beings contributing to the total functioning of the individual. For another thing, it represents a unique contribution anticipating research which was to follow, and substantiate Wechsler's position. For a third reason, it is a work which is less susceptible to individual interpretation (or misinterpretation) that is possible, and perhaps necessary, with clinical contributions. And finally, it holds the possibility for generating controlled experimentation and interpreting the nature and role of man in his society that is not found in the comprehensive sense in any other single contribution.

Wechsler joined Bellevue Psychiatric Hospital as Chief Psychologist in 1932. This began the period of his life most recognized by psychologists in current society. Already, he had published an article applying Freud's original three-stage description of psychosexual development to the significance of fingernail biting in children ("Incidence and Significance of Fingernail Biting in Children," 1931). He concluded from his observations that nail biting did not begin until about age 3 but showed a gradual and increasing rise until about age 12 in girls and 14 in boys with a marked increase in frequency to about age 14 for girls and about age 16 for boys. He compared these with the psychosexual developmental periods presented by Freud. Rather than place pathological significance on the incidence of nail biting, however, he reports that it is so common as to represent little more than a habit, but a habit which may be symptomatic of some more deep-seated problem. In the best clinical sense, then, he called for analysis of causation and not treatment of the symptom directly.

In conjunction with Schilder, Wechsler surveyed a group of children with a questionnaire sampling children's reactions to varied questions about death ("Attitudes of Children Toward Death," 1934). In addition, they employed eight pictures which allowed verbal reactions by the child. Finally, a toy doll was forcibly struck by the experimenter so that it fell and the child's reaction was sought. Case study material is reported and both general and specific conclusions drawn.

During the same period, he contributed a chapter on general intelligence and its role in the psychoneuroses for *The Psychoneuroses* by Israel S. Wechsler, David's brother and an eminent physician. He draws comparisons with the general population, and points to some specific disabilities that accompany psychoneuroses.

A significant paper was presented at the American Psychological Association convention in 1934 and later published in the *Psychiatric Quarterly* ("The Concept of Mental Deficiency in Theory and Practice," 1935). He takes the position that mental deficiency is not an entity, and certainly there is no group called "mental deficients" who are defined along any scientific lines. The principal component in correct application of the term revolves around the fact that the individual is incapable of applying whatever abilities he may possess of an intellectual type to concrete life situations. This article includes references then to the possibility that there is not only an intellectual defective, but also a social and emotional or moral defective.

Wechsler continued writing and research of an experimental type as well. Again with Schilder, he published "The Illusion of the Oblique Intercept" in the *Journal of Experimental Psychology* in 1936. This article fits well with a number of other articles on visual illusions found in the literature.

He concerned himself with some of the practical problems found in the educational setting. Included here is a study of reversal errors found in reading. A survey of the literature on reading errors indicated a tendency to include a variety of instances under the term "reversals." Wechsler and Pignatelli present a much more systematic basis for analyzing types of errors, based primarily upon the degree of axial rotation of letters ("Reversal Errors in Reading: Phenomena of Axial Rotation," 1937). Wechsler returns to this problem in 1964, devising a test to disclose kinds of errors which young children make in their perception of asymetric symbols ("Problems of Axial Rotation in Reading Disability," 1964). A survey of contemporary books on reading discloses that the field has not progressed beyond the position disclosed in the survey taken in 1937.

The first edition of *The Measurement of Adult Intelligence* was published in 1939. Wechsler had begun the work without support, had built the instrument, and standardized it completely by the time it came to the attention of the publishers. At the time, George Bennett was associated with the Psychological Corporation, heard of the work by Wechsler on his Bellevue Scale, and asked for the opportunity to see the test. He was much impressed, and the Psychological Corporation printed the edition as it stood. This began a long and very satisfactory association not only with the test publisher, but with the individuals—among them Seashore, Doppelt, Wesman, and Ricks—who have been associated with the firm throughout the years.

Wechsler actually began work on the Scale which was to bear the name of Bellevue Hospital before he became Chief Psychologist in 1932. With his appointment as Chief Psychologist, a problem of adult testing already recognized by him became more immediate and intense. Frequently, individuals referred to Bellevue presented problems for testing in that they might be multilingual and certainly offered diverse kinds of backgrounds and problems. Added to these were the differences in socioeconomic level, and consequently educational level, and the wide age range of individuals. No suitable adult scale was available and the children's scales, principally the Stanford-Binet revision, were employed in such situations even though they were recognized as being inappropriate. The inadequacies of the mental age as a score with adults had already been recognized and pointed out by Wechsler. Use of such a test score supplied a set of inappropriate norms for adult comparisons.

Extensive data had been published by this time from the use of the Army

Alpha in World War I. It was apparent from the data that there was a clear and consistent decline in score with age. Such data had been ignored or sloughed over by most psychologists of the day, but Wechsler recognized the importance of the finding and its application to measurement of adult intelligence. The development of both age and point scales with children had indicated the importance of chronological age in establishing norms. Wechsler realized that a similar account must occur in an adult scale. Estimating absolute level of ability was a practical concern, but at least of equal importance was being able to state relative levels of ability. Older persons may appear less competent than younger ones when performance is compared directly on intellectual tasks. Within his own age group, however, the level of performance may represent the same relative position for both the 60-year-old and the 25-year-old. The deviation I.Q. expresses such a relative ranking.

In addition to the practical issues such as those cited of relationships to age, it was necessary as well to employ perspective on the nature of intelligence so that an adequate definition might be stated. As mentioned earlier, Wechsler had concluded some limitations existed in the most frequently accepted definitions of intelligence as a unitary trait. Even the two-factor theory of Spearman seemed not to be an adequate substitute since its hierarchical nature and eclectic composition ignored the implicit importance of personality. As a result, Wechsler proposed a definition which considers the global capacity of the individual as the primary element and the effects of intellectual abilities to act purposefully, to think rationally, and to deal effectively with the environment as outgrowth of this global capacity. Given such a definition, one may hypothesize the interaction of a variety of abilities, only a portion of which may be cognitive in nature. Certainly cognitive abilities such as abstract reasoning, ability to learn, ability to adapt, and ability to solve problems are an important component, but the conative and affective traits of the individual also influence behavior.

The structure of the Bellevue Scale, and the subtests which compose it, reflects the essential elements of this definition. The number of subtests included is somewhat less important than the status that each subtest assumes within the structure. Wechsler decided to allow each subtest to contribute equally to total score. The test user should not assume by this that each subtest is ncessarily equally important. Indeed, Wechsler makes the point that he has accorded equal weights so as to avoid biasing for or against the individual on the basis of primarily verbal or primarily mechanical skills. The content of the test is to act as a medium or language by which the individual can express himself. Some individuals do this better verbally, others by responding to commands, others through manipulation of concrete materials, others by assembling things. Opportunities to demonstrate competence in any or all of these things are available in a test with the structure of the Bellevue and the following Wechsler Scales. It is both most feasible and reasonable to maintain such a structure since global intelligence, according to Wechsler, is multilingual just as is the brain. One may find fault with certain subtests, even advocate substitution of other intellectual abilities in certain instances, but these are relatively minor matters.

The question becomes: Can the psychologist interpret the score in terms of ability to cope with the environment more validly? Under the present structure, the Full Scale I.Q., and the component Verbal and Performance Scale I.Q.s, serve a useful function. Since neither this test nor any other can measure intelligence directly, the task of the test designer is to provide kinds of items which allow global intelligence the opportunities to reflect overt expression of purposeful action, rational thinking, and effective dealing with the environment in each of several different forms. This particular realization and inclusion in the scales by Wechsler is a brilliant addition to test function and theory.

At the same time, the role of the subtest is restricted to some degree by its place in the total structure. Analysis and prediction from subtest performance is limited not alone because of statistical problems reflected in lowered reliability, but by the total design and intent of the scale. Certainly comparisons may be made, and particularly in terms of diagnostic signs proposed by Wechsler, but the necessity for this "method of successive sieves" is essential. To ignore the information implicit in the I.Q.s, on some assumption that they are unnecessary or untrustworthy or biased, and utilize only subtest differences for comparison, may be dangerous for the client and is antithetical to the intent of the scale.

The definition and consequent organization of the Bellevue Scale permits the evaluation of nonintellective factors as well. Just as intellectual abilities as measured are not adequate reflections of general intelligence itself, neither is an evaluation of the intelligence of the individual complete without considering certain affective and conative traits which influence that dimension. Wechsler believes that the nonintellective traits may act to initiate, energize, and influence goal-directed behavior under certain circumstances. In the present day, Wechsler has extended his concept of nonintellective factors to include the capacity of the individual to perceive and to respond to moral, esthetic and social values. This position emphasizes once again the role of personality as the central factor.

Such an extensive position, however, implicit in the definition, was not so evident in the first volume of the *Measurement of Adult Intelligence*. At that time, Wechsler was content to describe general intelligence as a kind of energy which was neither definable nor measurable. Indeed, he stated at that time that "we know intelligence by what it enables us to do;" within this context, the elaborations that continued to the present time are plausible and possible.

It is certain that the Wechsler Bellevue I would have achieved great success in any event. A fortuitous circumstance, though lamentable in many ways, contributed to its success with the outbreak of World War II and the consequent need for intellectual evaluation in many contexts. Psychological and physical problems of war with associated trauma increased the need for reliable and valid measures of intelligence standardized on adults. The Army Wechsler appeared in 1942, and served to good purpose in the specialized areas and with the age groups for which it was most pertinent. A second edition of the *Measurement of Adult Intelligence* had appeared in 1941 and still a third edition in 1944, including much of the information garnered from the use of the Bellevue Scales in World War II. If there had been doubt about the place of David Wechsler in the mental test movement prior to 1939, all doubts were resolved by the demonstrated effectiveness of the Bellevue Scales. There followed the standardization and publication of the WISC, the WAIS, and the WPPSI. But Wechsler's contributions continued in diverse fields and research activities, further adding to his distinction as a psychologist.

The publication of the Bellevue I in 1939 offered the opportunity, indeed demanded, that comparisons be made to the Stanford–Binet. The latter was still the most widely used individual test in clinical as well as educational settings. Wechsler contributed research to questions concerning comparisons between the two scales for clinical use. With Balinsky and Israel, he studied their relative effectiveness in diagnosing mental deficiency, as defined by psychiatric commitment at Bellevue Hospital ("The Relative Effectiveness of the Stanford–Binet and the Bellevue Intelligence Scale in Diagnosing Mental Deficiency," 1939). Additionally, the role of subtests in the Bellevue Scale for diagnostic purposes was considered in a study published in 1941 by Wechsler, Israel, and Balinsky ("Study of the Subtests of the Bellevue Intelligence Scale in Borderline and Mental Defective Cases"). Such studies of the effectiveness of the subtests for diagnostic utility with specific clinical subgroups became increasingly popular with other psychologists. Much of the utility of the Bellevue Scale revolved around the fact that as a point scale it allowed certain kinds of comparisons among subtests. Indeed, some assumptions had been made about such utilization that have since been justified. Certainly one tribute which can be accorded to Wechsler is the fact that in all instances of publications of scales and manuals for the scales he has cautioned against the unwarranted use of subtest analysis due to the relatively low reliabilities of subtests and the problems of comparisons of difference scores.

The publication of the Bellevue again opened public debate on the issue of intellectual decline with age in adulthood. Wechsler analyzed data from several sources ("Intellectual Changes with Age," 1941) as disparate as Galton and Spearman to the testing of army officers during World War I. Some results from use of the Bellevue Scale during World War II to that date were available also. He drew the conclusion that intellectual ability follows the same general decline as physical ability with increasing age. This is an issue still much contested, and one which Wechsler admits finds him at some variance with much of the popular opinion as well as some degree of scientific opinion.

A second, and equally significant finding reported in the 1941 article, was that the types of abilities which make up general intelligence also show some decline, though possibly at different rates. This establishes the position that certain kinds of tests will show greater decline in performance with age than will others. Such an outcome, when demonstrated, should allow the possibility for measurement of mental deterioration and prediction of that deterioration. Wechsler does caution from his results in the same article that his conclusions are based on the measurement of intellectual abilities and that these abilities are only part of that which constitutes intelligence per se. Experience, wisdom, all the nonintellective factors, and other aspects of personality will continue to exert their influences with the result that decline in later age may not be as simplistic or straightforward as it appears from the measures obtained. In more recent times, Wechsler has stated that there is probably some loss of capacity with increasing age that may be compensated for by experience and know-how. The issue remains important, joined, and unresolved.

The fact that his interest continued in other aspects of personality functioning is demonstrated by the publication of "The Effect of Alcohol on Mental Activity" in 1941. This paper reviewed research done on effects of alcohol and makes the point that long-range or permanent effects have not been clearly defined. Data available to him from the Psychiatric Division of Bellevue Hospital made it possible to add a new dimension to such studies by analyzing long-range changes of individuals in subtest performance on the Bellevue. Furthermore, he closes with the point that scientific investigation is needed about the positive effects of alcohol, what alcohol does *for* the individual as well as the many studies which are conducted on its deleterious effects.

A major publication of the war years, major in the sense that it continues as a central feature of attempts to define intelligence, was published in the *Journal of Abnormal and Social Psychology* in 1943. Entitled "Nonintellective Factors in General Intelligence," this article was a direct statement of the limitations existing in currently accepted tests, the role of the nonintellective factors in test performance, and some attempts at defining what such factors might be. Recognition of these factors added dimension to discussions of diagnostic and clinical features which had occurred in the second edition of the *Measurement of Adult Intelligence* (1941).

The publication of the third edition of the *Measurement of Adult Intelligence* in 1944 stands as a major achievement for David Wechsler. The use of the Scale since 1939 in clinical settings buttressed by its extensive use during World War II, with all the resulting data, allowed a volume both complete in its scope and usable to a degree not previously found with any adult scale. Indeed, the content of the third edition was of such a nature that further refinement was not needed. The Bellevue, and its companion Manual, remained critically acclaimed and used until the publication of a newly standardized form known as the Wechsler Adult Intelligence Scale (1955), with its companion volume *The Measurement and Appraisal of Adult Intelligence* (1958). In the field of mental testing, and particularly in terms of the adult population, the 1944 edition of the *Measurement of Adult Intelligence* occupies a unique and distinctive place indeed. The content did not differ greatly from preceding versions. It must be remembered, however, that the 1939 edition represented a single-handed effort, published as Wechsler had built and standardized the scale. This third edition in 1944 became the ''proof of the pudding,'' the indication that despite limitations in standardization and the largely individual cataloging by Wechsler, the Bellevue Scale had validity which would make it the most usable and most used adult scale in the history of the testing movement. The WAIS does represent a considerable improvement, particularly in building the test and standardization. But the WAIS is possible only because of the brilliant effort in the Bellevue and the positive feedback about its qualities.

The 1944 volume also allowed confirming research to be conducted as well as spin-offs in other directions. In this context, for example, in 1945 Wechsler in conjunction with Levi and Oppenheim published a brief article on the clinical use of the mental deterioration index of the Bellevue Scale (''Clinical Use of the Mental Deterioration Index of the Bellevue–Wechsler Scale''). The findings confirmed in certain ways the plausibility of Wechsler's discussion of mental deterioration in Chapter Six of the 1944 edition of the *Measurement of Adult Intelligence,* and the type of predictive information which might be obtained from the ''hold'' and ''don't hold'' subtests.

At the same time, Wechsler continued to propose other measures which might be usable in the clinical setting, but not dependent upon measurement with the Wechsler Bellevue I. In this context, he reverted to the type of task used in his master's thesis dealing with retention and Karsakoff's psychosis. Additional subtests were added so that he developed a standardized memory scale, consisting of seven subtests, allowing the derivation of a memory quotient for adults. Age-related norms were included to permit a quick, objective, and usable appraisal of the memory function in individuals referred to clinic settings (''A Standardized Memory Scale for Clinical Use,'' 1945).

In yet another line, Wechsler published with Hartogs, in 1945, a method of measuring anxiety in an experimental fashion usable in the clinic (''Clinical Measurement of Anxiety''). They took the position that anxiety arises within the personality structure of the individual in terms of his personality integration. This is a contrast to the position that anxiety is a phenomenon, or drive, representative of motivational structures of the individual and directly accessible. To Wechsler and Hartogs, it is more sensible to accept a position that reflects a ''disintegration concept of anxiety.'' They devised methods of measurement, including a mechanical device which might induce a little anxiety in its own right.

Such efforts indicate a continuing interest by Wechsler in more than the immediately beneficial intelligence tests, a continuing subscription to the responsibility of the psychologist to remain active in dealing directly with the kinds of problems needing solutions in the psychological field.

By now, Wechsler was recognized as the prototype of the clinical psychologist in the institutional setting. It is not surprising, therefore, that he discusses the role of the psychologist in the psychiatric hospital ("The Psychologist in a Psychatric Hospital," 1944). The discussion is objective and frank. It includes problems and limitations as well as strengths in the role. There is a discussion, as well, of the type of training which the psychologist should bring with him to the clinic. The personality needed to do an effective job in such a setting is described by Wechsler. Indeed, the tone of the article deals more with the qualities the individual should possess than it does with the immediate rewards in the job. There is good reason for this, for, as Wechsler says,

> . . . This is perhaps a good deal to ask for a position which generally pays less than college teaching, but the requirements are indispensable not only because they are necessary for the personal success of the individual psychologist but for the prestige of psychology itself. In more ways than one the psychologist in the field represents the practical achievements of psychology, and the individual to whom this representation is entrusted should so far as possible be the most capable individual available.

The need for careful and extensive training and the superior qualities required for the psychologist remain today a point of major concern and dedication with Wechsler.

The decade of the fifties brought an opportunity to extend the variety of ideas already proposed by Wechsler, and to verify certain quantitative issues. An auspicious beginning for the decade occurred with the publication of "Cognitive, Conative and Nonintellective Intelligence" in the *American Psychologist* in 1950. A significant feature of the article is the enlargement and extension of the position about the relation of such nonintellective factors to intelligence. Whereas prior emphasis had been upon the residual nature of unaccounted-for variance as reflecting nonintellective factors, Wechsler now says they are more realistically referred to as personality components of general intelligence. Evidence available to him from his own work and others now indicated that conative functions like drive, persistence, will, and perseveration are a part of these nonintellective factors. Temperament also becomes important, reflected in variables such as interest and achievement. With the realization that personality and intelligence are not separate entities, but that intelligence is a part of personality, differentiation and scope of the nonintellective factors can more definitely be specified and studied.

Interest in intellectual development among children was reflected in the publication of the Intelligence Scale for Children in 1949. A matter of concern in all prior scales used with children remained with Wechsler: At what point is maturity reached so that there can be inferred no further incremental changes in performance? Wechsler deals with this problem in "Intellectual Development and Psychological Maturity" published in 1950. Intellectual maturity is defined in the usual operational way as the age level at which significant gains in mean scores on subtests are no longer found. But he extends this to psychological maturity by including other evidences of maturity as well. These he designates both substrate and behavioral in nature. The position becomes a most important one since it allows for establishing not merely a provisional limit, which he assumes to be around age 15, for intellectual maturity, but also for disclosing development of intellectual functioning over the period between ages 5 and 15. As a result, the WISC assumes a unique place in the testing movement because it offers assumptions and procedures quite different from those involved in an age scale and consequently an alternative view of the nature and meaning of intelligence of children. Though the measure has been used primarily for diagnostic purposes in clinical and educational settings, the issue is really not that simple. The WISC may be viewed in its scope and meaning in reference to a reflection of psychological maturity as well as intellectual development.

During this period, Wechsler also expressed his views on the nature and measurement of intelligence in an article dedicated to Piéron. This article was published in *L'Année Psychologique,* the journal founded by Binet. The article is a general one, expressing for a European culture the important ideas which Wechsler has developed over a lifetime.

A second edition of *The Range of Human Capacities* was published in 1952, allowing the application of more current research to ideas proposed as early as 1932. To Wechsler, variability in human traits is not a matter for science alone, but also a concern for human relationships. He believes that such social groupings as education, industry, and politics are influenced by human variability, and particularly involve issues extending into ethical relationships among individuals in such settings.

Science must be concerned in such matters because of the need to establish what Wechsler refers to as "natural constants." The known natural constants in psychology are very small in number. Wechsler says that, indeed, in terms of human capacities, whether or not natural constants exist is a matter largely unexplored. The central problem in psychology is that we have tended to highlight differences and to ignore likenesses. Despite measurement problems, Wechsler believes that it is possible to demonstrate the nature of human variability, and he firmly believes that this variability is much smaller than is usually supposed. The problem of comparative units for various kinds of measures remains a difficult one, so that he restricts himself to units of amounts rather than relative position. When this is done, Wechsler finds that the range of human capacities is indeed quite small. Obviously, differences are of importance in many areas, but the point is well taken that we may have exaggerated their importance.

Inferences are drawn from observations which are more limited than we should like to believe and perhaps even essentially unrelated to the kinds of conclusions which we make. A more scientific approach to the problem of human relationships and human problems, such as that advocated by Wechsler and implicit in this particular work, would be a healthy position in our society today.

The position of Wechsler on the range of human capacities certainly drew attention in a number of spheres. Tribute indeed, and one most pleasing to Wechsler, was the publication of a cartoon in the New York *Herald Tribune* on Sunday, October 4, 1953. Here, two youngsters, called the Duke and Duchess, discuss the implications of Wechsler's book *The Range of Human Capacities*. Fame has indeed occurred when one's technical work is recognized in the funnypapers!

The WAIS was published in 1955. The Manual for administration was published separately from the volume presenting the theoretical issues and implications underlying the scale and describing the use of the test. Yet Wechsler designed the Manual to contain information directly usable by the examiner in understanding the development of the scale and statistical use of scores. As a result, data on standardization, reliability, and standard errors of measurement, and administrative procedures to be followed were included in the Manual. As a separate volume, the *Measurement and Appraisal of Adult Intelligence* was published in 1958. More than an extension of prior volumes dealing with the Bellevue, the work offers to the psychometrician information necessary for interpretation purposes. The clinician who administers the WAIS, but makes little or no reference to the *Measurement and Appraisal of Adult Intelligence* will be a mechanic indeed. In many regards, the fourth edition of the *Measurement and Appraisal of Adult Intelligence* can stand alone. By contrast, the test cannot stand separate and alone from the fourth edition.

During the 1960s, Wechsler continued to be prolific in publication. He added a dimensionality greater than he had accomplished prior to that time. Though his reputation as a psychologist was firmly established, his dedication and responsibility to the field was in no way lessened. Basic issues in how the brain functions as the individual applies his intelligence, including the operations occurring then, were considered and discussed in the New York Academy of Sciences and published as "Intelligence, Quantum Resonance and the Thinking Machine" in 1960. Some comparisons of the processes in intelligent behavior to machine simulation were also made. The issues considered here were further expanded upon in the succeeding talks and publications.

There was the continuing interest in diagnostic procedures with both adults and children. A discussion of measures and their application for psychological diagnosis was included in a chapter for a textbook on clinical neurology by Israel S. Wechsler. An experimental application of the WISC for discriminating schizophrenic and nonschizophrenic children was published in 1965. The matter of memory as it is reflected during the aging process was discussed in 1961. It is in this article that Wechsler restates a principle reflecting his belief in a decline in intelligence with aging. Frequently, the individual shows greater wisdom with age and we are inclined to judge that as being sheer intellectual capacity. Wechsler makes a distinction, and a fair one. As he states: "Wisdom is necessary to make the world go round; intelligence, to make it go forward." The latter contingency is more frequently found with youth than old age.

Concern for the individual and the kinds of social bias which may operate even in a culture as democratic as ours was reflected in a chapter written for a book edited by Berg and Bass and entitled *Conformity and Deviation*. Wechsler points out that throughout man's history there has been a tendency to identify some individuals and families as superior, and consequently to accord their offspring superior position and honor. He discusses this history and makes applications to more current-day uses of the bias. Not only does he include the matter of presumed Aryan superiority in Nazi Germany, but even to more subtle reflections of assumed superiority in social groupings such as clubs or lodges, religious and political divisions, or any kind of socio-economic interest group. The effects may be insidious not only for those subservient to the power group, but even to members of the power group themselves since they are forced to conform to certain standards and values in order to maintain the status of the group.

An address, not published before this volume, he entitles "Intelligence in a Changing World." The address has been given in such diverse places as New York, Tokyo, Jerusalem, and Chicago, and to varied groups. If one were to choose a single statement which reflects both the history of development and the current feelings of David Wechsler, this particular paper might well be the one chosen. It is here that he takes a position defending not only intellectual differences among men, but the extreme importance of intellect in man. The need for understanding, the reflection of intelligence at work, is implicit. The problems facing individuals in a world which is changing as rapidly as ours perhaps have led to a willingness on the part of many individuals in today's society to dismiss intelligence as a significant human characteristic. Certainly, environmental circumstances conspire against the full utilization and development of intellect by a number of individuals. Wechsler has acknowledged this and pointed out the need for correction of social problems in order to allow the full implementation of the intellect of the individual. His position is not inconsistent with his idea that we are more alike than different, but there must be maintained the realization that differences exist in all aspects of personality with their consequent behavioral implications.

This issue is reflected in a more direct manner in a reaction to a policy decided by the New York City school system. In 1964, the issue of bias in the standardization and content of intelligence tests had become so pronounced and so volatile that the decision was made to discontinue the recording of intelligence quotients in pupil's records. The rationale was that intelligence tests reflected a cultural bias against those who came from deprived backgrounds and consequently led to educational decisions detrimental to the individual. Educational leaders resolved, for this reason, to eliminate the use of at least group intelligence tests and to use instead achievement tests. Wechsler responded to the issue and wrote for the New York *Times Magazine* a reaction to and against the policy. Among his points is the one that the primary opposition to intelligence quotients revolves around the way they are interpreted and used. He discusses some of the misinterpretations and misuses of such scores. Most important, however, is his point that the attacks on intelligence tests use the wrong target. He acknowledges the fact that results of intelligence tests reflect bias against disadvantaged children, to both children and adults who come from deprived backgrounds, to various minority groups. However, the intelligence quotient is not the responsible agent. Social conditions are. When these social conditions are corrected, the biasing elements within tests will no longer operate. We will then indeed have a single distribution of ability in all kinds of individuals regardless of color or background, and not overlapping distributions. The point remains, however, that the distribution will still be found.

Honors have been bestowed upon David Wechsler in many ways and forms over the years. He has served as president of the Division of Clinical Psychology of the American Psychological Association, president of the American Psychopathological Society, and as director and vice-president of the American Board of Examiners of Professional Psychology. Various groups have recognized his contributions for specific problems. Typical of such tributes was one accorded by the American Association of Mental Deficiency in May, 1972. The citation includes a single statement summarizing his work quite well:

> . . . David Wechsler has been active as clinician, teacher, researcher, writer, theory builder and test maker, and should anyone ask how he does so many things, one might give the answer attributed to Noel Coward in response to a similar question: "Superbly."

David Wechsler retired as Chief Psychologist at Bellevue Hospital in 1967. Perhaps the word "retired" is not the correct one. Though it is true that he gave up his duties as Chief Psychologist at Bellevue, he has not retired from active participation in matters affecting psychology particularly and mankind in general. He continues to travel, write extensively, lecture to various kinds of groups, and involve himself directly in scientific meetings. The Wechsler Intelligence Scale for Children appears in a new edition in 1974, and this work, as has been true for all scales since the 1939 Wechsler Bellevue I has been largely conducted by Wechsler in association with the Psychological Corporation.

Research interests have not abated. They include such matters as sex differences, not of the superficial types frequently debated in the literature, but more primary, intellectual types. The concept of collective intelligence has caught his attention and absorbed his energy in recent years. What constitutes "memory storage" has kept him writing, speculating, advocating research. He also has interest in what might be called "action at a distance" from the standpoint of tapping directly the mental functions of the individual rather than depending upon verbal communication or implicit signs in terms of facial expressions, attitudes, and the like.

In 1972, Matarazzo completed a fifth and enlarged edition of Wechsler's *Measurement and Appraisal of Adult Intelligence*. The work bears some features of the first four editions. However, it is, in Matarazzo's own words, a significant departure from prior efforts by Wechsler. The work will be of substantial interest and use to the psychologist. At the same time, it will not replace the *Measurement and Appraisal of Adult Intelligence*. Indeed, the psychologist will continue to need direct contact with Wechsler's works to establish and maintain understanding of the Scales and his significant theoretical contributions. The writings included in this volume will serve as one source for that purpose.

PART II

INTRODUCTION

Psychological literature has many instances of research not based on any clearly formulated theory or model. As a result, much of it seems unrelated either to other research or to practical problems. One of the strengths of the mental test movement is that most contributors have operated on some at least crudely formulated notion of implicit processes and outcomes. As a result, there is greater coordination despite the wide diversity of both models and tests.

David Wechsler became involved in the mental test movement during World War I and extended this involvement while a member of the Child Guidance Bureau in New York and as Chief Psychologist at Bellevue Psychiatric Hospital. He brought with him the attitudes and procedures of experimental psychology, plus a growing awareness of what, to him, represented severe limitations in the definitions of intelligence of that day. As a result, he formulated a definition which expressed the character of intelligence and within which he could devise a test consistent with the general statement.

The first selection included here, taken from the new edition of the WISC, succinctly and elegantly summarizes his concept of intelligence. His definition is widely recognized and widely quoted. What is not so frequently understood is the difference between intelligence and intellectual abilities. The second selection is taken from the 1939 publication, *The Measurement of Adult Intelligence*(2).[1] The definition evolved by him over several years was publicly cited here. He discusses the definition further to point to the dichotomy of global capacity (intelligence) and purposeful action, rational thinking and effective dealing with the environment (outcomes reflected from intellectual abilities). Obviously, the latter are all that may be measured, though we may have more pronounced interest in the former. As a result, we draw inferences about the former from our measures of the latter. There is a pitfall: we may define a number of intellectual abilities, crucial to dealing effectively with the environment. But no matter how cleverly done, we may not simply sum the measures of intellectual abilities to determine intelligence. Such a bundle hypothesis is rejected by Wechsler, and he includes his reasons in this selection. Additionally, there is the most important conclusion that: ". . . It would seem that, so far

---

[1]Arabic numerals refer to sequence of selections published herein.

as *general intelligence* is concerned, intellectual ability as such merely enters as a necessary minimum . . . [Italics added]."

The fact that tests do not measure intelligence as such, however defined, is not unique to Wechsler. Binet had made such a pronouncement about the 1905 Scale, and at least lip-service has continued. Such declarations may seem trivial and consequently to be ignored, but the distinction is valid and important. Wechsler indicates, as early as 1939, that there is no problem unless one attempts to equate intelligence with intellectual abilities. He discriminates the two clearly, and has continued to do so in his writings and research since that time. Later, he moves from the position of intelligence as entity to an aspect of personality. The distinction then is even clearer. There would be little quarrel with the position that measures of intellectual abilities, important and useful as they may be, are not equivalent to one's personality. Whether one prefers a "personality" approach or an "intelligence allowing personality" position is the lesser issue. In either event, the role and scope of intellectual abilities assumes the same position. Abilities are pragmatic, transitory in certain respects, invalid and obsolete to some degree. The definition offered by Wechsler reflects the difference clearly. It is consequently a major contribution and a guideline to consideration of other aspects of the "global capacity," however specified.

The use of measures of intellectual abilities, because of the kinds of limitations cited previously, brings problems in accuracy of interpretation and prediction. Regardless of the care in building and standardizing tests, some degree of unaccounted-for variance is found between the predictor and criterion. Test authors considered such residual variance as a source of error which should be controlled (but never really was). David Wechsler brought a more reasonable and beneficial viewpoint to the issue. Residual variance must include something more than mere "error." Indeed, some other aspects of the "global capacity" must be operating within the measurement procedure to influence the score and reduce the correlation between predictor and criterion. Such factors he labelled as nonintellective in nature, and attempted to specify them in at least a general fashion. In 1943, he had sufficient evidence to present his position in systematic form (3).

Nonintellective factors served more than one purpose. First, they could help determine reduction in predictive efficiency for the individual. Second, they could help account for differences among individuals in coping with the environment even though performance on intellectual abilities would not lead to such a prediction. Thus, the psychopath may function much more efficiently in the environment than the neurotic, though performing poorer on tests.

Wechsler conceived these factors as being conative and affective in nature, though only loosely defined in 1943. The position, nevertheless, adds dimension to Wechsler's definition. Use of his scales is also affected, allowing a dimension of interpretation not possible with prior tests.

More explicit discussion and definition followed in 1950 (4). By this time, he has concluded that general intelligence is itself some manifestation of personality. Measurement, however, in most instances, reflected a belief that intelligence is restricted to the intellectual abilities. Psychologists, dealing with problems of adjustment to the environment, could not accept any such limited position. A distinction in concepts is necessary, he states, and he presents means for measurement in this article.

Wechsler has restructured and redefined the role of the nonintellective factors as well by 1950. Prior to this time, the conative and affective factors have been considered nonintellective factors in intelligence. Now, he says, they are more realistically conceived as personality components of general intelligence.

In contemporary times, Wechsler has discussed definitions of intelligence in a book edited by Robert Cancro (5). He makes the important point, first, that despite the divergence in viewpoints which may be expressed, either in a symposium like the one represented in Cancro's book or in various independent sources, there is some implicit agreement that the term "intelligence" has meaning, whether or not this meaning is common to all individuals, it may be used to describe a trait and/or set of behaviors. There will continue to be different definitions of the term, any one of which may be accepted by the individual. Since intelligence is not an entity, in Wechsler's opinion, various behavioral expressions which represent definitions may be acceptable.

Definitions tend to be restricted because they are concerned only with a limited range of traits or abilities. As he points out, though intelligent behavior may utilize the traits or abilities specified, it is also dependent upon the nonintellective factors and the capacity of the individual to apprehend and respond to values of a moral, esthetic and social nature. This last point is an addition by Wechsler, further amending the concept of intelligence as a part of the personality of the individual. General intelligence is many-faceted indeed! It is not intellectual ability alone, yet not independent of intellectual abilities either. He discusses some alternatives to explanations to this state of affairs, and then repeats the definition which has been associated with him since at least 1939.

Yet Wechsler makes an important point at this juncture: whether or not intelligence is global or of some specialized type is more a theoretical than a practical matter. Tests show a similarity in their makeup despite the fact that they may differ in the way the content is organized and in procedures followed in administration and scoring. There are, after all, only so many legitimate tasks which may be included in a scale designed to measure intellectual ability, as he points out. Such tasks have indeed proved very useful since they call for behaviors which reflect the ability of the individual to act intelligently in much more wide-ranging aspects of the environment. Trite though it may seem, and unacceptable though it may be to many, the kinds of tasks included in a variety of intelligence tests are correlated with various criteria of intelligent behavior. In many cases, they are the best predictors of the behavior in question.

Aside from the issue of definitions of intelligence, their measurements and usefulness, Wechsler has discussed other expressions of intellectual ability as well. One of his more recent ideas, remaining of great interest and effort, is the matter of collective intelligence (6). He distinguishes this term from collective behavior. This latter concept, collective behavior, revolves around group contributions made by individuals to achieve some purpose or to solve some task. Collective intelligence is not concerned with the *nature* of the outcome as such. Instead, there may develop intellectual competencies in individuals that would not have been possible except for the group endeavor. Whether or not a particular goal is achieved by the group, a task solved, a problem resolved, is independent of this matter of collective intelligence. If such a position is feasible, Wechsler reasons that it may imply a type of thinking which is particular to the group and therefore collective in nature.

From the literature, he demonstrates varied discussions of collective behavior and their applications to the concept of collective intelligence. Those situations where individuals in the group develop a new awareness as a result of the joint endeavor would be instances of collective intelligence. The test of such a construct is the fact that such insight would not have occurred had the group not been composed and operated in the complex.

With this paper, Wechsler opens the possibility of a type of intelligence not previously considered even in the mass of writings dealing with collective behavior. The "unique integration," as he terms it, of the group effort may be necessary for certain outcomes to occur both for the society and subgroups within the society. It is not merely a matter of sharing, as he points out, but also a matter of deriving a different type of intelligent action. Always as the realist however, he points out that if there can be group intelligence there can also be group stupidity.

Two other papers are included in this section which are to some degree unique. The first of these is entitled "Conformity and the Idea of Being Well Born" (7), dealing with the need for conformity in societies in order to perpetuate status for the few and conformity by the many. Wechsler's discussion reflects an humanitarian bent. Certainly there is evidence here of his belief that many of the differences among individuals are imposed by external forces rather than innate ones. This idea fits with his conceptions of human capacities and their ranges, described in Part III.

The second paper was written by David Wechsler upon the decision of the New York Public Schools to remove I.Q.s from pupil's records (8). He discusses and dismisses the rationale proposed by the school system as well as alternatives which were espoused or tried. Perhaps the most important point is his discussion in the latter half of the paper dealing with the I.Q., its nature, its misuse and misinterpretation. Many of the arguments offered against the I.Q. and intelligence testing are directed at the wrong target. Abandoning the use of intelligence tests, or the recording of I.Q.s in pupils' records, will not correct for the social ills which beset such a large portion of our population. As he indicates, the treatment of social ills will indeed bring about some differences in the kinds of scores achieved by subgroups of our populace. A distribution of abilities will remain.

The address "Intelligence in a Changing World," delivered several times and in several forms over recent years, is the final selection included in this section. The form cited here is a compilation of the various alternatives and hopefully reflects the best of all of them. This paper gives much of the flavor of David Wechsler's beliefs, and his abiding concern for and about man. There is a certain redundancy of ideas presented in many other sources. There are also some ideas relatively new, but in concert with positions taken in the past by Wechsler. Perhaps one of the central of these is the discussion of common sense, at least as perceived by the layman, and its importance in man's behavior. As Wechsler states: ". . . in my opinion common sense is a much overrated trait. . . ." Both the layman and philosopher are challenged about the importance of common sense, particularly in terms of inventions which represent man's intellect at its best.

In this regard, he discusses the fear which the common man feels about the intellectual. As a result, society hesitates to trust the important positions in government to such individuals. Yet Wechsler maintains that in most instances the greatest intellects will be sensitive to those situations which might lead to the eventual destruction of mankind and proposes that in the long run brain will be much more satisfactory for solution of man's problems than will brawn. One might expect that today's youth would accept the responsibility for such assignment of the proper role of intellect in decision-making positions. Yet they hold the same fears as their parental generation, though the focus may be quite different. Wechsler discusses possible reasons for this and means by which the condition might be overcome.

There is a need to continue to respect and develop intellect on the part of all individuals in society. Wechsler makes reference to H. G. Wells' *The Time Machine,* where, in the far future in which the protagonist finds himself, the intellect of the populace is much like that of the six year old child of the year 1895. Though it may be both the glory and despair of a world changing as rapidly as ours, intelligence must be preserved to avoid such an outcome. Further, Wechsler's faith in intellect and the need for continuing to develop it is reflected in his reaction to the "Santa Claus" question posed by Virginia O'Hanley, first published in 1897. He restructures the situation, hypothesizing a letter written by an 8-year-old child who has been told she has a very high I.Q. She wonders about the dangerous nature of such a beast. Wechsler's response again reflects the meaning and necessity for intellect in man in all its meanings. No more positive statement of the essential worth and potential of mankind has been made by David Wechsler.

RATIONALE OF THE CHILDREN'S SCALE
What Intelligence Tests Test*

DAVID WECHSLER

Introduction

From the point of view of their avowed intent and wide use, intelligence tests are psychometric devices—in practice, sets of standardized questions and tasks, for assessing an individual's potential for purposive and useful behavior, at least in those aspects of it which one agrees to designate as intelligent. To be sure, there are many different definitions of intelligence, but nearly all intelligence scales appraise it in much the same way, namely by measuring a subject's mental abilities or current intellectual capacities. However, an intelligence test is not the same as a mental abilities test. Its primary intent and function is not to evaluate, as some assert, a subject's cognitive abilities, nor is its purpose, as proclaimed by those who are opposed to the I.Q. or the concept of general intelligence per se, to appraise his educational, vocational or other competencies. Intelligence tests inevitably also do this, but the information so obtained is, in the opinion of the author, relevant only to the extent that it establishes and reflects whatever it is one defines as overall capacity for intelligent behavior.

The Concept of Global Intelligence

The WISC is not predicated on any particular definition of intelligence, but like every attempt to appraise intelligence, it necessarily reflects the author's and eventually the user's own concepts. The author's views on the subject have been presented extensively in his *Measurement and Appraisal of Adult Intelligence* and other texts. Very briefly, they may be summarized by the following definition: Intelligence is the overall capacity of an individual to understand and cope with the world around him. Stated in these general terms this definition may impress the reader as perhaps not too radically different from many other definitions that might be cited. A careful comparison with these, however, would reveal that it differs from most of them in two important respects.

(1) It conceives of intelligence as an overall or *global* entity, that is, a

*Reprinted from *Manual for the Wechsler Intelligence Scale for Children—Revised*, The Psychological Corporation, New York, 1974.

multidetermined and multifaceted entity rather than an independent uniquely defined trait.

(2) It avoids singling out any ability, however esteemed (e.g., abstract reasoning) as crucial or overwhelmingly important.

In particular, it avoids equating general intelligence with intellectual ability.

Ultimately, intelligence is not a kind of ability at all, certainly not in the same sense that reasoning, memory, verbal fluency, etc. are so regarded. Rather, it is something that is inferred from the way these abilities are manifested under different conditions and circumstances. One can infer an individual's intelligence from how he thinks, talks, moves, almost from any of the many ways he reacts to stimuli of one kind or another. Indeed, historically, appraisal of such responses has been the usual way by which intelligence has been judged. Mental tests are a relatively new invention, a new method which psychologists think is a better or at least more scientific procedure. Accordingly, it is important to remember what tests of mental ability represent.

All tests of ability are essentially set tasks presented to a subject to elicit one or another kind of response that can be readily scored, that is, an artifice so contrived as to permit a subject to communicate meaningfully with an examiner. Thus, a verbal comprehension test is an artifice which permits a subject to answer certain questions by the use of words or verbal symbols; an arithmetic reasoning test, one which allows him to communicate with an examiner by manipulating numbers or numerical symbols; a visuo-motor (e.g., block design) test, a nonverbal task that enables him to show that he understands what an examiner wants him to do (by identifying and following visual patterns); and similarly for other tests. To the extent that tests are particular modes of communication, they may be regarded as different "languages." These "languages" may be easier or harder for different subjects, but none can be assumed to be necessarily more valid. Intelligence can manifest itself in many forms, and an intelligence scale to be effective as well as fair must utilize as many different languages (tests) as possible. It is also for this reason that WISC emphasizes the importance of intelligence probing in many different ways, that is, by as many different kinds of tests as one can marshal. It does so also because it assumes, as already mentioned, that intelligence is best regarded not as a single, unique trait, but as a composite or global one.

DEFINITION AND NATURE OF INTELLIGENCE*

DAVID WECHSLER

Some years ago when interest in intelligence tests was at its height, a prominent psychologist is reported to have answered an inquiry as to what he meant by intelligence by saying that it is what intelligence-tests measure. A similar attitude would not be maintained today by any considerable number of psychologists. But the continued failure of authors of intelligence-tests to declare explicitly what they understand by general intelligence would almost compel one to assume that they still maintain this circular position. The lay person is entirely justified in asking, as he does, "How do you know that your test measures intelligence?", and every author of a test should be ready to answer the question, however imperfectly. Obviously the more data the psychologist has, the easier his task will be. But he will be able to make no answer at all unless there is some provisional agreement between him and his challenger as to what they are willing to call intelligence, or at least intelligent behavior. We shall, therefore, begin by giving our own definition of intelligence and then consider its relation to the more important current theories on the subject.

Intelligence is the aggregate or global capacity of the individual to act purposefully, to think rationally and to deal effectively with his environment. It is global[1] because it characterizes the individual's behavior as a whole; it is an aggregate because it is composed of elements or abilities which, though not entirely independent, are qualitatively differentiable. By measurement of these abilities, we ultimately evaluate intelligence. But intelligence is not identical with the mere sum of these abilities, however inclusive. There are three important reasons for this: (1) The ultimate products of intelligent behavior are not only a function of the number of abilities or their quality but also of the way in which they are combined, that is, upon their configuration. (2) Factors other than intellectual ability, for example, those of drive and incentive, enter into intelligent behavior.

*Reprinted from "The Nature of Intelligence," in David Wechsler, *The Measurement of Adult Intelligence,* 1st ed., Baltimore, 1939, pp. 3-6. Copyright 1939, The Williams & Wilkins Co. Reproduced by permission.

(3) Finally, while different orders of intelligent behavior may require varying degrees of intellectual ability, an excess of any given ability may add relatively little to the effectiveness of the behavior as a whole. It would seem that, so far as general intelligence is concerned, intellectual ability as such merely enters as a necessary minimum. Thus, to act intelligently, one must be able to recall numerous items—i.e., have a retentive memory. But beyond a certain point this ability will not help much in coping with life situations successfully. This is true of even more important capacities, such as the ability to reason, particularly when specialized. The unusual reasoning abilities of the mathematician are more highly correlated with the thing that we ultimately measure as intelligence than sheer memory is, but possession of this ability is no surety that behavior as a whole will be very intelligent in the sense above defined. Every reader will be able to recall persons of high intellectual ability in some particular field, whom they would unhesitatingly characterize as below average in general intelligence.

Although intelligence is no mere sum of intellectual abilities, the only way we can evaluate it quantitatively is by the measurement of the various aspects of these abilities. There is no contradiction here unless we insist upon the identity of general intelligence and intellectual ability. We do not, for example, identify electricity with our modes of measuring it. Our measurements of electricity consist of quantitative records of its chemical, thermal and magnetic effects. But these effects are not identical with the "stuff" which produced them. General intelligence, like electricity, may be regarded as a kind of energy. We do not know what the ultimate nature of this energy is, but as in the case of electricity, we know it by the things it does or, better, by the things it enables us to do—such as making appropriate associations between events, drawing correct inferences from propositions, understanding the meaning of words, solving mathematical problems or building bridges. These are the effects of intelligence in the same sense as chemical dissociation, heat, and magnetic fields are the effects of electricity, but psychologists prefer the term *mental products*. We know intelligence by what it enables us to do.

Professor Thorndike was the first to develop clearly the idea that the measurement of intelligence consists essentially of some qualitative and quantitative evaluation of mental productions in terms of their number, and the excellence or speed with which they are affected. That is the only function which any measure of intelligence can possibly have. Abilities are merely these mental products sorted into different classes or types of operation. Thus, the class of operations which consist of effectually associating one fact with another and recalling either or both at an appropriate time is called learning; that of drawing inferences or educing relations between them, reasoning ability; that of merely retaining them, memory. The older psychologists were inclined to use a relatively small number of such classes based primarily on the type of mental process supposedly involved. More recently psychologists have begun to emphasize not only the processes but the content as well. They speak not only of memory but of auditory memory; not only of reasoning but of abstract, verbal or arithmetical reasoning. In a like manner some psychologists have begun to distinguish various kinds of intelligence. Thorndike, for example, has suggested subdividing intelligence into three main types: (1) abstract or verbal intelligence, involving facility in the use of symbols; (2) practical intelligence, involving facility in manipulating objects; (3) social intelligence, involving facility in dealing with human beings. . The significant thing about this classification is that it emphasizes *what* a person can do as well as *how* he can do it. This distinction between function and content is fully justified by experimental evidence. The rating which an individual attains on an intelligence examination depends to a considerable degree on the type of test used. His score on a test made up largely of verbal items may differ significantly from that obtained on a test involving questions of social comprehension and still more from another test made up of items involving predominantly psychomotor reactions and the perception of spatial relationships.

Though test results show that the rating which an individual attains will frequently depend upon the type of intelligence test used, they also show a contrary tendency. When large numbers of individuals are examined with a variety of intelligence tests, those who make high scores on any one of them tend to make high scores on the remaining ones; and the same holds for those who make low and intermediate scores. This dual characteristic of human abilities—their specificity on the one hand and interdependence on the other—has long been appreciated by psychologists. But unfortunately the reaction to this observation was not to accept it as a fact, but rather as a logical dilemma from which one had to escape. The older writers tried to escape it by accepting the scholastic formulated faculties; the modern ones, by their theory of independent unit or group traits. But more than 30 years ago, Professor Carl Spearman actually solved the problem by showing, through rigorous mathematical proof, that all intellectual abilities could be expressed as functions of two factors, one a *general* or intellectual factor common to every ability, and another a *specific* factor, specific to any particular ability and "in every case different from that of all others". This proof first appeared as a brief article in the American Journal of Psychology (1904). It has since been subjected to a great amount of discussion, criticism and experimental investigation. We cannot enter into all this here, but can only indicate our own position by saying that Professor Spearman's generalized proof of the two-factor theory of human abilities constitutes one of the great discoveries of psychology.

As has often been the case in the history of science, the proof of the two-factor theory, in addition to being a discovery, was also an explicit formulation of an hypothesis which workers in the field had unknowingly been assuming for some time. The fact is, that from the day psychologists began to use a series of tests for measuring intelligence, they necessarily assumed the existence of a general or common factor. This becomes immediately apparent if one recalls what the actual contents of intelligence tests are. They consist of various intellectual tasks which we call tests that require the subject to do such things as to define words, reproduce facts from memory, solve problems in arithmetic and recognize likenesses and differences. The variety of tasks used, their difficulty and manner of presentation varies with the type of scale employed. But so far as measuring intelligence is concerned, these specific tasks are only a means to an end. Their object is not to test a person's memory, judgment or reasoning ability, but to measure something which it is hoped will emerge from the sum total of the subject's performance, namely, his general intelligence. One of the greatest contributions of Binet was his intuitive assumption that in the selection of tests, it made little difference what sort of tasks you used, provided that in some way it was a measure of the child's general intelligence. This explains in part the large variety of tasks employed in the original Binet scale. It also accounts for the fact that certain types of items which were found useful at one age level, were not necessarily employed at a different age level. More important than either of these details is the fact that for all practical purposes, the combining of a variety of tests into a single measure of intelligence, *ipso facto*, presupposes a certain functional unity or equivalence between them.

NON-INTELLECTIVE FACTORS IN GENERAL INTELLIGENCE*

DAVID WECHSLER

Bellevue Hospital and New York University

As soon as one attempts to appraise intelligence-test ratings in terms of global capacity, that is, the ability or abilities to deal effectively with any and all rather than specific situations, it becomes strikingly evident that even our best tests of intelligence give only incomplete measures of the individual's capacity for intelligent behavior. This situation is reflected by various lines of evidence, the most familiar of which is the fact that individuals with identical test ratings (*e.g.,* IQ's) may differ markedly from one another in regard to level of global functioning as judged by practical criteria, that is, criteria against which the tests were presumably validated to begin with. The main reason for this, however, does not lie, as is generally assumed, in the unreliability of our tests; nor does it lie in the fact that many of our tests are influenced to a considerable degree by such factors as education, constrictive environment, etc. More basic than any of these is the fact that our intelligence tests as now constituted measure effectively only a portion of and not all of the capacities entering into intelligent behavior. Their limitations arise not so much from shortcomings of standardizations as from deficiencies of content.

The portions or aspects of intelligent behavior which our tests do measure effectively are those which are determined by the intellective factors of intelligence, whether by the general one "*g,*" or more specific ones such as verbal ability, abstract reasoning, arithmetical and other abilities which have been isolated by tetrad and multi-factorial analyses. These intellective factors do not, in my opinion, constitute everything which enters into intelligent behavior. Indeed, they do not even constitute all the factors which enter into our intelligence tests. That this is so is indicated by the fact that most studies with factorial-analysis techniques show a large unaccounted-for residual correlational variance. This residue, except in the studies of Thurstone, has amounted to as much as from 40 per cent to 60 per cent of the total variance. Professor Thurstone's opinion, I believe, is that the large residual variance has generally been due to the insufficiency in the number of variables entering into the correlational matrices. But the studies of Woodrow [1] and Morris [2] show that this cannot be the entire explanation. Morris, in his study, used no less than 32 variables but was able to account for only 35 per cent of his total correlational variance.[3]

A fact particularly worthy of note is that when tests forming part of a general intelligence scale have been used as the variables investigated, the correlational matrices have, on the one hand, furnished relatively few identifiable factors and,

*Reprinted from *Journal of Abnormal and Social Psychology*, 1943, **38**, 101-103.

[1] Woodrow, H. Common factors in 52 mental tests. *Psychometrika*, 1939, **4**, 209–220.
[2] Morris, M. A critical analysis of certain performance tests. *J. gen. Psychol.*, 1939, **54**, 85–105.
[3] There is good reason to believe that the amount of residual variance left unaccounted for is in a large measure contingent upon the type of tests entering into the correlational matrix. Thurstone was able to account for as much as 80 per cent of his correlational variance because most of his tests measured primarily the factors extracted and little of anything else. Morris, on the other hand, was able to account for only 35 per cent of the variance because his tests measured relatively little of the factors he identified and a great deal more of something else.

on the other, rather large variance residues. This is particularly true of test scales or combinations in which contrasting performance and verbal tests have been used. Such, for example, was the result obtained by Balinsky [4] in a recently completed factorial analysis of the Wechsler-Bellevue Scale, and before him by W. P. Alexander [5] in his study of "concrete and abstract intelligence." In Alexander's study, the residual variances after all identifiable factors had been extracted amounted to approximately 35 per cent; in Balinsky's study, from 40 to 70 per cent, depending upon the age of the subjects.

Alexander's study is of particular interest because he attempted to account for the residual variance. His interpretation of this variance was that it was due to factors entering into but not measured directly by the tests themselves. He also produced some evidence to show that these factors, provisionally named the "X" and "Z" factors, pertained not to abilities as ordinarily understood but to aspects of behavior historically looked upon as traits of temperament. They concern such traits as drive, persistence, and interest. These traits, he further observed, loomed large in certain kinds of achievement. Thus, reducing all loadings to a 100-per-cent basis, Alexander found that for success in science "g" (the inductive factor) contributed 10 per cent, "v" (the verbal factor) 31 per cent, and "X" (the temperament factor) 55 per cent. For success on one of the Otis scales "g" contributed 58 per cent, "v" 36 per cent, and "X" practically nothing. Again, for success on Kohs Block test, "g" contributed 54 per cent, "F" (the performance factor) 19 per cent, "z" (the other temperament factor) 27 per cent, and "v" and "X" nothing. From evidence such as this, Alexander concluded, on the one hand, that the "most important factor in educational achievement in some cases does not lie in ability, but in temperament;" and, on the other hand, that "there were factors necessary for achievement which intelligence tests did not test." To these findings, I would add the further conclusion that these factors (the "X"'s and "Z"'s, etc.), whether included or neglected by our current intelligence tests, form part and parcel of what is ultimately necessary for intelligent behavior. I would name these factors the non-intellective factors in general intelligence.

The degree to which the non-intellective factors enter into present day intelligence scales varies from test to test. Most verbal tests, particularly of the paper-and-pencil kind, contain relatively small non-intellective factor loadings, whereas some performance tests seem to contain them in relatively large amounts. But in neither case has any conscious attempt been made thus far to give them specific consideration. This accounts in part for the low forecasting efficiency of our intelligence tests in general, and the peculiar discrepancies between certain of them in particular. Why, for example, as in a recent study by J. C. Earle,[6] should mental defectives who do relatively well on verbal tests and poor on performance tests have a poor social prognosis, but those who do relatively well on performance and poor on verbal tests have a relatively good social prognosis? Or again, why, as indicated in a study now under way at Bellevue Hospital, should psychopaths score some 13 points higher than neurotics on the performance part of the Bellevue Adult Scale and some 13 points less on the verbal part, when both obtain approximately equal IQ's on the scale as a whole?

Differences such as these just noted cannot be entirely ascribed to the frequently posited differences in special ability. Actually, they are more broadly

[4] Balinsky, B. An analysis of the mental factors of various age groups, etc. *Genet. Psychol. Monogr.*, 1941, 23, 191–234.
[5] Alexander, W. P. Intelligence, concrete and abstract. *Brit. J. Psychol., Monogr. Suppl.*, 1935, No. 19.
[6] Earle, C. J. *Psychograph for morons.* This JOURNAL, 1940, 34, 428–448.

reflected in the capacity of the individual to cope with situations as a whole, that is, in his general capacity for intelligent behavior. Thus, psychopaths with modest IQ's (90–100) frequently show an excellent ability to manipulate their environment, often, to be sure, in a way disadvantageous to society, but nevertheless beneficial to themselves whereas neurotics, with considerably higher IQ's, often fail badly in managing their own lives with even a moderate amount of sagacity. I believe that the difference in effectiveness in the adaptive capacity of these individuals is largely the result of differences in amount of non-intellective intelligence possessed by each.

What now are these non-intellective factors in intelligence? In general they include all affective and conative abilities which in any way enter into global behavior. The phrase "enter into" is important. It is one thing if a child does poorly on an intelligence test because he is disinterested or emotionally upset and quite another if he does poorly on it because he is congenitally impulsive or emotionally unstable. In the first instance, the subject's emotional behavior is specific to the given situation or occasion; in the second, it represents a more or less permanent mode of response. In the former case, the subject might do much better if retested; in the latter, no such improvement could be expected.

The basic question which now presents itself is whether we can speak of conative and affective abilities in the same sense as we can speak of intellectual abilities. This has already been answered in the affirmative by the studies of Ach, Wynn Jones, Webb, and others. Summarizing these researches in his *Abilities of man*,[1] Spearman found it necessary to allow that affective and conative aspects of the mind may function as unitary factors in the same way as his cognitive "g." Specifically, he allows for a perseverative, a volitional, and a mental inertia factor. These factors, he finds, influence "g" only negligibly or not at all, and he accordingly lists them as representing independent traits or abilities. Nevertheless, because he seems to have been so completely sold on the idea that general intelligence is primarily determined by the amount of "g" possessed by an individual, he disregards these traits as factors actually entering into general intelligence. We are not however concerned with the question as to whether "g" does or does not play that important role, or whether the single-factor theory of cognition is invalid and needs to be replaced by a multiple-factor hypothesis. The main question is whether non-intellective, that is, affective and conative abilities are admissible as factors in general intelligence.

The contention of this paper has been that such factors are not only admissible but necessary. I have tried to show that in addition to intellective there are also definite non-intellective factors which determine intelligent behavior. If the foregoing observations are correct, it follows that we cannot expect to measure total intelligence until our tests also include some measures of the non-intellective factors. Attempts in this direction have barely been begun. Perhaps the nearest partial approximation thus far to such an approach are Doll's Social Maturity Scale and the writer's Bellevue Adult Scale. The suggestion now offered is that psychologists turn their attention to the construction of global intelligence scales which will include and measure there factors in a more comprehensive and more direct way. When our scales measure the non-intellective as well as the intellectual factors in intelligence, they will more nearly measure what in actual life corresponds to intelligent behavior. Under these circumstances they might not be so efficient in selecting individuals likely to succeed in Latin and geometry, but they should do a much better job in selecting those destined to succeed in life.

[1] Spearman, C. *Abilities of man.* London & New York: Macmillan, 1927.

COGNITIVE, CONATIVE, AND NON-INTELLECTIVE INTELLIGENCE*

DAVID WECHSLER

New York University

It is always a good omen for science when different men in different places make independent discoveries or arrive at similar conclusions. In the last two decades psychologists in their efforts to define the nature of general intelligence seem to have arrived at the threshold of such a situation. In this paper I wish to present to you what appears to me to be the germ of the impending re-orientation: it is this, that general intelligence cannot be equated with intellectual ability however broadly defined, but must be regarded as a manifestation of the personality as a whole.

From an historical point of view, the first one to argue against the identification of general intelligence with intellectual ability was Henri Bergson. Already in his *"Donees Immediate de la Conscience"* and more emphatically in his *"Evolution Creatrice,"* he pointed out the insufficiencies of the human intellect or, what was for him the same, normative logic, in dealing effectively with man's total environment.

I shall not here restate Bergson's arguments nor his attempted solution of endowing the human mind with a new faculty, creative intuition, and its generating force, the "elan vital." I wish only to call your attention to the fact that in our attempts at measuring intelligence we have persisted in treating intelligence as if it consisted exclusively of intellectual elements or factors. What, in fact, are these intellectual elements which we have continued to use and to posit in appraising intelligence? They are abstract reasoning, verbal, spatial, numerical, and a few other specified factors, all of which in some particularized manner deal with man's cognitive ability. Shades of Bergson, are we confirming his claim that human intelligence, as the psychologist conceives it, can only deal with geometric and logical symbols?

Now, the remarkable thing is that while this is what we are saying in our tests of intelligence, most of us don't believe it. What is more important, it isn't true! Our contemporary definitions of intelligence assert as much: intelligence according to these is not only the ability to learn, to abstract, to profit

*Address of the president of the Division of Clinical and Abnormal Psychology, given at Denver, Colorado, on September 5, 1949. Reprinted from *American Psychologist,* 1950, 5, 78-83. Copyright 1950 by the American Psychological Association. Reprinted by permission.

from experience, but also to adjust and to achieve. Everyone with clinical experience knows that the latter involve other capacities besides eductive, verbal, numerical, spatial, and the other intellective factors that have been demonstrated. Yes, but what are they? The answer is: they are *not* intellective. They are capacities and traits dependent upon temperament and personality which are not restricted to logical and abstract perception; they are, in my opinion, factors of personality itself. It is this point of view, independently sensed or suggested, at times only tangentially, by a number of investigators including Goldstein, Alexander, Wechsler, and more recently by Halstead and Eysenck, which I presented six years ago for the first time under the term *"Non-intellective Factors of Intelligence."* I wish now to present to you more fully the evidence in its support and to justify what appears to be not only the need for a re-orientation in our concept of general intelligence, but of a new psychometric that will, in fact, measure what is purported in our definition of intelligence.

Let me begin by restating the issue in terms of the actual psychometric problem. The crux of this problem, as we have already noted, is the discrepancy between what the clinical psychologist does and what he says he does in clinical practice. If we examine any of the current psychological tests of intelligence, we shall find them to consist of sample tasks measuring, by definition, a variety of mental abilities. One would imagine that any summary of the results obtained with such tests would be essentially a report of the degree to which an individual possesses these abilities and the manner in which they vary. However, it will be found that once a summative score is obtained from them, whether in terms of MA, I.Q., or whatnot, the clinical psychologist proceeds to enlarge his summary to include not only specific psychologic interpretations but broad social and biological implications as well.

An I.Q. is thus used, not only to determine comparative mental endowment, capacity to learn, presence of special abilities and disabilities, and evaluation of degree of mental deficiency, but also as a basis for school placement, for vocational guidance, for psychiatric diagnosis, and for the prediction of adjustment potentials in a variety of situations from infancy to old age, including such areas as child adoption, juvenile delinquency, fitness for military service, college success, and old age counseling.

Assuming that intelligence tests may be used in all these situations, and within limits I believe they may, the question arises how this is possible under the concept that general intelligence is a matter of a single basic or even a combination of a number of intellectual abilities. It is this question which I shall try to answer this evening. But I must first call your attention to the fact you are all aware of, that this is not the usual criticism of intelligence tests. The historic and continued objection to intelligence tests is not that they measure too much, but that they do not measure enough, or at least, not well enough.

You are all acquainted with the arguments against intelligence tests, and I shall not repeat them; the damaging criticism pertains, not as is generally emphasized, to the question of reliability, but to one of basic validity. Even such studies as those of Wellman, Goldfarb and others, showing changes in I.Q. produced by a variety of social and environmental factors, though relevant, are not crucial. The crucial instances are those where individuals obtain identical I.Q.s (say an I.Q. of 65) but, on overall appraisal, must neverthless be rated differently, say, one as a defective and the other as not defective. Such instances are not necessarily common, but neither are they rare exceptions. Here is a situation which needs explaining and cannot be by-passed.

The first to attack this problem was E. L. Thorndike. His answer, as always characteristic of his approach, was straightforward and to the point. Our tests measure intelligence to be sure, he said, but there is not just one unique, but several different kinds of intelligence, namely, abstract, social and practical. The first is manifested by the individual's ability to work with symbols, the second by his ability to deal with people, and the third by his ability to manipulate objects. Thorndike, himself, seems to have been primarily interested in the first kind of intelligence and, having made the above trichotomy, and along with it the distinction between tests which measure breadth, as against those which measure altitude, left the working out of these concepts to others. But relatively little has been done to verify or refute the hypothesis.

In the 1920's Moss published a test of social intelligence which consisted essentially of items involving memory and recognition of names and faces, and a series of multiple-choice questions involving social situations, in which the correct answer seemed to have been based on the notion that "the customer is always right." Although Moss's test for a time had some vogue among business firms, clinical psychologists, as far as I have been able to discover, seldom if ever make use of it.

The other important effort at producing a test of social intelligence is Doll's Vineland Social Maturity Scale. This Scale, as you know, consists of a series of questions listing a variety of social acquisitions, that is, of approved and useful acts and achievements, which a child may be expected to have learned from infancy to adolescence. The Scale is hardly a test in the ordinary sense of the term, since it involves no test performance or response by the subject, and can be completed, as it usually is, by other persons. But it does correlate fairly well with other tests of intelligence and has been shown by Doll and others to correlate positively and significantly with a number of practical criteria of social adjustment.

Clinical psychologists appear to have accepted performance tests, almost from the start, as a measure of practical intelligence. Only they seem to have regarded practical intelligence, as measured by these tests, as a kind of special aptitude rather than as a kind of intelligence. For many years the situation in clinical practice was something like this: a child would be given routinely a Binet test. Then, if his Binet MA did not seem to do justice to him, he would be given a Pintner-Paterson or similar performance battery as a supplementary test. But the child's score on the performance test, except in instances of language handicaps, would seldom be integrated with, or serve to alter, his Binet intelligence rating. Instead, it would usually be used as evidence of a compensatory useful special ability. Thus, if a child attained an I.Q. of 85 on the Binet, and one of 110 on the Pintner-Paterson, the reporting psychologist would ordinarily give the rating as "dull normal" intelligence with good practical or manipulative ability. It was not until the publication of the Bellevue Scales that any consistent attempt was made to integrate performance and verbal tests into a single measure of intelligence. The Bellevue tests have had increasingly wider use, but I regret to report that their popularity seems to derive, not from the fact that they make possible a single global rating, but because they enable the examiner to obtain separate verbal and performance I.Q.'s with one test.

The Aristotelian hierarchical white-collar concept of intelligence dies hard. This, in spite of the fact, that performance tests often can and do contain a larger amount of g than do the verbal tests. Thus, in his differential study of *"Abstract and Concrete Intelligence,"* W. P. Alexander, after correcting for communality, specific factors, and chance errors of measurement, found the theoretical g loadings for verbal and practical ability to be .60 and .81, respectively. Alexander concludes that "a perfect performance battery would be a better measure of g than a perfect verbal battery."

This and other findings by Alexander bring me to what constitutes the most compelling evidence for the reorientation in our concept of intelligence mentioned at the onset of this paper. I refer to the findings contributed by factor analysis. Here two important names appear on the horizon: Carl Spearman and L. L. Thurstone. I believe that the answers which they have given to the problem of the nature of general intelligence are incorrect. But I am sure that without the inspiration and without the tools which they furnished us, the solution of the problem would be altogether impossible.

Such a statement before a gathering of clinical psychologists may be unorthodox, because to many, factor analysis is almost anathema. But I can assure you, on the authority of expert consultants, that the mathematics of factor analysis is quite elementary, and on the basis of my own experience with it, extremely practical; and, with due apologies to Freud, even "sexy." For with what, in effect, does factor analysis concern itself, but with the bedfellowship of psychometric tests. For, mind you, it embraces matrices, correlational to be sure, and then tells you what test stays close to what other tests when axes are rotated. Now that, I submit, is what clinical psychologists want to know: what test, what factor, or, if you will, what function or what trait goes with what other factor, or function, or trait. And when the findings are examined some very interesting and unsuspected relationships come to light. For example, some tests of intelligence, like some human beings, are extremely promiscuous. Thus, vocabulary, the paragon of verbal tests, correlates very frequently, and to a considerable measure, with Block Designs, the perfect example of a performance test. But to return to a more serious vein, the importance of factor analysis is, of course, that it enables us to discover what our tests measure and the extent to which they measure the things they purport.

What are the elements which factor analysis has shown our intelligence tests to measure? The first is abstract reasoning. This is Spearman's g or eduction. Spearman argued that g was the only independent factor, and while he hesitated to identify g with general intelligence, his actual applications are tantamount to it. In equating g with general intelligence Spearman was in error, not because the tetrad equation is incorrect but because, in point of fact, it is not satisfied as he claimed. Spearman's answer to this finding was that we cannot expect the tetrad equation to be satisfied by all the tests of general intelligence but only by "good" tests of general intelligence, like analogies and mathematical reasoning which require eduction. But of course, if you select your tests, you can choose them so highly saturated with a single factor that the residuals vanish. This is all that the tetrad equation says, and it was the perceptive insight of Thurstone which recognized the tetrad equation for what it was, namely, a mathematically special case of a more general solution of the factorial problem. What was needed was a statistical analysis which would permit the emergence of other factors when present. By the use of his expanded technique, it has now been shown that intelligence tests, such as they are, contain not one but several independent factors. Some five or six have been definitely identified; they are, to repeat, induction, verbal, spatial, numerical, and one or two other factors. Notice, however, that these factors, like Spearman's eduction, are all cognitive.

At this point it is important to bear in mind what a factor stands for in factor analysis. Basically, it is an identifiable independent variable which accounts for a certain portion of the total test variance in a correlational matrix. The amount of variance it accounts for in any given test is called the test's factor loading. In a perfectly factorialized correlation matrix, the sum of the factorial loadings of the extracted factors should be 100 per cent, that is, account for the total test variance.

Now, it is a remarkable finding that when matrices of intelligence tests are factored, the amount of variance accounted for is seldom more than 60 per cent of the total, and, what is perhaps of equal significance, the greater the number of different tests included, the smaller, generally, the total per cent of variance accounted for; and this is seemingly independent of the number of factors extracted. In the case of our present intelligence test batteries, factors beyond the first 3 or 4 usually contribute so little to the already accounted-for variance that it is generally not profitable to extract them. It is the observation of this important finding that in the factorialization of batteries of intelligence tests, there always remained a considerable per cent of unaccounted-for variance, which began to arouse my interest some years ago. It seemed to hold the key to our problem.

If after successive attempts at factoring out all the components of intelligence, there always remained a large residue of these unknown elements, the obvious inference to be made was that our intelligence tests measured other things than those accounted for by the extracted factors. The second inference was that those other factors were numerous and occurred in relatively small amounts, because it was impossible to extract single additional factors which would account for any considerable portion of the residual variance. I assumed that the principal reason for this was that the test batteries usually factored did not include tests which contained sufficient amounts of these other factors, to enable some of the remaining tests to cluster about them. Provisionally I called these residual components the nonintellective factors of intelligence. But in terms of more recent findings, I believe they can be more justly designated as the personality components of general intelligence, which in fact they are.

The evidence for this conclusion comes from a number of sources. As early as 1913, Webb, (8), in factoring a battery of tests, along with a number of ratings which attempted to appraise traits of character, was able to extract a factor "W." "W" in a broad sense seemed to relate to a moral and conative propensity, which he called conscientiousness or purposeful consistency. A few years later, in Spearman's own laboratory, Lankes and Wynn Jones (7) demonstrated the existence of another non-intellective factor, "p," or perseveration, which characterized their subjects tendency to resist changes in set, and which Spearman related to his law of inertia. In 1921, W. M. Brown (2) discussed character traits as factors in intelligence tests, and in 1933, R. B. Cattell (3) reported correlations between tests of temperament and ratings in intelligence. But perhaps the most crucial findings are those of W. P. Alexander (1) who, in an extensive factor analysis of a large series of verbal and performance tests, supplemented by tests of achievement and academic marks, showed that in addition to the now familiar g, V (verbal ability), and P (practical ability), a considerable portion of variance had to be ascribed to two other extracted factors, namely, X and Z. X was a factor which determined the individual's interests and "concerns," in Alexander's words, "temperament rather than ability"; while Z was "an aspect of temperament related to achievement," in the case of Alexander's subjects, to school achievement.

The factor loadings of X and Z varied greatly from test to test, but even some of Spearman's ostensibly pure tests of g contained some Z and nearly all the performance tests showed considerable X or Z loadings. As might be expected, these factors played an even greater role in academic or technical achievement. For success in science, for example, the X factor loading was .74, as against only .36 for *g* loading. From these findings one might even infer that lack of intellectual ability, beyond a certain point, accounts for relatively little of school failures. Indeed Dorothea McCarthy (6) recently offered the "hypothesis," and I quote, "that emotional insecurity . . . is the basic cause of most educational disabilities and learning failures, which are not due to mental defect."

What are we to make of these two findings? First, that factors other than intellectual contribute to achievement in areas where, as in the case of learning, intellectual factors have until recently been considered uniquely determinate, and, second, that these other factors have to do with functions and abilities hitherto considered traits of personality. Among those partially identified so far are factors relating primarily to the conative functions like drive, persistence, will, and perseveration, or in some instances, to aspects of temperament that pertain to interests and achievement. This, to be sure, is just the beginning, but one of the reasons that not much more has been done is that psychologists have continued to assume that personality has little to do with intelligence. To Thurstone as well as to Spearman, general intelligence seems to be first and foremost a cognitive function, by Spearman to be accounted for by a single pervasive factor, by Thurstone by a number of factors.

It is curious that the clinical psychologist, so little impressed by or, at least, so little conversant with factor analysis, has almost from the start dealt with intelligence test findings as if the personality components in intelligence were already an established fact. For what does psychological diagnosis on the basis of intelligence test findings consist of but inferring adjustive capacities of the subject as a personna? It appears that the clinician, like the character in Moliere's *"Malade Imaginaire,"* has been speaking prose all his life without knowing it.

One might add that diagnosing personality and personality disorder, at the level it is being done, is not very difficult. Practically every good individual test of intelligence lends itself to such application to a greater or lesser degree, the Bellevue Scales and the new Children's Test of Intelligence perhaps a little more readily. This does not mean that they are tests of personality, but they do suggest that our intelligence tests contain elements which are essentially factors of the personality as a whole rather than specific cognitive abilities. When the neurotic does poorly on the Digit Span Test, it is not because of defective memory, but generally because of a basic anxiety mobilized by the test, as by any other situation, in which he is seemingly on trial. Conversely, when a mental defective does relatively well on the Maze Test, it is generally not because he has better planning ability, but because he is less impulsive. Similarly, a large variety of traits and personality factors may be inferred from test performance—for example, energy level from a subject's performance on the Digit Symbol, asocial tendencies from general comprehension, masculinity-femininity from the picture completion test. These are only a few of the traits and diagnostic constellations with which every clinician who has done psychological diagnosis is familiar.

The point here is not that personality traits can be discovered in psychometric performance, or, what needs no special argument, that personality and abnormal conditions influence intelligence test findings, but that personality traits *enter into* the effectiveness of intelligent behavior, and, hence, into any global concept of intelligence itself. It is one thing if a child does poorly on an intelligence test because he is disinterested or upset and quite another if he is congenitively impulsive or emotionally unstable.

One would naturally suppose that if intelligence is a function of the personality as a whole, one should find significant positive or negative correlations with measures of personality itself. Such, indeed, are the findings, but the results are extremely hard to evaluate. This is in part due to the fact that the studies in this area have been done primarily with the intent of discovering the extent to which intelligence accounts for variance in personality. In an article which appeared in 1940, Irving Lorge reviews the studies published to that date on the general and various measures or estimates of personality. The personality tests included most of the current and older inventories (Woodworth, Laird, Thurstone, Bernreuter, Allport, et al.), as well as the association experiment and the personality measures of Hartshorn, May, and Maller. Some 200 correlation coefficients were analyzed. The range of coefficients was from $+.70$ to $-.49$ with a median of $+.04$. Disregarding the signs, half of the ratios were between .00 and .15, and one quarter of them .30 and above. Lorge's general feeling about the findings is that the range is so "extraordinary that anybody can make any statement." Nevertheless, his conclusion is "that some correlation between intelligence and personality exists" (5).

All this is rather meager fare, but the findings are perhaps as satisfactory as could be expected. Apart from the known unreliability of paper-and-pencil inventories, there is the more disturbing fact of their uncertain validity and relevance. At times they do not measure the traits claimed for them, at others they measure only small segments of the personality, although in different ways; and at still other times, traits which are purely nominal. The latter, for example, was shown by Flanagan (4) to be the case with the Bernreuter Inventory dichotomies. In the original publication the test was scored for six different traits, which by factorialization were then reduced to two.

Flanagan's study is a good example of how factor analysis aids us in getting at basic components. Mere evidence of concomitant variation is not enough; in fact, it is often misleading. For example, defective hearing may have a measurable effect on both learning arithmetic and size of vocabulary, but, obviously, has no basic relation to either arithmetical reasoning or verbal ability.

A variable to be basic and scientifically significant must be independent. In the case of man's cognitive functions, these independent variables, in so far as they are relevant to general intelligence, have been pretty well identified. It may be possible to add one or two to Thurstone's list, but not many more. Those of personality are yet to be discovered. We have some knowledge of what the factors to be measured are likely to be, some on the basis of researches like those of Webb, Alexander, Guilford, Cattell, and Eysenck, others on the basis of general observation and clinical experience. The latter have thus far gone unrecognized, not only because we have no tests for them but because clinicians, like their more academic colleagues, still think of intelligence as consisting primarily of cognitive abilities. Any bit of behavior that seems concerned with or related to instinct, impulse, or temperament is ipso facto considered as having no direct relation to general intelligence.

Such, for example, is curiosity. This was one of the traits which Terman in his studies of genius found most frequently among his gifted children. But he did not have, nor do we as yet have, any test of curiosity. No attempt has been made to extract curiosity as a factor of intelligence. We all know how important curiosity is for biologic adaptation as well as scientific achievement. It is, to quote McDougall, "at the basis of many of man's most splendid achievements, for rooted in it are his speculative and scientific tendencies," and ". . . in men in whom curiosity is innately strong, it may become the main source of intellectual energy and effort." But what is curiosity? "It is the impulse to approach and examine more closely the object which attracts it," that is, an instinct, and according to McDougall, one of the basic instincts.

One need not be afraid or ashamed to acknowledge impulse, instinct and temperament as basic factors in general intelligence. It is indeed because I believe they are that I have brought before you the arguments and evidence presented. My main point has been that general intelligence cannot be equated with intellectual ability, but must be regarded as a manifestation of the personality as a whole. I have tried to show that factors other than intellectual enter into our concept of general intelligence, and that in everyday practice, we make use of them knowingly or not.

What is needed is that these factors be rigorously appraised. Factor analysis has been emphasized because, at present, it is the only method which enables us to demonstrate and discover independent variables. We already have some clues as to what the non-intellective but relevant factors of intelligence may be. What we now need are tests which not only identify but measure them. This in effect demands broadening our concept of general intelligence and calls for a revised psychometric to measure these added variables as sub-tests of all general intelligence scales.

To say that general intelligence can be social and practical, as well as abstract, was just a beginning. We had to know what basic components of the mind were responsible for making an individual effective in one rather than in another area.

To realize that general intelligence is the function of the personality as a whole and is determined by emotion and conative factors is also just a beginning. We now need to know what non-intellective factors are relevant and to what degree. This is the task which lies immediately before us.

References

Alexander, W. P. Intelligence, concrete and abstract. *Brit. J. Psychol. Monogr. Suppl.,* 1935, **6**, No. 19.

Brown, W. M. Character traits as factors in intelligence test performance. *Arch. Psychol.,* 1923.

Cattell, R. B. Temperament tests. I. Temperament. *Brit. J. Psychol.,* 1933, **23**, 308–29.

Flanagan, J. C. Factor analysis in the study of personality, Stanford Univ. Press, 1935.

Lorge, I. *Intelligence: its nature and nurture.* 39th Yearbook. National Society for Study of Education, 1940, Part I, 275-81.

McCarthy, Dorothea. Personality and learning. Amer. Coun. educ. Studies, 1948, Series I, No. 35.

Spearman, C. *The abilities of man.* New York: Macmillan, 1927.

Webb, E. Character and intelligence. *Brit. J. Psychol. Monogr. Suppl.,* 1915, III.

INTELLIGENCE: DEFINITION, THEORY, AND THE I.Q.*

DAVID WECHSLER

As you read the contributions which preceded mine, you may have been impressed by the diversity of the approaches to the topic and the differences in the points of view stressed. For a subject as broad and embracing as intelligence, this was perhaps inevitable. But if the topics treated in this volume are to be profitably studied, one must assume that underneath these and other differences there is a residuum of meaning to the term intelligence, acceptable to all who use it.

This does not mean that we must agree to any particular definition of intelligence nor, for that matter, abandon any preferred ones. But we must feel that, details disregarded, we are at heart talking about the same thing. It is possible to make this assumption because intelligence is not a unique entity, but a composite of traits and abilities recognizable by the goals and ends it serves rather than the character of the elements which enter into it.

The fact that intelligence has been and can be defined in many ways need not overwhelm us nor impel us to the view, sometimes advanced, that the term is best abandoned because "nobody really knows what intelligence is." Actually, we know much more about intelligence than about practically any other subject in psychology. Few topics have been as avidly researched and discussed, and at all levels of sophistication. It is a subject about which virtually

*Reprinted from *Intelligence: Genetic and Environmental Influences,* edited by Robert Cancro, New York, Grune and Stratton, Inc., 1971, pp. 50-55. Reprinted by permission.

everyone can speak on the basis of personal experience. I venture that nearly every person has had occasion to call somebody, justifiably or not, bright or stupid. As a matter of fact, recognizing and identifying degrees of brightness and stupidity is what intelligence testing is all about.

Of course, the last observation is an oversimplified statement. There are problems in and aspects to intelligence which perforce have to be specially considered and about which there exist and will continue to exist differences of opinion. But in discussing these one must be careful not to mistake the forest for the trees.

When one examines in depth the various definitions of intelligence, one soon discovers that they differ not so much by what they include as by what they omit. Thus, some emphasize primarily the ability to reason or to think abstractly; others, the ability to learn or to profit from experience; still others, the capacity to adapt; and, in recent years, increasing numbers, the ability to solve problems. None of these approaches can be categorized as incorrect, nor, when sufficiently elaborated, as failing to embrace basic mental operations. Taken individually, the definitions offered are restricted and incomplete because they concern themselves with only a modest range of traits and abilities that necessarily constitute the broad spectrum of intelligent behavior. Intelligent behavior, to be sure, may call upon abstract reasoning, the ability to learn, or to adapt, or to solve problems. It may manifest itself in any or all of these ways —though not necessarily at one time—and in many other ways as well. It is also dependent, to varying degrees, upon a variety of determinents which are more of the nature of connative or personality traits rather than of cognitive abilities. These connative and personality vectors are relatively independent of intellectual ability, and for this reason were originally designated by this writer, and since widely referred to, as the *nonintellective factors* of intelligence. They include such ingredients as drive, persistence, motivation, and goal awareness. Their impact on intelligence is attested to not only by direct observation, but also by statistical and factorial analytic studies.

Less often recognized than nonintellective factors of the sort just mentioned is another group which relates to the individual's capacity to perceive and respond to moral, aesthetic, and social values. These factors involve not so much knowledge and skills as the capacity to assess excellence and worthwhileness of human aims. They are manifested by such characterological traits as steadfastness to principles, respect for truth, concern with questions of right and wrong, and sensitivity to beauty in its varied manifestations. These are traits not everywhere or always esteemed, but, nevertheless, as in the case of honesty, they have been shown to correlate significantly with the more obvious and objective measures of intelligence.

General intelligence is thus a many faceted construct. It is not, as sometimes supposed, synonymous with intellectual ability; it involves much more. But if general intelligence cannot be equated with intellectual ability, neither can it be said to be independent of it. For an individual to deal effectively with certain situations may require more of one kind of ability than another. Consequently, some psychologists have found it useful to classify intelligence according to what they judge to be the major ability or abilities called for. This has suggested the view that there are in fact different kinds or types of intelligence. Cattel in Chapter 1 made a distinction between fluid and crystallized intelligence. Operationally, this distinction seems to differentiate between native and acquired intellectual capacity. More related to the type of situation than to the kind of operation involved is Thorndike's oft-cited classification of intelligence into abstract, social, and practical intelligence. Abstract intelligence, according to Thorndike, involves mostly the ability to deal with and use symbols; social intelligence, the facility to deal with people; and practical intelligence, the ability to manipulate objects. Each of these distinctions, and certain others that have been put forward, can be usefully applied.

I personally prefer to look upon general intelligence as a global capacity that manifests itself in different ways, depending upon the challenge presented and the assets which the individual possesses to meet it. But the question of a global versus special kinds of intelligence turns out to be primarily a theoretical one. In practice, i.e., when it comes to devising instruments or tests for appraising intelligence, it generally plays a minor role. Notwithstanding their theoretical views, authors of intelligence scales tend to make use of the same sort of tasks and items. Procedures may vary, but the tests themselves do not differ very much. The reason is that basically there are really not very many different ways of appraising intelligence. One is limited by the kind of reasonable tasks that can be set and the suitable questions that can be asked.

To act intelligently one must be able to perceive accurately, to recognize and recall what has been perceived, to think logically, to plan, and so on. These are not only important in and of themselves as descriptions of how the mind works, but, in addition, as manifestations of mental operations which lend themselves to objective evaluation and measurement. That is why they have been and continue to be used in tests of intelligence. When so employed, the measures involved call for such tasks as defining words, solving arithmetical problems, detecting likenesses and differences, putting blocks together, recalling words or numbers, and so on. But the abilities called for to perform these tasks do not, per se, constitute intelligence or even represent the only ways in which it may express itself. They are used and can serve as tests of intelligence because they have been shown to correlate with otherwise widely accepted criteria of intelligent behavior.

One may question whether the tests that have come to be employed are the sole or even the best ways of appraising intelligence. One will further want to know under what conditions the tests are given, the representativeness of the populations on which they are standardized, the suitability of the tests for subjects to whom they are now administered, and so forth. These questions have been asked and discussed ever since intelligence tests began to be used (more than sixty years ago). Contributors to this volume will no doubt pursue them again, particularly as they may relate to their specific topics and personal points of view. That is all to the good and fair game as a start. Hopefully, the greater parts of their discussions will not, as has so often been the case, be devoted to redundant criticisms and belabored reevaluations of the tests of intelligence in general. The validity and value of intelligence tests cannot be judged primarily by what they may or may not contribute to the nature-nurture controversy, any more than the answer to the problem of the relative importance of heredity and environment depends solely on the reported findings of intelligence tests. The role and implications of tests of intelligence are at once much broader and less crucial. It is important to distinguish between what tests are intended for and how they may be used. To do so one must know clearly what intelligence tests consist of and how they are put together.

There is nothing mysterious about tests of intelligence. Tests so designated consist ultimately of a series of questions or tasks which a subject is required to answer or perform. Depending upon the difficulty of the items used, the accuracy and speed with which they are completed, and the frequency with which they are passed, numerical values are assigned to the responses; these, in turn, are summed to give a total score. Scores so obtained are then used as a basis for defining different levels of intelligence.

The tasks or questions used in intelligence tests are, in the first instance, measures of selected skills and knowledge, like the ability to solve arithmetical problems or the size of one's vocabulary. But they differ from measures of achievement or special aptitude in that they are intended not so much to measure a particular skill or fund of information, as the degree to which successful performance on these tasks correlate with variously esteemed and otherwise desirable capacities commonly accepted as indicators of intelligence. If the tests correlate to a significant degree with any, and preferably several, of these criteria, and in addition satisfy certain other criteria, they are considered as having established themselves as valid measures of intelligence. Some of these conditions are that the tests consistently measure and reliably predict what they claim to, that the subjects employed in the standardization of the tests be representative of the population from which they were selected, and that the questions or tasks are not, for one or another reason, "unfair" to particular individuals or groups to whom they are likely to be administered.

Intelligence tests have been charged with failing in one or another, and even all, of these areas. Attacks have been both general and specific; often they have been based on political as well as scientific grounds. Particularly vehement have been the onslaughts against that widely publicized, denounced, and misunderstood feature of intelligence tests, the IQ or intelligence quotient. I believe that the opposition to the IQ is largely due to the misunderstanding of what an IQ really is and what it is intended to define.

An IQ is a numerical ratio, derived from a comparison of the score that an individual makes on a given test of intelligence with the average score which subjects of his own age have attained on the same or a similar test. In practice, this ratio is expressed in a percent notation in which the decimal point, for convenience, is left out. There are several ways in which an IQ can be computed. Sometimes the original scores are first translated into months and years and expressed as mental ages; at other times, more directly derived. However calculated, the result is an index of relative brightness. It is a measure not of absolute but only of *relative* ability. It purports to tell you how bright or dull an individual is compared to persons of his own age; or if a comparison is made between two groups, how the brightness of the average individual in the first group compares with the average individual of the same age in the second group.

All comparisons, of course, are odious, and comparing people's intelligence with one another, particularly so. Too much is at stake. Calling a child retarded or an adult mentally defective is much more serious than calling him delinquent or questioning his paternity. Education, a job, in certain situations one's legal rights may be at stake. One must obviously be careful as to how one interprets as well as how one arrives at an IQ. It is not, however, an inherent fault of the IQ that incompetent or mischievous people misuse it. Nor does the observation that educationally, economically, and otherwise deprived subjects generally score lower on IQ tests invalidate the IQ as an index. Of course, the factors that affect the IQ are important, but it is the social conditions that produce the factors and not the tests that are the culprits. No one, for example, would suggest the elimination of tests for tuberculosis in the public schools because it was found that children from deprived areas showed up more often with positive signs than children from "good" neighborhoods. Similarly, if the IQ test scores of children coming from deprived and depressed areas are significantly lower than those of children from better neighborhoods, the reason can no more be ascribed to the inadequacy of the IQ test than the greater incidence of tuberculosis to the possible limitations of the tuberculin test. The cause is elsewhere, and the remedy not in denigrating or banishing the IQ but in attacking and removing the social causes that impair it.

An equally important stricture on the IQ has to do with the trustworthiness of the measure itself—namely, its overall reliability. This is a legitimate concern. One needs to know not only by how much an IQ may diverge from its hypothetically true value, but for how long a time it may be expected to remain approximately the same. What are the changes that may be expected over time, to what extent, and in what direction? There is a vast amount of data and literature on this subject, although not all in agreement. It is too extensive for me to review here even briefly. But taken as a whole, the findings show that for most individuals an IQ once adequately obtained, does not change markedly. The average test-retest change amounts to some 5 points, or approximately one-third of a standard deviation. This is surprisingly small when compared with commonly accepted levels of variation in physical indices, like an individual's basal metabolism or electroencephalogram. Larger discrepancies than 5-point differences in IQ do occur, but with diminishing frequency the greater the difference. Thus, an IQ difference of 10 points on retest may be expected once in five times, a difference of 20 points approximately once in sixteen. These findings attest to the need of appraising each case individually and of avoiding definitive classification on the basis of a single examination. When a subject's IQ appears inconsistent with his past history, an obvious step is to retest him or reexamine him with other instruments. A large discrepancy is always suspect and should be explored. But one does not throw out the baby with the bath water. The IQ, whatever its defects, is still one of the most useful measures of intelligence available to us.

CONCEPT OF COLLECTIVE INTELLIGENCE[1]

DAVID WECHSLER

New York University College of Medicine

Is there such a thing as collective intelligence? And if so, does it involve something essentially different from an intelligence not so qualified? The answer necessarily depends not only on what one comprehends by the term collective, but how one defines intelligence. I confine myself in this article primarily to a discussion of the idea of collectivity as it has been or may be applied to the concept of intelligence.

In its broadest sense, collective means pertaining to a quality or trait that is shared in any way by two or more persons or things. What is shared is inferred from the nature and characteristics of the trait in question; how it is shared is inferred from the way the individuals concerned are affected by, or interact with, one another. Accordingly, intelligence may be termed collective when it involves, or is in some way the result of, group rather than individual mental effort. It also presupposes some degree of concerted endeavor, but mere conjoint effort or behavior is not enough. One must distinguish between collective behavior and collective intelligence.

Collective behavior occurs in almost any situation in which individuals come together by some mutual interest to pursue some common task. Implied here is that what is achieved is usually ascribed to the combined effort of the group as a whole rather than to the unique contributions of the individuals composing it. It is in this sense that one ordinarily speaks of the collective effort of farmers in building a grain elevator, of a group of businessmen raising a community fund, or of a team of engineers engaged in a scientific effort. In all these instances, the enhanced achievement, whether in terms of time required to perform the task, its quality, and the greater amount of work produced (if that is the case), is usually ascribed to a multiplication of the effort exerted or a summation of the skills contributed. In the case of collective intelligence, the nature of the outcome is not the central issue per se. The main question is not only whether a group of individuals working together may not, through concerted thinking, come up with a better solution (or for that matter a poorer one) but whether in doing so the individuals composing the group may not have acquired or made use of perceptions or insights not experienced or available to them

[1] Reprinted from *American Psychologist*, 1971, **26**, 904-907. Copyright 1971 by the American Psychological Association. Reprinted by permission.

when working or cogitating alone. If so, does this imply a way of thinking peculiar to the group?

Interestingly enough, it is not psychologists but sociologists who first put forward the idea of a group or allied concept of group mentation. The interest of sociological writers did not relate to the possible existence of a "collective" intelligence, but rather to the discovery of a hypothesis that could account for the myths and certain customs of primitive peoples or, again, as explanations of their aberrant behavior under certain conditions. Of the latter, the most widely discussed has been the concept of the "popular mind" put forward by Gustave LeBon to explain the predictably irrational behavior of crowds.

When part of a crowd, an individual acts as if he were an automaton, subject to the will of a leader and at the mercy of his unconscious drives and motives, according to LeBon.[2] He is suggestible, hostile, and lacking all sense of responsibility. Most important for evaluating and interpreting the mental reactions of the group is the sameness of behavior of the individual members that comprise it, regardless of their previous training, social status, or level of intelligence.

It is not clear from LeBon's descriptions whether members of a crowd behave in the same way because they all think, for the time being, the same way, or because they are no longer in control of their cognitive processes. According to LeBon, the intelligence of the crowd is always below the average of the population as a whole; the crowd, he says, is stupid. And the man in the crowd acts that way because his intellectual organization has been altered or transformed under the stress and impacts of his emotions. This transformation is an expression of the individual's unconscious drives and uninhibited impulses. And since all the members of a crowd are similarly affected, the behavior of the crowd takes on a sameness of direction and identity of purpose. LeBon interpreted this as a manifestation of a mass mentality or popular mind. It is "popular" because it is manifested by large numbers, perhaps also because it is pejoratively egalitarian.

It is important to note that nowhere does LeBon employ the terms common or collective as alternatives to the word popular. These two terms were linked initially with the word mind by other writers. The adjective common coupled to the noun mind seems to have been first applied and exploited by the anthropologist and sociologist Emil Durkheim. Durkheim arrived at the concept of the common mind (l'esprit commun) from an analysis of the myths, folklore, and ceremonies of certain primitive societies. He concluded that these practices and beliefs evidenced a kind of "mental force" or ideational activity characteristic of the group, which were no longer reflected in the cognitive and logical processes of the individual's contemporaneous mentation. To support this view, Durkheim

---

[2]LeBon defined a crowd as "an agglomerate of men under certain circumstances," in consequence of which "the sentiments and ideas of the individual comprising the group take the same direction."

claimed to be able to distinguish between human traits and abilities of primitive man, and classified them into two broad categories: those called on in group cultural ceremonies and practices, and those involved in the individual physical manipulations of tools, dress, etc. The former are said to give rise to or be based on what he termed "collective representations." They represent ideational constraints of the group and are considered as having a separate existence independent of the individual's personal experience. They are the beliefs and ideas that are handed down from one generation to the next. These collective representations, which in toto Durkheim designated as "la conscience collective," explain the recurrent myths and beliefs recalled in the mores and habits of primitive people.

A reprise and extension of LeBon's concept of the popular mind, but tied to his concept of the unconscious, is reflected in Freud's analysis of the "group mind." Freud accepted in essence LeBon's description of crowd behavior, applied it to other groups, and stressed the similarity between them. In doing so, he ascribed the untoward behavior of the group to the hostility between the intimidated horde and its relentless leader. The sexual jealousy of the primal father combined with his intolerance of any challenge are the roots of group psychology for Freud.

In this connection it should be noted that much of Freud's discussion of the psychology of the group is concerned with the role and impact of the leader, rather than the reactions of the people in the group that he dominates. The mechanisms used to explain the behavior of the groups are largely equated to those employed in explaining neurotic behavior, as, for example, the illogicality of group thought and the "primary process" of early childhood. This trend in Freud is due to the fact that he is not so much concerned with the characteristics of human thought as he is with the unconscious forces in the individual that motivate the thought. But the term collective unconscious, like the term collective intelligence, is nowhere used in Freud's discussions of group psychology.

The collectivity concept in relation to unconscious mentation, though perhaps implied by Freud, was actually first exploited by Carl Jung, who introduced and employed the term "collective unconscious" to describe "those deeper layers of the unconscious that are common to all humanity." It also furnished the basis for his more extended concept of archetypes.

To understand fully Jung's concept of the collective unconscious, one must bear in mind his basic distinction between what he defines, respectively, as the personal and impersonal unconscious. The personal unconscious consists primarily of the forgotten memories of childhood and the repressed and forgotten wishes and impulses of the adult as encountered in dreams. These are related intrinsically to the individual's own experiences. The impersonal unconscious, by contrast, is in no way derived from the individual's own experience, but consists of inborn attitudes and modes of perception assimilated from the experience of the group. The collective unconscious is the same. It is the impersonal unconscious and is defined by Jung as a separate psychic system "consisting of pre-existing forms of non personal character" that does not develop individually but is inherited.

Whether such a system is descriptive of a fact or fancy is a matter on which one can take sides. If it exists, one must concede the collective character that Jung ascribes to it. But this collective unconscious by its own definition applies to only a limited part of man's mental processes, namely, those which can be described or fall under the term unconscious. Disregarded, or at least not included, are all operations that are conscious and, in particular, those that are comprised under any definition of intelligence. In any event, the basic issue in evaluating the concept of collective intelligence is not whether the individual traits and competencies involved in its definition are conscious or unconscious, but whether they are considered primarily as manifestations of the individual's own assets and liabilities, or as the result of a new awareness evolved and sustained by the group. If the latter is the case, as I think it is, one must inevitably posit an intellectual capacity to account for this new awareness or level of perceptiveness that is often observed. It is a collective intelligence if the emerging insight is shared by members of a group involved in some joint enterprise and would not have emerged if the individuals composing the group had been left to their own resources.

Early writers on group intellectual behavior either did not observe or were not impressed by this phenomenon because they were mostly concerned with problems of *mass psychology*. A crowd, a mob, or similar gatherings constitute only some of the many situations in which people get together to act conjointly for a particular purpose. More numerous by far are the day-to-day conglomerations —public assemblies, conventions, protest meetings, conferences, scientific symposia, etc. Much has been written as to what happens and how participants interact at this type of congress. Many of the studies reported relate to the processes of group dynamics and, in recent years, increasingly to the subject of problem solving. The group dynamic studies, while often touching on the question of group versus individual impacts, are generally concerned with how conative and personality factors enter into and contribute to effective group relations. Those on problem solving are, as might be anticipated, more immediately germane; problem solving enters as an important element in most definitions of intelligence.

Problem solving has been investigated from various points of view, ranging from the part it plays in cognitive and learning processes to its role in decision making and creative productivity. These are all relevant. The one aspect of it, however, with which we are here concerned is whether and how it differs when performed by an individual from the way it functions when embarked on by a group.

Some of the things that have been investigated in this connection are the factors that favor successful problem solving, such as motivation, past experience, goal orientation, and others. These ingredients affect both individual and group activity. In the case of problem solving by groups, there are the additional factors of cooperation versus competition and the role of the leader.

More crucial to the efficacy and even emergence of group thinking in problem solving, as in other goal-directed activity, is the degree of homogeneity and level of inner organization of the group. A crowd, for example, is neither homogeneous nor organized and, therefore, incapable of collective intelligence (though, of course, not collective action). It fails to achieve it because the members are unable to deal other than single-mindedly with the problem at hand and are not afforded opportunities to participate directly in what is going on. But even when relevant conditions are met, as in scholarly symposia or scientific research, one still must find out how much of the end product is due to the contributions of the individual and how much to the interactions of the group.

One of the ways in which this question has been attacked is by comparing the relative effectiveness of individuals and groups at problem-solving tasks. In one such study, for example (Maier, 1970), comparisons were made between the output of subjects working alone in both of two trials; another in which an equal number worked alone on the first trial and cooperatively on a second trial; and, finally, a third group in which the subjects pooled their efforts in both trials. The results showed that solutions arrived at by subjects working in a group were superior to those arrived at by individuals working alone. But this obtained only when there was at least one individual in the group who had by himself reached a superior solution. In other studies, the results were not as clear cut. Sometimes the performance of the group came out superior, and at other times individuals working alone proved superior.

Perhaps too much emphasis need not be placed on whether solutions arrived at by groups are superior or inferior to those arrived at individually. Clearly, much depends on the type of problem dealt with, as well as on the nature of the objective pursued. Basic problems in science have been usually solved or best formulated by creative individuals working independently; practical ones, through cooperative effort. Striking examples of each are, respectively, the enunciation of the theory of relativity by Albert Einstein and the production of the A-bomb by the scientists working on the Manhattan project.

Summing up the evidence presented, one is impressed by the fact that there are many situations and areas of activity where the efforts of a group produce effective solutions that could not have been arrived at by individual pursuit. Part of this achievement may be ascribed to the fact that the group as a unit has a greater amount of knowledge at its disposal. More important is the fact that individuals when working in a group tend to influence each other's thinking.

The result is an interaction, explicable perhaps in terms of resonance phenomena analogous to those used to explain intellectual insight (Wechsler, 1960). From this interaction, something ''new'' in the creative sense emerges. Like necessity, cooperative thinking may be the mother of invention. The product may not be very impressive, but it is something that is the result of a unique integration. It has emerged because many have participated. A cross-fertilization of a kind has taken place. When this occurs, I think that one is justified in speaking of it as a manifestation of collective intelligence; and this not merely because it has been shared, but also because it is different.

A word of caution: If there is a group intelligence, there is also a group stupidity. *Vox populi, vox dei* is a misleading generalization as are most Latin dicta. A successful election or a miscarried campus confrontation no more proves the merit of its cause than the claim of a Madison Avenue ad proves the value of the product it advertises. But they all testify to the existence of group thinking.

Finally, can the collective intelligence just defined be considered an inherited modus operandi similar to what Jung claimed for his collective unconscious? That depends—depends, as we said on the concept of collective intelligence, on how one defines intelligence. If one equates intelligence, as many do, with adaptive capacity, one must allow that the capacity for collective intelligence is inherited, since much of human behavior described as adaptive is biologically transmitted. This is true of human goal-directed activities, no less than nest building in birds. In my opinion, however, the capacity to adapt is not the only basis of judging intelligent behavior, and more often than not the least innovative. One cannot always use the singular experiences of the past to solve problems of the immediate present. Intelligence requires much more.

References

Maier, N. R. F. *Problem solving and creativity*. Belmont, Calif.: Brooks/Cole, 1970.
Wechsler, D. Intelligence, quantum resonance and thinking machines. *Transactions of the New York Academy of Sciences,* 1960, **22**, 259–266.

CONFORMITY AND THE IDEA OF BEING WELL BORN*

DAVID WECHSLER

Bellevue Psychiatric Hospital and New York University

Insistence on compliance with decreed rules of behavior and disapproval of comportment not in accord with expectations has always been one of the core tenets of organized groups. Conformity is demanded so that the group's way of life will not be interfered with, deviancy frowned upon because the ends of the group are threatened by it. In general, the resulting disharmony can be explained in terms of conflicts between the needs and presses of the individual and the interests of the group. Much of the present book has been devoted to a consideration of the problems engendered by these conflicts. In addition, however, there are often historically determined beliefs and ideas which can account for persistent and recurrent attitudes of a group, not only toward the individuals which compose it, but also vis-à-vis other groups by which they feel threatened.

One of these beliefs is the idea of being well born, that is, the belief that some men are so favored by their Maker or so well endowed by nature that they are by right, divine or otherwise, destined to rule over their fellowmen. This is a very important idea, not only because of the mischief and misery which its exploitation has caused throughout history, but because it has been so widely and persistently held by so

*Reprinted from *Conformity and Deviation*, edited by I. A. Berg and B. M. Bass, New York, Harpers, 1961, pp. 412-423. © 1961, Harper & Row, Publishers. Reprinted by permission.

many different kinds of people, good as well as evil. In the past decades we have seen what heinous crimes have been committed in its name by a group of vicious and obscene men and their misguided or enslaved followers. It would be a mistake, however, to assume that the Nazis and their like have been the only ones who made use of this idea for their own ends. The greatly admired Greeks of the Periclean age likewise believed that some men were born better than others, and for this reason permitted slavery.

THE IDEA OF SUPERIORITY. Even more significant than the ubiquity of the idea of being well born is the large role which this belief has played in the philosophy and codes of those born to power and prerogative, or franchised to it. From the Pharaohs of Egypt to the Hitlers of modern Europe, from the Brahman priests to the Nazi Gauleiters, from the votaries of divine rights to the apologists of modern eugenics, there runs the same theme: master people, master race. Those born to power, those born to wealth, the would-be strong, the would-be rich, the would-be anybodies; their claims are the same: "We are the elite, we are the deserving." How this idea has manifested and maintained itself is a story too long to be detailed in a single paper. It begins with man's earliest effort to exploit his genealogy.

Forebears and Status

Genealogy is the oldest of human "sciences." The first records of literate man are ancestral rosters and social registers. In describing the heroes of the Trojan War, Homer never fails to tell us who their fathers were. Achilles, the Fleet of Foot, is not only the mightiest of Greek warriors but the son of Peleus; Agamemnon and Menelaus are always referred to as the Atridae, that is, the descendants of Atreus; and Odysseus of many devices, peer of Zeus in council, as the son of Laertes.

The modern reader may wonder why Homer has to identify the greatest of Greek warriors by reference to one Peleus,
a minor princeling, the king of one of the lesser Thesselian
tribes, who participated in the war against Troy. If so, he will
also find it hard to understand why the author of the first
gospel goes out of his way to prove that the son of God was
of the direct line of David. The explanation of both accounts
is not hard to find, if one bears in mind the epochs to which
the personnae are related. Three thousand years ago man
expected all his heroes to be of divine origin. Two thousand
years ago, at least his kings and prophets. Homer was re-
minding his readers that Achilles was of divine origin on his
father's as well as on his mother's side. Peleus was not himself a great hero but his father Aeacus was the son of Zeus.

Emphasis on the father's derivation, place of birth and
mother's maiden name, so curiously like the information
required on applications for country clubs or admission to
an Ivy League college, was ancient even in Homer's day.
The genealogies of the Iliad, like the "begats" of the Bible,
were seemingly an established custom practiced by the scribes
of Tutankhamen and the major-domos of the brick-writing
Sumerians.

HEROES AND HISTORY. From the beginning of recorded
history, men have expected their heroes to be well born. In
ancient times men meant that they were either related or
descended from the God-heads themselves; at other periods
a few select were permitted to claim this kinship. This kinship might be claimed both for the individuals or a clan or
a nation as a whole. In any case, the descent was described to
unique or a single pair of ancestors. Primitive genealogy always begins with the creation story, the progenitors of the
first man.

There are many legends or hypotheses as to how the first

man came to be. The one with which the peoples of the West
are most familiar is the story of Adam in Genesis. God created
Adam on the sixth day after he had finished with the heavens,
the earth and all living creatures. And God said, "Let us
make man in our own image after our own likeness and let
him have domination over the fish of the sea and the fowl
of the air and over the cattle and all over the earth" (Gen.
1:26). "So God created man in his own image, in the image
of God created He him" (Gen. 1:27).

The story of creation, as recounted in Genesis, is not
unique, nor original with the authors of the Bible. There are
many similar related stories in the legends of other peoples.
These differ in detail but are generally alike in two important respects. They asseverate man's special creation and
represent him as having been fashioned in his Maker's image.

OTHER VIEWS.   In opposition to the theory of special creation there has long existed the contrary hypothesis that man
was evolved from a lower form of life. This second theory is
at least as old as the first and, according to Frazier, almost
as widely distributed among primitive peoples. It is most
frequently encountered among Totemic, particularly African
tribes, who believe that their ancestors sprang from certain
animals or plants. It is also common among certain tribes of
American Indians. Thus, the Osages believe that they were
descended from the female beaver, the Iroquois from the
mud turtle, the Delaware Indians from the rattlesnake, and
the Indians of Peru from the puma. These legends indicate
that theories of evolution far from beginning with Darwin
or even Democritus, go back to the earliest speculations of
primitive man. Until recent times they seemed to have relatively little impact on major religions and social mores, particularly those of the Western world. We can only conjecture
what might have been man's outlook toward life and attitude

toward his destiny if the reverse had been true, but we can follow more definitely some of the consequences of the special creation theory.

BLOODLINES AND STATUS. One of these is the concept of uniqueness or exclusiveness; another, the view that those who did not share the heritage or origin of the group were in some way deviant or damned. These did not necessarily go together. The descendants of Abraham, for example, considered themselves the chosen people; and the descendants of Romulus and Remus thought of themselves as a noble line of conquering sons. But while they regarded the others as less fortunate, they did not look upon other peoples as inferior or species apart. The latter view seems to have been a later-day addition. Here again time does not permit me to enlarge on the manner in which this view developed, nor to detail the different forms it has taken. I shall skip some two thousand years and examine only one or two of its modern versions.

Modern Versions of Superiority

The most familiar example is the doctrine of Aryan superiority. This doctrine, most extensively espoused by peoples of northern Europe, began about the middle of the last century, following speculations of a number of philologists, particularly Frederick Max-Muller, Professor of Comparative Philology at Oxford, who sought to account for some striking similarities in the root forms of Indo-European languages. The evolved theory, as you will recall, was that the communality or similarity of these root words testified to the probable derivation of these languages from some original tongue. The tongue so identified was the ancient Sanskrit or hypothetical Aryan language. From a reconstructed Aryan language it was only a step to an assumed Aryan race. In fairness to Max-Muller, it should be noted that in his later years he denied there was any connection between blood and language. "If I say Aryans," he wrote, "I mean neither blood, nor bones, nor brain, nor skull. I mean simply those who speak the Aryan language."

The denial was of no avail; a new school of political and social anthropologists had already taken over the seeming implications of Max-Muller's theory and began using them as a base for their own doctrine, namely, that of a unique primordial stock from which this basic Aryan language was derived. The origin of this Aryan stock was variously located, among other places in the high plateaus of Persia, from whence after some wandering it supposedly settled in the hills of the Kush Mountains of India. Here lived a tribe known as the Aryas whom the original stock conquered and with whom it later intermingled. These Aryas or Aryans were pictured as a virile and aggressive people who at some unspecified date left their original mountainous abodes and eventually ended up somewhere along the shores of the Baltic. In their trek from Asia to Europe they left a trail of progeny behind them, which became the ancestors of the Indo-Germanic peoples. These prehistoric Aryas were, for the needs of the doctrine, described as a superbly endowed race whose superlative physical and mental traits determined not only the linguistic but the cultural destinies of the dominant peoples of Europe.

SKULLS AND SUPERIORITY.   A seeming aid to the Aryan doctrine came at about the same time from the new science of anthropometry which attempted, among other things, to classify peoples on the basis of certain measures of body physique. The measurement which seemed to give the most promising basis for classification is the now familiar cephalic index, that is, the ratio between the vertical and horizontal diameters of the skull. The cephalic index offered a simple way of classifying the crania into three main groups, the long heads (dolichocephalics), the short heads (brachycephalics) and the in-betweens (mesocephalics). When some early studies indicated that a large proportion of Swedes, Danes, and inhabitants of certain parts of Germany were predominantly dolichocephalic, the advocates of Nordic supremacy made use of this finding as additional proof that the Nordics were the lineal descendants of the Aryas. Dolichocephaly was then made a criterion for general superiority, and the last quarter of the nineteenth century produced many attempts to prove this theory.

Why the length of a man's head, any more than the length of his foot, should be associated with superior traits may be hard to understand. But, the fact to be borne in mind is that the object of this hypothesis was not to validate a possible correlation between physical and mental traits, but rather to exploit it as a biological argument in support of an already accepted theory. We need not go into these particular claims which have long since been discredited, nor stop to evaluate similar attempts to supplement dolichocephaly with other physical characters like fair skin and blonde hair as evidence for the existence of a picked race of men. Error is a protean monster which cannot be destroyed in one fell swoop. Like the Lydian hydra it may sprout two heads for every one that is cut off. Gobineau was followed by Lapouge and Aman; Chamberlain by a host too long to mention. The Gobineaus and Chamberlains of the late nineteenth century, no less than the Rosenbergs of the present one, were obviously not interested in scientific data, but an evidence, however spurious, that would support their prejudices.

The type of "evidence" exploited by groups claiming superior endowment has varied with the cultural sophistication of the eras at which it was entertained. Divine genealogy, historic philology and cranial measurements have largely given way, though not entirely, and been replaced by the popularized errors of modern genetics. We need not go into the question as to whether the particular traits posited are transmitted by way of heredity, actually very few, if any, have been demonstrated to be so; nor whether the traits in question are possessed to any greater degree by the groups that claim them than by those to whom they are denied. For example, whether the white are in point of fact more intelligent than the colored people, Nordics more adventuresome than Mediterraneans, the English less volatile than the French, and so on. The argument is still the same, except that endowment is no longer traced to divine ancestry but to genetic heredity. This is small gain for those who are excluded by either.

CLUBS, LODGES, AND THE NEW NEED FOR STATUS. The idea of being well born has generally been a belief entertained by dominant groups which by virtue of and in proportion to their dominance have been able to implant their philosophy on a people or a nation as a whole. But even in places or countries not so affected, one always finds numerous self-constituted groups who harbor the idea and, in one way or another, seek to exploit it. They may not be sufficiently strong to influence national politics significantly but nevertheless affect the cultural patterns of large portions of the population. They may consist of loose associations or well-knit organizations, tied together by religious, political or economic interests, and be inspired by old or new "isms." They may take the form of snob societies, military cliques, professional associations, splinter parties and almost any kind of socio-economic interest group. Sooner or later, they develop views regarding their own superiority and the conviction that those whom they seek to exclude are inferior. In this last respect the Daughters of the American Revolution and the eating clubs of Princeton are no different from various benighted and class prejudiced groups, although in terms of social goals and everyday behavior they may be far apart.

Political Aspects

These examples thus far cited have emphasized primarily the negative consequences of the idea of being well born. These are not inevitable sequellae but the most usual ones encountered. There are occasions, however, when it has been used in a positive way to emphasize obligations and duties as well as prerogatives either to account for a group's claim to unique origin or to justify the continuance of its special status. Such, for example, was the influence of Sparta's claimed descent from a line of demigods whose mighty and adventurous deeds form the first chapters of the nation's history, and served as a model for the mores of its rulers in later days. A similar role may be ascribed to legends pertaining to the origins of other ancient peoples. In other eras, the positive aspects of the idea were reflected in the self-imposed codes of honor among various orders of nobility. Familiar examples are the knight errantry of medieval feudalism, the special obligations assumed at times by royal houses and their followers, the assumed responsibilities of the gentry classes, the ideals expressed in the concept of the gentleman and in the codes of divers groups which include the concept of *noblesse oblige* as part of their ideology.

RESPONSIBILITY AND PRIVILEGE. But whether the idea of being well born has been employed to furnish a glorified account of a nation's early history, as a way of encouraging social responsibility or as a means of perpetuating special privilege, its basic significance for those who appropriate it has been that, by virtue of their origin, they constitute an elite or noble class. The original Greek word *eugenes* for nobility in fact meant being well born, and this has constituted its basic definition the world over. The implementation of the idea has varied from time to time, but while the codes of the Eugenes of Sparta, the Patricians of Rome, the Brahmins of India and the Peers of England have differed in certain details they are all in accord that the members of their class constitute a group apart. In most places this *apartheid* was ascribed to divine ordination, and was generally buttressed by a State religion, the priesthood itself constituted an elite class. But it has taken other forms as well.

The belief in class distinctions, whether considered innate or acquired, is of course, a philosophy not confined to groups imbued with the idea of being well born. It is an essential tenet of all groups who are afraid of being ousted or displaced, and in particular of totalitarian governments. And this obtains whether they are weak or strong. Contemporary communist states are striking examples of the latter. In spite of their egalitarian proclamations and claims to being a classless society, the leaders of these states regard themselves as in some way specially anointed, not by way of hereditary perhaps, but by a dialectic which crowns them as a select group entrusted with all the answers of how to organize a new world. The leaders do not, of course, designate themselves as a class apart, but so far as their treatment of demurring or minority groups is concerned, there is little to distinguish between their dictatorship of the proletariat and the dictatorship of any other sort. Thus, the Russian communist state, with its entrenched bureaucracy, as Milovan Djilas has shown, is just a new exploiting and dominating class with a philosophy vis-à-vis dissenting groups no different from other oligarchies, only more implacable. The commissars and members of the party are an elect, chosen to be sure not by an accepted divinity, but nevertheless tracing their lineage to an equated set of demigods (Lenin and Stalin). They thus constitute an elite class, and like all privileged classes, assert their power by the usual ukase, "conform or else." The communist code differs from historically similar ones in that it seeks to control the individual's thinking as well as his behavior. Thought control, per se, is not an entirely new technique. As practiced by the communists it is closely linked to otherwise widely accepted psychological theory. Brain washing and forced confessions are employed by them not merely for the purpose of intimidating future dissenters but also because, like the exponents of the hidden persuaders, they are firmly convinced that sooner or later thought may lead to action.

Thus far I have spoken more of conformity than nonconformity because it is the aspect of social behavior most often associated with the idea of being well born. Conformity is also easier to define than nonconformity, particularly if we focus our attention on the individuals rather than the terms descriptive of the concepts involved. A conformist is, broadly speaking, a person who does what is expected of him in any given society or subgroup of it, that is, complies with accepted rules of conduct. A nonconformist can be anyone who does not comply with the rules; but the ways in which he may demur from or defy prevailing thought or mores are innumerable. Nonconformists run the entire gamut of dissidents from the religious reformer and political maverick to the beatnik and delinquent. In the latter category they are also called deviants. Deviancy implies not only atypicality in the statistical sense, but abnormality in any one of a variety of meanings. A nonconformist may be disapproved, even thought of as eccentric, but seldom as immoral, antisocial. These distinctions are not mutually exclusive and actually involve considerable overlap. Much depends on the mores of the day, how threatening the views put forth, how ready the majority is for change, and so on. The nonconformist of today may be the conformist of tomorrow. This is particularly true of forerunners of religious thought and political change. I dare say Calvin, Luther, and Fox were considered the arch nonconformists of their day as have nearly all revolutionary figures from the Gracchi to some of the Fathers of the American Revolution in theirs. Some of these figures may have felt divinely inspired but seldom based their claims on the virtue of being well born. This status was generally bestowed or ascribed to them by their followers.

Summary

The idea of being well born is one of the oldest and most pervasive concepts in the history of Western civilization. It can be traced back to the early Greeks and beyond, and is still current today. Some examples have been given to illustrate its impact on societal interactions and in particular, of its mischievous influence on historical attitudes of groups vis-à-vis other groups. The main point made is that it has been used primarily to maintain privilege and special status, however obtained, and that one of the main instruments for doing so has been the insistence of conformity of the group in power to its own ideology. The idea of being well born is not the only concept so employed. In the long run it has not been as relentless as some others, for example, the class distinctions now employed by most of the communist states. Psychological determinants of conformity as related to the idea of being well born are many, but basic to all has been the feeling of insecurity of various groups induced by fear of being ousted or displaced from positions of power and privilege.

THE I.Q. IS AN INTELLIGENT TEST*

DAVID WECHSLER

IT IS NOW TWO YEARS SINCE THE NEW YORK CITY SCHOOL SYSTEM eliminated the I.Q. from pupils' records. Banned under the pressure of groups that claimed the I.Q. was unfair to the culturally deprived, it has been replaced by achievement tests. Meanwhile, a great deal of effort is being put into developing new, nonverbal scales to measure schoolchildren's abilities while eliminating the troublesome factor of language.

Neither of these substitutes is an adequate replacement for the I.Q. In my opinion, the ban was misdirected in the first place and we should restore the I.Q. to its former position as a diagnostic tool as soon as possible. The substitutes simply do not test enough of the abilities that go to make up individual intelligence.

To understand what I.Q. tests do, and why they are valuable, we must first be clear about what intelligence is. This is a surprisingly thorny issue. To much depends upon how one defines intelligence. In this respect psychologists are in no better agreement than the lay public. Divergency of view stems largely from differences in emphasis on the particular abilities thought to be central to the definition one envisages. Thus, an educator may define intelligence primarily as the ability to learn, a biologist in terms of ability to adapt, a psychologist as the ability to reason abstractly and the practical layman as just common sense.

One difficulty is similar to what a physicist encounters when asked to state what he means by energy, or a biologist what he means by life. The fact is that energy and life are not tangible entities; you cannot touch them or see them under a microscope even though you are able to describe them. We know them by their effects or properties.

*Reprinted from *The New York Times,* June 26, 1966. © 1966 by The New York Times Company. Reprinted by permission.

The same is true of general intelligence. For example, we must assume that there is something common to learning to count, avoiding danger and playing chess which makes it possible for us to say that they are evidence of intelligent behavior, as against learning to walk, being accident prone and playing bingo, which seemingly have little if anything to do with it.

Intelligence, operationally defined, is the aggregate capacity of the individual to act purposefully, to think rationally and to deal effectively with his environment. Although it is not a mere sum of intellectual abilities, the only way we can evaluate it quantitatively is by the measurement of various aspects of these abilities.

Any test is primarily a device for eliciting and evaluating a fragment of behavior. An intelligence test is one by which an examiner seeks to appraise this bit of behavior insofar as it may be called intelligent. Various abilities can be used for this purpose because manifestations of ability are the means by which a subject can communicate and demonstrate his competences. To this end it is not so much the particular ability that is tested which is important, as the degree to which it correlates with posited criteria. A test is considered a good measure of intelligence if it correlates, for example, with learning ability, ability to comprehend, evidence of capacity to adjust and so on. If it does so to a satisfactory degree it is said to be valid. But, even when a test has been established as valid, there still remains a question: For what class of subjects is it valid? The answer will depend in a large measure upon the population on which the test was standardized—for example, middle-class white children, Southern Negro children or recently arrived Puerto Ricans.

Thus I.Q. tests are attacked on the ground that they are overweighted with items depending on verbal ability and academic information. Individuals with limited educational backgrounds are obviously penalized, and non-English-speaking subjects are admittedly incapable of taking the tests at all. This is an important stricture and test makers, contrary to some opinion, are fully aware of it. One way of "solving" the problem would be to provide separate normal or average scores for different populations, but apart from the practical difficulty of obtaining such norms, there is always the stricture that they bypass rather than meet the central issue. A compromise approach is practiced in some school systems, where intelligence tests continue to be used—under the more acceptable name of "aptitude tests."

Almost from the start, psychologists have sought to cope with the problem of literacy and language disability by devising nonverbal tests of intelligence. Thus, soon after the Binet tests were introduced more than a half-century ago, two American psychologists, Pintner and Paterson, developed the Non-Language Individual Performance Scale for non-English-speaking subjects. Similarly, when the Army Alpha (the main verbal test of World War I) was devised for the military services, a companion nonverbal test (the Army Beta) was prepared along with it.

The Pintner-Paterson scale required the subject to give evidence of his capacities by filling in appropriate missing parts on familiar pictures, putting together form boards, learning to associate signs with symbols, etc. The Army Beta consisted of such tasks as following mazes, reproducing picture designs, counting cubes, etc.—with directions presented to the subject by gesture or mime.

Many similar tests—the so-called "culture-free" or "culture-fair" tests—have followed. The most recent one reported is the Johns Hopkins Perceptual Test devised by Dr. Leon Rosenberg and associates at the Johns Hopkins School of Medicine. This test was initially developed for children who did not speak or who were handicapped by certain functional or organic disorders; it has also been recommended as a more effective intelligence test for the very young and for culturally deprived children.

The Johns Hopkins Perceptual Test consists of a series of designs from which a child is asked to choose appropriate patterns to match others shown to him. Its primary merit is that it eliminates the factor of language. It is also claimed to be less dependent than verbal tests upon acquired skills, which, of course, depend to some extent upon a child's environmental experience. But this test, like other performance tests, does not measure a sufficient number of the abilities that go to make up the total picture of intelligent behavior.

Contrary to claims, the results of performance tests have been generally disappointing. The findings indicate that while they may be useful in certain situations, and for certain diagnostic groups, they prove quite unsatisfactory as alternates for verbal scales. They correlate poorly with verbal aptitudes and are poor prognosticators of over-all learning ability as well as school achievement. Above all, they have turned out to be neither culture-free nor culture-fair.

Culture-free tests fail to attain their end because, in the first place, the items usually employed are themselves subject to particular environmental experiences. A circle in one place may be associated with the sun, in another with a copper coin, in still another with a wheel. In some places a dog is a pet, in others a detested animal. Pictures, in the long run, are just symbols and these may be as difficult to understand and recognize as words; they have to be interpreted, as anyone who has attempted to learn sign language knows. Putting together blocks may be a challenge or a threat, working fast a sign of carelessness or an incentive to competition. Nonverbal, even more than verbal tests, need to be related to particular environments and, from a practical point of view, are both limited in range and difficult to contrive.

Finally, many performance items when increased in difficulty tend to become measures of special abilities rather than having any significant correlation with over-all measures of intelligence. Thus, while tests of visual motor coordination may be useful items on intelligence tests for young children they are no longer effective at later ages. Copying a diamond is a good test at the 7-year level, but whether a child of 12 can reproduce a complicated design has little to do with his general intelligence and represents at most a special ability.

The effect of culture on test performance is a subject that demands serious concern, but here one deals with the problem of what one understands by the word "culture." In the United States there is a strong trend among contemporary writers to identify the term with socio-economic levels. This is in contrast to the historic and broader meaning of the term, which covers all human as well as environmental influences that serve to characterize the intellectual and moral status of a civilization.

Not all the poor are culturally deprived. Although standards may differ widely, "culturally different" does not mean "culturally deprived." The Jews and Italians who lived on the Lower East Side had their culture, and so have the Negroes in the slums of Harlem. They differ widely in respect to almost any variable one might employ, and culture is no exception. What this implies is that "culture" no more than color of skin should be a basis for assessing individuals.

The comments relating to the question of cultural impact apply with equal force to the problem of racial and national differences. One may start with the hypothesis that such differences exist and not necessarily be overwhelmed by their importance. This, in the writer's opinion, is a reasonable position.

This opinion is based on studies done in the field and, in particular, on data from World War I and World War II United States Armed Forces testing programs. The data from World War I included not only tables for the overall draft population but for a great many subgroupings. Among these were separate test-score summaries according to national origin of the draftees, and a particularly detailed one comparing Negroes and whites. As might have been expected, differences between groups compared were found, and as might also have been expected invidious comparisons were immediately made and exploited. Particularly emphasized were the lower scores made by Negroes as compared with those made by white soldiers. Neglected, on the other hand, were the differences found between occupational levels and the more general ones between urban and rural populations.

It was not too difficult to correct the erroneous inferences made by the racists. But, in disposing of the racial claims, some authors went much beyond what the data warranted. Eventually, statements were made that other test findings revealed no significant differences between any national or racial groups—a fact which is equally questionable, and in any event still needs to be demonstrated. In the author's opinion, national and racial differences do exist—probably of both genetic and environmental origins, in varying degree. But the fact is that these differences are not large or relevant in the individual case.

We now come to the biggest bugaboo of intelligence testing—the I.Q. itself. The scientific literature on it is as large as its assailants are numerous. It has been attacked by educators, parents, writers of popular articles and politicians. During the Korean War it was investigated by Congress. Now that we are once more having trouble with draft quotas, the I.Q. will most likely be investigated again. It is doubtful whether the I.Q. can be brought into good grace at this time, but perhaps much of the fire sparked by the I.Q. can be quenched by an objective explanation of what it really is.

An I.Q. is just a measure of relative brightness. It merely asserts that, compared with persons of his own age group, an individual has attained a certain rank on a particular intelligence test. For example, a 10-year-old takes the Stanford-Binet test and attains a certain score, which happens to be that for the statistically average 8-year-old. We then divide the child's mental age (8) by his chronological age (10) and obtain a quotient, which we multiply by 100 simply to remove the inconvenience of decimal points. The result is called the Intelligence Quotient (or I.Q.)—in this case, 80. This particular figure tells us that, as compared with others in his age group, the child has performed below normal (which would be 100).

When this procedure of comparative grading is applied to a geography or bookkeeping test—when a teacher apportions class grades on a bell curve or a sliding scale—nobody gets excited. But when it is used with a mental test the reaction is quite different.

Opposition is generally focused not on the way that I.Q.'s are computed, but, more pointedly, on the way they are interpreted and utilized. One interpretation that has caused understandable concern is the notion that a person is "born with" an I.Q. which remains immutable. This is an allegation proclaimed by those who are opposed to the I.Q. rather than a view maintained by psychologists. What is asserted by psychologists, and supported by test-retest findings, is that I.Q.'s once accurately established are not likely to vary to any considerable degree. This does not mean that an I.Q. never changes, or that the conditions under which it was obtained may not have affected its validity.

The so-called constancy of the I.Q. is relative, but compared with other commonly used indexes, it is surprisingly stable. It is much more stable, for instance, than an individual's electrocardiogram or his basal metabolism level, which are accepted without question.

There are always exceptional cases which cannot be overlooked or bypassed. But one does not throw out the baby with the bath water. When for any reason a subject's I.Q. is suspect, the sensible thing to do is to have him retested. I.Q.'s, unlike the laws of the Medes and the Persians, are not irrevocable, but they should be respected.

While retest studies show that I.Q.'s are relatively stable, they also reveal that in individual cases large changes may occur—as much as 20 points or more. Thus, conceivably, an individual could move from the "dull normal" group to "average," or vice versa.

Much depends upon the age at which the original test was administered and the interval between testings. In general, I.Q.'s obtained before the age of 4 or 5 are more likely to show discrepancies between test and retest; those in the middle years least. Discrepancies are also likely to be larger as the intervals between retests increase. All this evidence points to reasons for not making a definitive intelligence classification on the basis of a single test, and more especially on one administered at an early age. This precaution is necessary not because the tests are unreliable but because rates of mental maturity are often factors that have to be taken into account. Such variations tend not only to penalize slow developers but also to overrate early bloomers.

Various skills are required for effective test performance at different age levels. The fact that they are not present at a particular age level does not indicate that a child who lacks them is necessarily stunted. It may only be that these skills have not as yet emerged. Early training has a bearing on test readiness, but it is not true that if a child has not had this training at one age, he will not develop the skills required at a later age. On the other hand, deliberately teaching a child skills in order to have him "pass" an intelligence test, as now seems to be the vogue, is not the answer to acquiring a high I.Q.

An important conclusion to be drawn from the above is that more, rather than less, testing is needed. Unfortunately, when this is suggested, one encounters the objection that extended testing programs in public schools would be too costly. The expensiveness of school testing has been greatly exaggerated, especially when considered in relation to the over-all cost of keeping a child in school (an average of $600 to $700 per child per year in most parts of the country).

Particularly neglected is the individual intelligence examination, which at present is administered in most public schools only to "problem cases." In the author's opinion, an individual intelligence examination ought to be given to all children as they enter school. Most private schools require such an examination, and there is good reason why the public schools should also provide it.

Allowing $50 per examination administered once over a four-year period, the cost would be a minuscule addition to the school's budget. In return, a systematic individual examination could serve as a means of evaluating a child's assets and liabilities before he was subjected to the hazards of arbitrary placement. Finally, it must be borne in mind that intelligence tests are intended as a means not merely for detecting the intellectually retarded, but also for discovering the intellectually gifted.

In discussions of the merits and limitations of intelligence tests, one important aspect, frequently overlooked, is their basic aim. This objective is most effectively summed up in the late Prof. Irving Lorge's definition of what intelligence tests aim to measure—namely, "the ability to learn and to solve the tasks required by a particular environment."

This definition implies a multiple approach to the concept of intelligence and intelligence testing. In the latter process, one is of necessity engaged in evaluating an individual's particular abilities. Of course, in doing so, one obtains information regarding a subject's liabilities and handicaps. This information is both useful and important, but is really only an incidental aspect of what one wishes to discover from an intelligence test.

When it is asserted that intelligence tests are unfair to the disadvantaged and minorities, one must be mindful of the fact that they are simply recording the unfairness of life. They show also, for example, that our mental abilities, whoever we may be, decline with advancing age. (Of course, this decline is in many cases counterbalanced by increased experience.)

Intelligence tests were not devised for the handicapped alone but for everybody. What then can be the reason for believing they may not be suitable for the major segments of our population—or for prohibiting their administration to the majority of children in a school system? The current New York City I.Q. ban is a case in point, and especially discouraging when one sees what is being used instead.

The tests that have been substituted are a series of achievement tests—in particular, reading tests. Of all the possible choices, one can hardly imagine a worse alternative. For of all areas in which the disadvantaged child is handicapped, reading heads the list. The main difference between an intelligence (or aptitude) test and an achievement test is that the former is less tied to curriculum content. If it is true that a low score on an intelligence test presents a misleading picture of a pupil's learning capacity, how much more unfair would be an even lower score on an achievement test. It is possible that the I.Q. was banned in New York because those who supported the ban wished primarily to combat what they believed to be a widespread view that the I.Q. is "somehow a fixed, static and genetic measure of learning ability." One may wonder, however, whether political pressures may not have played some role in the decision—and one may hope that the ban will soon be retracted.

The I.Q. has had a long life and will probably withstand the latest assaults on it. The most discouraging thing about them is not that they are without merit, but that they are directed against the wrong target. It is true that the results of intelligence tests, and of others, too, are unfair to the disadvantaged, deprived and various minority groups but it is not the I.Q. that has made them so. The culprits are poor housing, broken homes, a lack of basic opportunities, etc., etc. If the various pressure groups succeed in eliminating these problems, the I.Q.'s of the disadvantaged will take care of themselves.

INTELLIGENCE IN A CHANGING WORLD

DAVID WECHSLER

I am seemingly a person liable to multiple identification. Once, when in Athens, a number of people mistook me for a Greek; in Paris, I passed for a Frenchman and even in Tokyo I could, with a little squinting and bowing at the proper distance, be sometimes mistaken for a native. But while I was sometimes misidentified as to ancestral antecedents, I seldom passed unrecognized as the author of certain tests to which my name has become attached. This latter association was not always an asset, because nearly every place I was invited, I was expected to speak on these tests, or at least, some aspects of them. Perhaps, many in this audience may have entertained the same expectation, and would have been surprised if I had chosen a topic very different from the one on which I will speak this evening.

As you now know from the title of my address, I shall not entirely disappoint you. However, my talk will have little to do with intelligence tests or even with what they are supposed to measure. Rather, it will be concerned with the hopeful role of intelligence as a directive force in the administration of human affairs. Applying the term in this broad context, you might expect me to begin with an explicit statement as to what I mean by intelligence. I could do this, but prefer instead to let the general substance of my remarks convey to you its meaning. I also am avoiding any general definition of intelligence because I shall be primarily concerned with what I consider its central and, for us, relevant attribute, namely, the ability to perceive, to understand and to educe rational relationships.

The crucial word here is *understand*. To understand is to be consciously aware of what is involved, whether it be the implication of an idea, or the consequences of an act. To be sure, there are other factors, like persistence, drive and special talent, which also enter into effective intelligent behavior. But in my opinion, they contribute very little if not guided by understanding. In any case, it is about intelligence as manifested in understanding with which I shall be primarily concerned.

One of the more astounding, and at the same time dismaying, paradoxes of history is the minor role which intellectual ability has played in determining the political destinies of mankind. In spite of the fact that the man of intellect has been largely responsible for what may be broadly defined as human progress, he has seldom been called upon to participate actively in the decisions of government, or in shaping policies of state which determine the day to day course of human affairs.

One can only speculate why this has been so; why warriors and priests rather than philosophers and poets; why businessmen and politicians rather than scientists and sociologists, have been called upon to exercise this role. But, whatever the explanation for the events of the past, it is becoming increasingly clear that the changing state of society now requires a new type of leadership. Science and technology has made our society increasingly dependent upon the man of special talent and intellectual endowment. We are fast arriving towards a society which, in the apt phrase of Ralph Lapp, is keyed to the high I.Q. One should expand upon the meaning of this much abused term; but for our present purpose it will suffice to assume it to be synonomous with the intellectually gifted or mentally more able segment of our population. However, even with this delimitation, one is at once confronted with the increasing level of education; the communication gap between scientists and laymen has become greater rather than smaller.

Atomic fission and high-energy physics are not only hard to explain, but call for a mathematical understanding and research comprehension as well as a specialized vocabulary accessible to a relative few. Atomic and high-energy physics research aims are also expensive, and experiments in these fields are only possible through large government subsidies. It is estimated, for example, that by the end of 1972 the United States will have spent some five billion dollars a year on high energy research and development alone. This is less than what is spent by women in America on cosmetics but still a considerable sum. Could it not be spent more judiciously?

The average layman is not in a position to answer this question, but should the scientists alone be allowed to make the decision? The advances of science, behavioral as well as physical, have not only called for the selection of the intellectually gifted, but also for an increasing degree of specialization. It has led to the relative insulation of the scientists from the world of the layman, and brought with it the demoralizing consequences that result from the division of labor. It has led increasingly to what Karl Marx (in his more meaningful appraisals) called the estrangement of the worker from his product. But whereas Marx's appraisal referred primarily to the mill and factory worker, it is obvious that it has now begun to apply to the intellectual worker. What the machine and bulldozer did for physical labor, the computer and electronic devices are doing for the mental worker.

If all this were not enough to worry about, contemporaneous civilization is now confronted with the revolutionary changes in mass communication and electronic media which are reshaping and influencing nearly all social structures. Communication by printed word is becoming of limited value, and according to McLuhan, useful primarily to the advanced scholar. Most learning, he claims, takes place outside the classroom. The printed word for him is only an ''oblivious vault for posterity.'' What is needed is face to face confrontation with immediate reality, not with one or even a thousand persons, but a listening audience of millions. We are no longer being cautioned against the hidden persuaders, but alerted to the merits of the serialized soap operas and the advantages of audiovisual instruction.

The irony of all this is that many of McLuhan's claims are not without substance. Mass media are not only greatly in the public domain, but have given rise to an emerging special class, the television performer, the script writer and video commentator. Here is a new type of intellectual (pardon the expression of the term) with an impact and influence much more formidable than that of the scientist.

I have digressed somewhat from the topic, but only by way of calling your attention to the variety of new priesthoods as well as new problems to which our contemporaneous western civilization is exposed. Whether we want it or not, ours is a pluralistic world. We must account for the Hitlers and Stalins as well as understand the Einsteins and Russells; we must grapple with the implications of mass media as well as the contamination resulting from atomic fallout. A crucial factor for success on the various fronts will be the degree to which we are ready, willing, and able to utilize our intelligence. But for that, much will, of course, depend on what we comprehend under the term intelligence.

There are many definitions of intelligence and I could devote the rest of my address merely to quoting them. I shall not do this, but just note their most frequent common denominator: They are all concerned with the relative ability of the individual to perceive, to understand, and to deal with the world around him. Depending upon the modality emphasized, some definitions describe intelligence in terms of the ability to adapt, others the ability to learn, still others to reason abstractly, and so on. The really crucial term is the word *understand,* understand in the sense of not only an awareness of the logic of a situation, but of related moral and social values as well. These involve what I have called the nonintellective factors of intelligence. They involve not so much knowledge and skills as the capacity to assess excellence, and the desirability of human aims and goals. In this respect, intelligence differs from sheer intellectual ability which, however deep its insights, is not concerned with any value system.

However one defines intelligence and intellectual ability, there is still the problem of how to identify the people who possess either trait to an eminent degree. Most psychologists think that this can best be done by means of mental tests. Men of affairs are likely to insist that it should be based on practical criteria which take into primary consideration an individual's ability to accommodate means to ends. The latter is in line with historic attempts to distinguish between the man of intellect and the man of action. There is some basis for this distinction which can be of value in certain practical situations, but in my opinion is quite irrelevant to an essential definition of intelligence. The main effect of this distinction has been to perpetuate historic prejudices in the direction of overestimating the man of common sense and belittling the man of intellect.

The view that common sense is the core trait in general intelligence is typical of professionals and laymen alike. *In my opinion, common sense is a much overrated trait.* I say this with full awareness that in trying to defend this unpopular point of view, one risks taking on not only the man in the street, but some of the heavy weights of philosophy; for example, the great philosopher René Descartes. The distinction between intellect, intelligence, and common sense goes back to epochs much earlier than the publication of his famous *Discours sur la Méthode;* but its sponsorship by Descartes gave it broad acceptance and respectability.

Descartes' main argument was that common sense is so all important because "it is of all things in the world most equally distributed, for everybody thinks himself so abundantly provided with it that those most difficult to please in all other matters, do not commonly desire more of it than they possess." What could be more convincing to the average man than that? Particularly when bolstered by Descartes' further assumption that "what is called Good Sense and Reason is by nature equal to all men."

It so happens that Descartes was first and foremost a man of intellect, and though his view on common sense is frequently quoted, he is best remembered for his dictum "cogito ergo sum" and as the inventor of analytic geometry.

In any event, great and lasting as his contributions were to science and philosophy, Descartes' views on "bon sens" have since been disproved. *We know now that "bon sens" or intelligence, like any other human trait, is far from equally distributed.* There are people with inferior and superior intelligence as well as the great many in-between. Moreover, what is becoming increasingly apparent is the growing intellectual dependency of the many on the able few. This is an inevitable consequence of the ever increasing complexity of modern society. The trend has been going on for some time, but in the past 50 years has been greatly accelerated by a technological and intellectual revolution which is radically changing our ways of life.

This revolution has been most conspicuous in the physical sciences, but is increasingly evident in the advances of the biological and to some extent, in the behavioral sciences. The theories of relativity, quantum mechanics, the splitting of the atom, the discovery of DNA, and chromosomal coding, constitute just a partial list of the familiar advances. *In these, common sense played a very minor role indeed, often an impeding one.* The discoveries listed are all achievements of the man of intellect and not of common sense.

There is another side to the current intellectual revolution: Its impact on the thinking of the average man. While the man in the street may not comprehend the scientific complexities of these revolutionary advances, he is far from untouched by their implications. He respects the men who are responsible for the space ships, the electronic computers and the wonder drugs. But, as ever, he is suspicious and afraid of them. He is not merely afraid of the atomic bomb and the intercontinental missile or the biochemists' seeming ability to manipulate the basic materials of life, he is more immediately frightened by the thought that the men who can do these things will alter his day to day living. In democracies like the United States, he fears that his hope of a government by the common man will be replaced by a government of "behind-the-scene" experts. This concern, I think, is in some respects justified. Men of intellect have in the past been able to influence, in varying degrees, the events of history; but now for the first time scientists are in a position to determine mankind's destiny.

The great majority of scientists are, I believe, quite sensitive to the situation. It is the heads of governments that need to be convinced. Unfortunately, too many of them cannot or will not realize that we are living in a fast changing world, a world in which brains rather than brawn will, in the long run, determine its future. A new type of helmsman is needed for the modern ship of state.

But what chance, must we ask, has the man of intellect to attain this position in a world where he is both suspected and feared, especially in places where rule by any elite is regarded as a serious threat. To those of us brought up in a democratic tradition, or dedicated to an egalitarian philosophy, such possibility is more than a mere threat. The threat, to be sure, is largely theoretical, and due in great part to a certain emphasis on the form rather than the ends of government. People are naturally suspicious of any government by the few, whether oligarchs or any other self-proclaimed elite. The management of governmental functions by a small number of experts, however, is inevitable in our modern world.

The immediate problem is into whose hands shall decision-making functions be entrusted. The persons selected for these positions need, of course, to possess the obvious qualifications of leadership and a sense of social responsibility; *but they also need to be individuals of high intellectual capacity*. These traits are not, as sometimes claimed, incompatible. Indeed, we have. from time to time had men in high places who combined both; we need more of them now.

I believe the course of recent events has made people increasingly aware of this need, and there have been corresponding changes in attitude by leaders of industry and business, as well as government. However, we still have far to go. The man of intellect, whether consultant or expert, is still suspected and resented, though perhaps for new reasons. As Hofstadter put it, "the intellectual was once ridiculed because he was not needed, now he is resented because he is needed."

One may hope that this resentment will eventually disappear. In the meantime, our contemporaneous society has a number of more immediate problems confronting it. One is the attitude of our youth to the changing world, another of the difficulties they are facing in trying to deal with the problems confronting them. Many articles have been written on the subject, but I will mention only one; namely that of Mr. James Reston which appeared in the *New York Times* a few years ago. It is a report on the attitudes of young men in Britain, and includes the following remarks: "So far as a visitor can note, the young people who have grown up since the war are not dominated by the angry young men of Britain, or by the Weirdies or Beardies, who want to ban the bomb, in Trafalgar Square. The charge against this emerging generation is not that they believe in wrong things, but that they don't believe in anything." The question is why.

I shall not presume to know the answers; but I think that some of the explanations that have been offered are incorrect. For example, I do not think that our young men and women are more afraid than their elders of the atomic bomb; or that they are terribly worried about unavailable jobs, although that is a serious problem. This generation, more than any before, is seeking answers to deeper rooted questions. They want to know above all, "what to work for and what to live for." The college and university student today is uncertain as to the value and purpose of his education. *He is concerned with his place in a changing world, a world in which fewer and fewer are called upon to use their intelligence and talents in worthwhile activities.*

By way of illustration, consider the problem that confronted us in the United States a few years ago in the matter of the acknowledged shortage of young men going in for engineering. This is a profession highly esteemed and (at least until recently) well remunerated. Why the lack of appeal now to the American youth for the profession? In a small way it may have been due to the unnecessarily difficult admission standards set up by many of the schools. Beyond that, and more disturbing, have been the increasing reports by graduate engineers, attesting to the fact that the much publicized opportunities for creative work are seldom realized. Similar situations are encountered in other professions. In some, as in the case of the teacher, inadequate remuneration has often been an additional factor. But inadequate salaries or even job insecurity do not constitute the whole or even major part of the problem. Scientists and teachers do not leave schools and universities merely because they are not paid as much as in industry; often, it is because other values which they had hoped for are not forthcoming. The problem, where it exists, is not caused because young people do not want to extend themselves, but because they feel that the work does not permit them to participate in things that count. Intelligent young people want to be useful, not used.

I have emphasized the role of intelligence in our changing world as it involves young people because they will be affected most by it. But there will always be oldsters; so I will add a few remarks on the role of intelligence for those of us who have reached the age generally designated, and sometimes euphemistically, as the period of later maturity.

When I was younger, I favored the view that most human abilities decline significantly with age, and supported it with annoying statistics. The evidence presented, showed that the point of maximum intellectual virility occurred about age 25, and that intellectual ability, with some exceptions, declined systematically thereafter. As years went by, I acknowledged the possibility of a somewhat later downward inflection in the curve, and finally compromised the whole business with the conclusion that, while intellectual ability declined with age, sagacity and wisdom not only remained untarnished, but acquired a new lustre. This, I now confess, is an evasion, though it contains sufficient truth to warrant remedial action. Whether or not "life begins at 40," all of us can continue to learn for a long time thereafter, provided that such learning is purposeful.

At present, much concern and attention is being given to the problems of retraining, and important as this may be from an economic point of view, I do not think it is the most crucial one. Even if it is solved (and hopefully it will be), there still remains the problem of what to do when one retires, voluntarily or otherwise. As the age of retirement is reduced, the number of years envisaged for the succeeding periods of life will progressively increase. Retirement at age 65 or even earlier need not be calamitous, provided the individual is prepared to cope with his inevitable time changes. To this end, adult education can play a great role. The adult citizen needs continued education, not so much as a requirement for possible reemployment, but primarily to better understand and live in the changing world around him.

There are many other aspects to the role of intelligence in our changing world. I will consider just one more; namely, the heralded threat of the Faustian competitor of modern man, the automaton computer or thinking machine. The latest computers, either in the process of design or already in being, can perform mental operations almost at any level of complexity, from computing inventories to solving differential equations, from playing chess to composing music, and so on to a long list of phenomenal achievements. These achievements are not only in the field of practical engineering or applied mathematics, but in many areas of theoretical physics, biochemistry, and even recondite problems of psychology. Computers have been recently employed to make physical diagnoses, and one may expect them before long to invade the sanctuaries of psychoanalysis. In any event, there can be no doubt but that, by any reasonable definition of the thinking process, machines are able to think. The question is whether they can also be said to be capable of manifesting intelligence. Some people believe they can.

There is already a sector of computer science devoted to what is known as artificial intelligence. I have been seriously interested in this field and the work being done in it is nothing short of breathtaking. *But remarkable as have been the achievements of electronic computers, nothing they do, in my opinion, can be equated with intelligence.* This is not because the computer only does what it is told to do. In this respect, human beings are not much different from machines. However, the thinking machine lacks the one capacity needed for, and indispensible to, intelligent behavior—the capacity to understand. It is never aware of the implications or consequencss of its choices and decisions.

It is precisely because it cannot go beyond performance that the machine is unable to act as an intelligent human being. Thus, the computer may be able to detect unerringly a suspect object in space, and set off at the precise moment the intercepting missile which will destroy it. However, it can never be permitted to release the missile, because it cannot of itself know whether it should do so or not. There is still need for a human being that understands as well as knows what to do.

This does not imply that the atomic bomb and electronic computer are not serious threats to mankind's future. But I believe that the urge for survival in human beings is so ingrained that they are unlikely to give up without a struggle for some time. But at what price?

I recently read again that remarkable little volume by H. G. Wells, "The Time Machine," first published more than 80 years ago. As many of you who have read the book will recall, it is about a machine which permitted its inventor to move into the remotest past or the most distant future; and what he saw when he did so.

The inventor decides to try out the machine for a look into things to come. Within a few moments, he finds himself projected some 8000 centuries into the future. Since he was only traveling in time, he is still at the same place from where he started—a suburb of London. But it is now the year 802,701 C.E.

Naturally, there have been many changes; but the greatest is in the people now inhabiting the region. He sees groups of creatures, all about four feet tall, identically garbed, and romping like children in a garden valley. The grown-ups also look and act like children, and one cannot easily distinguish males from females.

It is a society with seeming total security. All needs of the community seem to have been provided for. Poverty and disease have disappeared. There are no hospitals, factories or food stores. The scientists of the past had eliminated the need for them. There are no armies and no one has to work. The inhabitants are sure that they are now living in "the best of all possible worlds": they have no worry about the past nor any concern for the future. But, adds the author, the mentality of most of the population impressed him as being at about the level of a six-year-old child in the year 1895.

I trust that our scientists will not too soon provide us with such a Utopia.

They will not if we can in some way preserve the intelligence, which is at once the glory and the despair of our fast changing world.

I should be stopping here if, as I was completing these remarks, I had not glanced at the editorial page of the *World Telegram* and spotted the famous letter of little Virginia O'Hanley written in 1897 to the editor of the old New York *Sun,* and reprinted every year since. Reprinted also is the editor's reply.

As you will recall, Virginia wanted to know whether there really is a Santa Claus. The answer, of course, was that there is a Santa Claus. With this reply most of us would agree, but not for the reasons given by the Editor. For either because of a need to fill up space or because he really wanted to explain himself further, he included a statement which I now quote in part. "In this great universe man is a mere insect in his intellect. . . ." It was this assertion that bothered me.

In a more benign mood, I might have agreed that the intelligence level of our species leaves something to be desired, but I resented very much the allegation that it is no better than that of the lowly ant. The Editor not only insulted me and my friends, but my children and my wife, and all my ancestors coming and going. Moreover, the statement is patently untrue, and I have been sufficiently influenced by Bertrand Russell to be persuaded that an untruth should not be permitted even in a Christmas story.

So, as my resentment rose, I thought how nice it would be if I were able to write to Virginia myself, not to the same Virginia of course, but to her great granddaughter; and not about Santa Claus but in response to a question to which today many children need an answer. Here is the imagined letter and my reply, of course, as editor.

Dear Mr. Editor:

I am eight years old and go to a public school in New York. Most of the children in my class say that if you are too smart you get into trouble.

Yesterday my teacher told my mother I had a very high I.Q. Is that dangerous?

Dear Virginia:

Yes, Virginia, a high I.Q. can be dangerous. But in the world we live in we need more and more boys and girls who, when they grow up, will not be afraid of danger. I am sure you are one of them.

Your friend,

DAVID WECHSLER

PART III

INTRODUCTION

David Wechsler considers as a major contribution to psychology, the series of papers and books dealing with the range of human capacity. The first of these was published in 1930 in the *Scientific Monthly* (1). The essential ideas, later developed in more complete form, are included in this article.

We are most often impressed by the individual who deviates most widely from the norm. For this reason, in considering possible limits of intellect, a Shakespeare or a Pasteur or an Enstein may be cited. This certainly does provide us a prototype and criterion against which to measure. The question is: To what degree are such intellectual heights possible for the individual? Wechsler takes the position that such instances are both rare and, for most of us, unobtainable. Instead, differences which separate one man from another in any capacity may be expected to be quite small. It is the purpose of this paper to demonstrate that such a position is not only tenable, but demonstrated factually.

At that time, investigation was difficult for several reasons. First of all, as Wechsler points out, data which might be used to test the hypothesis were indeed scarce. Certain physical measures were available and were included, but psychological measures were not so accessible. Quite often, as a second factor, the data represented summarized rather than complete information. It would be impossible to deal convincingly with the problem under circumstances where the total distribution were not available. A final difficulty is one which still haunts us today in the fact that mental measurements, indeed all psychological measurements, are not truly comparable with each other or with physical measures. As has been stated so often, a true zero point is not established and the problem is confounded by the fact that units of measurement are not equidistant, at least in a demonstrable fashion.

Nevertheless, it was possible for Wechsler to make certain comparisons from data of several types. A question remained about the extent of the range which should be considered. To avoid problems of extreme cases at either end, Wechsler decides any conclusions should be based upon performance of 998 out of each 1000 individuals. Thus the first and one thousandth person in a set of data would be eliminated from the analysis as atypical to a sufficient degree to represent a confounding element rather than a contributory one.

Comparisons were made in four general areas, though certain data were used in more than one such grouping. Physical, physiological, psychomotor and per-

93

ceptual, and mental capacities had been investigated in a way to yield usable measures for the purpose. Wechsler reports the procedures followed by him in computing the range and the ratio from this range. It is of more than passing interest to note that the particular formula used was

$$\frac{M + (3S.D.)}{M - (3S.D.)}.$$

The normal distribution is assumed and accepted within the limits commonly cited of $\pm 3S.D.$ This would, of course, account for over 99% of the cases in any given study, but would exclude a few quite deviant instances.

The resultant ratios are small, as hypothesized by Wechsler. The overall mean range ratio was 2.31 to 1 and the median, 2.30 to 1. Users of the Wechsler Scales will recognize the same assumptions operating in the range of scores for the Scales. The floor and ceiling of possible I.Q.s is limited, since Wechsler makes the assumption that, for all practical purposes, the range may be expected to be included within plus or minus three standard deviations where a mean of 100 and a standard deviation of 15 I.Q. points is accepted.

Limited though the data may appear, it was possible for Wechsler to draw certain conclusions which were later further substantiated. First, it will be noted that he does have evidence that the range of human capacities is quite small. Second, he concludes, along with Professor Cattell earlier, that the limits are about two to one for various traits when set in comparable units. Finally, and of great significance, is the conclusion that what is reflected here is the presence and action of a natural psychobiologic constant. One cannot assume equality in traits. But future events do substantiate that differences among men on a given trait are much smaller than commonly accepted. At least we have tended to overemphasize differences in a way not beneficial either to the nature of man or the welfare of society. From this standpoint, his discussion of the important social implications of his findings is significant as well.

In this context, he deals with such matters as equal wages among individuals for the same kind of job, a position much decried at the time except for the labor unions. Not only does he take the position that the argument may be unjust, but even specious. In defense of this statement, he cites data which indicate that the range of performance in a given task is about two to one between extremes. Thus, even the most efficient individual would not produce more than twice as much as the least efficient. Since most persons in such tasks will mass around the mean, the differences separating actual performance will be too small to differentiate much in the way of wages.

Wechsler believes that an even more vital implication is one that pertains to assumed and widely espoused racial differences. Differences between ethnic and racial groups are quite small and he rejects any statement of significant differences between races or between national groups as such. However, the emphasis at that time tended to exaggerate and overemphasize human differences, he states, and this has had social consequences not deserved from the facts. Again, it must be emphasized that he is not advocating total equality. Indeed, he concludes by pointing out that differences among men may be very important for practical purposes. The example which he gives certainly makes the point well.

> . . . I do not thereby mean to imply that these differences are insignificant or that, however small, they may not be extremely important for practical purposes. The capacity of a man who can jump six feet one exceeds by only one thirtieth that of another who can jump five feet eleven inches, but it may mean the difference between life and death if the leap required be across a six-foot chasm. Still, it is well to recall that the distance which separates the victor from the victim is often no greater than the breadth of a hair.

Wechsler gave a more precise documentation of procedures followed by him, with the underlying statistical rationale, in 1932 (2). After presenting the various formulas derived for the purpose, he concludes that there is some biological limit which is controlled by a law of organic rate of growth. He makes the point that it is impossible to define the true lowest limits of variability since there is no trait determined by a single factor. This does not obviate the possibilities of determining a true upper limit of variability of a trait no matter how many factors may influence the trait directly.

The first edition of *The Range of Human Capacities* was published in 1936. A second edition appeared in 1952 and Wechsler has included two selections from that volume in this book. The first deals with length of life of individuals based upon life expectancy tables (3). Though certainly environmental conditions do contribute to life expectancy, Wechsler concludes that the limit to potential length of life is primarily a matter of genetic factors. This position he documents with data from a number of sources.

He makes a distinction between life expectancy, the average duration of life which is reflected in actuarial tables, and span of life, which is a biological limit. Life expectancy in 1950 had shown a vast increase since the beginning of the century. Today, this increase continues. By contrast, life span, since it is genetically determined, is a fixed matter depending upon heredity. It is a straightforward matter to compute life expectancies; it is difficult if not impossible to determine life span. Despite the fact that there are problems, Wechsler does concern himself in this chapter from *The Range of Human Capacities* with determining what may be the actual upper limit of a human life. To do this, he cites case studies which have been authenticated for individuals who have lived to be at least 100 years of age. Adequately documented cases are, of course, extremely small. From those available (two in number), he concludes that the chances are about one in a billion that an individual will live to be

115 years of age. Theoretical considerations support this figure as well. Karl Pearson, for example, estimated a theoretical maximum limit of 110 years while Wechsler, using data from the deterioration curve of human intelligence and extrapolating, calculated a limit at about 150 years. Somewhere between these two figures is an actual true limit.

Wechsler also presents data on mortality curves, and demonstrates that there is a considerable irregularity in the plot. Pearson concluded from his data that there are really five age periods each of which has its peculiar mortality curve. Wechsler tends to accept the position and to speculate upon its meaning. He concludes, for one thing, that human life will be susceptible to death from different causes at different age periods. There may be, then, a series of life cycles for the individual. As a result, he says ". . . the child is father to the man in only a limited sense; each man in his time plays many parts but is no longer the same man when he plays them."

An important question remains of defining the possible range. If life is looked upon as a single span this leads to one kind of range ratio. If life is looked upon as a series of separate, but overlapping periods it will lead to a different estimate. Wechsler presents a table which depicts the range of life expectancy at different ages from 1 to 70. He shows that where life is considered as a single span, variability is enormous indeed and corresponds with no other human trait which may be defined and measured. As a result, he advocates rejection of this single-span concept to duration of life. Using the position that there are overlapping periods reduces the variability in longevity which is found in the former instance though it still leaves a much larger range ratio than for any other trait of man.

A portion of the chapter titled "Effect and Burden of Age" is included in this series of selections as well(4). Here, Wechsler discusses and dismisses the position that intellectual competence attained at maturity is relatively maintained to the end of life. He considers the contributions of recognized individuals as evidence. His work preceded that of Lehman, and the conclusions drawn by him, by several years. Combining results of studies including case studies from mankind's history, he concludes that recognition does not come to the individual at the age at which it should be given, primarily because of custom and social bias. Indeed, there is even the strong possibility that the individual is not allowed to accomplish at the age at which he would be most capable. He points out, for instance, the error implicit in judging merit of a creative work in terms of its completion no matter how long it may have taken. In this regard, he makes the provocative statement: ". . . who can say at what moment they showed their greatest brilliance? The only thing that can certainly be asserted is that, with the completion of these works, these moments must already have passed. . . ." As he notes, extremely gifted individuals continue to create to the benefit of mankind. There is still a place for wisdom that comes with experience, and competence that comes with practice. This viewpoint Wechsler accepts, though he does point out that in his opinion the importance of experience may be exaggerated.

Some variance with accepted dogma is reflected in writings which deal specifically with intellectual changes which may occur with age. Wechsler selected an example of his position in this regard to be included in this book. Previously[1] he pointed out that there had been little investigation of a scientific nature on how intellectual ability varied with age. He cited the monumental work of Francis Galton. The analysis of Galton's data which followed over several decades became the basis for plotting age curves which Wechsler uses in part in this paper. The physical and psychophysical measures of Galton show the characteristic increase to late adolescence, decelerating to a maximum around age 25, and then showing a small, but steady decrease throughout the rest of life. Using data from World War I, Wechsler demonstrates that there is a similar curve for tested intelligence. But such data might be biased by the select character of the subjects, since they became officers in the United States Army. Therefore, Wechsler uses other sources not so contaminated. These sources correspond in their findings to the plots reported for physical measures and for the Army Alpha scores from World War I. Further documentation was available from the standardization of the Wechsler Bellevue.

One should note he draws two conclusions from the data amassed and presented here. First, intellectual ability, at least as measured with tests available to that time, shows the same general decline in adulthood as is found with physical ability. Second, intellectual abilities which make up general intelligence must show a similar function though not necessarily at the same rate from one ability to another. This also is documented from the Bellevue standardization. Wechsler's position has remained essentially unchanged on both issues since that time. No empirical findings have accrued which would justify a change by him.

As always, he is not content merely to present data, but he discusses their meanings and implications as well. One important point revolves around the position that intelligence as such may not decline after age 25 or so. The reason for this, as might be expected from other writings over the years, is that intellectual abilities are not the same as general intelligence. Though abilities are important and must be considered in their own right, they are not the total picture of the individual. We measure change (and decline) in intellectual abilities. Some portion of such change represents differential effects of nonintellective factors as well. The picture we see from the results of our studies, important and valid as it may be, should not be construed to yield an unproven or incorrect generalization.

[1]"Intellectual Changes with Age." *In* Mental Health in Later Maturity: Papers Presented at a Conference Held in Washington, D.C. May 23–24, 1941. Washington, D.C.: Supplement No. 168 to the Public Health Reports. 1941, pp. 43–49.

If, as Wechsler believes and as seems evident from the data, there is an inevitable decline of ability with age, there must be consequent meanings for the aged population of this country. It is not the decline which is such a terrible thing since this may be shared at given age levels by all individuals. Our society, however, has become increasingly technical and depends less and less on the experiences which aging individuals may bring with them to a task. A technocracy defines restricted jobs and roles to the detriment of the intellectual nature of the individual. Wechsler concludes with the statement that ''. . . The problem of aging America is not merely that there are more older people, but that there is less for older people to do which younger people cannot do better or more cheaply.''

More fundamental issues of intellectual characteristics with increasing age are discussed in a section of a book published in 1955 (5). With increased age, there are special problems presented in measuring ability, problems which are both of an intrinsic and extrinsic nature. Of great significance, is Wechsler's position that abilities not only change with age, but may mean different things at different ages, and may bear different relationships to each other at different times. We currently use the same tests, the same materials for several different age levels, and even compare responses across age groups. Wechsler points out that perhaps we need a test of intelligence designed for older persons. Certainly we use different content for children; why not similar differences for levels of maturity? It is possible that intelligent behavior will require different kinds of abilities at different points in life. Probably the criteria for determining the intelligence of a person should differ at different times as well.

Again, he discusses the fact that intelligence declines with age just as do other human abilities. This finding is dependent upon the kinds of measures available, such as the Bellevue or WAIS. As a result, Wechsler describes limitations and strictures to the conclusion. One of these refers to time limits which may depress the scores of older individuals. However, when time limits were removed for a portion of the older standardization group of the WAIS, significant performance increments were not found. The second is, again, the matter of the complex nature of general intelligence and its consequent composition at different points in life. The role of experience, with the increased wisdom which usually follows, has led many to reject the concept of intellectual decrease with age. Wechsler makes the point that a person may be intelligent without great wisdom or wise without great intellectual endowment. In the last analysis, perhaps, it is true that one may define general intelligence either way. Under the circumstances the possibility of debate will continue.

Publication of the WISC allowed the collection of data reflecting intellectual development in children. Evidence from standardization data was discussed in an article published in 1950 (6), and led to a presentation of educational applications implicit in the data. Performance on WISC subtests indicated that, as advocated by other psychologists, different kinds of abilities emerge in children at different times and mature at different points. Though educators have tended to accept the position that the curriculum should reflect the developmental level of the child, the actual practices have been much closer related to traditional placement of subject matter areas. More to the point, however, may be the fact that the educational curriculum has usually represented a kind of hypothesized or observed "average development" for children of a given age level. Nowhere is this more evident than in the introduction to reading in the first grade, though there is abundant evidence that certain children are not developed sufficiently even in those factors defined by reading teachers in order to be successful in the first grade.

It is Wechsler's contention in this article that educators have, indeed, underestimated abilities of chldren. Often, administrators and teachers will speak of a lack of readiness or lack of capacity to learn when children do not achieve. Wechsler proposes that it would be more beneficial and worthwhile to devise methods and approaches which will allow children to utilize the abilities present to them so that they may achieve at a level congruent with abilities. Some of the contemporary approaches to education would seem to be more acceptable to his position than those in vogue at the time the article was written in 1950.

The publication of the Wechsler Preschool and Primary Scale required assumptions about intellectual development and maturity of children not yet in school. There are decisions which must be made about tasks, appropriate both to the intent of the scale and the age of the child. These matters are considered in an excerpt from the Manual for the WPPSI (7).

Wechsler believes that the child, by age 4, has matured to a sufficient degree that intellectual abilities may be measured. The child may be tested ". . . with a metric of moreness or lessness, rather than that of mere presence or absence, as one is constrained to do in the case of infants. . . ." Indeed, Wechsler believes that the mental abilities of a young child are the same as those which are found throughout life. The test author must be clever enough to tap these abilities in order to assess the overall functioning of the child.

The position departs markedly from that advocated by many developmental psychologists, including Jean Piaget. With sufficient use and experimentation with the WPPSI, the validity of David Wechsler's position will be clearer.

The matter of intellectual decline with age is incorporated with a discussion of memory in an article published in 1961 (8). The arguments presented for a decline in intelligence with increasing age are repeated, along with the belief that wisdom is not equivalent to general intelligence. However, the discussion of memory as it operates in the aging process presents a somewhat new dimension in this spectrum.

One conclusion drawn by Wechsler as a result of studies with the Adult Scale, and from other research, is the relative importance of memory at different ages in the life span. It has been commonly accepted that memory is particularly important in youth when we are beginning to learn and must learn a great many things in order to function adequately as adults. Wechsler concludes that memory is much more important in old age because of the great dependence upon memory which the aged must have. He cites evidence which is observational in nature, but related to the point. This matter of the increasing dependence upon memory as one grows older will be evident in other papers in this book, and documented to a considerable degree.

THE RANGE OF HUMAN CAPACITIES*

DAVID WECHSLER

WHEN we compare the mathematical genius of an Einstein or the scientific intuition of a Pasteur or the poetic gifts of a Shakespeare with the correlative abilities of the average man, let alone those of the moron or idiot, the range of human capacities appears well-nigh limitless. Flattering, however, as these summits of human achievement may appear to our vanity, they nevertheless represent only isolated peaks; actual measurements of the distances which separate the masses of mankind from one another, along any capacity we might choose to compare them, are extremely small. Indeed, not only are the differences relatively small, but what is more striking, the ratio between the extreme limits of the capacities maintains a constancy which, as I shall presently show, is nothing short of remarkable.

My interest in the problem of the range of human capacities was inspired by the early observations of Professor Cattell, who remarked that the range of a number of mental abilities, as measured by various psychological tests, approached roughly the ratio of 1:2. I was so struck by the possible importance of this observation that I decided to investigate its validity, and to see whether it held for only a few isolated psychological abilities, or whether it applied to the entire range of human capacities. The evidence which I present in this paper is the result of several years' intermittent analysis of available data.

The investigation of the problem presents several difficulties. The first and most important one is the paucity of reliable data. This is particularly true in the case of mental measurements, the plethora of psychological testing since the introduction of the Binet intelligence

tests, notwithstanding. It might surprise you to learn that until very recently there was no single study giving complete reaction-time measurements on as many as one hundred unselected individuals, although the reaction-time experiment was one of the first to be perfected in Wundt's laboratory. There have been published scores, one might say hundreds, of investigations, but in nearly every case the experiments were performed on half a dozen or a dozen subjects, usually university students, each with a distinct technique and not otherwise lending themselves to comparison.

In addition to the problem of the insufficiency of the number of cases and of the selected character of the population studied, one further encounters the difficulty of having summarized rather than fully presented data. What is needed for an analysis of the range of variability is a complete presentation of the original measures, that is, the total distribution of data selected. Until recently, however, most authors were content to publish merely measures of central tendency, whether average or median, only rarely including measures of dispersion and, indeed, often omitting to state unequivocally the total number of cases studied. Finally, in mental measurement we are confronted with the problem of the comparability of our units of measurement and of the location of the true zero point. If one is comparing, for instance, body weight, one can say that the man of two hundred pounds weighs twice as much as the one of one hundred pounds, but it is quite a different thing to assert that the child who solves four problems correctly has twice the mathematical ability of the one who

*Reprinted from *The Scientific Monthly*, 1930, 31, 35-39.

101

solves only two, or even to say that the first child can work twice as fast, unless we can be sure that the problems presented are of equal difficulty. The difference implied in the two illustrations is one which might be summarized by saying that in the first case we are dealing with natural, or at least equivalent, units, and in the other with arbitrary, or units of uncertain equivalence. The latter must first be equated before quantitative comparisons can be made, and as this has seldom been done in psychological measurements, particularly those which purport to measure various kinds of achievement, much if not most of the data otherwise usable does not lend itself to the comparison of the kind we have proposed for our present investigation.

In spite of the difficulties just enumerated, however, which make so much of the published anthropometric and psychological measurements unusable, I was able to find a goodly amount which can be trusted, and I shall, without much further ado, present the results which these data reveal as regards the method of measuring this range. The aim is to see how the highest or best individual compares with the lowest or poorest individual in any given ability. We shall thus have to compare the performances or measurements of the very extreme cases actually recorded. Now, aside from the fact that these extreme measures are generally not available because complete distribution of the measures is seldom given, the actual recorded extremes are generally not the most reliable cases to take. For if we did, we might thus, in the case of measuring cranial capacity, for example, have to include instances of hydrocephaly; or again, in studying visual acuity, individuals who are on the way to becoming blind, and so on. *A priori,* one would say that we have no right to reject any case. But it must be obvious that we are

merely doing violence to our notion of variability by including individuals that are clearly pathological, or in other ways accidental cases.

In a like manner, when studying the range of variation in mathematical ability, we ought theoretically to include a Gauss or a Newton on the one hand, and a vegetating idiot on the other. But here again, I am inclined to look on both these extremes as sports, the latter unfortunately more frequent than the former, but still relatively sporadic occurrences. At any rate, I shall claim for the statistics that I am about to present that they apply only to the mass of mankind, that is, if you will, to 998 out of every 1,000 individuals. Our task then ought to consist of comparing the 2nd with the 999th individual in every 1,000.

Many of the data from which I have drawn my conclusions do not include as many as 1,000 cases, but we can readily calculate by proper statistical methods what the value of the 2nd and 999th cases would be from our obtained measures, and often with greater reliability than if we had the actual figures. For, if we know the mean and standard deviation of our measured distribution, we can readily obtain the theoretical value of the 2nd and 999th case by first subtracting and then adding three times the standard deviation to the mean, since six times the standard deviation includes approximately 99.7 per cent. of the cases. It is this method which I have generally used in obtaining my extreme measures. The assumption which has to be made is that the distribution of the measures of the trait in question is normal—an assumption which we know holds for most biological traits and which I have verified wherever possible in these traits which I have included in my study. In any case, the errors which might be introduced if the assumption we have made does not hold would all tend to vitiate rather than to confirm the constancy of the ratio revealed. There is little doubt that the range of capacities if calculated from more complete data would reveal an even greater constancy than my present figures show.

Let us now examine the figures themselves. I have, for convenience, classified the available data under four groups: measures of physical, of physiological, of psychomotor and perceptual and, finally, of mental capacities. These are given in Table I arranged in the order just enumerated. The first column gives the source or compiler of the figures, together with the number of cases in which the measurements were made; the third column, the mean; the fourth the standard deviation; the fifth the range as calculated, namely, $\dfrac{M + (3 \times S.D.)}{M - (3 \times S.D.)}$; the sixth the numerical value of this ratio. In some instances the mean and standard deviation were not available and here actual extremes as furnished by the author are given in their stead. Many of the values presented in the table have been calculated from the raw data.

The table here presented, while not exhaustive, comprises by far the largest part of the data available, at least such as are published in English. It were highly desirable that fuller data were at hand; this lack, among other things, calls attention to the urgent need of a systematic remeasurement of the fundamental capacities of man, and it is to be hoped that one or another of the foundations that are interested in the study of human relations will make this investigation possible in the near future. The data, however, such as they are, nevertheless do permit us several generalizations which, I believe, augmented and improved data will only substantiate and reaffirm in more precise terms.

The first and fundamental conclusion

TABLE I

THE RANGE OF VARIOUS HUMAN CAPACITIES*

Source and no. of cases	Trait or capacity	Mean	S.D.	Range	Ratio
Galton (4,098)	Weight of body	148.9	20.23	209–88.2	2.29 : 1
Rezius (416)	Weight of brain	1400	106.3	1719–1181	1.45 : 1
Greenwood (302)	Weight of heart	11.04	1.92	16.8–7.3	2.30 : 1
Macdonell (80)	Cranial capacity	1476	122.4	1843–1111	1.66 : 1
Galton (4,098)	Strength of grip	74.6	12.51	112–37.5	2.99 : 1
Alvarez (1,066)	Blood pressure	130.0	13.4	170–89.8	1.89 : 1
Goring (500)	Pulse rate	74.2	11.02	107–43.2	2.48 : 1
Galton (4,098)	Vital capacity	221.8	39.0	339–104	3.23 : 1
Korosy (253)	Respiration rate	15.84	2.35	22.9–8.8	2.60 : 1
Lemon (113)	S. reaction-time	199.1	25.50	276–123	2.24 : 1
Galton (4,098)	Audible pitch	3586	492	5062–2110	2.40 : 1
Woodworth (100)	Snellen acuity	1.74	....	2.54–1.00	2.54 : 1
Terman (905)	Intel. quotients	100.7	12.02	136–64.6	2.11 : 1
Burt (200)	Binet mental age (both sexes, age 9)	9.4	1.24	13.1–5.7	2.30 : 1
Gates (197)	Memory span	7.5	....	11–5	2.20 : 1
Mean					2.31 : 1
Median					2.30 : 1

* Adult male, unless otherwise indicated.

is that the range of human capacities, at least as they pertain to the mass of mankind, is relatively small. Secondly, that the limits of most human traits, when measured in comparable units and from true zero points, may be approximately expressed by the ratio of $2:1$. Thirdly, that this ratio recurs so frequently and over so wide a range of traits as strongly to suggest that we are here dealing with a natural psychobiologic constant.

The figures upon which our generalizations are drawn actually only approximately bear out this ratio. It does not, to be sure, have the absolute mathematical constancy of the relation of the radius of a circle to its circumference. But when we consider the numerous causes of error to which the measures upon which they are based are liable, and even more when we consider the almost infinite numerical relations which might *a priori* have obtained between the limits of the measured ranges, I think it is rather remarkable that these limits can be expressed by such small numbers, and that these numbers so nearly approach the ratio indicated. My belief is that we are certainly dealing with what in the more precise sciences is defined as a natural constant.

From the statistical point of view, the relations established, even if only approximate, are extremely important, because they help in a way to prognosticate the range of yet incompletely measured traits or of such as are yet to come under observation. For if our generalization as regards the variability of traits is correct, we know in advance that it is extremely unlikely that any individual will be found that will measure more than twice as much as the smallest case, or less than half of our largest, however small the sample of population upon which our observations have been made. Indeed, the validity of the descriptions of a large part of physiological investigation, which generally involves infer-

ences drawn from a relatively small number of cases, really depends upon the fact that this assumption holds.

In concluding, it is not without interest to call attention to some rather important social implications which the results of this study seem to carry with them. One of the most persistent arguments of those who are opposed to social control, whether in politics or in industry, is that such control together with the standardization of compensation or reward that goes with it must be very unfair to the individual. To take a specific instance, a standard union wage is much decried because the superior and inferior worker are given equal compensation. If the range of capacities is as narrow as our ratio indicates, the injustice can not be very great and certainly not to very many individuals in the total population.

That the variations in individual efficiency are not very great, when taken in the large, is revealed by a comparison of the actual outputs of individuals engaged in diverse occupations. A series of such comparisons taken from Hull is given in Table II. The average range in variation of capacities is here as before approximately $2:1$; that is, the most efficient individual does not produce more than twice as much as the least efficient. And if we remember that the figures give the ratios of the very extremes and that by contrast most individuals are grouped about the mean, the differences in efficiency which separate the mass of individuals in any given occupation from another can not be very great.

Perhaps an even more vital implication is the one that bears on the current beliefs as regards racial differences. Scattered studies, especially in this country, have given rise to the belief in the existence of varying degrees of superiority and inferiority among different national groups. What these studies have

TABLE II

RATIO OF MOST TO LEAST EFFICIENT INDIVIDUAL ENGAGED IN DIFFERENT OCCUPATIONS§

Source	Occupation	Criterion	Ratio
Lovejoy and Monroe	Heel trimming (shoes)	Number per day	1.4 : 1
Elton	Loom operation	Per cent. of time loom kept working	1.5 : 1
Pollock	Hosiery maters	Hourly earnings	1.9 : 1
Wyatt	Loom operation	Earnings	2.0 : 1
Lovejoy and Monroe	Bottom scoring (shoes)	Number per day	2.0 : 1
Pollock	Machine operators	Hourly piece-work	2.2 : 1
Farmer	Polishing spoons	Time per 36 spoons	5.1 : 1
Median			2.0 : 1

§ (Abbreviated, from Hull.)

revealed are certain measurable trait or capacity differences, but those who have made use of them have almost altogether failed to appraise the significance of these differences. For certain purposes it may be useful to know that one group attains an average intelligence quotient of 87 and another of 92, but, from a social point of view, even more important is it to evaluate what such difference means. It is important, for instance, when you are grading school children, but practically negligible when you are comparing human beings. The comparison that may then have to be made is not between John Smith, IQ 87, and Tom Brown, IQ 92, but between John Smith, *Homo sapiens,* and the missing link, *Pithecanthropus erectus.*

This implication has generally been disregarded, and the tendency in recent years has been rather to exaggerate and overemphasize human differences, whether in the field of psychology, government or industry. Everywhere the search has been for experts or dictators, on the assumption that among all groups there is an inevitable minority so superior to the rest of the population that they alone are capable of ruling over and thinking for the group. Now every democracy and particularly our own is based on the very contrary assumption; and if the facts we have brought forward are at all correct this assumption is entirely justified, for the differences between men, when the totality of the capacities is considered, is surprisingly small. I do not thereby mean to imply that these differences are insignificant or that, however small, they may not be extremely important for practical purposes. The capacity of a man who can jump six feet one inch exceeds by only one thirtieth that of another who can jump five feet eleven inches, but it may mean the difference between life and death if the leap required be across a six-foot chasm. Still, it is well to recall that the distance which separates the victor from the victim is often no greater than the breadth of a hair.

ON THE LIMITS OF HUMAN VARIABILITY*

DAVID WECHSLER

In a paper delivered at the Ninth Congress of International Psychology,[1] I called attention to the fact that the range of a great many human capacities, when defined in terms of the number of times the uppermost measure is that of the lowest, approaches the ratio of 2 : 1. Further investigation has shown, on the one hand, that for a preponderant number the ratio is more nearly 2.5 : 1, and on the other hand, that for certain types of anthropometric traits, namely those of linear dimensions such as heights, it is considerably less, that is, about 1.3 : 1. Also, that in the case of some metabolic processes the ratio may be further reduced, so that, to take the most singular example, the case of normal body temperature, it may be as low as 1.03 : 1.

It appears that the 'simpler' the processes or capacities measured the smaller the variability, that is the ratio between the extremes, the term *simple* applying primarily to the method or conditions under which the measurements are obtained rather than to the intrinsic character of the trait or capacity considered. Thus height is classed as a simpler trait than weight, and oxygen consumption per minute as simpler than general intelligence; but it is obvious that even those traits which we may designate the simplest are in reality already very complex. Take, as an example, stature. For the purpose of practical classification we may call it or even assume it to be simple as compared to such a trait as vital capacity or general intelligence, but in point of fact we know it to be the resultant of an indefinitely large number of factors whose compounded cause or effect we term growth. And so on of any other human trait or capacity which we might choose. Now, to obtain the lowest limits of variability we should have to hit upon a trait which

*Reprinted from *Psychological Review*, 1932, **39**, 87-90.

[1] Printed in full in *Scient. Mo.*, 1930, **31**, 35–39. More extensive discussion of the entire problem of the Range of Human Capacities, and the data upon which the generalizations are based will appear in a book of the same title now in preparation.

is determined by only a single factor. Such an ideal case, however, is non-existent, and for this reason the calculation of the lower limits of human variability is not possible. But it can readily be shown, as I propose presently to do, what inevitably are the true upper limits of variability of any trait or function, however complex its character, that is, upon however many factors it may depend.

I start with the assumption which experience amply justifies, namely, that all human traits are complex variables dependent upon a large number of factors. Of the variability of these ultimate or 'single' factors we know nothing other than that taken individually they must be small, since when already compounded they give small values (*e.g.*, height 1.26 : 1, body temperature, 1.03 : 1). Now let T be any trait which in our present argument is dependent upon an indefinitely large number of factors, $a, b, c, d, e, \ldots n$. Then as,

$$T \propto a, b, c, d, e, \ldots n$$
$$T = a \times b \times c \times d \times e, \ldots \times n.$$

Calling V_T the variability [2] of T, then, if the function is continuous, as all measurements of human traits in fact are, it can be shown mathematically that

$$V_T = V_a \times V_b \times V_d \times V_d \ldots \times V_n, \qquad (1)$$

where

$V_a, V_b, V_c, \ldots V_n$ are the corresponding variabilities of the individual factors $a, b, c, d, \ldots n$.

The variability we are here concerned with is the total range for whose measurement we take the ratio between the extreme or limiting values. Call T_0 the lower limit of the trait; then the upper limit, T_u, may be defined as $T_0 + dT$, where dT is a difference less in magnitude than T_0 (as actual data shows it to be). Then by definition

$$V_T = \frac{T_u}{T_0} = \frac{T_0 + dT}{T_0},$$

which may be rewritten,

$$V_T = 1 + \frac{dT}{T_0}. \qquad (2)$$

---

[2] Where the variability, V, is defined as the ratio between the extremes; for practical ways of calculating this, see paper already cited.

In the same way, V_a, V_b, V_c, . . . V_n, may be written as

$$V_a = 1 + \frac{da}{a_0}$$

$$V_b = 1 + \frac{db}{b_0}$$

$$V_c = 1 + \frac{dc}{c_0}$$

. . . .

. . . .

$$V_n = 1 + \frac{dn}{n_0}.$$

Substituting in (1)

$$V_T = \left(1 + \frac{da}{a_0}\right)\left(1 + \frac{db}{b_0}\right)\left(1 + \frac{dc}{c_0}\right) \cdots \text{to } n \text{ factors.} \quad (3)$$

Whatever the value of V_T, V_a, V_b, V_c, . . . must necessarily be smaller; also as we increase the number of factors, a, b, c, . . . , the values of da/a_0, db/b_0, dc/c_0 . . . will progressively diminish and the differences between them even more so, so that if we take n indefinitely large, the differences will become negligible, that is,

$$\frac{da}{a_0} - \frac{db}{b_0}, \quad \frac{da}{a_0} - \frac{dc}{c_0}, \quad \frac{db}{b_0} - \frac{dc}{c_0}, \cdots, \text{etc.,}$$

will all approach zero as a limit. Whence by equating them, we get

$$\frac{da}{a_0} = \frac{db}{b_0} = \frac{dc}{c_0} \cdots = k.$$

We do not know the value of k, other than that it is small and must be less than 1. Let $k = 1/x$; then by substituting in (3) we get,

$$V_T = \left(1 + \frac{1}{x}\right)\left(1 + \frac{1}{x}\right)\left(1 + \frac{1}{x}\right) \cdots \text{to } n \text{ factors, or}$$

$$V_T = \left(1 + \frac{1}{x}\right)^n \cdots. \quad (4)$$

The value of the term in the parenthesis depends on the relative values of x and n. We do not know what is the value of $1/x$ but do know that as n increases $1/x$ becomes decreasingly small, or what amounts to the same thing, x becomes increasingly large. As n approaches infinity x will also approach infinity, and hence by taking n sufficiently large, we may substitute n for x, and (4) becomes

$$V_T = \left(1 + \frac{1}{n}\right)^n = 2.7182 \cdots, \tag{5}$$

that is, our old friend epsilon (ϵ) or the limiting value of organic rate of growth that seems characteristic of all biologic phenomena.

It thus appears that human variability is limited biologically by the law of organic rate of growth and that therefore under normal conditions we may not expect the total range ratio to exceed the amount of 2.718 : 1. The fact is that measurement of a large number of traits and abilities shows this to be true in most cases. There are some exceptions, but in my opinion these are due to the uncertainties of our units of measurement and to some special factors the discussion of which, however, is beyond the intent of this paper.

DAVID WECHSLER

60 W. 68TH STREET
NEW YORK CITY

[MS. received September 17, 1931]

LENGTH OF LIFE AND THE CHANCES OF SURVIVAL*

DAVID WECHSLER

Like all living things, human beings have a limited span of life, but within this limited span there are wide individual variations. Some die at birth or even before, while others live on to a ripe old age. A select few reach the 100 year mark but the unborn, still-born and the centenarian constitute a comparatively small percentage of the total; and even though we add to these numbers those who die capriciously (and needlessly) owing to man's ignorance and cruelty, the duration of life at any given epoch is relatively circumscribed and inevitably determined. One can, for example, forecast with reasonable certainty that of every thousand males born in the United States in 1940, less than half (actually 46.7 per cent) will survive the biblical promise of three score and ten, and less than a quarter can hope to reach the age of 80. These are mean expectancies; that is, expectancies as to the number who will die before or survive until a certain age. But, of course, who will die and who will survive no one can tell. For though the Angel of Death makes his unfailing rounds with mathematical regularity, it is not possible to know at whose door he will stop or whose he will pass over.

Life expectancies are calculated from mortality rates euphemistically called life tables; that is, from cumulative frequencies of the number of persons per 100,000 dying, at all ages, beginning with any given year. The mortality rates are basic data, but the expectancy tables are derived indirectly and involve a number of calculations. The latter usually require: (1) the

*Reprinted from David Wechsler, *The Range of Human Capacities*, 2d ed., Baltimore, 1952, pp. 73-84. Copyright 1952, The Williams & Wilkins Co. Reproduced by permission.

number of persons surviving at any given age (x); (2) the number dying between that age and the succeeding age $(x + 1)$; (3) the total number of years lived by the base group (referred to technically as the cohort) between ages x and $x + 1$. This enables one to calculate, (4) the total number of years lived by the cohort from that age until all have died. To obtain the life expectancy or the average number of years of life remaining to a person of any given age, (5) one divides the number of years lived by the entire cohort by the number of persons attaining that age. Thus, at year 10, the number of persons per 100,000 who survived at that age being 93,601 (males, U. S. 1939–41), and the total number of years lived by the group, 5,337,876 years, the average life expectancy for males surviving to age 10 is 57.03 years[1].

Life expectancies have varied widely in different places and at different times. The last two centuries and particularly the last fifty years have shown marked increases in longevity as inferred from life expectancies, but enormous geographic variations still obtain. Thus, according to actuarial historians, the average length of life rose from an estimated 18 years in the early Bronze Age of Greece, and 22 years at the beginning of the Christian Era in Rome, to an estimated 33 years in medieval England, 40.9 years in 19th century Britain and 66.7 years in contemporary United States (1946). Almost as wide differences, however, still exist in different parts of the globe, so that the life expectancy for women in Australia (1934) is given as 67.14 years and in India (1933) as 26.56 years[2].

While life expectancy or the chances of survival are dependent on the variety of environmental conditions, the limit to potential length of life seems to depend primarily on genetic factors. Among these, the most easily demonstrable one is that of sex. It appears that whatever the life expectancies of a given population at any given place or period, the differences noted

[1] Cf. Dublin, Louis I.; Lotka, A. J.; Spiegelman, M. S. (*44*).
[2] Loc. cit. pp. 26–79.

between the sexes are always in favor of females. The order of difference found is shown in Table 8. The advantage in favor

TABLE 8

*Examples of national and sex differences in life expectancies**

COUNTRY & PERIOD	LIFE EXPECTANCY	
	Male	Female
Australia (1881–90).............	47.7	50.84
Chile (1926–30)................	40.65	43.06
Finland (1931–40)..............	54.45	59.55
France (1933–38)...............	59.94	61.64
India (1881)...................	23.67	25.58
Japan (1935–36)...............	46.92	49.63
Sweden (1755–76).............	33.20	35.70
Sweden (1936–44).............	64.30	66.92
U. S. (1900–02)...............	48.23	51.08
U. S. (1946)..................	57.49	61.02

* Adapted and abbreviated from Dublin, Lotka and Spiegelman (44).

TABLE 9

*Sex differences in life expectancy at different ages (U. S. whites 1939–41)**

AGE	MALE	FEMALE	DIFF.
Birth (0)	61.81	67.29	5.48
10	57.03	60.85	3.82
20	47.76	51.38	3.62
30	38.80	42.21	3.41
40	30.03	33.25	3.22
50	21.96	24.72	2.76
60	15.05	17.00	1.95
70	9.42	10.50	1.08
80	5.38	5.88	0.50
90	3.06	3.24	0.18

* Adapted and abbreviated from Dublin, Lotka and Spiegelman (44).

of females obtains not only at birth but for all ages. This is evidenced in Table 9 which gives the life expectancies for both sexes in the United States, based on mortality rates for year 1946. Why women should thus be favored is not clear; perhaps Nature in her wisdom esteemed the female of the species more useful for the preservation of the race. In this connection it might be noted that the advantage diminishes as the end of a woman's childbearing period is approached (50 yrs.) and disappears almost entirely toward the limit of human life span (age 80).

At this point it would be well to distinguish between life expectancy and the span of life. Life expectancy refers to average duration of life, and it is this average with which actuarial tables are primarily concerned. Average duration of life has, as already was noted, been enormously increased over the centuries and particularly in the last 50 years. Span of life, on the other hand, refers to the biological limit to human life, that is, the maximum age which human beings have or can hope to attain, and this limit does not seem to have changed significantly over the ages. According to eugenicists, life span is genetically determined, which means that the maximum age that an individual may hope to attain depends primarily on his heredity. Heredity is, however, a long range affair, and the average person may well be content with the increase in his life expectancy that has resulted from medical and social progress in the last century. Nevertheless, the question of maximum life span has direct bearing on the problem of range and merits further discussion. We need to know what are the actual upper limits of human life.

Authentic birth dates for persons who have lived over 100 years are difficult to obtain. The oldest "authenticated" life span cited, authenticated in the sense that it is accompanied by what appear to be fairly reliable records, is the case of a Dane, Christen Drakenberg, who is cited in the literature[3] as having attained the extraordinary age of 146. He is reported to have been born on November 18, 1626, and to have died on October 9, 1772. Among other unusual achievements in his long life, he is reported to have married a 60-year-old widow when he was 111 years old. There is no record of children by this lady who

[3] Loc. cit. pp. 3–5.

died shortly after the marriage, but Christen seems to have retained his virility for many more years, since at the age of 130
he is said to have proposed to several women "although without
success".

Several other cases of persons attaining the extreme age of
120 years and over are cited in the literature, among them the
famed English farmer, Thomas Parr[4], who is alleged to have
died in 1674 at the age of 152, but most investigators are inclined to doubt the authenticity of these cases. Amram Scheinfeld (*137A*), who made a thorough study of the longevity claims
for these persons, calls attention to the significant fact that in
every one of these cases the reports are about people who lived
long before reliable records were kept; modern records fail to
reveal any life span approaching the Parr and Drackenberg
claims. The two oldest persons both whose birth and death
dates Scheinfeld was able to authenticate are those of a Cana-
dian subject, Pierre Joubert, who died at the age of 113 in the
year 1814, and of a spinster, Miss Catherine Plunkett, who died
in Ireland in 1902 just a few days short of her 112th birthday.
If we accept these two cases and for good measure add two
more instances that might have occurred but passed unnoticed
in the past 100 years, the chances are still less than one in a
billion that any individual will live to be 115 years; the chances
are nil that anyone will ever attain the life span of Methusalah.
This conclusion must be accepted not only the basis of actual
cases but also on the basis of theoretical considerations. Karl
Pearson in his essay, *The Chances of Death* (*123*), estimated
that the theoretical maximum limit should fall somewhat under
110 years; the present writer (*162*) by quite a different method
(extrapolation of the deterioration curve of human intelligence),
calculated the theoretical limit at approximately 150 years. It
is probable that the true limit falls somewhere between these
two estimates.

Pearson arrived at his estimate of human life span from the

---

[4] For age records of Parr and others see Scheinfeld, A. (*137A*).

study of death rates in France and Great Britain toward the
end of the last century, and more specifically from the death
rates in England for the period 1871–80. Modern actuarians
have since accumulated much fuller and to some extent more
accurate records, but none has treated the subject more pro-
foundly. What perhaps is more surprising is that no one seems
to have taken up the challenging ideas which Pearson brought
to light in his analysis of the so-called mortality curve.

A mortality curve is a graph which describes the year-by-
year variations in the death rates of a given population. This is
accomplished by plotting the number of persons per thousand
dying annually, beginning with a given year when all are known
to have been born and continuing until all are assumed to have
died. On examining such mortality curves, and in particular
one which he himself drew up from the death rates in England,
Pearson was much impressed by their anomalous appearance,
anomalous in the sense that they were quite unlike all other
frequency curves he had previously encountered in biometric
studies. The mortality curve (English death rates for the period 1871–80) which first challenged Pearson is reproduced in
Fig. 7. As the reader can see at a glance, the main graph (the
line connecting the cross hatches) describing the variation in
mortality over the entire life span is decidedly irregular. To
some extent this irregularity may have been due to the paucity
or peculiarity of the data, and indeed in more recently published mortality curves (see Fig. 8), wherein much of this irregularity (except for the high death rates in early infancy) seemingly disappears. But the obliteration of these irregularities is
an artifact, and it is rather fortunate that the defects in Pearson's data, such as they might have been, served to increase
rather than to attenuate the irregularities, for they led him to
conclude that human mortality could not be adequately described by a single curve. It appears that man is at the mercy
of not one but several Angels of Death competing, as it were,
for their victims, and yet, as if by agreement, dividing man's

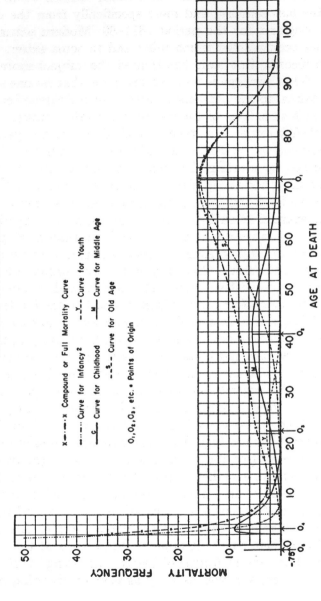

Fig. 7. Deaths per Annum of 1000 Persons Born in the Same Year (English Mortality, Males, 1871–1880). The full curve for infant mortality is not shown on this graph Redrawn from Pearson's *Chances of Death (128)*

For description of same see text and Pearson, loc. cit. p. 26.

116

life span into periods over which each retains an allotted prerogative. More prosaically, what Pearson found was that the variation in human mortality with age was not a simple continuous function, but a resultant of several components which could not be summated by a single integral. He accordingly

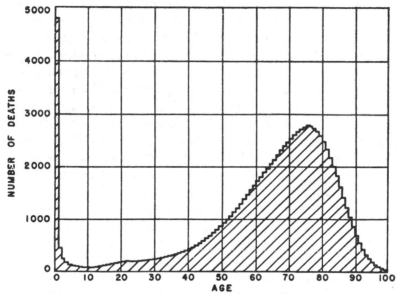

FIG. 8. MORTALITY CURVE FOR WHITE MALES (U. S. 1939–1941). DEATHS WITHIN ONE YEAR AFTER ATTAINING EACH SUCCESSIVE AGE, OUT OF 100,000 LIVE BORN
(Reproduced from *Length of Life*, by Dublin, Lotka and Spiegelman, The Ronald Press, New York.)

divided the overall mortality distribution into successive segments and fitted separate curves to each of them. These curves described successively a mortality of infancy, of childhood, of youth, of middle and of old age.

It is of some interest to compare the curve which characterizes the entire mortality data with the component curves (see Fig. 7) which describe the delimited mortalities defined by the five age periods. The overall curve starts with a high death rate in infancy, falls rapidly to a minimum at age 13, then slowly increases but with some unevenness in the twenties, until "hardly one in 10,000 remains for death to aim at in the 100th year of life"[5].

The characteristics of the component curves considered in their reverse sequence[6] are briefly as follows: (1) *Old Age Mortality:* The peak death rate in this component falls approximately at the 73d year (mode 72) with a mean at year 67 and a range which continues backwards to almost infancy and forward to the 106th year. The curve is markedly skewed toward youth and falls very rapidly after age 80. (2) *Middle Age Mortality:* The curve for this period, unlike that of old age is almost symmetrical. It shows negligible skewness and resembles altogether a typical normal frequency distribution. The highest death rate is in the early 40's with the mean at age 42, standard deviation 12.8 years. (3) *Mortality of Youth:* The third component is again practically without skewness. The mean falls at about age 23 and has a standard deviation of 7.8 years. (4) *Mortality of Childhood:* This curve is markedly skewed; shows a maximum death incidence in the third year but with a mean at 6 years and a standard deviation at 3.52 years. (5) *Mortality of Infancy:* Fitting a curve to this period presented a special problem. If one started with a view that human mortality can only be figured as beginning with birth, the actual data falling into the infancy period could not be fitted by any known frequency curve. To get any fit at all, the curve had to be started approximately nine months before birth, that is, almost at the moment of conception. We know, of course, that human mor-

[5] The modern overall mortality curve (see Fig. 8) does not differ significantly from Pearson's in its main characteristics. There is still a high rate noted in infancy, a minimum more nearly at age 10 instead of 13, and again a maximum in the 70's, but the curve, as already pointed out, is decidedly more regular.

[6] In analyzing his data Pearson first treated the population at the extreme right of the distribution (old age) and fitted the remaining component curves by successively subtracting each of the segments of the included population from the total.

tality of some sort occurs before birth, as shown by occurrences of miscarriages, still-births, etc., but it is very revealing that such deaths could be anticipated on purely theoretical considerations. Pearson calculated that somewhat more than one third[7] of all children conceived died prior to birth, the total postnatal mortality being 246 as against 605 antenatal deaths. The theoretical mean for the entire period of infancy occurs in the last antenatal month, but the curve, as might be expected, is markedly skewed.

It is probable that with fuller and more modern data some of the constants of the curves described by Pearson might require modification; but their main trends and the inferences to be drawn from them would seem to need little qualification. Particularly clear is the evidence that the single mortality curve based on continuous death rate is really a composite of several lesser curves which delimit different mortality periods. Accepting these curves as real, the question arises as to what significance they may have. One implication is the fact that human life is subject to varying mortality causations at different age periods. Thus, infants do not die of arteriosclerosis nor old men of whooping cough. Cancer is essentially a disease of middle and later life whereas measles and scarlet fever occur in early life, and so on. More intriguing, however, is the speculation that these different mortality curves represent successive life cycles in the individual and, therefore, point to a discontinuity in the birth to death span which is usually understood as defining duration of life. We do not, like insects, pass through a pupa and chrysalis stage, but no one observing "the infant, mewling and puking in the nurse's arms" can see him as "the soldier full of strange oaths and bearded like a pard" or forecast from "the whining schoolboy. . . ,the justice in fair round belly with capon lined." The child is father to the man in only a

[7] According to theory one would expect 605 antenatal deaths for every 1,000 births alive. Of these 605, 391 were to be expected to occur in the first 3 months.

limited sense; each man in his time plays many parts but is no longer the same man when he plays them.

Whether we conceive life as a single span or as a succession of distinct though overlapping epochs does not, of course, affect its actual duration. It does, however, affect our way of appraising length of life and, more particularly, that aspect of it with which we are seeking to define its determinable range. If we evaluate life as a single span, calculation of its range is a rela-

TABLE 10

Range of life expectancy when lower and upper limits are set at the 1st and 99th percentile

AGE	UNIT OF MEASURE-MENT	NUMBER (BASE COHORT)*	MEAN	EXTREMES	RANGE RATIO
1	year	95,188	64.98	91.8–3.4	27:1
10	year	93,601	57.03	82.8–6.9	12:1
20	year	92,293	47.76	72.9–3.4	21:1
30	year	90,092	38.80	62.9–2.6	24:1
40	year	86,880	30.03	53.0–1.9	27.6:1
50	year	80,521	21.96	43.0–0.87	49.4:1
60	year	67,787	15.05	33.8–0.43	78.6:1
70	year	46,739	9.42	25.8–0.18	143.0:1

* Where base cohort at birth is 100,000.

tively simple matter. Defining range and range ratio as before, one may obtain a direct estimate of them either on the basis of life expectancies at birth, or from a count of actual survivals between the ages of the population when only one tenth of one per cent of the initial cohort is still alive and all but one tenth of one per cent has died. Calculated either way, but beginning with year 1 instead of 0 to avoid the abnormally high death rate in the first year of life, one obtains the total range ratio of duration of life which turns out to be approximately 400:1. The figure becomes somewhat smaller (100:1) if the range of life expectancy is calculated from year 10 instead of birth, but the values begin to mount from then on until they reach or even exceed the initial values. To show this trend as well as the variability[8] of life expectancies with age, I have calculated the range ratios from year 1–70 by ten-year intervals, using as measure of range the ratio between the 1 and 99 percentile case (rather than the 0.1 and 99.9 percentile). The found values are given in Table 10. Inspection of this table shows that if duration of life is considered as a single span, then its variability is enormous and is significantly out of line with that of any other human trait. This may be reason either for rejecting the idea that longevity is a trait in the ordinary sense of the term, or for rejecting the single span concept of duration of life. I am inclined to the latter view. It would seem that life expectancy, like mortality, covers overlapping periods which need to be separated from one another. Such separation would involve in the first instance an elimination of all accidental causes of death, including all but degenerative diseases. If disease and accidental causes of death could be eliminated, length of life would not only be more predictable, but also much more delimited though, of course, longer. The enormous variability in longevity now observed would then greatly diminish, and while still much larger than those of any single trait or variability, might then be expected to fall within some modest limit which would be equal to some small power of organic rate of growth[9].

[8] Published life tables do not give the standard deviation for the recorded life expectancies at any age; nor the raw data from which they might be calculated. One can, however, with some labor, derive them by indirect calculation. I have calculated the standard deviation for life expectancies for year 1 and for years 35 and 63. They are as follows: year 1—mean 65.0, S.D. 52.6; year 35—mean 34.4, S.D. 24.7; year 63—mean 13.3, S.D. 6.5. Ages 35 and 63 are chosen because at 35 the mean life expectancy is about equal to the number of years already lived by the average individual, and age 63, the age at which the average individual will have completed his full life expectancy when calculated from date of birth.

[9] That is e^x, for example; e^2 or e^3.

THE EFFECT AND THE BURDEN OF AGE*

DAVID WECHSLER

I wish now to dispose of yet another line of "evidence" which has been put forth as "proof" of the fact that individuals maintain their intellectual virility at approximately its maximum level right up to the end of their natural life. I refer to various genetic and statistical studies of genius, particularly those that involve estimation of age of maximal virility from dates of publications of greatest works or ages at which men of eminence and genius have supposedly made their greatest contribution.

We may begin by calling attention to the fact that the statistical study of men of genius and their achievements is subject to various difficulties and pitfalls which make inferences based upon them far from incontrovertible. There are, to start with, the difficulties of selection: First, there is the question of the validity of any investigator's choice of the individuals included in his list of men of eminence; second, the individuals being admitted, of the legitimacy of his particular choices of what are or are not to be counted as their *magnum opus*. The selections when made by a single judge are always influenced by personal bias or individual preference, and as such are subject to large errors of judgment. In this respect, some of the earlier and also some of the more recent writers on the subject (e.g., Dorland) are open to much criticism. Since Galton showed the way, however, attempts have been made to reduce this source of error, either by basing selections on composite ratings of several judges, or by arriving at them independently through statistical analysis of biographical compendia of various sorts.

*Reprinted from David Wechsler, *The Range of Human Capacities,* 2d ed., Baltimore, 1952, pp. 111-119. Copyright 1952, The Williams & Wilkins Co. Reproduced by permission.

Thus, in some of his studies, Thorndike[12] chose his subjects partly on the basis of the amount of space given them in the Dictionary of National Biography and in the Encyclopedia Britannica, the general theory being that in the long run, the space given an individual would be proportionate to his historical importance. This might, at first thought, seem to be a very flimsy procedure, since what it does is simply to shift the onus of choice to some unknown person (the author of the article), and makes it dependent upon the bias or verbosity of the individual who happened to have been assigned to the task of writing the biographical sketch[13]. The stricture cannot be entirely dimissed, but is in part to be discounted by the fact that the choice of individuals is supposedly based on established historical evaluation, and in part by the fact that personal idiosyncrasies have been more or less compensated for, by the use of not one, but several encyclopedia. In any case it would be difficult to replace this procedure with a less arbitrary one[14].

A much more serious source of error is the localization of the age or moment of greatest mental virility of one's subjects, however chosen. In the case of statesmen and men of affairs for example, the periods at which they exerted greatest authority, the epochs at which they were able to carry through their most important projects or received their greatest honors, and hence the moments at which they have generally been judged as having attained the zenith of their careers, will only seldom correspond to the years of their greatest intellectual virility. Nevertheless, most writers on the subject have fallen into the error of identifying the two. Thus Dorland (*40*) takes 1801 as the year which marked the zenith of Jefferson's intellectual virility (when Jefferson was 58), seemingly, for the

---

[12] Adult Intelligence (*152*), p. 303. See also Galton (*51*) and Cattell (*24*).

[13] Or perhaps literary ability of the biographer. Thus Johnson owes the large amount of space alloted to him in the Britannica to the fact that his biographical sketch was written by Macaulay.

[14] For justifications of the method see Cattell, loc. cit.

mere reason that it coincided with the date of his ascendency
to the presidency. But while the presidency is the supreme
American symbol of social recognition, nothing ·that Jefferson
did during that year or in the remaining years of his tenure
compares in brilliance with his drafting of the Declaration of
Independence, achieved at the age of 33. So also does this
author take the years of Disraeli's premiership as the period
of the great stateman's intellectual zenith, forgetting that owing
to political, social and other circumstances, Disraeli had to
wait nearly 30 years for the opportunity of exercising the
abilities which he had already displayed more than two decades before.

In the case of men of science, much error results from the
easy habit of identifying the acme of a man's intellectual
powers with the date of publication of his *magnum opus*. A
good example is here furnished again by Dorland who places
Copernicus' age of maximal intellectual virility at 75, the year
in which was published his *De Revolutionibus Orbium Coeles-
tium*. This assumption, however, is certainly not justified. In
the first place, the date of publication of the De Revolutionibus
does not even remotely coincide with the epoch of its completion. Actually it was finished many years before, and had
been kept under cover by Copernicus for 13 years, because of
his fear of persecution by the Church. Secondly, and more
seriously perhaps, to accept the date of publication of the book
as coincident with the period of the author's greatest fertility,
would be to disregard almost entirely the long years which he
labored over the opus before its completion. We know now
that Copernicus came to the belief of the heliocentric theory
of the universe long before he announced his "discovery".

The foregoing instances illustrate the inevitable error to
which the identification of social recognition or political ascendency with ages of greatest intellectual power will generally
lead. In most cases such identification will advance the posited
age of the individual's intellectual zenith by a greater or lesser

number of years. Either through custom or established practice, positions of importance and authority have nearly always
been reserved for older men, and often definitely closed to
younger ones. Thus, by law, no man may become president
of the United States before he is 36, and where there is no
legal limitation the established order generally requires the
individual to pursue a graduated ascent of political stepping
stones before giving him access to the higher places. By that
time he is usually well beyond middle age.

It is only in the case of social upheavals, where trust and
power fall into hands of those who are best able to wield it, or
in the case of accidents of royal birth, where the individual is
endowed with special privileges, that youth finds no bar to
opportunity. Thus it is that the French Revolution brings
forth Robespierres and Napoleons and not Clemenceaus and
Joffres. The case of military leadership is particularly instruc-
tive. In times of peace seniority and politics are largely the
basis for advancement, so that in the beginning of a war at
least, it is the older men who lead the armies, but in the free
for all during times of upheaval, or when special circumstances
intervene, as for instance, the accident of royal birth, youth
has a chance to come to the fore. At any rate, it cannot be by
pure chance that the greatest of military captains have for
the most part been young men.

Alexander conquered Persia before he was 25. Hannibal
crossed the Alps before 29, and even Caesar when he completed the conquest of Gaul was only 44, this after having
subjugated Spain several years before. As for Napoleon,
whether we choose his victories at Lodi or the triumph before
Austerlitz as his greatest achievement, he is still a man under,
or but a little over 30, who has already reached the acme of
his genius.

It thus appears that custom and social bias contrive, in
many fields, to postpone the age at which an individual will be
afforded recognition, and what is more serious, opportunity of
doing the things he could do at the age at which he is most

capable of doing them. These factors, to be sure, make themselves most felt in the case of statecraft (politics), religion, and the military arts in ordinary times. Their effect is less handicapping in the field of art, literature and science, where achievement is to a certain extent independent of immediate social appraisal. On the other hand, in the case of literary and scientific productions, we must take into consideration the fact already mentioned, that the year in which an author's opus is completed does not necessarily represent the period of his most assiduous labors. When, therefore, to the foregoing fact we add that the throes of parturition have been preceded by a greater or shorter period of travail, it is apparent that the so-called dates of greatest achievement, if taken at their face value, are likely to give a false idea as to the age of greatest fertility. To do so would often lead to a type of error that might be made if we judged the merit of a great painting by the excellence of the artist's last stroke. Leonardo is said to have spent 14 years on *The Last Supper*, Dante no less than 20 on his *Divine Comedy*, and Darwin almost as long on his *Origin of Species*. Who can say at what moment they showed their greatest brilliance? The only thing that can certainly be asserted is that, with the completion of these works, these moments must already have passed. When due allowance is made for this discrepancy, it is my opinion that, using even such data as we have, a careful investigation would show that the acme of a man's intellectual and artistic virility, even when measured by the date of his magnum opus, would certainly be not much over 40, and probably much nearer to 35.

The conclusion which I have just drawn does not deny that there have been men of genius who have made great contributions in later life. The persistence of achievement in later life is perhaps in itself one of the sure signs of genius, but the contributions of a genius cannot be compared with those of the average man, for the output of genius in its dotage may still be superior to that of mediocrity in its prime. It is rather a comparison of earlier works of men of genius with their own later ones that must be undertaken[15]. When this is done, the evidence is not in doubt. Even a layman can detect the wide gap between the Shaw who wrote *Candida* (1898) and the one who wrote *The Apple Cart* (1931).

It would be a laborious but not difficult task to show that the effect of age is to diminish the individual's creativeness in practically all realms of human endeavor[16]. I shall restrict myself to examples from a single field, namely the so called new[17] physics, in which one generally includes the quantum theory, the wave mechanics and recent advances in nuclear physics. The greatest contributions in these fields are almost exclusively the work of young scientists: De Broglie,[18] Heisenberg,[19] Dirac,[20] Schroedinger,[21] Fermi,[22] to mention only the outstanding, were nearly all under 35, and some only in their twenties. It is true

[15] It is surprising how often the first works of an author turn out to be his best; one may recall in this connection the frequent complaint of critics about young authors, particularly novelists, not living up to their promise.

[16] Since these lines were written (1933) the task has been accomplished by Professor Harvey C. Lehman who has studied the relation of age to creative endeavor and unusual achievement in the arts, science, literature, music, philosophy and various professions including sports. His overall findings are that while many gifted individuals continue to be productive throughout their normal life, outstanding masterpieces or greatest works have come with few exceptions from persons under 45 or even 40. For details and differences in various fields see Lehman (*83–94*).

[17] These lines were written in 1933.

[18] De Broglie, Prince Louis, derived the wave properties of matter in 1925, at the age of 33.

[19] Heisenberg, Werner, founder of the quantum matrix mechanics, promulgated when its author was in his twenties.

[20] Dirac, P. A. M., at 24 discovered the relativistic quantum equations and predicted the existence of the positive electron which was experimentally discovered 3 years later.

[21] Schroedinger, Edwin, founder of the wave mechanics (1926) when he was in his late thirties.

[22] Fermi, E., born in 1902, who with Dirac discovered a quantum statistics named after them.

I am indebted for this information to my friend, Mr. Alexander W. Stern, himself one of the important younger American mathematical physicists.

that they were inspired by the work of Planck, Bohr[23] and Einstein[24], but the great discoveries of these geniuses were similarly made when they too were relatively young men.

The decline of vigor with age, which the above adduced facts show to be the general rule in the field of intellectual endeavor, is even more apparent in the realm of affective life, although it is less easy to marshal numerical evidence for the conclusion. But the absence of statistical proof is more than compensated by the accumulated experience of mankind, whether as revealed in the homely assertions of the practical man, the guarded reflections of the physician[25] or the penetrating observations of the great poets. However, for those who insist upon objective evidence, one may point to such facts of physiology as that, with age, breathing becomes harder,

[23] Bohr, Neils. His work on the quantum theory appeared in 1915. He was then in his early thirties.

[24] Einstein's first paper on relativity appeared when he was only 26.

[25] See for example the famous remarks of Osler in his 1905 address at the Johns Hopkins University. The speech is quoted at length in "His Life", by Harvey Cushing. The following excerpts give the general tenor of his attitude toward the influence of age on our abilities: "I have two fixed ideas . . . which have a direct bearing on this important problem. The first is the comparative uselessness of men above forty years of age. This may seem shocking, and yet read aright the world's history bears out the statement. Take the sum of human achievement in action, in science, in art, in literature— subtract the work of the men above forty, and while we should miss great treasures, even priceless treasures, we would practically be where we are today. It is difficult to name a great and far-reaching conquest of the mind which has not been given to the world by a man on whose back the sun was still shining. The effective, moving, vitalizing work of the world is done between the ages of twenty-five and forty—these fifteen golden years of plenty, the anabolic or constructive period, in which there is always a balance in the mental bank and the credit is still good. In the science and art of medicine, young or comparatively young men have made every advance of the first rank. Vesalius, Harvey, Hunter, Bichat, Laennec, Virchow, Lister, Koch—the green years were yet upon their heads when their epoch-making studies were made. To modify an old saying, a man is sane morally at thirty, rich mentally at forty, wise spiritually at fifty—or never. . . .

"My second fixed idea is the uselessness of men above sixty years of age, and the incalculable benefit it would be in commercial, political, and in professional life if, as a matter of course, men stopped work at this age."

the heart slower, and the general reactions of the body more sluggish, just as our senses become more blunted. Indeed the statement that we grow cold with age is literally true. The temperature of the body is nearly a whole degree less at 60 than at 10.

Data testifying to the decline of human ability with age are kinds of facts which most people find hard to accept. This seems to be largely due to what Professor Spearman has called "the alarming consequences" which the view that our abilities decline with old age, seems to imply. "The suggestion arises," he says, "that a man becomes too old for his work, not at 70 or even at 50 but already at 30." And some of the alarming consequences which he fears are that, "the boy or girl on quitting school, instead of as now proceeding to work his or her way up in the world would everywhere. . .straightway assume command," and "thenceforward, as gradually as may be, plane downwards". The answer to all this is that it is just a fancied specter and not a necessary conclusion. It may be true that human capacities attain their zenith before the age of 30, and yet it need not follow that boys and girls in their twenties be put at the helm of our social, industrial, and political ships, for the simple reason that successful operation of these enterprises does not depend upon native ability alone. There are, of course, other factors,—tested knowledge and experience, to mention only the most common, which may be more important, and these, of course, take time to acquire. One may, for example, concede far greater intelligence to a young physician just out of medical school, and yet legitimately have more confidence in a less gifted old practitioner, because of the latter's greater experience. In practical life particularly, the situations that arise are often too complicated, and the need for prompt action too urgent, to permit elaborate examination of the problem at hand. What is needed here is quick recognition of the difficulty, and an acquaintance with consequences of past results in similar situations; and this knowledge accrues with age. All this may be termed experience, and I have, of course, not argued that experience is a negligible factor in practical life, although my personal view is that its importance is greatly exaggerated[26].

Again, the fact that man's capacities reach their zenith at 30 does not necessarily mean that he becomes "too old" for work at 50. It simply means that at 50 he is probably beyond the age at which he can do his best work, and may only imply that he ought to switch to a less creative, a less energy-demanding job. That is a more obvious conclusion and, if its cogency is overlooked, it is seemingly because its logic is obscured by some emotional factor, most often the harrowing phantasy of the dismissed pilot or the discharged employee. This fear has in recent years been augmented by the callousness with which many industrial organizations have treated their older workmen, and the spectre has arisen as to what would happen if the practice of dismissing or penalizing with reduced wages, workers who, after years of service, have become less efficient (or if you wish, less economic) were extended. My personal view is that faithful service ought not thus be rewarded; society should be beholden to its workers for what they have already done, and not measure its rewards by the value of their immediate services alone; we do as much for race-horses, why not for men?

---

[26] One might point out, en passant, that the general effect of relying on experience in practical life, is to eliminate thought and obviate inquiry. The "experienced" man knows what things "work" and what's "the right thing to do", because he "knows what's going to happen", or has seen such cases before. As the practical man usually only does what's been tried and proved, such knowledge is extremely valuable. It makes the world go round, as the saying is. But while experience may make the world go round, it cannot make it go forward. For this intelligence is necessary.

THE MEASUREMENT AND EVALUATION OF INTELLIGENCE
OF OLDER PERSONS*

DAVID WECHSLER

IN discussing the changes of performance in relation to age, I shall confine my remarks to a consideration of the sort of performance or ability which psychologists have used to measure and define general intelligence, and more particularly to the impact of age on intelligence test scores of older subjects. The appraisal of intelligence of older persons in terms of test performance presents a number of special problems, both intrinsic and extrinsic. Under the extrinsic problems one might mention the investigators' greater dependence on voluntary participation, the higher selectivity of available subjects, the greater difficulty in obtaining subjects for test purposes, any and all of which factors tend to impair the representativeness of the population studied. Among the intrinsic problems there is, first, the suitability of the test materials available and, second, the difficulty of interpreting the data as obtained with the tests. Tests may be unsuitable or even unutilisable because the individual is inaccessible to or incapable of responding to the stimulus at hand. Infants, for example, cannot be tested with verbal and certain motor tests because they lack the tools of expression. Comparably, older persons often cannot be tested because they may no longer effectively utilise these tools. You cannot, for example, test older persons for intelligence with tests involving visual discrimination because of impairment of vision, or with certain motor tests because of loss in speed and motor co-ordination.

But even when the above difficulties have been satisfactorily met there still remains the question whether an identical test, identically performed, measures the same function at one age as it does at another. In the case of young children, for example, repeating digits, reproducing designs, and manipulating blocks are fairly good tests of intelligence. In the case of older persons they are certainly not equally effective. The question then arises what are we measuring when we measure intelligence in terms of success or failure in any given performance. I cannot at this time go into this complex and basic problem. I have merely brought it up to indicate that I am not unaware of the difficulties which comparisons of performance at different ages present. My own view, briefly, is that not only do human abilities change with age but that the significances of the abilities themselves are altered at different ages. Indeed, they are not only altered with age but also with different levels of function at the same age levels. Practically, this means that at different age

*From *Old Age in the Modern World*, report of the Third Congress of the International Association of Gerontology, London, 1954. Reprinted from *Old Age in the Modern World*, Edinburgh and London, E. and S. Livingstone, 1955, pp. 275-279.

131

levels we may be dealing with different psychological parameters although employing the same test materials and obtaining similar kinds of response. If this is so it would seem that we ought to have special tests of intelligence for older individuals just as we now have them for young children. This not only because the abilities called for in the exercise of intelligent behaviour differ widely, but also because the thing we call intelligence at different ages is evaluated in terms of quite different criteria.

With these considerations in mind one can briefly summarise the findings regarding the changes of intelligence test scores with age. Intellectual ability as we measure it follows very closely the curve of growth and decline observed in other human traits of ability. It is a logistic curve which begins to level off in most instances at about age 15. From this age on test scores show negligible increments with age until a maximum is reached in the age interval 20 to 25. Beyond this age all test scores begin to decline. The decline at first is relatively slow, but after 35 becomes increasingly apparent. The decline is continuous for most abilities and by age 60 amounts, on the average, to a drop of about 25 per cent. in test score. Some test scores decline more than others; thus the drop in Vocabulary and Information is relatively small, whereas the loss in rote memory (Digit Span) and Block Design is considerable; but the decline is uninterrupted and increasingly significant (2).

From the above it is clear that if we evaluate intelligence in terms of measured abilities taken singly or in combination, one must conclude that intelligence like other abilities declines with age. Two strictures are possible in rebuttal to this unpleasant conclusion. One has already been indicated, namely, that intelligence tests, such as they are, do not measure the same kind of intelligence in old people or in the same sort of way as they do at other age levels. I shall return to this point shortly. The second stricture, and one which has been emphasised by Professor Irving Lorge, is that the tests we now use unduly penalise older adults, because they are so heavily weighted for speed. Professor Lorge sought to demonstrate this point by giving subjects whose ages ranged from below 20 to over 70 two different types of tests, the Army Alpha and the Otis in which speed is heavily weighted, and the Thorndike CAVD Test in which speed is seemingly a minor factor and in which in any case the time factor was eliminated by permitting the subjects to take as long as they wished to finish. Professor Lorge found that the older made lower scores than the younger on both types of test, but that when he kept CAVD scores constant the decline of the older subjects on the speeded tests, although considerably less, was still substantial. From this he concluded that older subjects can perform as well as younger subjects only more slowly and, by implication, that decline of intelligence with age is an artifact (1). I have elsewhere discussed the results of this study (3). Its main limitation apart from the indicated selected character of the subjects was that no attempt was made to reverse the conditions of the experiment, in an effort to see what would happen to the scores of the older subjects on the non-timed tests if the scores on the timed tests had been kept constant. I believe that if this had been done one could have found that the older subjects continued to fare almost as poorly on the non-timed test.

More recent data available from the current restandardisation of the Wechsler Intelligence Scale for Adults has made possible a more direct attack on the problem of the influence of time on intelligence test performance of older subjects. As part of our standardisation, opportunity was afforded us to examine a cross-sectional segment of the older population of Kansas City, in conjunction with a study which was being conducted by the Chicago University Committee investigating the ageing problem in its various aspects. The subjects consisted of random samples * of the older population of Kansas City, ages 60 and over, to whom the revised Wechsler Adult Scale was administered in two ways, one in which the subjects were allowed fixed times to complete the task assigned and another in which the subjects continued with the items until they said they were finished or indicated they could do no more. This permitted us to obtain two scores for each subject and to compare the differences in score on the same tests when timed and when not timed.

The results are shown in Table I. The average increment in raw score per test when subjects were allowed unlimited time was only about 5 per cent., and the ratio between the mean differences of the compared test scores and the standard deviation of these differences never exceeded a critical ratio of 0·92. This is a difference in level of performance considerably less than what would be expected from chance variations at the 1 per cent. level of confidence. The differences between timed and untimed performances of the other age groups tested (not shown in table) were of the same order. Altogether, our findings show that the older subjects were negligibly, if at all, penalised by a speed factor, at least so far as the tests of the Wechsler Adult Scale are concerned. I believe that the same would hold for most other well-standardised tests of intelligence.

With regard to the first point, the evidence is increasingly clear that the concept of general intelligence is a multi-variate construct, the differentiæ of which alter with successive periods of the individual's life span. In the case of older people it seems that the thing we wish most to include under the term " intelligence " is what William James long ago referred to as sagacity, and which may

---

* The sampling was accomplished as follows: The entire city was mapped out according to block dwellings, and from the 300,000 dwellings so mapped out 2,400 were randomly and cross-sectionally listed. About 1 per cent. of the entire dwelling population of the city was thus earmarked for interviews. For testing purposes every alternate individual 60 years and over within the sampled population was invited to take the test. Of this total the examiners encountered only 14 per cent. refusals, some 9 per cent. were too ill to be tested, and 2 per cent. died in the interval between the initial designation as a potential subject and the time it was possible to contact them. The total number of persons tested was approximately 450. These were equally divided between the sexes and almost equally divided among the successive age groups, 60 to 64, 65 to 69, 70 to 74, and 75 and over.

be broadly defined as the ability to deal with life's situations in terms of integrated past experience. It is often assumed that sagacity can be equated with intellectual ability. This is certainly not so. Sagacity in older persons, even less than intelligence in younger persons, is not identical with intellectual ability and certainly not a substitute for it. There are many highly intelligent people who lack wisdom and many wise people who are limited in intellectual endowment. The problem again comes down to what we want to accept as a definition of general intelligence. As mentioned above, I do not think it is possible to define it by a single continuous concept, that is, one that holds for the entire span of human life, because life itself is only continuous in a chronological sense. One cannot predict " the justice in fair round belly with good capon lined " from " the infant, mewling and puking in the nurse's arms," nor even from " the soldier full of strange oaths and

TABLE I

EFFECT OF INCREASING TIME ALLOWANCE ON SCORES OF THE FIVE TIMED TESTS OF THE W.A.I.S. (KANSAS CITY OLD-AGE STUDY)

| Subject of Test. | Age Group. | N | Males. | | | | Ratio $\frac{M_2}{M_1}$ | CR.* |
| | | | Timed. | | Untimed. | | | |
			Mean Sc.	Standard Deviation.	Mean Sc.	Standard Deviation.		
							Per cent.	
Arithmetic	60 to 64	52	10·13	2·91	10·27	2·85	0·98	0·28
	70 to 74	51	8·78	3·25	8·96	3·22	0·99	0·32
Picture completion	60 to 64	50	9·50	3·98	9·82	3·97	0·98	0·40
	70 to 74	47	8·88	4·86	9·18	4·73	0·99	0·29
Block design	60 to 64	46	23·43	10·21	25·57	10·64	0·96	0·72
	70 to 74	44	18·77	9·30	21·18	9·21	0·96	0·92
Picture arrangement	60 to 64	45	16·10	5·78	16·72	6·11	0·96	0·36
	70 to 74	41	14·16	5·86	14·65	6·13	0·97	0·33
Object assembly	60 to 64	46	22·72	7·88	23·28	7·68	0·97	0·24
	70 to 74	40	19·55	8·26	20·55	8·43	0·98	0·59

$$*CR_\sigma = \frac{M_2 - M_1}{\sqrt{\sigma_{M_1} + \sigma_{M_2} - 2r\sigma_1\sigma_2}}.$$

bearded like a pard." Special ability, intelligence, and wisdom are not identical and we cannot always measure one in terms of the other.

To sum up, sheer ability of all kinds, intellectual included, certainly declines with age. In so far as measures of these abilities are used as measures of intelligence, they force us to the conclusion that intelligence declines with age and, furthermore, that this decline is not due to any time factor penalty. There remains, however, the question of whether there is not an added aspect of intelligence in later maturity and old age which is not measured by our test, namely, sagacity. It appears that in the light of life experience (as well as test performance) we might supplement the old French aphorism, *Si jeunesse pouvait, si vieillesse savait*, with the more encouraging adage, *Vieillesse peut, par ce qu'elle sait.*

REFERENCES

1. Lorge, I. (1936). *J. educ. Psychol.*, **27**, 100.
2. Wechsler, D. (1944). " The Measurement of Adult Intelligence," 3rd ed. Baltimore.
3. Wechsler, D. (1952). " The Range of Human Capacities," 2nd ed. Baltimore.`

INTELLECTUAL DEVELOPMENT AND
PSYCHOLOGICAL MATURITY*

DAVID WECHSLER

New York University

In discussing the problem of intellectual maturity, or indeed psychological maturity in general, I think it is important first to define maturity and second to differentiate between what one may call substrate and behavioral evidences of maturity. As regards intellectual abilities, one can define maturity operationally as the attained level of psychological functioning beyond which measures of performance no longer increase significantly with age. This definition circumvents, to be sure, the question of integration as an aspect of maturity but it only restates, I believe, the assumption underlying most objective measures of intellectual functioning, at least as regards specific abilities. In any event it is the one which I shall use in discussing the data in this paper.

The second distinction is not so generally made and perhaps would not be altogether acceptable to workers in the field. By substrate aspects of maturity I mean those segments of mental and other allied functions which develop relatively independent of training and special education. Thus, walking and talking would be substrate abilities, whereas riding a bicycle and language facility would be behavioral. In the case of the higher functions the distinction between substrate and behavioral performance is not so easily made. For example, it is difficult to determine to what degree arithmetical reasoning as measured by tests is a manifestation of sheer native ability and to what extent it is due to training and instruction. Another difficulty in evaluating intellectual ability, especially in the early ages, is our lack of unequivocal measuring rods or tests. It is important to distinguish between our inability to measure a given function and an implied absence of that ability merely because we are unable to elicit it by the means at hand. Thus, if we restrict ourselves to a similarities test as a measure of abstract reasoning ability then we might conclude that children below six or seven years are incapable of abstract reasoning because, in point of fact, average children under that age are unable to give likenesses or differences. Children under that age are, of course, capable of certain types of abstract reasoning and certainly of generalization, but it is almost impossible to devise a simple series of tests which would continuously measure the function and thereby enable us to say precisely at what age below five the ability first emerges.

Psychologists and others have for a long time sought to discover at

*Delivered at the Symposium on the Concept of Maturity from the Anatomical, Physiological, and Psychological Points of View at the meetings of the Society for Research in Child Development, New York, December 28, 1949. Reprinted from *Child Development*, 1950, **21**, 45-50. By permission of the Society for Research in Child Development.

what age a child can do what things, but this has been mostly at the descriptive level. Such descriptions are, of course, of some value and Gesell's books may be cited as illustrations of their usefulness, but on the whole contribute little to the maturation problem which confronts us because they are concerned primarily not with questions of basic abilities, as such,

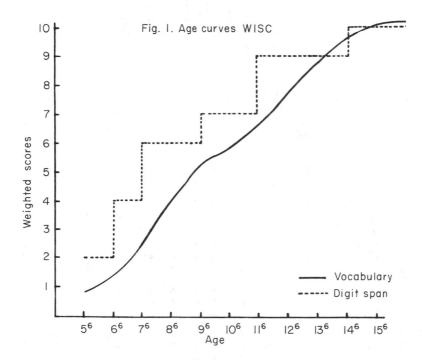

Fig. I. Age curves WISC

but with their behavioral aspects. The material which I wish to present deals with none of these but with intellectual functions that can and have indeed been measured continuously over a considerable span of the child's life. Much data are already available in this field but the material which I wish to present as a basis for our discussion is data derived from the recent standardization of the Wechsler Intelligence Scale for Children (WISC) which covers the ages from 5 to 15 years.

The Scale consists of 12 equated tests which may be said to involve as many different, though to a considerable degree overlapping, intellectual abilities. Since the tests have been equated not only in terms of equivalent units of amount, but also in terms of equivalent age scores, it is possible to appraise maturity levels in terms of the degree to which performance at any given age approximates the score of the age beyond which mean scores no longer increase. Year 15 has been provisionally chosen as this age. Curves of growth have been established by transmuting raw scores of mean performance at every age into weighted scores for year 15. This was done for all the tests of the Scale. Figure 1 illustrates type of curves obtained. The unbroken curve shows the increase of vocabulary with age, the broken line that of memory span for digits. Table I gives the transmuted scores for all tests (at four-month intervals) from which the curves of growth of the remaining functions may be derived.

TABLE I

Weighted Scores at Mean of Each Age when Base of Comparison Is Equivalent Standard Score of 15–4 to 15–7

Inf.	Com.	Ar.	Sim.	Voc.	D.Sp.	Test Age	PC	PA	Bl.D.	O.A.	Code	Maze
½	1	½	1	¾	2	5– 2	3	½	½	½	—	2
½	1	½	1	¾	2	5– 6	3	1	½	1	—	2
1	1	1	2	1	2	5–10	3	1	½	2	—	2
1	1	1	2	1	2	6– 2	3	1	½	3	—	2½
2	2	1	2	1	4	6– 6	4	2	2	3	—	3
2	2	2	3	2	4	6–10	4	2½	2	3	—	3
2	2	2	3	2	4	7– 2	4	3	3	4	—	3½
2	3	2	3	2½	6	7– 6	5	3	3	4	—	4
3	3	3	3	3	6	7–10	5	4½	4	4	—	4
3	4	3	3	3½	6	8– 2	5	5	4	4½	3	4½
4	4	4	4	4	6	8– 6	5	5½	4½	5	3	5½
4	5	4	4	4	6	8–10	5	6	5	5	3½	5½
4	5	4	5	4	7	9– 2	6	6	5	6	3½	7
4	5	5	5	5	7	9– 6	6	6½	5½	6	4	7
5	5	5	5	5	7	9–10	6	6½	5½	6	4½	7
5	6	5	6	5	7	10– 2	7	7	6½	6½	4½	8
5	6	6	6	5½	7	10– 6	7	7	6½	6½	5	8
5	6	6	6	6	7	10–10	7	7½	6½	6½	5	8
6	7	7	7	6	9	11– 2	8	8	7½	8	6	9
6	7	7	7	6½	9	11– 6	8	8	7½	8	6½	9
6½	7	7	7	7	9	11–10	8	8	7½	8	6½	9
7	8	8	8	7½	9	12– 2	8	8½	8	9	7½	9
8	8	8	8	8	9	12– 6	8	8½	8½	9	7½	9
8	8	8	8	8	9	12–10	8	8½	8½	9	7½	9
9	9	9	9	8½	9	13– 2	9	9	8½	9	8½	9
9	9	9	9	8½	9	13– 6	9	9	9	9	8½	9
9	9	9	9	8½	9	13–10	9	9	9	9	8½	9
9½	9½	9	9½	9½	10	14– 2	9	9½	9½	10	9	9
9½	9½	9	9½	9½	10	14– 6	9	9½	9½	10	9½	9
9½	9½	9	9½	9½	10	14–10	9	9½	9½	10	9½	9
10	10	10	10	10	10	15– 2	10	10	10	10	10	10
10	10	10		10	10	15– 6	10	10	10	10	10	10

General characteristics of the curves of growth for most intellectual abilities resemble the growth curve for vocabulary. This is characterized by a rapid rise in test scores in the first years with a gradual slackening as age 15 is approached except for a brief acceleration somewhere between ages 10 and 12, a rise sometimes referred to as the pubescent hump. While most of the abilities tested on the WISC conform, with slight variations to this logistic curve, which characterizes a great many other functions studied including those of most physical traits, there are one or two exceptions in our findings. These are most clearly revealed by the age curve for memory span. Here it is not possible to apply the characteristic ogive. Instead, the line connecting the mean scores at successive age levels consists of a series of rises separated at irregular intervals by plateaus of greater and lesser breadth. The plateaus may be due in part to the fact that the units of measurement are too large or insufficiently discrete. But they might also be interpreted as showing that mental capacities are, contrary to current views, discontinued functions, that is, quantities which can increase or decrease only by certain amounts or quanta. If this were generally true the ogive type of curve found for functions like vocabulary might only represent an artifact due to the cumulated effects of learning.

More immediately important, however, from the point of view of maturation, are the differential rates of increase revealed by the curves (see Table I), and more especially the fact that though most abilities increase up to age 15, they do so at progressively decreasing rates. Thus, the mean scores in the Maze Test increase up to age 15, but the increase after age 10 is so small that for all practical purposes it may be said to be negligible. And even this small increase with age will only show up if we take the performance of the theoretically average 15-year-old as the base for comparisons. But average performance is not, of course, defined by a single point but by a range; thus, if we take the actual mean height of the native adult American male at 5 ft. 8½ in. we could still call a man of average stature when his height falls between 5 ft. 7 in. and 5 ft. 10 in. In the same way, though the mean score on the Maze and other tests at age 15 is 10, the lower limit of normality (—1 P.E. from mean) is eight, and if we take this score as the base of comparison we find that children approximate the adult level of performance at even younger ages. This is most clearly seen in the case of functions which are relatively independent of learning, as in the Maze, Picture Completion and Digit Span tests.

What are the implications of these findings? The first, and one that has often been pointed out before, is that different abilities emerge and mature at different times. Education, to be most effective, should be related to the maturation levels of the child. This is, of course, an accepted principle in education. But while posited in theory, it is applied only to a limited extent in practice. And this for two reasons: first, because ages of maturation of different intellectual functions have not been fully established and, second, because of the difficulties in combating long-held misconceptions and cultural. biases. Consider, for example, the many work hours or, if you will, play hours, wasted every year in teaching children to play musical instruments before they are ready for them; or again, the even greater number of hours in teaching reading to children in the first year of school, because at some time in the distant past somebody decided that reading was a first-grade subject. But even more egregious are the sins of omission than those of commission. Educators have systematically underestimated the abilities of children and have tended to ascribe poor achievement to lack of learning readiness or even lack of capacity rather than to the inadequacies of teaching methods. This tendency, it is gratifying to report, is gradually being shaken, and in some progressive schools, at least, there is a growing movement to introduce "difficult" subjects earlier in the curriculum. Thus, I was recently surprised to have my son of nine explain to me the atmospheric pressure principle involved in the experiment of forcing an egg through the mouth of a milk bottle which had been demonstrated to him at school that morning. It was not until I was in the seventh grade that I was exposed at all to scientific experiments and not until I was in high school that I heard the term atmospheric pressure. I can testify that the youngster who is not precocious understood the principle, as one may assume did most of the children in the class. This can be expected if our data regarding maturation of intellectual functions are correct, for they show that all intellectual capacities are pretty well "mature" by the age of 12, in the sense that little further development in the substrate abilities occur beyond that age. This does not, of course, mean that basic endowment cannot be influenced by socio-economic and cultural factors. Even I.Q.'s, as we know can be raised, but that is not because the child's native endowment is altered, but because the factors which have inhibited it have been removed. This distinction is important because it points to the fact that the aim of education should not be to create abilities which it cannot, but to utilize them which it does not.

While I have concerned myself only with phases of intellectual maturity, I think it would be useful to emphasize that the same sort of problems confront us in the evaluation of emotional maturity. Unfortunately, we here enter into an area where no general definition seems to exist. It appears that emotional maturity means a type of behavior which the sponsoring author conceives as his adult ideal. Without attempting to review any of these diverse ideals one needs first to call attention to the fact that, except in a very broad sense, we cannot speak of emotional maturity because it involves a variety of emotions. For example, an individual may be mature as regards his fear reactions but remain immature as regards his sexuality. Moreover, there is definitive evidence that the individual develops emotionally and instinctually at different rates in different areas in the same way as he does in the intellectual spheres. Unlike the case of intellectual abilities we do not have precise ways of appraising affective capacities and more especially the substrates as compared to the behavioral aspects of emotionality. In general, however, it seems quite certain that emotional maturity at the substrate level, occurs much earlier than is generally supposed. For example, the anger and fear reactions, as Watson has shown, occur as early as the first few weeks of infancy, and while their pattern is not identical to what we get in adulthood, the essential form of the reaction is already present. Similarly, we could run down any list of emotions and show that their basic manifestation appears long before adolescence. It is interesting to note also, as in the case of intellectual abilities, some appear earlier than others. Thus while the child, even as an infant, shows capacity for love, it is not until he is five or six years of age that he manifests hate in the ordinary sense of the term.

It is unfortunate that in order to meet their economic and cultural pattern various societies have prolonged the child's period of infancy. They have done this by being blind to the individual's relatively early emotional as well as intellectual development, and by setting up artificial criteria of maturity which prevent the young person from entering into adult activities of the group. It would take us too far afield to point out the many deleterious effects of this process. One of them, however, is worth mentioning because it is not so obvious. It is this, that prolongation of the infancy period serves in a certain sense to nullify our advances in longevity. While we have been adding to the span of adult life by extending it at one end, we have at the same time been curtailing it at the other by delaying by years his participation in it.

RATIONALE OF THE WECHSLER PRESCHOOL
AND PRIMARY SCALE*

DAVID WECHSLER

Les petits enfants sont des
génies méconnus. – A. France

The years 4 through 6 are in some ways a nodal period in the intellectual growth of the child. Although often treated as an in-between age and referred to as pre-this and pre-that, this age period constitutes a well-defined landmark in the young child's mental development. It is also the period when he is exposed for the first time to some sort of formal education and is deliberately brought into wider social contacts with children of his own age. By 4 or 5 he is no longer intellectually a baby but, so to speak, a "little man." Insofar as experience and language enable him to do so, he can now think for himself and profit from his mistakes. He may not be able to tell you what makes clouds move, and he is still several years away from grasping set theory, but he knows that if he crosses the street against the light he may get run over, and that if you cut an apple in half it makes two pieces. Moreover, he has arrived at a stage where he is both ready and willing to carry out tasks of reasonable difficulty. The intelligence of the 4- to 6-year-old is not, as sometimes claimed, primarily sensory-motor or predominantly anything else. His abilities are not restricted to any specific modalities. On the contrary, he can express himself in a variety of ways; and he can do a great many things in a great many ways, provided, of course, his interest and attention are sufficiently engaged.

The *Wechsler Preschool and Primary Scale of Intelligence (WPPSI)* is based on the assumption that the 4- to 6-year-old not only possesses the foregoing potentialities, but that they may be systematically appraised through an appropriate battery of tests. It continues the methodological and theoretical approaches to the measurement of mental ability which were the guiding principles in the construction of the *Wechsler Intelligence Scale for Children (WISC)*. Like the *WISC*, it consists of a battery of subtests, each of which when treated separately may be considered as measur-

*Reprinted from "Introduction: Rationale of the Scale," in *Manual for Wechsler Preschool and Primary Scale of Intelligence,* The Psychological Corporation, New York, 1967, pp. 1-2.

142

ing a different ability, and when combined into a composite score, as a measure of overall or global intellectual capacity.[1]

Also like the WISC is the division of the test battery into Verbal and Performance test groups, not because the author believes they represent different kinds of intelligence, but because the dichotomy has proved diagnostically useful. The same may be said with regard to the further breakdown of the *Scale* into tests purporting to measure different abilities. The aim here is not merely to highlight possible differences of maturation or endowment but to alert the examiner to the manner or degree to which a subject's assets and liabilities may influence his overall functioning.

The realization of a preschool scale along the lines indicated depends upon whether the abilities of the preschool child can, as in the case of the older child, be tested with a metric of moreness or lessness, rather than that of mere presence or absence, as one is constrained to do in the case of infants. An affirmative answer implies that the mental abilities of the preschool child are, in essence, the same as those encountered in later years. This does not mean that they necessarily manifest themselves identically at all ages. It merely presumes that mental abilities are continuous and not disparate, and that consequently one can use the same or similar tasks in appraising them. The practical question is at what age one can begin to do so.

Some three years were devoted to the investigation of the above question, and resulted in findings which showed that most of the WISC tests, with slight modifications, could be employed with children beginning at age 4. These tests were tried out in preliminary studies of some 300 children and, after further combing, assembled with the addition of three new tests into the battery which now constitutes the WPPSI. The outcome, however, has not been a mere pulling down of, or an addendum to, the WISC, but a separate scale, optimally suited for the mental examination of the 4- to 6½-year-old child.

---

[1] For fuller discussion of the relation of ability to intelligence, see Wechsler, D. *The measurement and appraisal of adult intelligence.* Ed. 4. Baltimore: The Williams & Wilkins Co., 1958, pp. 15-16.

INTELLIGENCE, MEMORY, AND THE AGING PROCESS*

DAVID WECHSLER

IN APPRAISING HUMAN ABILITY after 60, personal experience plays a greater role than recorded opinion; and attitudes toward old age vary with both time and place. Recently I was attracted to a "boxed" quotation from the collected letters of Adams and Jefferson, in the Book Section of the *New York Times,* in which the aging ex-President, Mr. Thomas Jefferson, writing to the aging ex-President, Mr. John Adams, makes this personal comment: "The rapid decline of my strength during the last winter has made me hope sometimes, that I see land. During summer I enjoy its temperature, but I shudder at the approach of winter, and wish I could sleep through it with the dormouse, and only wake with him in Spring, if ever." It is possible that had Jefferson lived in Florida, or been less sensitive to cold, he would have been more optimistic. By contrast, some 2,000 years ago, the elder Cato, living in a more sunny clime, perhaps because he, when well over 70, had taken unto himself a buxom young Roman matron, found little cause to complain about his old age. And Marcus Tullius Cicero, even while awaiting proscription, felt urged to write his famed, and since oft quoted *de Senectute,* in which he not only denied the evils ascribed to old age, but enthusiastically praised its advantages. Here is how the implacable prosecutor of Catiline introduces his defense of old age. "When I reflect on the subject, I find there are four reasons why old age is regarded as unhappy. First, it withdraws from active employment; second, it impairs physical vigor; third, it deprives us of sensual pleasure; and fourth, it is the verge of death."

Cicero then proceeds to examine these four reasons, refutes them in turn, and then goes on to show that old age has assets of its own, which more than make up for its alleged disadvantages. We need not go into his arguments; as might be expected from so great an

*Reprinted from *American Psychopathological Association Publications, Vol. 17: Psychopathology of Aging,* edited by Paul H. Hoch and Joseph Zubin, New York, Grune and Stratton, 1961, pp. 152-159. Reprinted by permission.

advocate, they are quite convincing and indeed, so well chosen that they have been quoted and requoted ever since. The modern reader, however, is likely to be struck by one omission, possibly deliberate on the part of the author, but none the less difficult to explain. Among the infirmities of the senium, Cicero barely refers, if at all, to the now frequently alleged decline of mental ability in old age. He does, at one point, mention the complaint of faulty memory, but quickly disposes of it with the remark that it only occurs when one does not have occasion to remember: "The old remember everything that concerns them, the appointments at court, who owes them money, and to whom they owe money." Cicero was undoubtedly basing his impressions on observations of elderly persons of his own social stratum—senators, lawyers, *equites*, and from his last remark, I would judge, also money lenders.

Modern appraisals based on less selected population samples are not nearly as encouraging. The fact is that, whenever attempts have been made to measure memory and other mental abilities, results always point to significant decline with age. The average older person in the modern world has many other things to worry about than keeping appointments or checking on who owes him money.

In the past two decades there have been a considerable number of studies reported on the changes of mental ability with age. These are too numerous to review even briefly in a short paper. For the purpose of this address I shall merely recall the main findings. They are as follows:

All test performance, when plotted against chronological age, after reaching a peak somewhere between 20 and 30, or thereabouts, shows progressive decline with age. The peak age and the rate and amount of decline vary with the ability measured. For example, verbal fluency declines less than arithmetical reasoning, visual-motor organizations more than visual perception, fund of information least, new learning most, and auditory memory span somewhere in between. Age curves are now available for many tested functions, and all show, so far as one can see, negative correlations with age. This is true for tests which enter into intelligence scales, whether taken individually or as composites. Thus, the respective correlation between age and test score for the Wechsler Adult Intelligence Scales[4] are as follows:

—.27 for the Verbal part of the Scale.
—.53 for the Performance part.
—.42 for the Full Score.

If level of score on an intelligence test is a measure of general intelligence, then one has to conclude that intelligence, like all other abilities, after reaching a peak, tends to decline with age.

Of course, acceptance of this conclusion will depend upon how one defines intelligence and on the confidence one has in the efficacy of psychological tests in measuring it. On both, there is far from universal agreement. As regards the latter, there have been at least four objections; the first is that intelligence tests are unfair to older subjects, because they are heavily weighted for speed; second, that scores obtained on them are largely dependent upon education and stored information; third, that the findings regarding decline of ability have generally been based on cross-sectional rather than horizontal studies; and finally, that tests such as we have are not really measures of intelligence. As one who spent some 25 years devising tests of intelligence, and has some vested interest in them, I could hardly be expected to accept these strictures. However, the objections can be and, in my opinion, have been answered on more substantial grounds.

This is not the occasion to go into the pros and cons regarding the validity of using tests to appraise adult intelligence. I shall only summarize my own point of view by saying that I believe intelligence tests can and do measure intelligence of older persons. I also believe that they do not measure all of it, nor equally at all ages. A more troublesome problem than the question regarding the validity of the test, is that we are inclined, and to some extent compelled, to define intelligence differently at different ages. At younger ages, definitions of intelligence are likely to emphasize mental alertness, ability to learn, and capacity to see new relationships. In older ages, one is likely to be more concerned with what is broadly covered by the terms wisdom and sagacity, where by sagacity one means the ability to deal with life's situations in terms of past experience. This is understandable and perhaps also legitimate. But, as I have previously asserted, intellectual ability, intelligence and wisdom are not identical. Wisdom is necessary to make the world go round; intelligence, to make it go forward.

As regards the changes of memory with increasing age, there is much less controversy. Practically all studies, as well as common experience, testify to its progressive decline in later years. The finding that has caused most surprise, is that memory as measured on intelligence tests does not decline as rapidly as some other abilities, as for example, abstract reasoning, which was generally thought to remain unimpaired much longer. Thus, Jones and Conrad, in analyzing the results of their very comprehensive study of an entire community with the Army Alpha found that oldsters fell off much more on tests of analogies than they did on tests of general information, and subsequent studies by Jones[2] showed that this was not an artifact. Jones interpreted the findings "as indicating that the age pattern differences between the two tests is due to the tendency for general information to reflect the mere documentation of verbal or factual knowledge, while analogies had more to do with problem solving, adaptation and flexible use of mental resources."

The degree of loss in memory functions or learning ability in later maturity depends in a good measure upon the areas of memory investigated. This was clearly demonstrated in the studies of Gilbert[1] who compared the scores made by persons ages 60-69 with scores made by persons 20-29 on a variety of memory tests, the subjects compared having been previously matched on the basis of vocabulary test scores. The loss varied considerably with type of material the subject was asked to remember. Thus, the loss for auditory memory span for digits was 12 per cent; that for repeating sentences 21 per cent; for retention of paragraphs 40 per cent; memory for designs 46 per cent; and retention of paired associates 55 per cent.

The examples of memory loss just cited are in areas generally calling for what is usually designated as reproductive memory. Recall of this sort—that is, reproduction of learned associations—has often been distinguished from the ability to recall or relive personal experiences such as what happened at a certain time, what one did, or what one thought on certain occasions. These were differentiated by Bergson into memories which "repeat" and memories which "represent," and more recently by Reiff and Scheerer[3] as "memoria," in contrast to what they designate as "remembrances." The historic view has been that old age primarily suffers from inability to retain or acquire memoria rather than from a loss or an inability to recall remembrances. This opinion is open to much doubt. There are no important studies which have attempted systematically to investigate the hypothesis. Such a study, if feasible, would require not merely a count of the memories one can recall at a given moment, but an estimate of the proportion which this number represents of the totality of the individuals' past experiences. This proportion, if it could be arrived at at all, would necessarily be very small, and when compared with the proportion of retained facts one may have acquired in school or elsewhere, would be even infinitely smaller. In any event, I am of the opinion that we recall much more of what we have learned than of what has happened to us. I venture the guess that older people do better on television quiz-shows than on psychoanalysts' couches.

Interesting as the last speculation may be, I leave it in order to consider more objective observations which have increasingly intrigued my interest during the past few years. These have to do with the importance of memory and the so-called general factor of intelligence relative to the aging process. At this point it may be useful to state what, for the purpose of this paper, I wish to comprehend under the term intelligence. I say *for the purpose of this paper* because I realize that there are many possible definitions of the term, that pronouncements on the subject differ widely, and that some psychologists have even expressed the opinion that nobody really knows what the world means. The last point of view carries modesty a bit too far. In point of fact, there is much more implicit agreement than disagreement as to what is involved in intelligent, at least among those who have devoted their time to measuring it rather than philosophizing about it. Whatever else it may embrace, most psychologists would agree that intelligence, first and foremost, implies the capacity to perceive relevant relations. This capacity does not constitute all of intelligence, but is the one unequivocal and requisite element of it. Since Carl Spearman first demonstrated this broad factor, it has usually been designated by the letter g. It is found whenever intercorrelations of any battery of intelligence tests are systematically investigated by a method which has come to be known as Factor Analysis.

I will not detain you here to explain the merits and demerits of the method, but merely recall that it is a statistical technique for determining the smallest number of variables that need to be posited in order to account for the observed variance which enters into the measures one uses. These are what are now often referred to as the primary "factors of the mind." In the case of intelligence test batteries, some 4 to 5 factors are generally sufficient to account for nearly all the extractable variance. Among the factors so extracted are verbal ability, abstract reasoning, memory, visual motor organization, and, above all, g. Translated into practical terms, this means that an individual's composite test scores, or what he achieves on the tests, may be explained as being due to the degree to which he possesses the designated primary abilities or factors. Also to be noted is that the factor g is not only always present, but contributes by far the greatest amount of variance, usually 3 or 4 times that of all others combined. For example, in the case of the Wechsler Adult Intelligence Scale, at ages 20-24, g accounts for about 54 per cent of the variance; the

Verbal factor 5.2 per cent; the non-Verbal 4.5 per cent; the Memory factor 2.3 per cent; and so on. This finding is similar to results obtained in the factor analysis of other test batteries, and is quite familiar.

What has intrigued me during the past few years is not so much this finding, but what change, if any, there may be in the relative contribution of the factors with the aging process, and in particular in the relative contributions of the *g* factor and the Memory factor. You will recall that *g* is the over-all factor which is considered as the main source of intellectual capacity and which for practical purposes may be equated with the basic indicator of general intelligence itself. Thus translated, the question I am trying to investigate is the relative roles played by over-all capacity or general ability and the more delimited capacity involved in memory or the ability to recall and reproduce learned material. To do this I have examined Cohen's Bifactor Analysis of my Adult Scale, which allows us to compare the contributions of these two factors at different age periods. The periods which I have chosen for the comparison are ages 25-34, which is the period of maximal intellectual ability, and the age interval 60-75, where, by all criteria, the decline in ability is admitted as having already set in. The percentage of variance contributed to the total is as follows:

PERCENTAGE OF VARIANCE CONTRIBUTED TO TOTAL VARIANCE

Age Period	g Factor	M Factor
25-34	50.0	1.7
60-75	42.1	6.1

The meaning of this finding is that with increasing age *g* declines and memory becomes increasingly more important.

What are we to make of this? On the one hand we started out with a well known and repeatedly demonstrated fact that memory in later years is considerably impaired, and now one finds that, in spite of this loss, the older person is more dependent for effective over-all functioning on his ability to remember than on his basic *g* endowment. Here is a paradox indeed. What has always been believed is that memory is most important at age periods when we are supposed to be still learning; actually it turns out that in old age we may be much more dependent on it. Once we get over the surprise, however, we can recall examples which support it. This is particularly true in cases where pathology has set in, and those of you with wide clinical and neurological experience will be able to recall many instances.

Consider, for example, the helplessness of the Korsakoff or arteriosclerotic with severe memory defects, the organic case with aphasia, or even ordinary amnesia at whatever age. Of what value is it to the patient to know who is President of the United States, to add, multiply and divide, or to operate a typewriter or play a piano, if he does not remember who he is. Here is a loss of awareness of self, a loss which if extensive, may end in complete separation of the individual from his past. The loss is the most disabling as well as distressing of all. There is no longer any point for pursuing "la recherche du temps perdu," when old remembrances cease to exist.

Is the progressive loss of one's past as we grow old inevitable? So far as one can see, the answer must be yes. But there is some indication that this loss may be postponed and, to varying degrees, arrested. I say this primarily on the basis of certain research findings in psychopharmacology which seem to hold out encouraging hopes for controlling impairment of memory along with other physical processes. If they are realized, I should be ready to agree with Cicero that old age has assets of its own. In the meantime, the following verses by Oliver Wendell Holmes may be of some comfort.

The Last Leaf

They say that in his prime
Ere the pruning-knife of Time
   Cut him down,
Not a better man was found
By the Crier, on his round
   Through the town.

My grandmamma has said—
Poor old lady, she is dead
   Long ago—
That he had a Roman nose,
And his cheek was like a rose
   In the snow;

But now his nose is thin,
And it rests upon his chin
   Like a staff,

And a crook is in his back,
And a melancholy crack
   In his laugh.

I know it is a sin
For me to sit, and grin
   At him here;
But the old three cornered hat,
And the breeches, and all that
   Are so queer!

And if I should live to be
The last leaf upon the tree
   In the spring,
Let them smile, as I do now,
At the old forsaken bough,
   Where I cling.

REFERENCES

1. Gilbert, J. G.: Memory loss in senescence. J. abnorm. soc. Psychol. 36:73-86, 1941.
2. Jones, H. E.: Age changes in mental ability. *In:* Old Age in the Modern World. London, 1957.
3. Reiff, R., and Scheerer, M.: Memory and Hypnotic Age Regression. New York, 1959.
4. Wechsler, D.: The Measurement and Appraisal of Adult Intelligence. Baltimore, 1958.

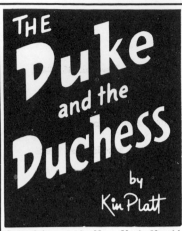

PART IV

INTRODUCTION

Brain function in expressions of intellect have been of interest to David Wechsler throughout his professional life. From the publication of *The Range of Human Capacities* and the first edition of *Measurement of Adult Intelligence*, he has included discussions of relationships which he believes exist between intelligence and brain function.

The fourth edition of *The Measurement and Appraisal of Adult Intelligence*, published in 1958, includes such a section. He has chosen this particular selection (1) to include in this collection. Scientists are concerned with the way the structure of the brain, studied descriptively, may be related to the cognitive and abstract components of mental activity, on the one hand, and direct relationships which may exist between particular portions of the brain and given mental functions, on the other. Direct evidence was not, and is not, available. Inferences may be drawn, however, from indirect sources.

In the practical sense, as Wechsler notes, local insults and injuries to brain tissue seem to have much less effect on general or global intelligence than they do on specific kinds of abilities and competencies. Particularly in adult life, rather severe damage may be done to particular sensory functions and yet the I.Q. remain at the same level as before the accidental insult.

Though the more specific the ability, the more directly related to some delimited area of the cortex, any direct expressions remain rather obscure. Certainly, with quite abstract behaviors, pointing to specific cortical areas of damage is nearly impossible. This position, of course, should have its meaning for a number of educational difficulties encountered by students as well as the more obvious physical and sensory ones. The field of reading has in recent years begun a deliberate search for relationships between reading disability and brain dysfunction. At the present time, the search would seem to be more hopeful than realistic. Even if one were to assume that such a relationship exists, what areas would be involved remains unstated and consequently what to do in an ameliorative or training fashion undetermined.

There is very little known about the brain and its function beyond a highly descriptive notation of cell composition and function. There remain, for example, those areas of the brain which, under excision, seem not to have effect upon the function of the brain totally. Wechsler points to the intriguing possibility that we have not yet discovered ways in which these portions of the brain may be used. Perhaps the behaviors ascribed to such areas have been incorrectly labeled and researched.

Such issues bring up the point as to whether intelligence is mediated by particularized areas in the brain. Wechsler surveys the historical positions taken on this point and concludes a negative answer to the question. This leads him to both the observational and empirical position that: ". . . intelligence deals not with mental representations, but with relations that may exist between them, and relations cannot be localized. . . ." Intelligence, then, has no specific locus in the brain.

There follows a discussion of intelligence as a physical construct. As he notes, there have been the theoretical positions from history as well as more contemporaneous research in neurology and physiology attempting to correlate behaviors with specific actions of the nervous system. Such work does not offer evidence about the possibility of a physical basis for intelligence, though Spearman did include a theoretical position that G is some form of mental energy.

It is possible, with the use of computers, to simulate performance analogous to mental ability. Such mental abilities, as Wechsler has stated on several occasions, are not the same in sum or substance as general intelligence. The computer may disclose ways in which mental operations are carried out, but will fail in attempts to relate such operations to outcomes and goals, the function of general intelligence. The importance of the work that has been done with computers in simlulating human thinking is too great to overlook, and as a result Wechsler discusses some of this work and its implications. He points out, however, that the computer is limited as compared to the intelligence of man since it must follow directions only and cannot use its experience for further direction.

The crux of the matter lies in the distinction between intelligence and abilities as he conceives them. The work and conclusions of A. W. Stern are pertinent since he used a mathematical model consistent with physical theory. More importantly, the model serves to point again to the inconsistency of attempting to assess global intelligence by measuring intellective abilities and summing their performance qualities. Wechsler concludes by pointing out that it will not be possible to build a test where the total variance is accounted for by the test itself because, in intellectual functioning, there is some integration and combination that is not expressed in performance scores directly. The need for tests which will come closer to this goal remains.

The ideas expressed in this selection from the fourth edition of *The Measurement and Appraisal of Adult Intelligence* are the basis, then, for the three succeeding articles in this section. The first of these involves not only the relationships between intelligence and machine function, but also the idea of quantum resonance implicit in the work of Stern (2). Wechsler points out that the measure of mind is now conceived scientifically to be a function of how the brain operates.

As a result, physics may be a more usable source for explanation of psychic processes than philosophy ever could have been.

This paper considers two questions. The first involves the physical events that may occur in the human brain as the individual acts or manifests intelligence. The second relates mental activity to the kinds of logical operations that may be simulated in machine function.

The physical structure of the brain is described, with emphasis on the current concept of integration. Wechsler raises a basic question as to the description of integration in physical terms. The brain may be conceived in machine terms, with consequent screening and sorting among stimuli. However this will not serve as an adequate model for intelligence. So, he returns at this point to the physicists' construct of collectivity as a possible explanation of the general nature of intelligence. Reviewing the work of Niels Bohr, with his proposal of a principle of complimentarity, Wechsler points out that neurons perform not only in terms of individual behaviors, but also in a collective sense. Based upon this, he hypothesizes that: ". . . all mental processes, including those of consciousness and cognition, are manifestations of collective behavior of the elementary systems in the encephalon. . . ." These manifestations may take several forms and may be overtly expressed in various ways, only crudely measured to the present.

Now Wechsler addresses himself to the physical equivalent of intelligent behavior. What are the events that take place in the brain as the individual manifests intelligence? For this purpose, he turns to the idea of resonance. The mechanical concept of quantum resonance is extrapolated to physical events in the brain. The conclusion is: ". . . mental events in the brain consist of the creation of successive molecular systems when activity in any one group of cells is reinforced or inhibited by the reverberation to particles in some other group of cells. . . ." Degrees of intelligence may be related to the presence of more or better resonators. Furthermore, he takes the position that the effects of environment are relatively limited in their influence upon this function.

A more direct comparison of machine and human thinking is included in an address of that title included here (3). In the latter half of this paper, he turns to the concept of memory, both of a machine and human nature. This issue is an important one since differences exist in the ability to combine data into meaningful configurations.

The machine can serve certain usable and worthwhile roles, so that Wechsler discusses both strengths and limitations. Since they are tireless and efficient, machines assume many of the tasks required of the human and do them in a more economical fashion. He concludes that they will become increasingly important in assuming "mental work" of human beings, and that the results of this are less desirable than most of us might expect or wish.

The final paper included in this section deals even more specifically with the matter of memory, both as historically conceived and as analyzed by Wechsler himself. The paper (4) is entitled "Engrams, Memory Storage and Mnemonic Coding." The basic question revolves around the events in the brain that allow one to recall an experience which no longer has a physical excitation. Historical explanations are reviewed as well as more contemporary research. Wechsler takes the position that the mechanism of memory essentially uses a matching process. Engrams, applied by experience, are stored like genetic codes, transmitted as genetic information, and reused through a matching process. Such matching may be on either a chemical or electrical basis.

This position, while dealing with the basic question, leaves unresolved the issue of storage as such. Again, Wechsler reviews current viewpoints on memory storage and rejects them primarily because he takes the position that memories as such are not stored at all. Obviously, there are changes in the brain as a result of excitatory processes. Such changes should not be equated with the original conditions that were involved at the time.

Memory is conceived by Wechsler as having an essential function of coding and transmitting information as it may be needed. He admits a machine quality may exist, but on a genetically established and in a working state without having to be programmed in any fashion. Experience determines the information coded and transmitted. However, experience plays a relatively minor role in the process itself and, indeed, Wechsler maintains that the information thus acquired is only a small portion of the potential total engram store which memory possesses.

The popular view of memory as a machine function is not acceptable to Wechsler for two reasons. First, the brain is relatively much slower in transmission than the electronic computer. Second, memory processes cannot be accounted for on the basis of probabilities alone. Instances and arguments for each of these positions are cited.

His position that the memory process is not stochastic, at least in its essential nature, does not mean that both learning and recall are random processes. Indeed, he believes that certain general principles do relate to learning and recall and may be identified. However, the conditions that may influence the effectiveness of memory are not the same as the processes which describe the memory function. This becomes a basic difference between the reality of the human memory and the imitation of that reality by the machine.

INTELLIGENCE AND BRAIN FUNCTION, AND INTELLIGENCE AS A PHYSICAL CONSTRUCT*

DAVID WECHSLER

In dealing with the brain as an "organ of the mind," its investigators have been concerned chiefly with two questions: 1) the manner and the degree to which brain structure is related to mental activity, and 2) assuming that mental activity is dependent upon brain structure, which parts of the brain are associated with which mental functions. More progress has been made on the latter, but no satisfactory answers can be given to either of these questions. Particularly vague is our knowledge as to where and how intelligence is mediated.

Like all mental functions, general intelligence may be said to depend upon the condition and structure of the brain, in the broad sense that no intelligent behavior is possible without at least partially intact cerebral hemispheres. But in this broad sense, the statement does not explain very much. In particular, it does not distinguish the possible role of the brain in the mediation of intelligence from the part it plays in sensory, motor, perceptual and other processes, since injury or removal of various parts of the cortex can involve one without the other. Especially challenging is the fact that except in cases of injuries involving the speech areas, human beings can apparently continue to function intellectually after considerable loss of brain substance, whereas much less damage areawise is sufficient to impair severely or destroy entirely specific sensory functions. In general, measures of global intelligence are less affected by local injuries than are measures of specific ability. A missile injury may severely impair visual, auditory or tactile discrimination without noticeably affecting the subject's IQ.

Findings of this kind and more especially observations of sequelae of cerebral lesions in animals (306) and man (392) have led to a distinction between at least two kinds of effect that may result from brain injury: (1) specific dysfunctions associated with circumscribed and generally small brain areas; (2) general intellectual impairment unassociated with any particular locus, and usually involving larger cortical areas. This distinction oversimplifies what actually happens in most cases. But it has been convincingly shown that disabilities, like scotomas, generally result from very circumscribed lesions, while other dysfunctions, such as loss of

*Reprinted from "The Nature of Intelligence," in David Wechsler, *The Measurement and Appraisal of Adult Intelligence,* 4th ed., Baltimore, 1958, pp. 17-23. Copyright 1958, The Williams & Wilkins Co. Reproduced by permission.

ability to discern hidden figures may ensue "irrespective of localization of lesions and presence or absence of other symptoms" (490).

Thus, the question of whether the locus of brain injury is or is not "a differential factor in performance increment" cannot be answered exclusively one way or the other. Some disabilities, namely those principally involving sensory, motor and simple perceptual functions, are established with delimited cortical areas; others involving more complex discrimination functions appear tied to such areas to only a limited degree; still more complex abilities, such as the capacity to profit from past experiences, are only negligibly or not at all established. This does not mean that levels of intellectual ability or of global intelligence are impaired by only certain kinds of brain lesion or are independent of either the size or locus of the lesion. On the contrary, subjects with severe brain lesions anywhere, when compared with normal controls, nearly always show significantly lower levels of performance (287). Nevertheless, there exist large portions of the cortex the suppression or removal of which, whether by trauma or excision, seems to have little effect on the function of the brain as a whole. These are the so-called "silent areas" of the cortex. Whether they are really silent or merely functioning in ways which we have not yet discovered still remains to be answered. It is possible that the limited changes observed after removal of these areas may be due to the fact that investigators are appraising functions historically imputed to them, but seldom, if at all, on the basis of actual proof. According to Penfield and Evans (392), the negligible role of the silent areas may be due not only to the fact that "there is bilateral representation of the function involved" but also to the fact that (in some cases) "the function is only weakly encephalized while the essential mechanism remains in the diencephalon."[13]

The points just discussed pose the problem of whether intelligence in any sense may be conceived of as being mediated by any localized area of the brain. Historically it has been asserted not only that "different parts of the brain are specialized for different functions" but also that "in the course of this development certain portions of the brain and especially the frontal cortex take on or are concerned with all the highest and latest acquired functions" (222a). This led to the view not only that the frontal cortex and oftener that the prefrontal lobes were primarily involved, but also that they constituted the centers of or seat of intelligence. Unfortunately for this point of view, neither direct experiment nor clinical observation gives support to the superior role of the frontal cortex. Most striking, as already pointed out, has been the finding that elimination of substantial portions of the frontal lobes or even complete removal of them, produces little effect on specific intellectual performance or on global intelligence ratings as

---

[13] The effect, however, is not so negligible as sometimes reported. See, for example, studies of Gardner, Karnash *et al.* (181). Also the discussion of the general problem on p. 217.

measured by tests. Equally damaging to the claim of pre-eminence for the frontal lobes is the fact that comparative studies of the sequelae from injuries to various parts of the cortex have shown that resultant decrements in intellectual performance, if there are any at all, far from being greatest, are actually least for injuries in the frontal lobes (489). These findings have been repeatedly confirmed, but in spite of the negated findings (39, 366, 370a) several authors have sought to maintain the dominance of the frontal lobes as centers of intelligence by distinguishing between different kinds of intelligence. W. C. Halstead (230), for example, makes a differentiation between what he terms "psychometric and biologic intelligence,"[14] the former merely representing intellectual ability as measured by tests and the latter a basic capacity for nervous and mental organization by which "the nervous system contributes to man's survival." Halstead assigns the mediation of this "biologic intelligence" to the frontal lobes. Apart from the fact, however, that the definition of "biologic intelligence" is derived by its author from the performance of subjects in psychometric tests, one must note that the capacity to survive, and in general to adapt, even if equated with intelligence is a function oftener described as being mediated by various other parts of the nervous system, for example, the thalamus or even the brain stem. And so far as co-ordination and organization of conscious behavior are concerned, the frontal lobes seemingly play an even more minor role. For, whereas the entire frontal area of the cortex may be removed without any loss of consciousness, any considerable damage in either the diencephalon or the midbrain produces immediate unconsciousness. In the opinion of Penfield and Rasmussen (394) the most important means of co-ordinating the functions of the cortical areas are not the association mechanisms within the cortex. Such co-ordination, they state, is produced largely by the integrating action of the subcortical centers which lie in the mesoencephalon and the diencephalon.[15]

Not only does the bulk of contemporaneous experimental and clinical evidence dispose of the role of the frontal lobes as unique centers of intelligence, it also counter-indicates the possibility of its exclusive localization in any other part of the brain. The effort to locate centers of intelligence, like the search for seats of consciousness, as I. S. Wechsler has clearly shown (529), must inevitably end in disappointment, and for the same reasons, namely, that intelligence like consciousness "is not a single entity . . . (but) the result of numerous integrations of simple and complex neural activities." In this connection, the recent investigations of Magoun (346a and c) on the arousal and activating function of the reticular system in the brain stem further testify to the complex interrelationships of the

[14] Also two other kinds, namely, clinical and neurological intelligence. According to Halstead these are associated with and dependent upon different primary factors which are "differentially represented in the cerebral cortex" (230), p. 204.

[15] p. 235.

various parts of the brain in the mediation and production of higher mental processes. According to Magoun, "its cephalic influences upon the cerebral hemispheres provide the substrate of the state of wakefulness upon which most higher functions of the nervous system depend." (346b). In brief, neither electroencephalographic nor neurological evidence substantiates the existence of loci in the cerebral hemispheres that serve as centers for either consciousness or any specifically defined mental processes. But apart from neurological considerations, one cannot expect anything like fixed centers of intelligence for purely logical reasons. Intelligence deals not with mental representations but with relations that may exist between them, and relations cannot be localized. A man is bigger than a mouse and a five dollar bill is 'bigger' than a one dollar bill. One might conceivably posit the percept man, mouse and dollar bill as having some sort of cortical representation, for example as engrams, but where or how could one locate the logical relationship *bigger than* which has no spatial or substantiative existence. As a cognitive process, intelligence involves primarily the perception of relations, or to use Spearman's more precise phrase, *the eduction of correlates*, and this process is independent of the specific modality in which the terms are perceived. For effective functioning intelligence may depend more upon the intactness of some rather than other portions of the brain, but in no sense can it be said to be mediated by any single part of it. Intelligence has no locus.

Intelligence as a Physical Construct

Psychologists, like philosophers, have sought from time to time to account for the workings of the mind in terms of physical processes. The efforts[16] have concerned themselves primarily either with the general (and metaphysical) problem of the relation of the mind to matter or with the attempt, as in more recent years, from the cues of neurology and physiology, to account for the correlates of the specific actions of the nervous system.

[16] The earlier efforts usually ended with a *deus ex machina*; Leibnitz' monad and Descartes' cybernetic soul housed in the pineal gland are perhaps the most famous examples. Subsequent to the publication of Newton's *Principia*, and up to the middle of the 19th century, the models of brain function for the most part consisted of vague mechanical analogies supplemented later by hypotheses derived from the newly developed chemistry and the laws of thermodynamics. The mind in terms of these formulations operated as a complicated clockwork or self-regulating chemical engine. With the dramatic discoveries in electricity, and particularly its practical applications to communication and recording devices, the models became primarily electric. By the beginning of the present century the brain and its operation were most often compared to a telephone switchboard. This comparison can still be found in the textbooks of physiology of a generation ago. The telephone switchboard has now given way to more complex electrical relay systems involving built-in controls, feedback circuits, and black box properties.

These have resulted in some theories as regards the possible physical basis of sensation, perception and association but, so far as we have been able to discover, there has been no comparable attempt to explain intelligence. Spearman's interpretation of *g* as a kind of mental "energy" may perhaps be considered an exception, but he did not carry the physical analogy very far. More recently still, the remarkable performances of the automaton computer have suggested analogies between the physics of its operations and human thinking and by implication of the human intellect itself. It should be noted at this point that the achievements of the automaton computer, apart from furnishing physical models for the nervous system, present types of performances which, psychologically speaking, are most nearly identifiable as abilities.[17] These mental abilities can be directly explained in terms of the physics of the computer. Accounting for mental abilities, however, presents quite a different problem from that of general intelligence. The first seeks to explain the nature and manner in which mental operations are carried out; the second, the relevance and relation of these operations to certain ends and goals. But the achievements of the analogue and digital computers[18] are in many ways so similar to those of the human intellect that it will be useful to discuss in what way they are alike and in what way they are different.

The analogue and digital computers are remarkable machines. They can perform complex calculations, solve differential equations, compute trajectories and unravel codes. They can store information of a complex nature and give it back at a moment's notice. As already perfected, the digital computer can do many things which have hitherto been considered purely mental or restricted to human capability. For example, it can be made to exhibit retention and recall, make alternative choices, check its own mistakes (which it seldom makes), translate Russian into English, and if put to it, play a game of chess (454). But for all these remarkable "abilities" it lacks certain basic potentials of which only man and certain animals seem capable. The computer cannot initiate action, or learn from experience. It can only do what it is told to do, that is, what has been built into it. In short, it can only follow instructions.[19] Perhaps the most important thing to be said about the computing automaton is that while it can do things, it cannot understand them. It has abilities but these abilities do not go beyond performance.

[17] Such as performing arithmetical computations, storing and reproducing information, etc.

[18] The principles upon which these computers are built are too complex to be considered here. For an exposition of them the reader is referred to the masterful article by von Neumann in the Hixon Symposium on the cerebral mechanisms in behavior (501).

[19] But in this respect it does not really differ much from the average human being.

The distinction between intelligence and abilities emphasized in earlier pages is the crux of the matter. There is no doubt that machines can now be designed and have already been constructed that manifest mental abilities of various sorts, *i.e.*, perform many intellectual tasks including that of logical reasoning. But for the same reasons that abilities cannot be equated with intelligence, the electronic automaton cannot serve as a model for it. What is needed is a conceptual scheme that would yield some insight into the functioning of the brain, not only in terms of its individual components but also collective action as a whole. Here the idea of complementarity borrowed from quantum mechanics, rather than concepts derived from the mathematics of electric circuits, may shed some light. Such an explanation has recently been made available in a remarkable article by A. W. Stern (478), that should greatly modify our thinking regarding the nature of intelligence.

Stern begins by distinguishing between human abilities, mental factors and the interacting process by which the latter are integrated into intellective behavior; he correctly concludes that they cannot be consistently treated in any mathematical statistical scheme if they are posited to exist as purely isolated factors. Primary mental abilities, like the elementary particles of physics, exhibit a collective as well as an independent behavior; they have group as well as individual properties. Because of their group character the primary intellective factors, according to Stern, possess the basically important property of *connectivity*. This property is manifested psychologically as a *coupling* among the separate intellective factors. Furthermore, "the two modes of behavior form a fundamental *complementarity* suggestive of the complementarity exhibited by the well known wave-particle duality of quantum theory."[20] In terms of quantum mechanics, the wave-particle duality arises because "it is impossible to separate the behavior of the elementary particle from its interaction with the system representing the apparatus." In the case of mental functioning involving intellective behavior, the dual properties of the primary factors arise from the fact that the mind (brain) is an interacting system, "and the environmental situation of the mind plays a role similar to that of the experimental situation in physics under which the phenomena occur." Postulating the above, Stern concludes that "intelligence is the resultant collective behavior among the intellective factors," and *g* "the measure of the strength of the resonance evoked by the coupling process."

The foregoing is an epitome of the major points in Stern's paper on *g* and the nature of intelligence, which in turn is a summary of his mathematical analysis of the problem. The important implication of Stern's paper for psychology is that it presents a mathematical logical model which

[20] *Loc. cit.*; the other quotations are from the same article (478).

not only is consistent with current physical theory, but explains the existing inconsistency of psychologists' trying to measure global intelligence through the summation of intellective abilities. The point here is that while intellective abilities can be shown to contain several independent factors, intelligence cannot be so broken up. Hence, no amount of refinement of tests or addition of factors will account for the total variance of an intelligence test battery, because the variance in intelligence test performance is due not only to the direct contributions of the factors themselves but also to their collective behavior or integration. In order completely to measure intelligence, it is insufficient to extend the range of abilities measured, though this is needed too; we must also find tests which manifest both greater coupling potential and greater resonance characteristics.

INTELLIGENCE, QUANTUM RESONANCE, AND THINKING MACHINES*

DAVID WECHSLER

Department of Psychiatry, New York University College of Medicine

Speculation about how the mind works is as old as philosophy itself but, while there is a discernible continuity in the concepts employed to account for the way man perceives and thinks, modern views differ from former theories in at least one important respect. These views are more concerned in what takes place in the brain as a physical apparatus than with what older philosophers called the attributes of the soul. This change in interest began with René Descartes who, while distinguishing sharply between mind and matter, nevertheless located the soul in the brain and, once having conveniently housed it in the pineal gland, left it little to do other than to serve as a sort of detached, albeit divine, observer. Since then the soul has gradually lost even this modest role. To contemporaneous science, how the mind works means how the brain works: such factors as sensation, perception, and cognition are manifestations of brain activity and neural interaction. These are regarded as physical events – events which, as Bertrand Russell (1929) has pointed out, happen to take place in terminal neurons of the central nervous system. Psychology now turns more and more to physics for its ultimate "explanations" of psychic processes.

The subject I shall discuss will concern itself with some of the physical explanations or hypotheses of how the brain works intellectively. More specifically, I shall consider the following two questions. (1) What, in the light of recent advances in neurophysiology and quantum mechanics, is the likely physical event that takes place in the human brain when an individual is said to manifest intelligence? (2) In what way is human mentation as involved in intelligent behavior different from the logical operations performed by thinking machines? In trying to answer these questions, it will be useful to summarize contemporary views on two germane topics. The first is the neurophysiologist's concept of how the brain operates as a physical apparatus and, second, the physicist's concept of *connectivity*.

*This paper was presented at a meeting of the Division on January 18, 1960. Reprinted from *Transactions of The New York Academy of Sciences,* 1960, **22,** 259-266.

The human brain is now generally regarded as a complex neural network whose main function is to serve as a vast clearing house of incoming and outgoing messages. For this purpose it is conceived of as a complex automatic information exchange or self-regulating intercommunication system. Parts of the nervous system (such as the sense organs) collect information that is then transmitted through synaptic barriers to various centers, although not necessarily fixed loci, where it is eventually integrated. Transmission and integration are achieved through interlacing systems of inhibiting and facilitating reverbatory circuits, and the brain itself has been recently described as a complex of such circuits in continuous activity. A gap unaccounted for in this hypothesis is that much of the received information is unused; one needs to explain what becomes of unused information and, especially, in what manner it is "edited." This hiatus did not present a problem to Descartes, because he provided the brain with a divine editor; the helmsman of modern cybernetics is just another automaton regulating, and regulated by, feedback circuits.

The key work in contemporaneous neurophysiology is integration, generally described as a complex of neural activity or pattern of excitation taking place in or between certain regions of the brain. One of the interesting facts recently demonstrated is that while this organized activity, particularly of the higher functions, such as memory and learning, may be associated with the integrity of certain parts of the cortex, it is not exclusively dependent upon them, since this integration can continue in spite of cortical interruptions. For this reason it has been posited that initiation and regulation of the higher processes may take place and be mediated through regions other than the cortex: for example, parts of the thalamus, various reticular tracts, and other intracephalic communicating systems.

Regardless of where or how integration occurs, however, one is still confronted with the underlying question: To what does this integration correspond and to what can it be equated? Is it a kind of electrical activity that, on reaching a certain level, merely initiates or delimits a particular set of motor responses? Does it represent special cortical patterns that serve to define one or another type of perception? Is it just a state of awareness associated with or defining particular kinds of neural activity? One must distinguish here, as W. Koehler has emphasized, between what a process is and how it is achieved. It is the difference between describing the structure and mechanism of an atomic pile and and trying to account for the fission phenomena in terms of the properties or behavior of the elementary physical particles that produce it. It is the former type of description that now constitutes the physical models of how the brain works (Asby, 1947).

The current definition of the brain that has met with greatest acceptance among neurophysiologists is that it is essentially a screening and sorting organ, a complex electrochemical servomechanism that in some respects functions like a multiple television system with built-in screening generators and, in others, like a high-speed automaton computer. In either case it is eventually conceived as a thinking or logical machine.

The concept of the mind as a logical machine is not new, but the remarkable achievements of the recently developed digital computers have lent much support to the suggested equivalence between intellectual and computer operations. It is not altogether clear which is the model for which, but that there is strong resemblance between them cannot be doubted.

One of the earliest computers and, perhaps, the only strictly logical machine, that of the English logician Stanley Jevons (1913), was mechanically quite a simple affair. In general appearance it resembled the small upright organ with a keyboard containing twenty-one keys. Sixteen of the keys represented the usual terms employed in logical notations *(A,a; B,b; C,c; D,d);* the remainder designated possible logical operations: for example, one for the copula, one to designate equality, and one for disjunction. To work the machine it was necessary only to press the proper keys designating the signs and letters of the logical proposition and, after thus inserting one's minor and major premises, collect the indicated conclusions by pressing a finis lever. The machine as described by Jevons was not only able to indicate conclusions but would also, to quote Jevons, "detect any self-contradiction between the premises presented to it." The one big drawback and limitation of the machine was that the problems that it solved were primarily those in which only the academic logician was likely to be interested. The modern automaton is infinitely more versatile (and more complex), but deals with many problems that even an average bank clerk or business executive can understand. It can perform many more practical operations. It is a computer, not a logician.

The remarkable tasks that electronic computers can achieve are now fairly familiar. These machines perform complex calculations, solve differential equations, compute trajectories, and unravel codes. They can store information of a complex nature and give it back at a moment's notice. The latest models of the digital computer can do many things that have hitherto been considered purely mental or restricted to human capability. With proper programing such a machine can be made to exhibit retention and recall, make alternative choices, check its own mistakes (which it seldom makes), translate Russian into English and, if put to it, play a fair game of chess. However, for all these remarkable "abilities" it lacks certain basic potentials of which only man and certain animals seem potentially capable. The automaton computer cannot initiate action, or profit from experience, without external intervention. It can do only what it is told to do: that is, what has been built into it. The most important limitation of the computing automaton however, is that while it can do things, it cannot understand them; it has abilities, but these abilities do not go beyond performance.

The basic distinction between intelligence and abilities, namely, that of understanding as against merely performing a task, is the crux of the matter. There is no doubt that machines can now be designed and have already been constructed that manifest mental abilities of various sorts including that of logical reasoning. However, for the same reasons that abilities cannot be equated with intelligence, the electronic automaton cannot serve as a model for it. What is needed is a conceptual scheme that would yield some insight into the functioning of the brain, not only in terms of its individual components but also collectively, as a unit, as well. It is here that the physicist's construct of *collectivity* offers a promising lead.

The physical concept of collectivity is derived from the particle-wave duality of quantum mechanics, which was so well elucidated by Niels Bohr's complementarity principle, which aims to reconcile the contrary aspects of the (dual) behavior of the elementary particle. These are its wave and particle characteristics which, although they cannot be observed simultaneously, together form a complete description of the behavior of the basic entities present in nature. This duality of behavior is ascribed not to the intrinsic properties of the elementary particle, for example, the electron, but to its interaction with other particle congeries or systems, such as the apparatus used. The elementary particle is thus conceived of as being capable of manifesting two types of behavior: one in which it acts, as it were, alone or independently, and another in which it acts communally or collectively. Contemporary physics teaches that the properties of molecular and atomic systems arise essentially from their interaction or their contiguous presence.

What seems to characterize the behavior of the elementary physical particle might give us a key for understanding the elementary units involved in neural activity. One might reasonably assume that the individual neurons of the nervous system, like the electrons of the atom, may have a collective as well as an independent behavior. When we say neurons we mean, of course the fine particles in the neurons and particularly those in the cortical cells. However, the important thing to be emphasized is that there is a collective as well as an individual behavior of the neuron cells and that the characteristics of this behavior are due to interaction processes and not merely to the inherent properties of neural protoplasm.

In light of the foregoing I venture the hypothesis that all mental processes, including those of consciousness and cognition, are manifestations of collective behavior of the elementary systems in the encephalon. Different spatial and electrochemical field patterns define various psychological processes, and these are aroused or constituted when they attain a sufficient intensity due to the collective activity of the generated behavior. This activity may be manifested externally either as various kinds of electric rhythms in the form of short-lived waves (EEG, alpha, and beta) or, as recently shown, by less fluctuating or so-called quasi-steady currents.

We now come to the possible physical equivalent of what we have termed insightful or intelligent behavior: namely, the event or the events that take place in the brain when an individual may be said to perceive, is aware of, or educes a relation. Note that I have said, again, equivalent and not a correlate of: I look upon perception, cognition, and insight not as concomitant physical events in the brain, but as the events themselves. These events are at once both mental and physical. They are different only in the way they are described.

With the foregoing as a point of departure, it would seem that insight as a physical fact could be intelligibly described as a collective response of the elementary systems in cortical cells in one or another region of the brain. This interaction must be conceived as occurring not through the transmission of impulses, in the manner classically postulated, along axons or nerve trunks, but rather as a *resonance* phenomenon.

The resonance with which we are most familiar is the kind manifested in the re-echoing of sounds through reflection or its prolongation through reverberation. It is the response of a system or object, such as a tuning fork, having a given vibrating frequency to another periodic stimulus or vibration of the same or nearly the same frequency. Similar phenomena characterize the reinforcement and impedance conditions of electric circuits, but perhaps what would be immediately pertinent for our conceptualization of mental processes are the behavioral properties of the individual elementary particle. One of the most important of these is the property of *quantum* mechanical *resonance*. The quantum mechanical resonance of an elementary system differs in a basic respect from the performance of macroscopic bodies such as, for example, the prongs of a tuning fork. In the latter, the reinforcement of sound vibration results from a simple addition or superposition of one series of amplitudes onto that of another. In the case of quantum mechanical resonance, "the separate wave components are no longer considered as existing independently. The resultant amplitude formed by superposition of other states is not a simple sum of the amplitudes of the interacting components. The wave interaction of one set of particles with another results in a new state or system" (Stern, 1956).

In the light of the foregoing I suggest that mental events in the brain consist of the creation of successive molecular systems when activity in any one group of cells is reinforced or inhibited by the reverberation to particles in some other group of cells. Mental phenomena are patterns of such resonances, or recurring quantum mechanical systems, activated in one or another part of the brain. Insight is the perception or psychological equivalent of a certain type of resonance: the type that happens to have meaningful implications for the individual experiencing it. Intelligence is a sequence of such insights leading to purposeful or practical behavior. An intelligent person may thus be defined as one who has been endowed with more or better resonators. This does not exclude the possible influence of environmental stimulation, but it does support the view of Paul Weiss that any pattern of behavior "is developed by the laws of its own embryonic differentiation without aid of sensory input from the outside world."

Two additional remarks are required. First, whatever the nature of the physical process, the phenomena must be understood as occurring initially at a molecular and not at a macroscopic level. To be sure, they may be later amplified macroscopically. Gross stimulation of the brain, or damaging it, as by cutting or extirpation, while capable of furnishing useful information to the neurologist, is of little value in telling us what is taking place in the brain. By the same token, attempts at altering its function will depend more on how we can modify its molecular structure. For this reason electric and chemotherapies, in spite of their negligible contributions to date, hold out much more hope for effective change of human behavior, but not necessarily for the better, than do psychological procedures. However, the chemotherapies of the future, of course, may necessarily involve techniques quite different from those presently in vogue.

The second remark to be made concerns thinking as a psychological phenomenon. The so-called laws of thought, as Bertrand Russell has pointed out, are not descriptions of psychological processes, but only a set of rules for testing the validity of logical propositions. Human thinking only occasionally follows such rules. As introspectively described, valid thinking is more generally achieved through sequential associations and sudden insights than by logical analysis. At times thinking is also evaluative, that is, it involves judgments as to the appropriateness, desirability, and usefulness of its conclusions. In such instances it is also intelligent.

The answer to the question as to whether machines can think does not, of course, depend solely on the manner in which they achieve their end, nor is it necessarily tied to any specific hypothesis (Wisdom, 1956): for example, the hypothesis that the chief mechanism of the central nervous system is one of negative feedback. The brain may or may not function predominantly in this way.

Nevertheless, if by thinking one comprehends primarily the capacity to process, sort, and utilize information, to execute logical operations, and to solve rational problems, one must agree that machines can think. One is forced to this conclusion, not only from an appraisal of the tasks that the digital computers are already known to perform, but also from the theoretical considerations of their potentials as described, for example, by Norbert Wiener, J. von Neumann (1951) and A. M. Turing (1951).

However, while I have been convinced that machines can think, I find no indication that they are capable of any type of a performance that I call intelligent. My chief reason for this view is, as I have already indicated, that while the digital computer can do many things that have previously been considered characteristic of human mentation, the abilities manifested do not go beyond performance. Although capable of making decisions, the digital (or analogue) computer cannot evaluate its own work, that is, understand either the relevance or purpose of what it is doing. It may be able to solve complex differential equations but will not, unaided, set up a simple experiment. It will go on calculating if its house is on fire or the problem it is trying to solve is no longer relevant or necessary.

We have just conceded that machines can think and, we may add, that they can make decisions. However, these decisions are always statistically determined: that is, they depend on the totality of combinations that the input information makes available. Once the computer has been programmed, it must go through a predestined routine. Compared to the human mind, it may have to do an inordinate amount of work even in solving a simple problem. The fact that it can perform it very much faster and more accurately does not make it intelligent. Intelligence, like creativity, presupposes avoidance of what Henri Poincaré (1951) has termed "sterile combinations," that is, combinations that in the long run are irrelevant and useless. "The inventive individual," he once said, proceeds not "like a purchaser before whom are displayed a large number of samples, and who examines them one after another to make a choice; here the samples would be so numerous that a whole life would not suffice them . . ." Actually, "the sterile combinations do not even present themselves to the inventor."

Thus far, it will have been noted, I have not offered any succinct definition of intelligence, although the title of this paper indicates that I should attempt to formulate one. I have refrained from doing so, not only to avoid dilating on a construct about which there is so much disagreement, but because I have hoped that my own concept of intelligence might be inferred from the context in which I am using the term. I have presented elsewhere a formal definition of intelligence that may or may not be better than others that are more familiar. Space is lacking to discuss the latter, and I do not think that my own concept of it would settle matters. In concluding, therefore, I shall state only what I think intelligence is not, and I shall designate the one attribute which in my opinion, is its *sine qua non*. Intelligence (Wechsler, 1958) however defined, is not the equivalent of any ability, however esteemed, particularly not of learning or even of abstract reasoning ability. Something more than performance must be involved. That something, as I have already indicated, is awareness of the meaning and purpose of performance on the part of the operant. I have called this aspect of intelligence understanding. Behavior that does not involve understanding is in my opinion not intelligent. Machines do not possess understanding; hence, by my definition, they are essentially stupid or, they are at best, idio-savants.

Digital computers may be able to think, to learn, and eventually, perhaps, also to reproduce themselves; but they cannot understand what they are doing. In this respect they may not differ very much from the way human beings function much of the time; all of which may mean simply that men usually behave like machines. However, sometimes they do not; and then they build machines.

References

ASHBY, W. R. 1947. The nervous system as a physical machine. Mind. 56: 44-59.

JEVONS, W. S. 1913. The Principles of Science. 2nd ed. Repr. London, England.

NEUMANN, J. VON. 1951. General and Logical Theory of Automata. Cerebral Mechanisms of Behavior. L. A. Jeffress, Ed. Wiley. New York, N.Y.

POINCARÉ, H. 1951. Mathematical Creation. The World of Mathematics. 4. J. R. Newman, Ed. Norton. New York, N.Y.

RUSSELL, B. 1929. Mysticism and Logic. Schuster. New York, N.Y.

STERN, A. W. 1956. The Nature of G and the Concept of Intelligence. Acta Psychol. 12: 282-289.

TURING, A. M. 1951. Can a Machine Think. The World of Mathematics, J. R. Newman, Ed. Norton. New York, N.Y.

WECHSLER, D. 1958. The Measurement and Appraisal of Adult Intelligence. Williams & Wilkins. Baltimore, Md.

WISDOM, J. O. 1951. The hypothesis of cybernetics. Brit. J. Phil. Sci. 2: 2; 1956. General Systems. 1: 111-112.

MACHINE AND HUMAN THINKING[1]

DAVID WECHSLER

In discussing machine versus human thinking, it will be useful to preface the remarks with a definition of terms. As regards the word *machine,* I shall employ the term in the very general sense of any contrivance that performs work and whose operations can be described and accounted for in terms of the laws and established language of physics. In this sense I regard a digital computer or Ashby's homeostat no less than the gas engine and dictophone as examples of such contrivances.

Defining thinking is a much more difficult task. Psychologists are far from agreement as to what constitutes thought and what goes into the process. It would take me too far afield to attempt even a brief summary of the issues involved. I will only recall that the term thinking has been used to designate some or all of at least four distinct steps or processes. The first is the mere recognition of an object on the basis of sensory cues, as when observing a number of ships in the harbor, you might point to one and say, "This is a submarine." A second meaning is that of grasping a fact or situation. A young lady is walking down the street, hears a chorus of whistles and without the benefit of further explanation correctly infers what the whistles purport. Third and most common, thinking means to have an opinion or belief or a judgment. Thus, many think, that is believe, that the aim of the Soviet Union is to communize the world. Finally, to think means what humans, perhaps also some animals, do when they try to solve a problem. It is this aspect of thinking which is primarily involved in the performance of thinking machines and with which I shall, for the most part, be concerned in this paper.

That machines can solve problems is nothing new. What is so impressive and even astounding, is the ever increasing complexity and variety of kind of problems which now can be entrusted to them. These have been so widely publicized that even laymen are now fairly well acquainted with the remarkable tasks which modern electronic computers can perform. These, as you know, include such diverse tasks as computing trajectories for intercontinental missiles, translating languages, doing factor analyses, and playing chess. The question no longer is whether machines can "think," but how well they can think, not whether they can solve problems but what kind of problems and finally,

[1] Paper delivered before a research group at The Johns Hopkins University.

in what ways the thinking machines are like and differ from the thinking of human beings.

In general, the thinking of machines can be described as an ability to follow directions without making mistakes. It is a method of successive trials, but not of trial and error. A computer solves problems by literally figuring them out, that is, by a method of continuous computation. The problems it deals with are primarily arithmetical and logical or such that can be reduced to mathematical form. This is true whether the machines compute inventories, solve differential equations, or play a game of chess. All these tasks are concerned with quantitative relations and answer questions of how much or how likely.

There are a great many problems which do not involve such relations. They pose questions of a different order. They ask not ''how much'' or ''how likely,'' but ''what now.'' And in these instances electronic computers are not at present of much service. You cannot expect a digital computer to tell you whether to support the Red Cross or UNICEF or help your wife choose the dress to wear to the Jones's party. These examples are seemingly trivial and are hardly the kind that scientists or businessmen are likely to want the computer to answer for them. They nevertheless represent a numerically large and practically important kinds of problems which automata cannot deal with. These are problems calling essentially for value decisions, ''What should you do when,'' ''How worthwhile is it,'' ''Should you do it at all?'' No amount of computing could have informed President Truman as to the wisdom of dropping the A-bomb on Hiroshima, and another kind of advice rather than a more expert intelligence service is what President Eisenhower needed to appraise the U-2 incident.

Another limitation to the type of problem which current thinking machines can deal with derives from the prescribed language to which they are restricted. This is particularly true of digital computers which can seemingly use only two words—yes and no. There are many questions that cannot be directly answered by ''yes'' and ''no.'' For example, those that ask ''how good,'' ''to what extent,'' ''what difference does it make,'' and so on. To be sure these and other needed terms can be translated by sequential dichotomies into ''yes'' and ''no'' series, but apart from the fact that this procedure may require an inordinate number of intermediate decisions, it necessarily puts the greater burden for solution on the programmer rather than the machine.

Mention of the role of the programmer brings up the most common objection made against equating the performance of automata with the act of thinking, namely, that the machine does only what it is told. The most direct answer to the latter stricture is that in this respect, human beings behave in much the same way. The main difference is that the instructions which they have received have for the most part been built in at birth, that is, are genetically prescribed. Human beings are more flexible; they can alter, change or refuse instructions. This often gets them into trouble. The machine is much more docile; it never disobeys, it never talks back. This is not inevitable. Newer models are more neurotic. Their answers often contain more than has been asked of them, and to this extent may be said to show some potential for productive thinking.

All computers necessarily start out with a decoding device that enables them to obtain the information which they will subsequently have to make use of. They are also provided with a storage device or a memory that permits them to use the information as needed. In the computer this memory is often a magnetized spot on a drum which when ticked, triggers off a relay. In the brain it is a sensitized cell or group of cells which when stimulated triggers off another series of cells. The neurons in the brain do not, like the coded spots on the drum, contain pictures or any other type of permanent imprint. Thus, if asked what you had for breakfast, and you answered ham and eggs, it would not be necessary to posit that somewhere in the brain there were cells coded with specific engrams for these things. The ham and eggs were not engraved in your brain before you were asked the question any more than the sensation of pain existed in your arm before it was pinched, or a melody in the piano before somebody played it. Memory is primarily a capacity to respond. What is "remembered" is an order and sequence. This does not constitute the entire process of memory, but is all that is necessary for a designer of thinking machines to take into consideration.

The capacity to store information is, of course, basic to thinking because in order to make selective decisions, an organism must be able to recall past experience. But this is not enough. It must be able to combine past data into meaningful configurations. Moreover, in order not to be swamped, it must be able to do this without necessarily making use of all antecedent data, that is, without actually having to process all of its accumulated bits of information. This is a key concept in all theories of thinking. It means uniting elements and parts so as to form wholes, a procedure with which, of course, mathematicians are familiar, and use when they apply algebra or the calculus in solving certain types of problems.

Since a machine can be programmed to solve integral equations, it may also be said to possess the capacity to integrate. Like the calculus, however, it can only proceed by adding bits together. This is only one way of obtaining wholes and is effective in the solution of many problems, but is inappropriate in those types of problems in which sums do not necessarily add up to wholes; for example, those involving interlacing structures—a house, a face, a set of principles, and in the opinion of some psychologists, all complex mentation. This does not imply that mental processes do not involve some type of calculus, but merely that they require some other techniques which do not necessarily assume that the whole is equal to the sum of its parts. Psychologically the whole often equals much more and, nearly always, something different. Parts add up not only to a sum but also to patterns or configurations. It is a great achievement of Gestalt Psychology to have demonstrated this and to have formulated experimentally principles which account for the process. These are the so-called laws of *gute gestalten,* like the law of closure and the principle of *Praegnantz.*[2]

As to the possibility of thinking machines serving as models of how the brain works, it is very unlikely that they represent, except in some minor details, how the brain or at least the mind actually functions. I say this primarily because I am not convinced that the mind works as a stochastic system. Probability theory may be able to explain what decisions we might, or even should make, but not those we actually do make. If the brain operates in mathematical ways, they are certainly not predominantly algebraic. I would venture that its mathematics, such as it is, more nearly resembles those of geometry and topology, and these branches of mathematics have been called on, it seems to me, not nearly as much as they deserve in the designing of the thinking machines.

In evaluating machines as organized systems capable of thinking, it is important to remember that to be successful, they need not operate, let alone look, like the model they try to emulate, in this case of course, the human brain. Nor do they have to, in my opinion, illustrate or validate psychological theory. I do not wish to imply thereby that physicists and psychologists cannot profit from an interchange of ideas, but there is always the danger of misapplying borrowed constructs. For example, there is no need for physicists to be implicated in the psychologist's concept of purpose and adaptation anymore than for the psychologist to worry over the physical constructs of entropy and antimatter. A machine, like a man, should be judged by what it does. A machine can store and reproduce information implanted in it and therefore, may be said to show memory; a machine may present behavior modified by past events and therefore, said to evidence learning; a machine may be empowered to make selective responses and therefore said to be capable of making decisions; a machine can solve problems and therefore be said to think. The latest computers can do all these things, sometimes better, and generally faster than human beings.

Now what can't a machine do? It cannot make moral, aesthetic, and in general, value judgments. Above all, it cannot go beyond performance. When one says that thinking machines do not go beyond performance, one implies that they are incapable of understanding what they are doing, that is, are incapable of insight. They cannot show insight because they are essentially logical devices. They cannot go beyond what is already contained in their programmed instructions, because the logical process cannot add anything to what is not already contained in one's premise or hypothesis. Logic is essentially a method of

---

[2]The degree to which the organization of a field tends toward optimal clearness or simplicity.

proving and not of finding out things. This limitation of the logical process explains why we cannot expect machines to effect productive or creative ideas.

To sum up, one must concede first, that machines like digital and analogue computers can think; not necessarily in the same way as human beings, but in the areas that they do, as thoroughly and generally more efficiently. They are best at solving problems requiring computation. To do this they must be able to process information, remember and make decisions. On the other hand, one must acknowledge that they are incapable of making evaluative judgments or of creative productions in the broad sense of these terms. Their thinking is essentially reproductive, not productive. That they can only do what they are told is no serious indictment of their performance because, in this respect, they do not differ very much from what human beings do in school or in their day-to-day activities. It is probable that as time goes on the machines will progressively take over much of the "mental" work now done by human beings. This, in my opinion, is to be regretted not so much because it may throw people out of jobs (new ones can and undoubtedly will be created for them), but more important because it will condemn most human beings to kinds of work that have little human dignity.

ENGRAMS, MEMORY STORAGE, AND MNEMONIC CODING*

DAVID WECHSLER
New York University College of Medicine

Although the subject of memory has been investigated more than most topics in psychology, many of its basic problems remain discouragingly unsolved. Prominent among these are questions concerning how the human brain records, stores, and transmits information. These are broad topics, and I propose to discuss them here, not so much with the aim of presenting definitive answers, but rather in an attempt to reformulate some of them in the light of recent advances in physics and biochemistry.

The first, and in many ways the basic question, is what happens in the brain that enables one to "recall" past experiences in the absence of excitatory stimuli which originally provoked them. The historical answer has been that all such stimuli produce some enduring physical changes in one or another part of the brain which, in virtue of the effects produced, are subsequently capable of redintegration. These after effects have been at various times differently designated and in recent years generally referred to as engrams or memory traces. The term engram was introduced by Richard Semon a little after the turn of the century and defined by him (1921) as the "change left behind in the irritable substance of the brain after excitation has died down." Semon conceived of it as an enduring, if not permanent change, produced somewhere in the nuclear material of the brain cell. Here he came close to the contemporaneous point of view that it involves primarily a molecular change. Thus, in discussing the possible locus of the engram, he wrote, "most probably neither the cell nor the nucleus of the cell is able to possess it [the engram]." Again, without being acquainted with current genetic theory, he speaks of an elementary *protomere* or "a minimum segment of irritable substance capable of retaining possession of the inherited engram." As a biologist, Semon was more interested in what we now think of as genetic characters but believed, and I think correctly, that the same laws applied to the transmission of the acquired memories.

Semon's view as to how the engram is represented in the brain is less explicit. His statement on the matter is that "each mnemic excitation is related to the original one much as a reproduction of a picture relates to its original" (Semon, 1921). This is the historical point of view.† I do not think that Semon intended

---

*Reprinted from *American Psychologist*, 1963, 18, 149-153. Copyright 1963 by the American Psychological Association. Reprinted by permission.

†Thus, according to James Mill, "our ideas spring up or exist in the order in which the sensations existed, of which they are copies" (Boring, 1929, p. 213).

it to be taken literally, but it did serve to reinforce the widely held concept that a memory trace is a sort of facsimile of the stimulus or excitation which produced it, in much the same way as an image of an object is represented on the retina. The analogy in any case is misleading. There is no evidence that a memory trace, however constituted, is a kind of pictogram or any other analogically defined replica. All that is known is that it involves some structural change in some part or parts of the nervous system. The structural changes have at various times been posited as occurring at some points in the course of transmission of the neural impulse such as at the neural synapses, or as now more generally agreed in the nuclear elements of the involved receptor cells.

Not less easy to answer is whether the structural changes which are the bases for engram formation are spatially localized. The answer depends in a measure on what one understands by locus or localization. If by a locus we mean a particular area in the brain or a particular cell in any particular place, there is no such thing as engram localization. The findings regarding stimulus equivalence and equipotentiality of the brain areas would indicate that memory, unlike sensation, does not depend upon the excitation of particular cells at some points in the nervous system. As Lashley (1960b) has amply demonstrated "there is no specialization of memory areas outside of the primary sensory field."

On the other hand, if by localization one thinks primarily of a structural change that takes place in one rather than another part of the cell, e.g., the part containing deoxyribonucleic acid rather than other particles in the nucleus, then structural changes posited for engram formation necessarily imply some specifiable locus. It is precisely through investigation of molecular reorganizations which take place at such times that biochemists have, in recent years, discovered where and how genetic changes take place. The chemist's description of the way this information is laid down and transmitted strongly suggests the possibility of a similar mechanism in mnemic coding. It seems likely that engrams, like genetic codes, eventually involve rearrangement of atomic structures. This might be effected, as has been shown in the case of genes, through the formation of characteristic molecules (polymeres) from less complex molecules (monomeres) in the acids of the nucleus (Blum, 1961).

What is of special interest and suggestive to the psychologists is the chemical process by which these polymeres are formed and duplicated, particularly those involved in the construction of the so-called biologic templates. A biologic template is at once a code and a method of reduplication and, in virtue of this dual characteristic offers a basis for explaining, at least analogically, the process of engramatization. Even more significantly, it supplies a key as to how memory patterns are kept intact and revived. My view of the memory mechanism is that it consists essentially of a matching process. This is in contrast to the explanation of it in terms of reverberatory circuits by McCulloch (1951). The matching hypothesis may be described in purely psychological terms, but it is encouraging to discover that the chemist and physicist have furnished us with descriptions which show that many of the changes in molecular structure take place essentially in a similar manner. I believe that acquired engrams are laid down like genetic codes, are transmitted as genetic information and revived and assembled into memories by some matching method. The matching may be either chemical or electrical and at some levels of neural organization of the sort we identify with frequency radio tuning or electrical resonance. That the brain, or a certain part of it, shows continuous electrical activity is a well established fact. The question is whether a complex electrolyte like the brain lends itself to electrical resonance is something that would have to be demonstrated. While this has not yet been done, there is reason to believe that under certain conditions, it is not theoretically impossible (Wechsler, 1960).

Another of the unresolved problems in the description of the memory process is what happens to the engram or memory trace between the moment it is first imprinted and the moment it is revived. This is the problem of storage. The common view on the matter is that there are certain areas or reserved places of the brain in which memories, so to speak, are locked and at the same time kept available for future use. These spaces are often compared to filing cabinets or storage cellars. The designated comparisons are presumably presented to begin with merely as metaphors or analogies, but more often than not are preserved as literal explanations. Actually it is not important whether one regards the various parts of the brain as a series of intercommunicating compartments or an assortment of filing cabinets. The main source of confusion resides in the belief that memories as such are stored at all, in the usual sense of the term.

When I say that there are no stored memories, I do not wish to imply that the excitatory processes in the brain, which serve to evoke whatever it is that is later revived, effect or leave behind no changes, but only that these changes must not be equated with the ones that are involved in the production of the original percepts or ideas. The elements out of which these were constructed were laid down long before and in most instances genetically.

Thus, if we conceive of learning as a linking of sequential responses or facts, it is not the facts but the links between them which are altered by the learning process. Nothing was implanted which was not laid down before. What has been modified is the organism's capacity to respond. Memories, like perceptions, and eventually sensations, have no separate existences. The memory of what you saw yesterday has no more existence until revived than the pain you felt in your arm before it is pinched.

A view not unlike the one just put forward was suggested by Ewald Hering as long ago as 1870. Thus, in discussing the existence of unconscious memories, he asserted that: "They do not exist as ideas; what is preserved is the special disposition of the neural substance in virtue of which it gives out today the same sound as it gave out yesterday, if properly struck" (Boring, 1929). In short, for the experiencing individual, memories do not exist before they are revived or recalled. Memories are not like filed letters stored in cabinets or unhung pictures in the basement of a museum. Rather, they are like melodies realized by striking the keys on a piano. Ideas are no more stored in the brain than melodies in a piano or any other musical instrument. An almost identical view was expressed by Lashley (1960a) when he stated that "The anatomic structure of engrams is fixed like the keys of a piano; behavior patterns play over the structure as the fingers of a musician, producing the characteristic chords of G or F sharp minor throughout the range of the keyboard." I would only add that the brain probably consists of many different keyboards, intercommunicating to be sure, but not always in tune and, of course, not all with a Steinway quality. Some, I am afraid, remind us more of penny whistles or cigar-box ukes.

It is interesting to speculate on how the information possessed or acquired by the brain is ordered and transmitted. In view of the all-or-none, or nearly all-or-none type of responses which characterizes neuronal excitation, it has been generally posited that the feat is accomplished by a relatively simple stop-go, open-close switching device. The advantage of such a system is that it requires a minimum of circuitry and makes possible utilization of the switching system itself as a coding device. For this reason, among others, a stop-go switching system has generally served as a model in the construction of computers and devices for artificial intelligence. There is considerable neurophysiological evidence that some such step system may actually be employed in the transmission of nerve impulses, whether mediated by some form of neurobiotaxes or acetylcholine-esterase interactions. It is possible to conceptualize and implement a switching system which, if properly organized, could fulfill the entire memory functioning by itself, and indeed even explain logically the activity of the brain as a whole. This is what Warren McCulloch and his co-workers have suggested and tried to show in their description of the brain as a computing machine (McCulloch, 1951).

The main objection to the view that the brain functions as a computer is the fact that, so far as one can observe, it does not operate in this manner. In the first place, the brain's switching operations are much too slow to carry out a step-by-step process at speeds one would have to require of them. The rate of neutral transmission is at least 10^{-6} times slower than even a moderately fast electronic computer. If this is true, the brain could not solve any but the simplest problems within the order of time limits we know it does, if it were compelled to do so by any method of sequential counting. On the other hand, consider how fast the mind works in responding to a simple question, requiring straightforward recall, for example, of responding to a question like, "Who was the Secretary of War in Lincoln's second administration.'' I cannot say how long it would take a well-programed computer to furnish the correct response, but I am sure the computer would not produce the answer as quickly as a high school student with only a modest knowledge of American history. Of course, the reason why the student could come up with an answer more quickly is because he would not have had to ''calculate'' it; he would merely have had to ''remember'' it.

The second reason why I do not think that the memory processes are carried on by computer methods is that I do not believe that these processes, like many other activities of the brain, can be accounted for stochastically, that is, can be wholly predicted on the basis of probability theory. If they could, it would be necessary to assume a beforehand knowledge of the probabilities of most, if not all, of the sequences of events involved in any given process. I do not think that such knowledge can be posited in the case of memory because association between mental events depends not merely on antecedent concomitance and frequency, but also for purely idiosyncratic reasons. Consider, for example, a simple free association experiment where it is possible to anticipate, on the basis of previous data, what the frequency of any specified response to a given word might be. Thus, in a normal population one might expect the following frequency of responses to the word *sickness: health* approximately 35 times in a hundred, *death* 14 times in a hundred, *illness* 8 times in a hundred, *medicine* 2 times in a hundred, and so on. But unique or idiosyncratic responses could not be predicted. Thus, one could not anticipate a response like *Brooklements* given by a schizophrenic girl, which was encountered once and probably would never be met with again.

What has just been said about the responses of expectancy problems in simple situations like a word association test would, of course, apply with much greater force to more complex situations. Consider for example, an experience like the one which Amundsen recounts in his autobiography, that occurred during one of his trips to the North Pole. He had left his ice-locked ship one morning for a brief walk and had not gone very far when he saw a hungry looking bear not many yards ahead of him. Amundsen decided to turn back, but the bear, equally determined, began to follow him. Amundsen quickened his pace; the bear did likewise. Sensing the danger of what might happen, Amundsen started running toward the ship. As he reached the gangplank he tripped and fell. Various thoughts passed through his mind but none which, in view of his predicament, anyone would have thought likely. He was not at all frightened nor in anyway concerned with immediate danger. Instead, he saw himself sitting on a curb corner of Piccadilly Circus in London, counting the ladies' hairpins scattered about him.

Although I believe that the mnemic process is essentially nonstochastic, I do not thereby wish to imply that these processes are entirely nonpredictable, much less to conclude that learning and recall do not conform to certain general principles. Above all, we must distinguish between the conditions which favor or inhibit memory from the processes which account for it. Here, we must rely upon knowledge gained from the basic sciences rather than be tempted by the practical models offered by the engineer. Such models, effective as they may be, do not necessarily correspond to what goes on in the brain; nor do they need to, in order to achieve their ends. Thus, the intriguing systems now employed in computers, however effective in equipping them with memory storage, do not represent, in my opinion, what actually goes on in the brain. There is little evidence to show that the brain uses the same or even similar devices to fix and recall the information that it receives. It does not rely on tape inputs, acoustic relays, or magnetic cores. Information is received and transmitted more directly, and while no definitive mechanisms have been established, it seems clear that coding and transmission of information in the brain more nearly resembles genetic replication and resonance phenomena than the devices currently employed in automata.

References

Blum, H. F. On the origin and evolution of human machines. *Amer. Scientist,* 1961, 49, 474-508.

Boring, E. G. *A history of experimental psychology.* New York: Century, 1929.

Jeffress, L. A. (Ed.) *Cerebral mechanisms in behavior; the Hickson Symposium.* New York: Wiley, 1951.

Lashley, K. S. Cerebral organization of behavior. In F. A. Beach, D. O. Hebb, C. T. Morgan, & H. W. Nissen (Eds.), *The neuropsychology of Lashley.* New York: McGraw-Hill, 1960. (a)

Lashley, K. S. In search of the engram. In F. A. Beach, D. O. Hebb, C. T. Morgan, & H. W. Nissen (Eds.), *The neuropsychology of Lashley.* New York: McGraw-Hill, 1960. (b)

McCulloch, W. S. Why the mind is in the head. In L. A. Jeffress (Ed.), *Cerebral mechanisms in behavior; the Hickson Symposium.* New York: Wiley, 1951.

Semon, R. *The mneme.* New York: Allen & Unwin, 1921.

Wechsler, D. Intelligence, quantum resonance and thinking machines. *Trans. N. Y. Acad. Sci.,* 1960, 27, 259-266.

PART V

INTRODUCTION

Wechsler's contributions to the role of diagnosis are widely recognized in psychological literature. The publication and use of the Bellevue Scale in 1939 was the impetus for this view. This section contains selections related to the general matter of diagnosis.

The second edition of *The Measurement of Adult Intelligence,* published in 1941, contained a chapter detailing possible diagnostic and clinical features for the Bellevue investigated or hypothesized to that time (1). Wechsler points out that the central feature of an intelligence test is to give some valid and reliable measure of global intellectual capacity, or at least some estimate of it. Beyond this job, however, it is possible for a well-designed test to yield information of more detailed use. He specifically refers to such things as the examinee's motor reaction, any special abilities or disabilities which may be disclosed by performance on subtests, even the possibility of inferences about the personality of the examinee. But he also makes the point that such deductions are basically dependent upon the examiner's clinical experience and wisdom. The design of the Bellevue Scale allowed more direct judgments about such matters, and to this purpose the content of the chapter here quoted is directed.

Given the essential purpose of an estimate of global ability, the next type of data immediately available to the clinician is yielded by performance on the two scales: Verbal and Performance. Wechsler does point out, however, the fact that a considerable amount of variation between scales may be expected as a function of normal variability as well as test error. Particularly will such differences be found among those individuals whose general ability is at either extreme. Furthermore, as he notes, certain differences may be built in as a result of group and cultural backgrounds and experiences, and these will need to be interpreted appropriately in analyzing any differences found between Verbal and Performance Scale scores.

A second useful feature of the scale lies in comparisons that may be made for the different abilities tested by the Bellevue at all levels of functioning. Test patterns may be used, at least for comparisons within age groups, to determine on what abilities a given individual varies from his overall performance. This involves the procedure of determining diagnostic signs, a procedure described explicitly by him in this source and applied to test characteristics of clinical groupings. Though the fourth edition of *The Measurement and Appraisal of*

Adult Intelligence published in 1958 contains much elaboration and clarification of the procedures and applications, the essential elements are present here.

After a more detailed description of clinical groups and performance on subtests in the Bellevue Scale, Wechsler returns to some of the problems of diagnosis. The sign procedure advocated by him must be interpreted with the same care as is done with physical systems in medicine. As he says, ". . . a listing of mere symptoms met with in different diseases would show relatively little correlation between any one sign and any one specific disease entity, for the reason that the same symptoms are met with in many different diseases. . . ." One may show a temperature of 101 and this may be characteristic of several possible diseases. The high temperature alone, as Wechsler so aptly points out, cannot be used to diagnose any particular disease. Other physical signs will help the physician designate much more directly which of the possible diseases is the more likely one as a diagnosis. This is the very procedure which Wechsler advocates in the use of diagnostic signs in applying the Bellevue Scale, and later in the WAIS. It is possible, then, to have a description of clinical groups and their usual performance in diagnostic sign terms on the subtests. The greater the congruence between the performance of a given individual and that pattern, the more likely the apt application of the label. As one digresses from the same performance as the diagnostic group, then the application of the term or label becomes less certain. There remains of course, how much of a departure from the catalogue description is acceptable. The experience and wisdom of the clinician enter this decision to a large degree.

There is the problem of a differential or critical score as well, particularly as this would determine appropriate diagnosis. He gives no such critical scores, intentionally. He also gives his reasons for not doing so. It is worthy to note his principle reason: ". . . The writer would have been extremely loath to present such critical scores for fear of conveying the impression that all that is necessary to make a diagnosis is an ability to look up a table of interpreted scores. . . ." He points out that many tests of personality attempt to do such a job, with varying degrees of success and error. Unfortunately, there are instances in the literature where other individuals have done exactly the same thing with the Wechsler Scales. This, it should be noted, is neither advocated by nor faithful to the work of David Wechsler.

Wechsler includes case studies and a reference to certain qualitative indicators which may assist the clinician in making a tentative judgment. Overall, the care and concern for appropriate procedures in making judgments about individuals is clearly evident in this selection. The intervening years, with their clinical experience, have done nothing to reduce that concern. Indeed, one might say that it is more explicit with the continued work in developing and applying the Scales to patients.

The matter of ageing has appeared earlier in this volume, and particularly in terms of normal changes with age. One such change, though one may quarrel with whether it is normal in nature, is in terms of mental deterioration. From the 1944 edition of *The Measurement of Adult Intelligence,* Wechsler has included the chapter on the problem of mental deterioration (2). The first concern is to define the term mental deterioration, and this Wechsler does both in the general and specific sense. He points out the fact that mental deterioration may have two different meanings in the diagnostic sense. The first of these is what might be considered a "natural" deterioration that occurs for all of us once we have reached maturity and lived beyond that point. The second type concerns a deterioration which is a concommitant of extraordinary sources, and these are of greatest concern to psychologists and neurologists. From the psychological point of view, Wechsler believes that the difference between the two is academic except for the rate at which the deterioration occurs.

To indicate the normal rate of deterioration, information from *The Range of Human Capacities* (referred to in Part III of this volume) is cited. Intellectual abilities seem to show greater impairment with time or age than do physical abilities, despite the common belief in the reverse. To Wechsler, mental ability certainly does decline with age and, furthermore, is a part of a general organic process affecting all of us. Indeed, he takes the position that the phenomenon itself begins fairly early in life, showing the same linear function that is true of other abilities.

The question remaining, then, is how to measure mental deterioration. The most precise method would use some reliable present measurement of functioning and compare it with equally reliable measurements of previous functioning. Quantitative differences, if any, could be determined and would be an expression of the degree of deterioration occurring over the time interval between the measures. The arguments which Wechsler presents for this procedure are acceptable despite limitations in the measures which may be used to judge them. Frequently, of course, there is no initial measure available on such a test as the Bellevue or the WAIS for a comparison with present performance. As a result, the most common procedure is to assume, in the absence of other evidence, that the individual conformed rather closely to the average for his age group at the earlier level. Since this presents some problems, other data will be used as a means of making the judgment more realistically. Wechsler advocates a close appraisal of the individual's educational, vocational, and social history. How he has functioned in the past in coping with society will be a useful indicator of whether or not he has shown deterioration at the present time.

Wechsler notes that psychometric tests of the type which he devised with the Bellevue, and more recently with the WAIS, offer the opportunity for disclosing small differences in ability from one measured trait to another or in the measurement of a given trait from one time to another. The more accurately they do this job, the more usable are the differences in diagnostic settings.

Particularly, if measures with the same test have been taken over time, such comparisons become more meaningful and usable. However, even in the absence of such information, it is possible to make certain types of comparisons by looking at the age curves of groups of individuals over time. He has done this and notes the fact that performance on certain subtests seemed to remain more stable over time than performance on other subtests. General Information, for example, rarely shows a decline in performance over time with the majority of society. However, Digit Symbol performance will certainly show decline with age, only partly because of physical changes.

As a result, Wechsler was able to designate certain tests which he called ''hold'' tests because of their relative performance stability, and other tests which he called ''don't hold'' because they were expected to show a decline over time. He carefully selected subtests which would show functional similarity between the contrasted measures. Given these, he proposed the use of a differential test score method to make judgments about mental deterioration of the individual. As stated earlier, the arguments and procedures may be valid despite inadequacies in the test to do a sufficiently reliable job. Certainly, since the proposal in 1944, the use of a mental deterioration index from the Wechsler Scales has not fared well under research. That in no way reduces the significance of the theoretical position; indeed, it requires that tests better suited and designed for the purpose be devised and applied.

Wechsler's discussion of the nature of deterioration as a process in ageing individuals is of considerable interest and importance. Its generalized nature, in most instances, reflects the fact that the brain does act as a unit and where there is impairment the effects may be quite generalized. Indeed, the fact that disorganization may be expressed along one line more strongly than another is of only secondary importance. This leads to the conclusion that it is relatively unimportant what test might be used in detecting deterioration so long as the tests themselves are sensitive to intellectual functioning. Therefore, it is not surprising that the best types of measure involve speed of response, learning, and perception of new configurations. Such tests, whatever their content specifically, require a type of functioning on the part of the individual which will not be plausible if deterioration is present.

The remaining three selections deal with aspects of the general diagnostic procedure relative to specific measures. The first of these, for example, was published in 1926 and concerned itself with the influence education had on measured intelligence reflected in the Binet–Simon Test (3). The intent of the paper is to indicate an increase in variation in mental age scores with increasing chronological age. Wechsler assumed that such increases would reflect the influence of education on intelligence as measured by the scale. His data are derived both from that of Louis M. Terman in this country and Cyril Burt in England.

He accepts Burt's data as more definitive and as a result draws his major conclusions about the influence of education from the English sample.

It is interesting to note his conclusion that the major influences of education on intelligence test performance occur after age 10 or 11. Wechsler believes this is the point at which there is less emphasis on sensory input and elementary concept development, and greater dependence on abstract cognitive experience.

The publication of the WISC in 1949 offered a viable alternative to the use of the Stanford–Binet Revision. However, many clinicians and educators had become accustomed to the reporting of a mental age as the score on the test. The WISC made no such provisions, since Wechsler believes that the mental age concept as an absolute measure of level of intelligence is invalid. The expressed need for a mental age led him to derive test ages which might be compared in certain ways to an M.A. though they are not quite the same score expression. The source published including these equivalent tests in mental ages is included (4) and reports procedures followed in the calculation of the ages as well as the equivalent test ages. The table containing age equivalents for WISC raw scores is now published in the WISC Manual as well.

A final selection (5) is included here because of its discussion of the role of the psychologist in the clinical setting. Primarily emphasized is the role of the psychologist in diagnosis and care of individuals who may be temporarily or permanently committed to psychiatric institutions. Wechsler points out the traditional role of the psychologist in this setting, that of appraisal of intellectual functioning. This assumes more than the global report, and particularly where information from subtests relative to possible clinical diagnosis may be made as with the Bellevue and WAIS. Other kinds of instruments also must be used and evaluated by the psychologist in this setting. Beyond this, other roles may be played by the psychologist and these are delineated by Wechsler.

There is also a discussion of the possibilities for research in mental hospitals. Unfortunately, there is less time for this role than for most others since there is the immediate problem-oriented atmosphere that must exist. Nevertheless, Wechsler takes the position that research should be expanded and encouraged if progress is to be made. Most research in such settings has not been done by psychologists but by psychiatrists and neurologists, due to the fact that the psychologist is rarely trained in experimental procedure which he may apply appropriately in such settings.

Perhaps the major feature of the article is the comment by Wechsler on training of the psychologist. Though certainly there will be differences in the training offered from one area to another, and though the roles played by the psychologist will differ from institution to institution, there are some "givens" which should be present in every instance. Wechsler describes the type of curriculum which might be taken by those clinicians who plan to enter the profession, with particular emphasis on practicum experiences which offer direct contact. He also describes personality characteristics which the clinician must bring with him to the mental hospital setting. Overall, the picture reflects the best combination of traits desirable, even necessary, for the clinician concerned with the welfare of patients. Perhaps the description may be compared to the professional life of David Wechsler.

DIAGNOSTIC AND CLINICAL FEATURES OF THE
WECHSLER-BELLEVUE SCALES*

DAVID WECHSLER

Although the primary purpose of an intelligence examination is to give a valid and reliable measure of the subject's global intellectual capacity, it is reasonable to expect that any well conceived intelligence scale will furnish its user with something more than an I.Q. or M.A. In point of fact, most intelligence examinations, when administered individually, make available a certain amount of data regarding the testee's mode of reaction, his special abilities or disabilities and, not infrequently, some indications of his personality traits. At present, the amount of this sort of adjuvant data which may be derived from an intelligence examination is in a large measure dependent upon the individual examiner's clinical experience and sagacity. No doubt this will always remain true to a greater or lesser degree. But much also depends upon the intrinsic merits and diagnostic possibilities of the tests themselves. The following remarks are accordingly directed to a discussion of those features of the Bellevue Scale which either preliminary analysis or subsequent experience have shown to be of clinical and diagnostic value.

The most obviously useful feature of the Wechsler-Bellevue Scales is their division into a Verbal and Performance part. We have already discussed the general significance of this division. Its à priori value is that it makes possible a comparison between a subject's facility in using words and symbols and his ability to manipulate objects, and to perceive visual patterns. In practice this division is substantiated by differences between posited abilities and various occupational aptitudes. Clerical workers and teachers, in general, do much better on verbal tests, whereas manual workers and mechanics do better on performance. The correlations are sufficiently high to be of value in vocational guidance, particularly with adolescents of high school age.

Apart from their possible relation to vocational aptitudes, differences between verbal and performance test scores, particularly when large, have a special interest for the clinician because such discrepencies are frequently associated with certain types of mental pathology. Whenever a mental disorder produces a change in the individual's functioning capacity, the resultant loss is generally not uniform, but affects certain abilities more than others. This fact is frequently made use of in a

*Reprinted from David Wechsler, *The Measurement of Adult Intelligence*, 2d ed., Baltimore, 1941, pp. 145-162. Copyright 1941, The Williams & Wilkins Co. Reproduced by permission.

crude way in psychiatry and neurology where specific disturbances or defects are considered pathognomic symptoms of various disease entities. Familiar examples are the disturbances of association (flightiness of ideas) in manic depressive insanity and the memory defects in chronic alcoholism of the Korsakoff type. In so far as the diagnostic significance of large differences between verbal and performance ability as a whole is concerned, the general finding is that in most mental disorders impairment of functioning is greater in the performance than in the verbal sphere. This holds for psychoses of every type, organic brain disease, and to a lesser though still large degree, in most psychoneuroses. On the other side of the fence there are only two groups. One is the adolescent psychopath (without psychosis) and the other the high grade mental defective. Both of these do better on performance than on the verbal tests. It is interesting to note that both psychopaths and mental defectives differ from other psychopathic states in that they represent failure of functioning due to a 'lack of—' rather than a disturbance or disorganization of functioning ability.[1]

In appraising differences between verbal and performance test scores one must naturally allow for variability even among normal individuals. For subjects with I.Q.'s not far from the average, a variation of 8 to 10 points between verbal and performance in either direction is within the normal range. But the amount as well as the direction of the differences also varies with the age and intelligence level of the individual. Subjects of superior intelligence generally do better on the verbal, and subjects of inferior intelligence do better on the performance part of the examination. There are also racial (group) and cultural differences. We have made no systematic study of this aspect of the problem but experience shows that the psychometric patterns of colored subjects for example, need special interpretation. Our general observations also confirm the findings of older studies which show that Jewish children do better on verbal and Italian children on performance tests. Among adults, the nature of the subject's occupation is frequently an important factor, so that carpenters, as might be expected, will generally score higher on performance and lawyers, on verbal tests. All this means, of course, that a significant difference between a subject's verbal and performance score cannot be interpreted *carte blanche* but only after due

---

[1] Appreciation of this 'lack' helps us to understand why psychiatrists of the older generation used to refer to certain classes of psychopaths as "moral imbeciles". This appraisal of the psychopath agrees with Kahn's definition of psychopathic personalities as individuals characterized by quantitative divergences in impulse, temperament . . . etc.

weight has been given to the various factors which may have contributed to it. With these limitations in mind, the data given in table 30 may be accepted as clinically valid.

The second clinically useful feature of the Bellevue scale, is that the different mental abilities tested by it, may be compared at all levels of functioning. This is achieved through the fact that the same type of material is used throughout the scale, and because the individual subtests of the scale have been equated. This makes it possible to compare a subject's individual test scores and to look for significant test patterns. For any pattern analysis it is necessary to know the subtest score for any given total score, and the variations in these scores which occur with age. Since each of the subtests have been equated, the mean expected score on any given subtest for any given total score may be obtained with good approximation by dividing the total score by 10.

TABLE 30
Clinical Groups Scoring Higher on Verbal Tests
Organic brain disease
Psychoses
Psychoneuroses
Clinical Groups Scoring Higher on Performance Tests
Psychopaths (adolescent)
Mental defectives

Thus, if a subject makes a total score of 95, the mean expectancy for any given subtest is 9.5; or, since the performance and verbal scores do not contribute identically equal amounts to the total score, a somewhat better approximation is obtained by dividing the sum of the verbal tests and the sum of the performance tests by 5 respectively. Thus, for a subject making a total score[2] of 95 with verbal and performance scores of 50 and 45 respectively, the mean expected scores for verbal tests would be 10 and for performance tests 9 points each. For the variations in subtest scores with age, separate data are, of course, necessary, and these data have been furnished in Tables 40 and 41, page 214.

The problem next arises as to what constitutes a significantly varying score. This necessarily has to be established both through clinical and statistical validation, and here again, not only for any given score but for all possible combinations of scores. While the data is available for such complex analysis, the multiple tables necessary for it have not

[2] These are, of course, the weighted scores.

been made, but again may be had with sufficient approximations, by the following rule of thumb: For total scores on the full Scale lying within the limits 80 to 110,[3] a difference of more than two points from the mean subtest score is significant.   Thus, a subject making a total score of 95 with the following distribution of subtests:

Comprehension	11
Arithmetic	9
Information	10
Digit-span	7
Similarities	13
Picture Arrangement	9
Picture Completion	6
Blocks	11
Object Assembly	10
Digit symbol	9

would manifest significant variations or differences in the Similarities, Picture Completion and Digit-span tests.

For subjects having total scores beyond the limits 80–110, the deviation of the individual's subtests from their mean, defining a significant difference may be roughly obtained by dividing the mean subtest score by 4.   Example: Subject A makes a full score of 56.   The mean subtest score is accordingly 5.6 points; one fourth of this is 1.4 points. Hence, any of his individual subtest scores which deviate by more than 1.5 points from this mean would be significant.   Again, Subject B obtains a full score of 132; mean subtest score is 13.2.   Hence, for subject B any individual subscores would have to deviate by 3 points (actually 3.3 points) from the mean of the subtests in order to be significant.

The amount by which a given subtest must differ from the mean of the various subtests in order to be significant, is roughly proportional to the magnitude of his total score.[4]   In certain instances where the discrepancy between performance and verbal is very large, it is desirable

[3] This represents a deviation of approximately ±1 S.D. from the mean of 95 at ages 20 to 35.

[4] This may be assumed if the correlation between variability and ability is small.   Such seemingly is the case at least between the ages 20 and 40.   Though the *r*'s between them have not been calculated, a low correlation between ability (total score) and variability $\left(\dfrac{\sigma}{M}\right)$ would be in accord with the findings of most other investigators.   Cf. *Bown, M.D.*, Variability as a Function of Ability, etc. Doctor's Thesis, Columbia Univ., 1941.

and often necessary to treat each part of the examination separately. This is particularly true in certain organic cases which show large dis crepancies between verbal and performance as a whole but relatively

TABLE 31

Test characteristics of various clinical groups

A. Organic Brain Disease
  1. Verbal higher than Performance
  2. Information: relatively good
  3. Comprehension: relatively good
  4. Arithmetic: poor
  5. Similarities: poor
  6. Memory Span: very poor, particularly digits backwards
  7. Block Design: very poor
  8. Object Assembly: poor
  9. Digit Symbol: very poor
  10. Small variability when verbal and performance test scores are considered separately

B. Schizophrenia
  1. Verbal higher than Performance
  2. Information: good
  3. Vocabulary: high
  4. Comprehension: generally good but occasionally poor
  5. Arithmetic: poor
  6. Memory Span: unpredictable; usually high on digits forward, often poor on digits backwards and generally poor when taken together
  7. Similarities: low (paranoid)
  8. Picture Arrangement: low in certain types of paranoids
  9. Picture Completion: low in hebephrenics and relatively high in simple schizophrenics
  10. Digit Symbol: low
  11. Block Design: better than Object Assembly
  12. Large interest discrepancies

C. Psychopathic Personality (adolescents)
  1. Performance higher than Verbal
  2. Object Assembly: high
  3. Information: high
  4. Comprehension: unpredictable
  5. Arithmetic: poor
  6. Similarities: poor
  7. Picture Arrangement: relatively good
  8. Picture Completion: frequently poor
  9. Sum of Block Design and Picture Completion test scores nearly always less than sum of Object Assembly and Picture Arrangement test scores
  10. Intertest variability: moderate

TABLE 31—*Concluded*

D. Neurotics
  1. Verbal higher than Performance
  2. Vocabulary: high
  3. Information: good
  4. Arithmetic: unpredictable but generally poor
  5. Digit Span: generally poor, frequently showing no difference between number of digits repeated correctly forwards and number repeated correctly backwards; sometimes better on digits backwards than on digits forwards
  6. Similarities: relatively good
  7. Object Assembly: low
  8. Digit Symbol: generally low but with some exceptions
  9. Interest variability: unpredictable but generally less than schizophrenics

E. Mental defectives
  1. Performance higher than Verbal
  2. Digit Span: relatively good
  3. Similarities: very poor
  4. Object Assembly: relatively good
  5. Block Design: low
  6. Interest variability: limited

little variation between the subtests constituting the two parts. Case *O-1* given below is an example.

Having determined how much of a test score difference constitutes a significant deviation, the general clinical problem of test patterning consists of establishing associations between particular test score divergences, and specific clinical entities. This may be done in several ways, but the method which the author has found most adaptable for clinical use is that of "counting" or integrating signs. A "sign" or symptom is a low test score which has been found to be characteristic of, or associated with, a particular type of mental disorder or disfunction. Thus, if a low Performance and a particularly low Block Design test score has been found characteristic of organic brain disease cases, then a subject who does badly on both these items will be assumed to show two "signs" of possible organic involvement. This, of course, does not mean that it is necessarily an organic case, because there are other conditions which also show these "signs". But the first step always consists of noting the number of instances of relatively low or contrastingly high scores in the subject's test score distribution.

The above procedure, of course, implies a prior demonstration of the existence of established associations or correlations between particular test "signs" and disease entities. The extensive statistical work which is required for such correlations has not yet been done, but the author has accumulated sufficient clinical experience with the Bellevue Scale to warrant a presentation of certain empirical findings which he believes will be of use to the clinician in his attempts at diagnosis. These have been put together in Table 31 which attempts to summarize the test patterning met with in various common mental disease entities. By test patterning here, is merely meant a summary of the various tests on which patients suffering from various mental disorders have been found to do particularly poorly or have shown significantly contrasting score differences.

COMMENTS

1. *Organic brain diseases.* The category organic brain diseases covers a large group of syndromes ranging all the way from brain tumors to chronic alcoholism. The cases cited are not intended as examples of differential diagnoses between any specific disease entities but rather as illustrations of the disorganization of the intellectual processes observed in most organic brain cases irrespective of type. The most general symptoms of organic brain cases are disturbances in the visual motor spheres, a loss of shift, various memory defects and a falling off of capacities involving organization and synthetic ability.

Organic brain cases, with few exceptions, do consistently better on verbal than on performance tests. Most diagnostic is their inability to do the Block Design test, which is systematically associated with disturbances in visual motor organization. Next in order of frequency to a low score on the Block Design are low scores on the Digit Symbol, and depending on the type of organic involvement, the Object Assembly test. Memory defect is reflected in low memory span score, particularly on digits backwards. Certain cases also do badly on the Similarities test and this may reflect either a loss in conceptual thinking or, more frequently, an increasing rigidity in thought processes. All new learning is markedly affected. This accounts mainly for the organics low score on the Digit Symbol test, although visual motor disturbances also play a rôle in it.

Some groups of cases, like the paretics and arteriosclerotics, often show a generalized deterioration, that is do badly on nearly all tests. In general, they do better on verbal than on performance, but show no great variability as regards the tests which constitute each part of the Scale. This fact is often of value in differential diagnosis, for example, as between traumatic brain injury where the defects are uneven, and general paresis where the intellectual processes are more or less equally impaired.

2. *Schizophrenia.* Schizophrenia or dementia-praecox comprises a related group of affections rather than a single disease entity. Although the classical division of dementia-praecox into the four types, catatonic, paranoid, hebaphrenic and simple, is more theoretical than factual, it does suggest what experience demonstrates, that schizophrenics may vary widely among themselves both as to symptomatology and general picture. Moreover, the general diagnosis of schizophrenia itself is often contingent upon the orientation of the psychiatrist or the school to which he may belong. A case which in one hospital is diagnosed as schizophrenia may, very well at another, be labelled manic depressive, and vice-versa. In view of this situation it is obvious that no single list of signs can be either sufficiently comprehensive or free from exceptions if not contradictions.

Intellectually the most general effect of the schizophrenic process is the impairment of the subject's mental efficiency. This loss is evidenced by the low scores which he makes on most tests calling for immediate and directed effort. Occupationally, this is shown by the fact that the schizophrenic's vocational adjustment is often considerably inferior to what might be expected of a person with his original endowment. Supplementing the impairment in mental efficiency, the schizophrenic is further characterized by a marked slowing up of his thinking, a loss in mental shift and a tendency toward perseveration. As often noted, he does much better on verbal tests. This relative superiority of the schizophrenic is of special interest because ordinarily one does not think of him as a verbalist. Clinically he is continually being referred to as a shut-in, uncommunicative person. The inconsistency, however, between the two findings is explained when it is discovered that the verbal tests on which the schizophrenic does well are precisely those which do not require much verbalization. When they do make this demand, as in the case of the similarities test, he is likely to fail. This failure is not due to a lack of either understanding or linguistic facility, but to a distortion in the patient's ideational processes. The schizophrenic misinterprets words just as he misinterprests reality, and his incongruent replies, like his bizarre ideas, are a product of this misinterpretation.

Another characteristic of the schizophrenic is his inability to deal with concrete and specific situations. He is oblivious to details and does not perceive ordinary likenesses and differences, difficulties which are often reflected by the poor scores he attains on either the Similarities or Picture Completion tests or both. Last but not least is the schizophrenic's unpredictability, so that now and again one finds patients who do well on one or several of the tests, failure on which we have listed as characteristic of schizophrenics. A thorough acquaintance with a particular case generally makes it possible to account for the contradictory findings, but the occurrence of such exceptions shows that the diagnosis of schizophrenic through psychometric "signs" or "patterns" is not a cut and dried affair. The cases we have used as illustrations are typical only in the sense that they are of individuals who manifest most or many of the signs characteristic of the schizophrenic group as a whole.

3. *Psychopaths*. The most outstanding single feature of the adolescent psychopath's test pattern is his systematic high performance score as compared with his verbal test score. Occasional exceptions occur but these generally reflect some special ability or disability. Also worthy of note is the good score frequently made by the psychopath on the Picture Arrangement test, a finding that is surprising because this test has been interpreted as measuring social intelligence. If this interpretation is correct, a distinction must be made between understanding and resultant behaviour. Psychopaths generally have a grasp of social situations, but they are inclined to manipulate them to their own advantage in an anti-social way. The point cannot however be pushed too far because there are many exceptions to the rule, particularly in the case of extreme psychopaths who are not only perverse in their behaviour, but distorted in their social comprehension. The psychopath's test performance as a whole is characterized by a breeziness and self-assurance which contrasts markedly to that of a neurotic. He is not bothered by contradictions and, when not ornery, takes everything in his stride. His abstract thinking is generally below average and this is frequently indicated by a low score on the Similarities test. His subversive and egocentric tendencies are often shown by the quality and content of his responses. The replies of the extreme psychopath to the Comprehension questions are occasionally bizarre and resemble those obtained from schizophrenics. An interesting finding by Joseph Levi, who is working on the problem of psychopathic pattern, is that psychopaths make systematically higher scores on silent reading than on arithmetic tests. The explanation for this finding is not yet clear, but the observation is so consistent as to make the concurrence a valuable additional sign for adolescent psychopaths.

4. *Neurotics*. The neurotic generally does poorly on tests which re-

quire immediate effort.   He is inclined to look upon each task as a challenge and is apprehensive of the impression he may make on the examiner.   The result is that he is often "blocked", over critical and erratic.   These characteristics may be evidenced on any test but are best revealed by the neurotic's performance on the Object Assembly and the Digit Span.   Though the neurotic seldom puts the Object Assembly together in an absurd fashion his effort is characterized by a great deal of trial and error.   The absence of absurd configurations is what often distinguishes neurotics from organic cases who also make low scores on this test.   The neurotic's successes and failures on the Digit-Span test are unpredictable.   He often fails on an easier digit series and passes on a harder one; frequently too, he repeats as many and sometimes more digits backwards than he does forwards.

Although the neurotic's performance is generally lower than his verbal score, exceptions are not uncommon, particularly in hysterics and obsessives.   Many of the latter are preoccupied with numbers and often do surprisingly well on both the memory span and on the arithmetic tests.   Neurotics engaged in clerical work may also get relatively high scores on the Digit Symbol.   The low score of the neurotic on the Picture Arrangement test is frequently associated with lack of social alertness and reflects their common inability to deal with social situations.

Neurotic anxiety often manifests itself in the subject's hesitation, unexpected failures and balking at various test items.   Patients with anxiety neuroses and neurotic depression require, as might be expected, continued reassurance.   Neurotic patients generally overestimate their own intellectual ability.   Test variability in neurotics is greater than that of normal subjects but less than that of psychotics.

5. *Mental defectives.*   Mental defectives do not ordinarily present any special diagnostic problem except where the social rather than the intellectual prognosis is the paramount issue, and in a small number of cases which have to be differentiated from simple schizophrenics.   In differentiating between simple schizophrenia and mental deficiency, the most critical tests appear to be Similarities and Block Designs. Schizophrenics may on occasion get high scores on either or both of these tests, but the mental defective, almost never.   These two tests also differentiate between borderline and the definite mental deficiency.[5] In a recent study comparing these two groups we did not find a single

[5] A Study of the Sub-tests of the Bellevue Intelligence Scale in Borderline and Mental Defective Cases by D. Wechsler, H. Israel and B. Balinsky.   American Journal of Mental Deficiency, 1941, XLV, 555–558.

mental defective who attained a score equal to the lower limits of normality. This is in contrast with what happens in the case of the Digits-Span and the Object Assembly tests on which defectives will not infrequently obtain non-defective and even average scores.

The data given in table 31 will be valuable to its user in proportion to his familiarity with the scale as a whole and his clinical acquaintance with the disease entities. They are not intended, nor can they be used as psychometric short cuts to psychiatric diagnosis. But they can be of considerable differential aid if the examiner is aware of the statistical and nosological problems which all such tables present. Thus, a careful examination of the table will show that the same tests are recurrently failed by different clinical groups. For example, all groups except the psychopaths and mental defectives do less well on performance than on verbal tests. Again, Digit Symbol as a "do-bad-on" test is common to the neuroses, organics and many psychoses; and nearly all subjects with mental disorders do relatively well on Vocabulary and Information. Accordingly, it is not merely the incidence of a given "sign" but the character of the other "signs" associated with it in combination, that determine its diagnostic significance. In general, the problem of diagnosis by test score differentiae resembles medical diagnosis through physical signs. A listing of mere symptoms met with in different diseases would show relatively little correlation between any one sign and any one specific disease entity, for the reason that the same symptoms are met with in many different diseases. An elevated temperature is characteristic of pneumonia, erysipelas, abscess of the arm, etc. None, therefore, would make a diagnosis of pneumonia on high temperature alone. However, if the high temperature were accompanied by consolidation of the lungs, it would quite obviously indicate an active pneumonia; if it were accompanied by a "butterfly" rash with raised edges, erysipelas, and so on.

In addition to assuming a correlation between "sign" and disease entity, the diagnostic technique just illustrated also assumes some differential or critical score method of evaluation.[6] But as the reader

[6] The method of counting and subsequently interpreting "signs" suggested above is, of course, only one of several possible ways of evaluating the sort of data we have been dealing with. Instead of treating the individual test scores separately, an obvious next step would be to try combinations of certain selected tests, as for example, the sum of the Object Assembly and Picture Arrangement versus the sum of the Block Design and Picture Completion test, etc. Or, instead of dealing with sums, one might use ratios between the scores of certain tests or combination of tests, as I. Rabin has done, (Test Score Patterns in Schizophrenia and

defective, although presence of the added "signs" would indicate that we were dealing at the same time with an unstable and not easily adjustable defective.

On the other hand, it is sometimes extremely useful to distinguish between what might be termed "soft" and "hard signs". "Soft signs" are differences in test scores which deviate only slightly from the normal or expected mean, but which are nevertheless similar in direction to those met with in given disease entities. "Hard signs" are test score differences which show marked divergence from the normal or expected mean score. "Soft signs" are ordinarily passed over because they are within the normal range of variation. But their systematic presence is very important because they sometimes enable one to make a diagnosis before definite or full blown physical symptoms are in evidence. A striking case of this kind was that of a 19 year old boy who was admitted to the hospital after an attack of dizziness and transient loss of memory. He had experienced several similar attacks before, which the mother described as of short duration. She said, "IIe (the patient) did not seem to remember and couldn't get himself together". The only event which the patient himself associated with his last attack was that on the night before he had "drunk two coca-colas". A neurological examination on admission was essentially negative. He improved very quickly and was discharged after a short period of observation with a tentative diagnosis, largely based on the patient's attitude toward his illness, of conversion hysteria. During this first stay, a psychometric examination (Bellevue Adult) revealed a number of "soft signs" which led the psychologist to suggest the possibility of organic involvement. As there was no medical substantiation at the time of an organic brain disease, no special regard was paid the psychologist's observation. Three month's later the patient was readmitted to hospital with a fullblown brain tumor.

We shall now present a series of cases to illustrate the diagnostic possibilities of the method above described, making uses, so far as possible, of the tabular data given on pages 149–150.

ILLUSTRATIVE CASES

Organic Brain Disease

Comprehension.........	12
Arithmetic............	9
Information...........	14
Digits.................	13
Similarities...........	11
Verbal..............	59

Case O-1. Male, age 34, showing definite neurological signs including marked hydrocephalus, facial weakness, slight tremor, absent abdominals. Also suggested Babinsky on left side with mild postural deviations on same side. Diagnosis— post Meningo-encephalitic syndrome. At age will have observed, no attempt has been made to furnish such critical scores for any of the disease entities listed. There are several reasons for this omission. In the first place, none has been statistically validated. But even if this had been done, the writer would have been extremely loathe to present such critical scores for fear of conveying the impression that all that is necessary to make a diagnosis is an ability to look up a table of interpreted scores. That such apprehension is not unwarranted, is attested by the wide incidence of such tables furnished by the authors of personality, neurotic inventory and delinquency scales. A more important reason for omitting critical scores which might be used directly for diagnosis is that our list of "signs" is concerned only with the presence or absence of significant test scores. Such simple dichotomy obviously does not take into consideration the factors of configuration and of degree of concomitance of "signs," which, as we have just noted, are at the very root of the problem of valid diagnosis. The appraisal of concomitance and interpretation of configurations cannot be made through simple statistical procedures, and at this stage of our knowledge, is provisionally best replaced by clinical judgment and experience.

In general, the greater the number of "signs" associated with any given mental disorder manifested by a psychometric, the greater the probability of a correct diagnosis being made on the basis of the examination. However, the presence of only one or two "signs" when very marked, may be definitely pathognomic. For example, a very low Block Design score combined with a very low Object Assembly test score is definitely indicative of organic involvement, although some of the other signs may be absent. Sometimes, the "signs" are more numerous but not very decisive, and in these cases adjuvant aids must be taken into consideration. For example, mental defectives occasionally show test score distributions very much like that found in psychopaths. In such a case, the global intelligence rating of the individual may well be the most important differential determinant. For example, if along with the other "signs", the subject had an I.Q. of 65, the chances would be that we were having to do primarily with a mental

---

Non-Psychotic States, April 1941 meeting of Eastern section of A.P.A.) and as we have suggested in the discussion of indices of mental deterioration (p. 66). Finally, there is the technique of the multiple regression equation. This would be the most valid method of all, but its application to the problem of diagnosis would be beset with many difficulties, not the least of which would be the inability of most clinicians to apply it.

Picture Arr.	9
Picture Comp.	8
Block Design	4
Object Ass.	1
Digit Symbol	3
Performance	25
Verbal I.Q.	115
Performance I.Q.	74
Digits forward	8
Digits backward	6

of 6 months patient had an injury with sequelae lasting 6 months, which was diagnosed as meningitis. This case shows the four most conspicuous signs of organic brain disease: large discrepancy between Verbal and Performance in favor of the former, very low Blocks combined with even lower Object Assembly and very low Digit Symbol. While all of the test scores on the verbal part of the examination are average or above, the two lowest are Similarities and Arithmetic which are in line with the organic picture. The only exception is the Digit Span which is good for both forwards (8) and backwards (6).

(Vocabulary)	10
Comprehension	11
Arithmetic	6
Information	11
Digits	9
Similarities	7
Verbal	45*
Picture Arr.	7
Picture Comp.	10
Block Design	7
Object Ass.	11
Digit Symbol	4
Performance	39
Verbal I.Q.	103
Performance I.Q.	103
Digits forwards	7
Digits backwards	4

Case O-2. Male, married, age 54, fireman. Entered hospital with complaints of headaches and forgetfulness. History of old skull fracture. Physical examination, including blood-Wasserman and flat plates were negative. While under observation referred by Neurological service for psychometric. On Bellevue Adult patient attained a rating of average intelligence with subtest score distribution as indicated in summary at left. The distribution shows the following organic signs: Arithmetic—low, Similarities—poor, Blocks—poor, Digit Symbol—very poor. Digit Span appears to be unimpaired, but actually average score of 9 was due primarily to subject's relatively good span for digits forward (7); backwards span was only 4 digits. A very low digit backwards in a person of otherwise normal intelligence is generally characteristic of organic brain disease. This patient, when his age is considered, manifests relatively little deterioration but is of special interest because he shows many of the signs of organic brain disease; the one conspicuous exception is the relatively high Object Assembly score; but a good Object Assembly is occasionally found in organic cases who have not as yet deteriorated markedly.

Schizophrenia

Comprehension	10
Arithmetic	10
Information	15

Case S-1. Male, age 41, war veteran, 3 years college. Long history of inadequacy and maladjustment. Has been at various mental hospi-

---

* When Vocabulary is included, the Verbal score is obtained by taking 5/6 of total.

Digits	14
Similarities	11
Verbal	60
Picture Arr	˙8
Picture Comp	13
Block Design	10
Object Ass	12
Digit Symbol	4
Performance	47

Verbal I.Q.	116
Perform. I.Q.	95

Comprehension	6
Arithmetic	6
Information	10
Digits	6
Similarities	0
Verbal	28
Picture Arr	4
Picture Comp	10
Block Design	0
Object Ass	2
Digit Symbol	2
Performance	18

Verbal I.Q.	80
Perform. I.Q.	70

Comprehension	11
Arithmetic	6

tals and repeatedly diagnosed as paranoid praecox. Latest admission followed threats of violence to mother. Well preserved, no hallucinations or delusions elicited; but insists that mother and veterans hospitals are against him. Patient is of better than average intelligence. The schizophrenic signs in his psychometric are: Verbal much higher than Performance, low Picture Arrangement,⁻ very low Digit Symbol simultaneously with high Digit Span, large discrepancy between Information and general Comprehension in favor of the former. High intertest scatter within Performance group.

Case S-2. White, male, age 39, elevator operator. This patient shows marked deterioration, generally seen only in old cases but occasionally also in cases of relatively short duration. In his case, reported onset of disease was about six months prior to administration of test. First indication that something was radically wrong with patient occurred when he left his job with no apparent reason; said he was nervous and had no peace of mind. Later complained police were after him. On admission to hospital was bewildered, kept to himself but was passively cooperative. Although diagnosed as paranoid schizophrenic, general behaviour was that of a simple or mixed type. Psychometrically, he showed the following schizophrenic signs: Verbal higher than Performance, low Digit Symbol with much better Digit Span, low Object Assembly, zero scores on Similarities and Block Design, high Information. Most outstanding of all, very large intertest variability ranging from a score of zero to a score of ten. The very low scores on the Object Assembly and Digit Symbol together with zero score on the Block Design taken alone would suggest organic brain disease, but in that case we would also get a low Picture Completion and not an average score on this test. The inconsistency here is what definitely shows this case to be schizophrenic. Similarly, only a schizophrenic would give an average score on Information and a zero score on Similarities.

Adolescent Psychopaths

Case P-1. White, male, age 15, 8th grade. Continuous history of stealing, incorrigibility

Information........... 10
Digits................. 6
Similarities............. 5
   Verbal................ 38
Picture Arr............ 12
Picture Comp.......... 10
Block Design.......... 15
Object Ass............. 16
Digit Symbol.......... 12
   Performance......... 65

Verbal I.Q.............. 90
Perform. I.Q........... 123

Comprehension........ 8
Arithmetic............. 6
Information........... 6
Digits................. 6
Similarities............. 6
   Verbal................ 32
Picture Arr............ 10
Picture Comp.......... 8
Block Design.......... 7
Object Ass............. 11
Digit Symbol.......... 9
   Performance......... 45

Verbal I.Q.............. 82
Performance I.Q....... 92

Comprehension........ 14
Arithmetic............. 13
Information........... 14
Digits................. 10
Similarities............. 13
   Verbal................ 64
Picture Arr............ 10
Picture Comp.......... 14
Block Design.......... 15
Object Ass............. 12
Digit Span............. 9
   Performance......... 58

and running away. Several admissions to Belle-vue Hospital, the last one after suicidal attempt. While on wards persistently created disturbances, broke rules, fought with other boys and continuously tried to evade ordinary duties. Psychopathic patterning: Performance higher than Verbal, low Similarities, low Arithmetic, sum of Picture Arrangement plus Object Assembly greater than sum of scores on Blocks and Picture Completion.

Case P-2. Male, age 16, schoolboy, 8th grade. Readmitted for observation from Correctional Institution where he was reported to have thrown acid into face of one boy and was suspected of pushing another into an open fire. History of outbursts, of violent temper and cruelty from early childhood. Would throw objects at least provocation and took pleasure in inflicting pain on others. Once pushed a boy, who he knew could not swim, off dock in hope of witnessing a drowning. Psychopathic patterning: Performance higher than Verbal, good Object Assembly, sum of scores on Object Assembly and Picture Arrangement greater than sum of scores on Block Design and Picture Completion. This subject does not show all the psychometric signs of the psychopath but the sum of Object Assembly plus Picture Arrangement is markedly higher than that of Picture Completion plus Block Design, and that in itself is almost pathognomonic.

Neurotics

Case N-1. Male, age 25, college graduate, "Y" secretary. Complaints: easy fatigability, lack of concentration, sexual difficulty, and general symptoms associated with Neurasthenia. Has been under psychiatrist's care. Neurotic patterning: Verbal higher than Performance, high Comprehension and Information with relatively low Digit Span. Low Picture Arrangement and low Digit Symbol, Object Assembly less than Block Design. Negative sign: relatively good Arithmetic, but in this connection account must be taken of fact that subject is a college graduate with B.S. degree.

Verbal I.Q.............. 113
Performance I.Q........ 125

Comprehension.........	10
Arithmetic.............	6
Information............	10
Digits.................	7
Similarities............	7
Verbal...............	40
Picture Arr............	7
Picture Comp..........	9
Block Design...........	10
Object Assembly.......	7
Digit Span.............	8
Performance.........	41

Verbal I.Q.............. 93
Performance I.Q........ 87

Case N-2. Female, age 15, school girl, High School—1st term. Difficulties began when subject entered high school. Commercial course, which subject has been failing, obviously unsuited to girl's ability. Main symptoms: gastric distress and vomiting, unhappiness at school. Physical examination essentially negative. Diagnosis: Conversion Hysteria. Neurotic patterning: poor Arithmetic and Digit Span with relatively good Information and Comprehension, low Picture Arrangement, Object Assembly less than Block Design. However, total Verbal and Performance scores are not markedly different. This is not uncommon in duller neurotics (especially of Hysterical type). Also to be taken into account is the fact that the subject comes from bilingual home. Low Similarities in this case only an indication of subject's limited intelligence.

We shall conclude our discussion of the diagnostic material elicitable from the Bullevue Scale by adding a few notes on what might be termed "qualitative indicators". These indicators are significant items which reveal themselves either in the form or in the content of the subject's responses. The perseverative, redundant quality of the schizophrenic's definitions on the Vocabulary test is an example. Another is the negativism which reflects itself in a subject's tendency to say or to do the opposite of what is requested. This is frequently brought out by the subject's responses to the Similarities test on which, instead of giving the asked for likenesses, he responds with gratuitous differences. The tendency to give differences when likenesses are called for, is also encountered in subjects of limited intellectual endowment (e.g., young children and mental defectives). But when given repeatedly by a person of above dull normal or better intelligence it is almost always pathognomic of schizophrenia. The following, for example, are the responses to the Similarities test questions, made by schizophrenic patient (case S-2) who insisted upon giving differences even after repeated correction, and ended by making a zero score on the test:

Orange-banana: orange is round, banana is long

Coat-dress: a coat hangs over the dress

Dog-lion: a lion is larger

Wagon-bicycle: wagon has four wheels, bibycle has two wheels

Daily paper-radio: you hear news on radio, read stories in newspaper
Wood-alcohol: alcohol is white, wood is any color
and so on for all twelve test items.

Sometimes a patient merely persists with a stereotyped reply, "they
are not alike". In such cases it is generally impossible to change his
set, but even when one succeeds in so doing, the usual result is to elicit
a difference instead of a likeness. For example, one patient after systematically answering "not alike" to the first four Similarities questions,
altered his reply after much urging to the fifth question (Newspaper-
radio) "one is for news, the other is for entertainment."

A common characteristic of schizophrenics and occasionally of certain
types of psychopaths is the "spoiled" or contaminated response. The
subject first gives a good or passing response, but then "spoils" it by an
irrelevant or eccentric addition. Such responses are most frequently
elicited by the Comprehension questions, occasionally, also, by the
Similarities questions. Thus, *Why are shoes made of leather?*—"It fits
(the foot) easily, it is an old custom." (schizophrenic) *Why does land
in the city cost more than land in the country?*—"In the city land becomes more valuable because people need space while in the country
acres are not so much in demand. In that way the law of supply and
demand becomes counterbalances." (schizophrenic) *What is the thing
to do if you find a letter, etc?*—"Might mail it, but first I'd open it up
to see if there was any money in it." *Suppose there wasn't any money
in it?*—"Tear it up." (psychopath).

Sometimes abnormal trends are indicated by the question which a
subject may ask. Thus, before answering the arithmetical problem,
*If a man buys 6¢ worth of stamps and gives the clerk 10¢ how much
should he get back?*, a schizophrenic wanted to know whether they were
"2 or 3 cent stamps". At other times a casual question by the examiner
will be equally effective in eliciting a telltale response. The following is a
rather amusing example. *How far is it from New York to Paris?* *Patient*:
"I don't know." *Examiner*: "try to figure it out." *Patient*: "Well, it
takes about a week to get from Paris to New York. There are seven
days in a week and twenty four hours in a day; so multiply 24 by 7 and
you get 161 which equals the hours in seven days or one week. Now
there are twenty blocks in a mile; so multiply 161 by 20, and this gives
you 3,220. The distance from Paris to New York is 3,220 miles."
The arithmetic is not quite accurate but more important than the slight
error in multiplication is the way in which the subject arrived at the
almost correct answer. The response was made by a schizophrenic
with manic features.

THE PROBLEM OF MENTAL DETERIORATION*

DAVID WECHSLER

In speaking of mental deterioration much depends on what one means by "mental" and how one proceeds to define deterioration. By mental we shall mean primarily intellectual abilities,[1] and by deterioration any conspicuous falling off or loss in these abilities. Concretely, a person will be considered as giving evidence of mental deterioration when he is no longer able to carry on his intellectual tasks with the speed, accuracy or efficiency previously characteristic of his functioning level. The only condition to be added is that the loss must not be one which is due merely to lack of practice.

The definition of mental deterioration which we have just given is much broader than what is generally understood by it. Most psychiatrists and neurologists would not consider a mere falling off or loss in general capacity as an indication of mental deterioration. This is because they are primarily acquainted with mental impairment when associated with some organic or brain injury. But mental decline may and does occur independently of any specific mental disease. It is characteristic not only of such conditions as general paresis, cerebral arteriosclerosis, or chronic alcoholism but of all senescent decline. Nevertheless, for diagnostic convenience, mental deterioration may be said to be of two sorts—that which occurs after maturity with the natural increase of age, and that which is consequent to some brain lesion or prolonged mental disease occurring at any age. Psychiatrists and neurologists have been primarily concerned with the latter and have almost entirely disregarded what for want of a better term, we shall refer to as "normal mental deterioration". Psychologically, however, there is little difference between the two, except as regards the rate at which deterioration occurs and, in the case of traumatic injury, as regards the number of mental functions involved. The deterioration met with in normal old people is similar to that met with

---

*Reprinted from David Wechsler, *The Measurement of Adult Intelligence,* 3rd ed., Baltimore, 1944, pp. 54-69. Copyright 1944, The Williams & Wilkins Co. Reproduced by permission.

[1] This is an arbitrary delimitation of the term. Emotion is no less mental than intellect, but the delimitation of the term when used in connection with deterioration corresponds to what is generally implied by it in clinical practice. Thus psychiatrists distinguish "emotional" from "mental," that is to say, "intellectual" deterioration.

in most organic brain diseases. Senility,[2] or extreme mental deterioration, is merely a terminal state of certain processes which begin relatively early in life and continue progressively with age. The net result of the accompanying changes is to impair all original endowment. Whether we wish to reserve the term mental deterioration to cover only the extreme losses of ability or prefer to apply it equally to the entire senescent decline is a matter of convenience. For an understanding of the impairment as a whole, however, it is essential that we have as full knowledge as possible of all changes which occur in human ability with age. It is these changes which we propose to discuss in this chapter.

The changes in human capacities which occur with age fall into two self-limiting epochs: (1) The period during which they increase and (2) the period during which they fall off with age. The first of these is the well known period of growth which need not detain us here. The second period is that of gradual decline, regarding which there is still much difference of opinion but whose main trends have been sufficiently established to warrant a general description. We have elsewhere summed up the main facts regarding the decline of capacities with age[3] but for the sake of completeness will briefly summarize them again.

Every human capacity after attaining a maximum begins an immediate decline. This decline is at first very slow but after a while increases perceptibly. The age at which the maximum is attained varies from ability to ability but seldom occurs beyond 30 and in most cases somewhere in the early 20's. Once the decline begins it progresses continually. Between the ages of 30 and 60 it is more or less linear. In the case of most abilities the decline between these ages may be described with good approximation by an equation of the first degree. These facts are graphically summarized in figure 3. The bold-faced curve is the smoothed line of means of Bellevue intelligence test scores for subjects from age 15 to 65; the light curve, that for Vital Capacity measures for the same age period. Both have been reduced to comparable scale units.[4] As will be seen the maximum of both curves

[2] Senility, unlike "senile psychosis," is not a clinical entity. Even the latter is seldom used alone. Usually there is some qualifying condition added; thus: senile psychosis with arteriosclerosis, senile psychosis with Alzheimer's disease, and so on.

[3] Wechsler, D.: *The Range of Human Capacities.* Chapter VII.

[4] The test-score means were derived from an abbreviated 8-test scale; the actual means for the Full Bellevue Scale are given on page 118. Those for Vital Capacity will be found in an article by Ruger and Stoessiger, *Annals of Eugenics* 1926, vol. II., pp. 85 and 104.

occurs in the age period 20 to 25, with that of Intelligence somewhat earlier than that for Vital (Lung) Capacity. Another point of interest is that the Intelligence Test curve declines at a faster rate than the curve of Vital Capacity. This may seem strange but is not an artifact. Contrary to common belief many of our intellectual abilities show greater impairment with age than do our physical ones.[5] The actual decline in any given case, however, varies with the ability in question.

The curve of mental decline shown in figure 3* is a composite curve. It is composite, first, in the sense that the points used in plotting it have been derived from measurements obtained on large groups and

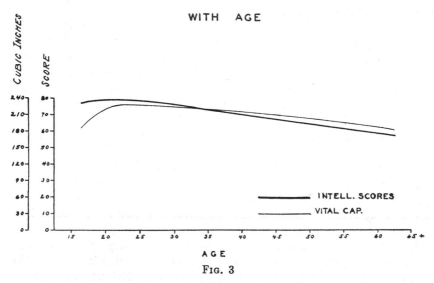

VARIATION OF INTELLIGENCE SCORES AND VITAL CAPACITY

WITH AGE

FIG. 3

not on single individuals. But it is also composite in the sense that the decline described represents the age changes in mental capacity, not with respect to any specific ability, but with respect to the average of a large number of abilities. The groups of abilities here considered are those represented by the tests which happen to constitute our

[5] The most conspicuous decline of all is shown in the sensory field. Vision and hearing fall off rapidly after 30. Their curves of decline, however, are far from straight lines. See on this point Ruger and Stoessiger, *op. cit.*

* See also figure 2, p. 29. The curve of mental decline shown by the heavy line in figure 3 has been "reduced" to make it comparable to the Vital Capacity curve given along side of it. It has also been "smoothed".

scale. A scale made up of a different set of tests might furnish an age curve which differed significantly from the one we obtained. To determine whether such were the case one would have to examine the same group of individuals with a large variety of scales, each as different from the other as possible. We were unable to do this. But, as a possible alternative approach, we compared the age curve obtained with the Full Scale with age curves obtained from combinations of only certain of the tests[6] and also with age curves obtained from the individual tests, taken separately. Individual age curves for six of our ten tests are given in figures 4 and 4A.

As will be seen from their examination, the form of all these curves is the same as that of the generalized curve given in figure 3. The decline of any given ability, like that of any combination of them, is essentially linear. The main difference between them pertains to the age at which the initial decline begins and more particularly to the rate at which the decline proceeds. Different mental abilities decline at different rates. That they do is psychometrically fortunate, because these differences can be made use of in determining mental deterioration.

The decline of mental ability with age is part of the general senescent process of the organism as a whole. Hitherto the common view has been that our mental abilities, unlike our physical abilities, remain relatively unimpaired until rather late in life (senility), except as an occasional consequence of disease or traumatic injury. This was an unsubstantiated hypothesis tenable only so long as no facts were at hand to oppose it. But the view still persists even though such facts are now available. Most people, including scientists, hate to believe that they are not as mentally alert at 50 as they were at 20. Part of this is due to a confounding of mental with practical ability, that is, a failure to differentiate between intellectual endowment and the success had in applying it. The latter is naturally dependent in no small measure upon experience. What one has lost through a falling off of native ability one may often replace by acquired knowledge. An old clinician may be a better doctor than a younger one, even though he possess less actual understanding of disease processes.

Another item which contributes to the biased attitude towards the facts of mental decline is the historical distinction between physical and mental. According to this distinction the latter is conceived of being higher, better or more important. Accordingly few people are

---

[6] For example, curves obtained from verbal tests alone, or performance tests alone.

concerned when told that at 40 they cannot hear or fight as well as when they were 20, but are quite "het up" when informed that they probably also cannot calculate or reason as well. There also exists a kind of hierarchy of relative values as regards the various mental

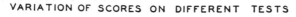

VARIATION OF SCORES ON DIFFERENT TESTS

WITH AGE

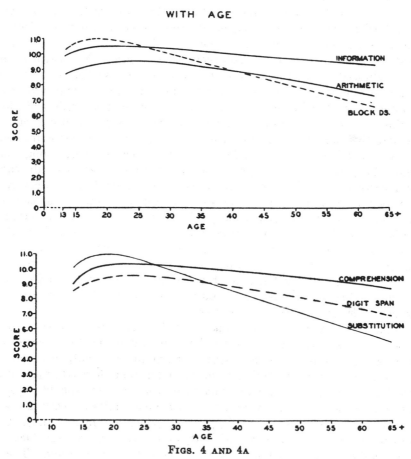

FIGS. 4 AND 4A

abilities themselves. Professor Cattell long ago called attention to the fact that people are ever ready to complain about their bad memory, but seldom of their poor judgment or common sense. But it is certain that memory is not the only mental capacity which declines with age, nor the one which is always most impaired by it.   Conrad and Jones,[7] for example, found that older people (individuals over 50) did much better on the Army Alpha Test calling for general information, than on the one calling for abstract reasoning (the Analogies Test), and we ourselves have found that they do better on repeating digits forwards than in detecting similarities.

We have put forward the hypothesis that the decline of mental ability with age is part of the general organic process which constitutes the universal phenomenon of senescence, and have insisted upon the fact that the phenomenon begins relatively early in life.   The evidence we have adduced for this hypothesis is the observed parallelism we have found in the rate of decline of various physical and mental abilities. Another line of evidence is furnished by neurological studies of the brains of senile individuals.   These are not always clear-cut cases because they may be associated with special trauma or organic disease. If our hypothesis is correct, however, the same changes, though of course to a lesser degree, ought to be expected much earlier in life, say from 20 years onward.   Up to the present, experimental data supporting this view have been lacking.   This may be due to the fact that neuropathology has not been particularly alive to the problem, or, as is more probable, to the fact that neurological techniques are not sufficiently advanced to detect very small and gradual alterations[8] which may, and undoubtedly do, occur in brain tissue.   There is, however, some indirect evidence that alteration of the brain begins at an early age, which may be considered as supporting our view.   We refer to the progressive change in brain weight with age.

It has been known for some time[9] that the mean weight of the adult brain declines with age.   The skull thickens and the brain shrinks. It we accept the brain as the organ of the mind, it is only reasonable to assume that even gross changes such as alterations of weight may also affect its function.   Assuming that to be the case, we should expect that the changes in brain weight show some concomitance with alterations in general intellectual ability,—a fact which we thought might be demonstrated by an analysis of both in relation to the age factor. The graphs in figure 5 represent the results of such a study.   They

[7] *Genet. Psychol. Monog.* 1933, pp. 260–261.

[8] Probably because most of these are atomic or molecular and therefore not discernible under the microscope.

[9] Pearl, R.: Variations and correlation in brain weight. *Biomet.*, 1905, vol. IV, pp. 13–104.

are the age curves for intellectual ability and brain weight for ages 15 to 65. Necessarily they were not obtained from the same subjects. The age curve for intellectual ability is that obtained for subjects given the tests which were used in standardizing our Bellevue Scale; the brain weight curve is that computed from figures for brain weights of autopsied subjects of comparable ages, collected by Rössle and Routlet.[10] For purposes of comparison, the curves have been reduced to approximately the same scale. Inspection of these curves reveals a close parallelism between loss in brain weight and decline in mental

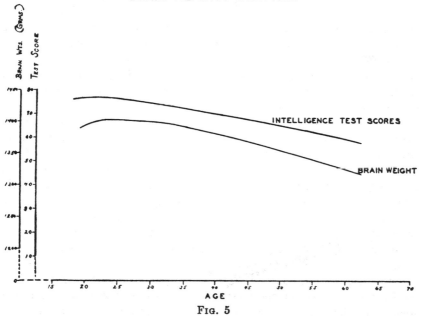

VARIATION OF INTELLIGENCE TEST SCORES AND BRAIN WEIGHTS WITH AGE

Fig. 5

ability with age. It is probable that, with a different series of brain weights and a different series of tests, the similarity between the two curves would not be so marked. But the general parallelism cannot be ascribed either to chance or artifact. It is much better than that found between most physical and mental traits and as good as that found between curves for many mental abilities taken separately.

[10] Data given in Wertham's, F.: *The Brain as an Organ.* New York, 1934. The brain weights are those of males 16 years and over, averaged for five year periods.

The decline in the weight of brain, like that in intellectual ability, is essentially linear.[11]   After reaching a maximum, at about age 20, the brain begins to decline in weight, somewhat irregularly at first, but after 25 or 30 at a fairly constant rate.

If our generalizations regarding the influence of age on mental deterioration are correct, it follows that mental deterioration in human beings begins at a relatively early age.   However, to speak of a person in his early 30's as showing signs of deterioration because he already manifests some measurable decline of ability, would be stretching the term beyond its usual connotation.   Clearly that is not what is implied by deterioration in the ordinary sense.   It would seem desirable to restrict the term to only such impairment or losses in ability as are significantly greater than those due to the age factor alone.   To do this we must necessarily know what the normal loss of ability is for the average individual and the mean limits of variability at all ages for the normal population.   But even with these facts at hand we are only at the beginning of our task.   To evaluate deterioration we must be able to measure it quantitatively.

The measurement of mental deterioration involves three separate problems: (1) The reliable measurement of the individual's actual or present functioning ability; (2) the evaluation of his previous functioning level; (3) the expression of the difference between the two in meaningful, quantitative terms.   Up to the present, none of the three problems has had complete solution.   We say none, although as regards the measurement of present functioning ability this statement is not altogether correct.   We do have considerable means of measuring an ndividual's functioning ability, but these means, in general, are unsuitable for precisely those groups on whom they are most needed in studying mental deterioration, namely, the older adults.   What we have said regarding the inadequacy of available general intelligence scales for the measurement of adult intelligence, holds equally for individual tests of mental ability.   They have seldom been standardized for adults.   The Bellevue Scales presented in this book are an attempt to furnish the necessary adult norms for such tests.   By means of the tests which compose them we are now able to measure a fairly large number of intellectual abilities throughout the greater part of adult life, that is, up to the age of 60, and in some instances up to the age of 70.

The second step in the measurement of deterioration, namely, the evaluation of an individual's previous functioning level, presents a

---

[11] For further evidence on this point see Pearl, R.: *Studies in Human Biology.* Baltimore, 1924, pp. 58–65.

much more difficult problem. The reason is that in most cases we have no psychometric data by which such evaluation can be made. Few persons examined for mental deterioration have ever had a previous psychological examination. Yet, in order to make an accurate estimate of a person's normal functioning ability, we should have not only one but a series of psychometric examinations on him, done at various intervals and so far as possible with the same or comparable tests. That, however, is an ideal situation which cannot be realized at present.

In practice, it is necessary to turn to other sources of data that will enable us to appraise the subject's previous functioning ability. The data usually consist of facts gleaned from the subject's educational, vocational and social history. Thus, if from a subject's history we learn that he is a high school graduate, that he has held responsible positions for a number of years and that he attained some social recognition in his community, we can safely assume that he must have been a person of at least average endowment and that he should be able to perform certain mental operations which may be expected of individuals of comparable endowment. But information of this sort is of value only where the discrepancy between an individual's actual and expected functioning is considerable. Thus, if a formerly successful business man at age 45 attains an I.Q. of only 70, is unable to do simple calculations and can no longer repeat 5 digits, we should know at once that he has deteriorated. Degrees of deterioration of this sort, however, can ordinarily be detected without standardized psychometric examination.

We do not need tests to discover deterioration in an old paretic. The merit of psychometric tests is that they can show us small differences of ability, and their usefulness in the clinical field depends upon how well they can do this. Their value in determining mental deterioration must reside in their ability to detect changes in mental functioning long before they have so disorganized the behavior of the individual as to make them patent to all. For such purposes a general social and psychiatric history is insufficient as a base for comparison. We must either have psychometric records of previous examinations with the same or similar tests, or be able to use the results of the mental tests given at any specific examination as a means of inferring the probable previous ability of the individual. However, as already mentioned, few adults who come up for psychometric examination have had previous mental tests, and even fewer were done sufficiently long ago to enable us to make a comparison between their present and their former functioning. It is here that the age curves for separate abilities which we give in figures 4 and 4A are of value.

One of the interesting facts revealed by the age curves for different abilities obtained on the same groups of individuals, is that certain abilities decline more slowly with age than others. Thus, the abilities called for by the General Information and General Comprehension Tests hold up much better than do the abilities called for by the Substitution and the Memory Span for Digits Tests. This difference in rate of decline of various abilities suggests a possibility of estimating previous functioning levels. Thus, if the abilities which do not decline significantly with age were precisely those which were least affected by the deteriorative process, one could assume that scores which individuals attain on tests measuring these abilities represented their original or permanent endowment. If now we combined a number of these tests into a rounded scale, such a scale would furnish us a means of measuring mental deterioration as well as past functioning levels in terms of present functioning abilities. All that would be necessary would be to compare the mean score which a subject attained on the tests which remain relatively unimpaired with age, with the rating which he obtains on a group of tests which are relatively much impaired with age. The ratio or difference between their rates of decline would give us the required measure.

The method outlined above for comparing previous and present functioning ability in terms of test scores obtained in a single examination of a subject may be termed the *differential-test-score method* of measuring mental deterioration.[12] As we have just seen, it makes use of the fact that some abilities decline relatively little during adult life and others to a considerable degree, and assumes that the difference between their rates of decline in any given individual expresses his relative degree of deterioration. The usefulness of the differential-test-score method for evaluating deterioration necessarily depends upon the availability of tests with full age norms. Ideally, we should have to have available age curves for many different abilities, each measured in as many ways as possible with tests whose validity and effectiveness had been previously established. At present such tests are all too few, but the eleven subtests made available by the standardization of the Wechsler-Bellevue offers the possibility of trying out the method just discussed.

---

[12] Some attempt to use methods like the one just outlined has already been made by a number of psychologists. (Babcock, H., *Arch. of Psychol.*, 1930, no. 117; Gilbert, J. D., *Arch. of Psychol.*, 1935, no. 188; Shipley, W. C., *J. Psychol.*, 1940, 9, 371–377; Hunt, H., *J. Appl. Psychol.*, 1943, 5, 375–387.)

The first step in the application of the differential test score method is the optimal allocation of tests to the "Hold" vs. "Don't Hold" groups. In general, the tests which drop most markedly with age belong, as might be expected, with the "Don't Hold" and those which drop least, with the "Hold" tests. But another factor must also be considered, namely, the type of ability measured by the tests. There must be some functional similarity between the opposed or contrasted tests. If this is not the case, we risk making test combinations which, though showing significant differences, are likely to give spurious discriminants. For example, most abilities tapped by performance tests decline much more rapidly with age than those involved in verbal tests. At first thought it might appear that this situation could be capitalized by using verbal tests against performance tests as a ready means of obtaining measures of "Hold" *vs.* "Don't Hold" abilities. This, however, would be a mistake because, if we accepted differences between the scores on verbal and performance tests as a criterion of deterioration, all individuals who have relatively good verbal capacity would inevitably show greater mental deterioration as they grew older. This would follow from the fact that the differences between verbal and performance abilities automatically increase with age. On the other hand, people who are relatively good in performance tests would show lesser deterioration or indeed none at all, because the discrepancy between their verbal and performance scores would become smaller and smaller as they grew older. Accordingly, in assembling our "Hold" vs. "Don't Hold" batteries we have brought together approximately the same number of verbal as performance tests. The tests combined in each of the proposed categories are as follows:

Tests which hold up with age
Information
Comprehension
Object Assembly
Picture Completion
Vocabulary

Tests which do not hold up with age
Digit Span
Arithmetic
Digit Symbol
Block Design
Similarities
(Picture Arrangement)

To obtain a measure of deterioration, one compares the sum weighted scores of the "Hold" tests with that of the "Don't Hold" tests, allowing for the difference in number of tests in each group, or for a more strict comparison the sum of the first four tests of the "Hold" with the first four tests of the "Don't Hold" group. The resulting comparison may be expressed either as a ratio or difference between the two sums. Naturally, if the result is given as a difference it must be expressed as a percent difference in order to take into account the absolute magnitude of the sums compared. Thus, if the sum of a subject's "Hold" subtest scores is 50 and the sum of his "Don't Hold" subtest scores 40, he shows a deterioration loss of 20% and efficiency quotient of .80. Deterioration is indicated if the percent loss is considerable or the efficiency quotient low, that is considerably below 100.

The problem, of course, is to define what is meant by considerable or significant loss. In the long run such a definition would have to be statistical in character and be based on a distribution of individual percents of loss or calculated deterioration quotients of a sufficiently large number of cases both normal and pathological. These data are not yet available, but it is possible to arrive at effective approximations by the use of tables 39 and 40 given in appendix 2. This table contains the mean scores of all the subtests at successive age periods. Summing the subtest scores of the tests composing each of the batteries compared, we can obtain the total weighted score that may be expected for the "Hold" and "Don't Hold" batteries at different ages. Next, it only remains to treat the resulting sums in the manner described above, and obtain what may be termed "normal" or average deterioration expectancies. These are given in tables 6 and 6A.

Table 6 was obtained as follows: at each age level sums were obtained of the mean test scores of the Information, Comprehension (or Vocabulary[13]), Picture Completion and Object Assembly tests, (Hold tests), and of the Digit Span, Arithmetic, Block design and Digit Symbol tests, respectively. The sum of the "Don't Hold" tests at each level was then subtracted from the sum of the "Hold" tests and the difference divided by the minuend. The result is expected normal percent deterioration loss. If instead of expressing deterioration in terms of a difference one wishes to express it as a ratio the sum of the "Don't Hold" tests is

---

[13] In practice it will be found safer to use the Vocabulary than the Comprehension test.

divided directly by the sum of the "Hold," and the results so obtained constitute deterioration quotients. These are given in table 6A.

We may now define deterioration in the pathological sense: An individual may be said to show signs of possible deterioration if he shows a greater than a 10 percent loss, and of definite deterioration if a loss greater than 20 percent[14] than that allowed for by the normal decline with age. Obviously the larger the loss the greater the probability that we are dealing with true deterioration.

TABLE 6

Average (Normal) Deterioration Loss at Different Ages

(In percent)

HOLD − DON'T HOLD ÷ HOLD	AGES							
	20–24	25–29	30–34	35–39	40–44	45–49	50–54	55–59
Calculated Values........	0.5	0	4	4	9	11	14	16
Smoothed Values.........	0	1	3	5	8	11	14	16

TABLE 6A

Average (Normal) Deterioration Quotients at Different Ages

DON'T HOLD ÷ HOLD × 100	AGES							
	20–24	25–29	30–34	35–39	40–44	45–49	50–54	55–59
Calculated Values........	99.5	100	96	96	91	89	86	84
Smoothed Values.........	100	99	97	95	92	89	86	84

We shall now present a few applications of the procedure described above, restricting ourselves to the percent of loss technique as the preferred method.

On page 161 is cited a case of a man age 54 with symptoms of headache, dizziness and history of an old skull fracture. The case was used to illustrate the organic brain impairment pattern. But the psychometric also serves to illustrate what is not so obvious, a test score distribution indicating marked mental deterioration. This is not suggested by the subject's test performance as a whole, since his I.Q. is 103 and

[14] Losses of 10 and 20 percent correspond roughly to deviations of −1 P.E. and −2 P.E. from the mean at age 20–25. The mean loss at this age is, of course, 0. The equivalents at other ages may be assumed to be roughly of the same order, but the percent of loss must of course be calculated from the altered means at these ages (see table 6).

shows no discrepancy between his total Verbal and total Performance ratings. If, however, we compare his scores on the "Hold" and "Don't Hold" tests we find the following: Information—11, Comprehension—10, Object Assembly-12, Picture Completion-10, Arithmetic-7, Digit Span-6, Block Design-7. The sum of the "Hold" tests is 43, that of the "Don't Hold" 24; from which by applying the method outlined above, the deterioration loss $\left(\dfrac{43-24}{43}\right)$, is found to be 44 percent or, allowance being made for his normal decline with age (see table 6), a net loss of 30 percent. This is obviously considerable; actually, the subject was unable to continue at his job. The method just described will be most useful in determining mental deterioration in organic brain cases, but it may also be applied in cases of Schizophrenia. Here special considerations arising from the peculiarities in test patterning of this group must be borne in mind. Thus, the not uncommon low score of the Schizophrenic on the Comprehension and still lower ones on the Picture Completion test (see Case S-2); or, again, the fact that schizophrenic patients do systematically worse on the Object Assembly than on the Block Design, and so on.

Another possible application of the method is in the appraisal of the reported effects of shock treatment, negative as well as positive. Here in addition to some of the considerations already mentioned, there is also the problem of practice effect inherent in all retest procedures, and in particular its differential effect on the various tests used. But perhaps the most serious limitation to the method as a whole is the assumed very high reliability of the tests themselves. Such high order of reliability does not in fact exist. For some of the tests, such as the Vocabulary, it is reassuringly high and perhaps sufficient, but for most of the others no such claim can be made. Nevertheless the method does prove effective in practice, and if the limitations discussed are borne in mind, may be applied with reasonable confidence.

A particular point worth calling attention to is the frequency with which certain functions are involved in the deterioration of mentally ill patients irrespective of the disease entity. Thus alcoholics (Korsakoff type), paretics, seniles and schizophrenics all do badly on Digits Backwards, Hard Associations, Reproducing Designs and the Digit Symbol Test. They do not, however, do so for the same reason. The paretic and alcoholic fail on repetition of Digits Backwards and on the Digit Symbol Test because of definite retention and learning disabilities; the dementia praecox patient because of poor attention. self-preoccupation and general inability to concentrate.[15] Nevertheless, from certain practical points of view, the disabilities may amount to the same thing. Both types of patients cannot be trusted to execute simple tasks or to follow complicated directions.

This brings up again the interesting question of the nature of the deteriorative processes. There is no doubt that, as a result of certain traumatic injuries, individuals show special disabilities. But the recurrence of like disabilities in different traumatic injuries strongly suggest the generalized nature of the deteriorative process. The brain acts as a whole and its impairment in one place affects its functioning as a whole. The fact that its disorganization is greater along one rather than another line is of secondary importance. · For this reason it is perhaps not particularly important what tests are used in detecting it, providing they are such tests as are especially sensitive to the patient's intellectual functioning.

In general, mental deterioration is best revealed by measuring speed of response, learning and the ability to perceive new configurations, particularly spacial ones. Ordinarily, it is not the form of the test but the function it calls forth that determines its diagnostic value. One can measure speed of response almost equally well by counting the number of words the subject gives in three minutes, or by the number of A's he can cancel on a printed page in a like period. But it makes considerable difference when we study learning ability, whether we use "old" or "new" paired associates. Chronic alcoholics, for example, tested with a list of paired associates such as *come—go* and *Boston— Massachusetts* show little impairment, but when tested with a list of hard paired associates like *crush—dark* and *Appleby—Texas* will show considerable impairment. The reason is that while the test is of the same form, the functions involved are quite different. One requires the formation of new, the other merely the recall of old associations.

We have defined deterioration primarily as an impairment or loss of function. Sometimes this impairment manifests itself as a disorganization, sometimes as a mere regression to primitive types of response. Both occur in various types of organic brain disease. The disturbances met with in the visual motor field are particularly striking and have been extensively studied by Lauretta Bender by use of the Wertheimer

---

[15] This is the usual psychiatric interpretation. For a very different explanation, see Babcock, H.: *Dementia Praecox*. N. Y., 1935.

figures which she has standardized into a visual-motor Gestalt test.[16]
We have applied her test to patients variously diagnosed as seniles,
and found that the figures are reproduced by these patients as primitive
loops or segments of large arcs, perseverated in a wavelike manner.[17]
This is precisely the kind of thing that Bender found to be characteristic
of children's efforts prior to the maturation of the psychomotor function, (at M.A. level of approximately 2 years) and in particular of mentally defective children of about this M.A. level.   Veritably we must
add another stage of Shakespeare's Seven Ages, the age of just plain
sans everything.

[16] Bender, L.: The Visual-motor Gestalt Test and Its Clinical Use. *Research
Monographs*, Amer. Ortho. Psych. Assoc., New York, 1938, particularly Chapter
VIII.

[17] It is interesting to note that these changes are precisely those observed in
patients with severe sensory aphasia.   Seniles are, of course, frequently aphasic.
Cf. Bender, L.: *Arch. of Neur. & Psych.*, 1933, XXX, 514–537.

ON THE INFLUENCE OF EDUCATION ON INTELLIGENCE AS MEASURED BY THE BINET–SIMON TESTS*

DAVID WECHSLER

The Psychological Corporation, New York

The object of this paper is to present the results of a study on the variability of intelligence, as measured by Binet mental ages, with increasing natural age, and to show what light these results throw upon the problem of the influence of education on intelligence.

Experimental attack on the question of the influence of education on intelligence as measured by the Binet-Simon scale, has been hitherto primarily along two lines. The first approach has been through the method of partial correlations. In this method the procedure has consisted of obtaining measures of educational attainment, and of other possible contributing factors, in conjunction with intelligence ratings as furnished by the tests, and then inferring the contributing influence of each of the factors measured upon the intelligence ratings, from the nature of the final partial correlation ratios obtained.

The second line of approach has been through the comparison of successive intelligence ratings obtained from retests. Here the procedure has consisted of examining the same subjects with the same scale after different intervals of time, and noting whether or not there were significant differences between the successive IQ's so obtained.

The most thorough study of the influence of education on intelligence by the method of partial correlations is that made by Burt. Complete analysis of this study is to be found in his book on *Mental and Scholastic Tests* (pp. 180–183). I shall here only briefly summarize Burt's method of procedure and general results.

In his investigation Burt obtained the following data on some 300 children between the ages of 7 and 14 years: (1) The child's age; (2) his scholastic attainment as measured by educational tests and corrected by teachers' estimates; (3) his native "intelligence" as measured by a special reasoning test and his teacher's estimate; (4) his mental age as obtained with Burt's revision of the Binet-Simon tests. Having these data Burt next correlated the ratings obtained with each of these measures, and then by the method of partial correlation eliminated successively one or more of the "factors" as contributing influences to the mental age score.

*Reprinted from *Journal of Educational Psychology*, 1926, **17**, 248-257.

The results of the intercorrelations were as follows: Binet mental age and school work correlated to the extent of .91; Binet mental age and intelligence (as measured by the reasoning tests) .84; school work and intelligence .75; Binet mental age and school work after both intelligence and chronological age were eliminatd .61. This last coefficient was the highest of any of the coefficients of the second order coefficients obtained (*i.e.*, those obtained after any two factors among the various combinations had been eliminated).

In view of the high value of the coefficient of correlation between Binet mental age and school attainment .91, and its persistent high value, .61, after the factors of intelligence and age were eliminated, Burt concludes: "There can therefore be little doubt that with the *Binet-Simon Scale* a child's mental age is a measure not only of the amount of intelligence with which he is congenitally endowed, not only of the plane of intelligence at which in the course of his development and growth he has arrived; it is also an index largely, if not mainly of the mass of scholastic information and skill which, in virtue of attendance more or less regular, by dint of instruction more or less effective, he has progressively accumulated at school." (*Loc. cit.*, p. 182.)

Excepting the words, "largely or mainly," the above conclusion appears to me a valid inference, providing one accepts Burt's reasoning test as a true measure of native intelligence. The assumption that it is such might, of course, be questioned but perhaps no more effectively than any other single criterion. It must furthermore be borne in mind that the reasoning test ratings were combined with teachers' estimates of the child's intelligence. Taken as a whole, Burt's data show that intelligence as measured by Binet mental age ratings is unquestionably influenced by academic education. What they do not show is precisely how great this influence is, and to what extent if any, the diagnostic value of the Binet-Simon tests is reduced thereby.

Let us now consider the second array of evidence from which conclusions regarding the influence of education on intelligence have been drawn. This evidence, as already mentioned, is derived from studies on the constancy of the IQ, and consists of data furnished by retests of individuals with the same scale after varying intervals of time. The results of such studies made with the Stanford revision of the Binet-Simon tests in the United States have been recently summarized by Colloton and Rugg,[1] and with Burt's revision in England by Gray and Marsden.[2]

---

[1] *Journal of Educational Psychology*, 1921, 12, pp. 315–322.
[2] *British Journal of Psychology*, Gen. Sect., 1924, 15, pp. 169–173.

Upon analyzing the results of the various reports reviewed, Rugg and Colloton found that the average difference in IQ between first and second testings was approximately 4.5 points for the middle 50 per cent of the groups tested. This difference was not far from the average figures reported by most of the investigators individually, but was not distributed equally in either direction. These authors summarize their findings thus: "For all studies the positive differences are nearly twice as large as the negative, the typical positive difference being somewhat less than six points and the typical negative difference approximately three points." The magnitude of these differences have been shown by Terman to be not much greater than those obtained by immediately succeeding retestings, that is tests made within a day or two of each other instead of after intervals of one, two, or three years as in the studies reviewed by Rugg and Colloton.

The results of Marsden and Gray were very much the same as those of Rugg and Colloton. They report: "The middle 50 per cent of changes in IQ lie between the limits of 5.1 points decrease and 6.0 increase," or, in terms of the probability of the IQ not varying beyond certain limits, from one examination to another, "the chance of an IQ showing an increase by as much as 5.5 points is 1 in 5; as much as 11 points 1 in 5; as much as 16.5, 1 in 20; as much as 22 points, the chances are 1 in 100."[1]

The general conclusion of Gray and Marsden and of the other authors cited is that an individual's IQ remains fairly constant, and that the results obtained from retesting of subjects after varying intervals of time show that the changes in IQ which do occur are not significant. The first part of the conclusion, I believe, is warranted by data reported; the second part, it seems to me, is a very doubtful inference.

The studies on the constancy of the IQ have usually been undertaken with the view of ascertaining the prognosticating validity or diagnostic value of the IQ rating. In the light of this criterion, results of the retest investigations seem to indicate quite clearly that the IQ is sufficiently constant to assure the examiner a reasonable amount of confidence in the exactness of his rating. The chances are good that if the same individual were tested on a different occasion or at a sub-

---

[1] In the case of two investigators (Stenquist and Fermon) these differences were considerably larger. Rugg and Colloton are inclined to these exceptional results as having been "caused primarily by the non-uniform scoring of the responses."

sequent date, with the same scale, his intelligence rating would be substantially the same. Nevertheless, measurable differences are found in the majority of the cases and in many of the cases these differences are rather large. The chances are only even that an individual's IQ will not vary by more than 5.5 points (Gray and Marsden) at two successive examinations. And this difference must be doubled if we wish to increase the range of possible variability so as to include 83 per cent instead of only 50 per cent of the cases. Now, while this margin may not seem too wide for practical diagnostic purposes, it does seem too large a quantity to be lightly passed over. The variability of 11 points in 100 (the theoretical mean IQ of the average normal child) within a range of 2 PE's is hardly an insignificant variation and certainly seems to need accounting for. Some effort to do so has, to be sure, been made. It has been explained, for instance, as being due to the influence of practice, the inexpertness or difference in methods of scoring of different examiners, and the varying emotional adaptation on the part of the subject on the different examinations. But the evidence is not clear that these are the only or even the most important influences, and whether there be not some other constant factor or factors which contribute to the magnitude of the variation.

The factor whose presence or absence we are particularly desirous of ascertaining is that of education or academic training. Unfortunately the studies on the constancy of the IQ do not permit us to conclude anything definite on this question owing, in the first place, to the limitations of the data themselves, and, in the second place, to the disturbing influences inherent in the method of retesting, such as the effect of practice, variations of emotional attitude on the part of the subject at different examinations, etc. I shall present a method of approach to the study of variability of intelligence ratings, which seems to eliminate these difficulties, and which, I believe, permits the attack of the problem of the influence of education on intelligence in a more rigorous way.

The method about to be considered consists of analysis of the range of variability of intelligence as measured by Binet mental age, at the different chronological year levels over which the Binet-Simon scale extends. The theory of this procedure is that if education influences the intelligence ratings, the variability of these ratings should be modified as the individuals tested have been more or less subjected to that influence, that is as they grow older. If the effect of education is to make us more alike, the variability should become smaller with increasing age; if it tends to make us more unlike, the variability should become greater as the individual grows older. On the other hand, if the range of variability should be found to remain approximately constant, the influence of education might be said to be negligible.

In order to answer the above questions about any particular scale it is, of course, necessary to have original distributions of mental age ratings for each of the chronological years embraced by the scale employed.[1] The next step is to obtain the mean mental ages and their standard deviations for the different chronological age levels. These means and standard deviations calculated from the original distributions of both the Terman and Burt revisions of the Binet Scale are given in columns (3) and (4) of Tables I and II. (The year levels below 6 and above 14 were omitted from consideration, owing to both the diminished reliability and the inherent limitations to variability at the extreme ends of the scales.) Having the means and standard deviations it is, of course, an easy matter to obtain an expression of variability by dividing the latter by the former and multiplying the quotient by 100 (Pearson's coefficient of variability). The coefficients of variability thus obtained together with their probable errors are given for each chronological year in columns 5 of Tables I and II.

Inspection of the coefficients reveals that, with some exceptions, their absolute values tend to become smaller and smaller as the ages of the subjects increase. This fact appears more outstandingly in Burt's than in Terman's data. It is, however, not possible from inspection of the figures alone to evaluate the nature of the variability indicated. The question is whether the differences revealed are significant. The answer to this question can be obtained by calculating[2] the probable errors of the differences between the coefficient of

---

[1] I wish to express my indebtedness to both Professor Terman and Dr. Burt for furnishing me these data.

[2] I am indebted for these computations to Mr. B. Malzberg, statistician to the New York State Board of Charities.

The formula used for the calculation of the PE's of the differences is:

$$\text{PE of } C_I - C_{II} = \sqrt{e_I{}^2 + e_{II}{}^2}$$

where C_I and C_{II} are the coefficients of variability and e_I and e_{II} their respective probable errors. The PE of the coefficient of variability is given by the formula,

$$\text{PE of } CV = \frac{.67449\, V \left\{ 1 + 2\left(\dfrac{V}{100}\right) \right\}^{\frac{1}{2}}}{\sqrt{2N}}$$

where V is the coefficient of variation and N the number of cases.

variability of each chronological age and that of every other chronological age in the group. This has been done in Tables III and IV. A difference is considered significant when it is equal to three times its probable error. Where such is the case, the figures in the table are given in bold face type.

The results are extremely interesting. In neither Burt's distributions nor Terman's is there any significant increase or decrease of variability between the ages of 6 and 9. In Burt's data this continues to be the case through year 10. But beginning with year 10 in Terman's distributions and year 11 in Burt's, significant differences begin to appear. In Burt's distributions there is a very sharp change at this point. From here on nearly all coefficients of variability show significant differences. The coefficients of variability become smaller with increasing age. The PE's of all the differences are significant with the exception of those between years 10.5 and 11.5, and 12.5 and 13.5. Out of 26 differences (comparing the coefficients of year 10 through 14 with each other and with those of every other year in the table) 2 are insignificant and 24 are significant and positive.[1]

Terman's distributions show no uniform changes of variability until we reach the age of 14. Until this age is reached the significant differences encountered are more or less sporadic. There is a significant difference between the year 10 and 6, year 11 and year 9, year 13 and years 7 and 10. Year 14, on the contrary shows significant differences when compared with all the other years in the table except years 10 and 9. Out of 30 differences compared 21 are insignificant and only 9 are significant, and of these some are negative.

There is thus a discrepancy in the results obtained from the data of the two revisions of the Binet-Simon Scales. Terman's data indicate no significant change of variability in intelligence with mental age; Burt's data, on the contrary, indicate a very clear cut alteration in variability, the change occurring at a very definite point in the course of the child's development. We have reason to ask ourselves, therefore, which of the data are to be accepted and the possible reasons for the discrepancy revealed.

In the opinion of the writer, the results obtained from analysis of Burt's data are more to be trusted, and for the following reasons: In

---

[1] A difference is positive when the coefficient of variability of the higher chronological year is smaller than the coefficient of the lower chronological year, for instance when the coefficient of year 12 is less than that of year 11. Positive differences thus indicate decreased variability.

the first place, Burt's data were obtained on the average from about twice the number of subjects. The Stanford Revision is based on less than 100 cases per year level, roughly in equal distribution between each sex. Burt's standardization, on the other hand, is based on 200 cases per year level (roughly, 100 boys and 100 girls). In the second place, the differences of variability revealed by the analysis of Burt's data is so clear cut that it is extremely unlikely that they are due to chance. The only alternative explanation is that these differences are due to the operation of some constant error or errors, but of these there is no evidence. Finally, and most important, is the fact that the point at which the significant differences begin to appear is precisely that at which we should expect it, if education did influence mental age ratings, namely when formal academic instruction begins to be the important source of the child's intellectual acquisitions.

If we compare the contribution which academic training makes toward the mental equipment of the child, with that which he acquires through natural growth, it is not hard, I think, to show how relatively small the former is. Compare, for instance, a child's learning to read with his acquisition of the fundamental concepts of language, meanings of words, etc., in the course of his natural development. Or, again, the motor coordinations in learning to write with these involved in speech or general orientations of the body. The first few years of formal education, indeed, emphasize the training of the native sensory, perceptual and conceptual powers of the child. The acquisition of the three R's to which the major portion of the child's first four years of schooling is devoted consists primarily in a systematic training of these powers. Learning to read consists primarily in the formation of certain visual and motor percepts and the acquisition of certain fundamental concepts; learning to write of acquiring some specialized neuro-muscular habits; in arithmetic attempt is made to give the child the fundamental concepts of number and numerical relations.

The early years of the child's education then even in the school are concerned with the training of his sensory perceptual and elementary conceptual powers. In the average school system this instruction is emphasized for approximately the first four years of the school curriculum. Beginning with the fifth year more and more emphasis is begun to be placed on the acquisition of facts, information and cultural material. History, geography, literature, science are given progressively more and more time. The child begins to acquire knowledge.

Now, analysis of Burt's data shows that from the age at which the acquisition of knowledge begins to play an important role in the schooling of the child, as compared with the training and development of his perceptual and conceptual powers, the influence of formal education on mental age ratings begins to make itself felt more and more. In short, the acquisition of knowledge, or what we shall now use as a synonomous term, education, seems to have a significant influence on intelligence as measured by the Binet-Simon tests. The influence of education is to make us less variable, that is, to make us more alike.

Summary and General Conclusions

In this paper the writer has attempted to attack the problem of the influence of education on intelligence as measured by the Binet-Simon tests through a study of variability in mental age with increasing chronological age. This was done by calculating the coefficients of variability of mental age for each of the chronological year levels from years 6 through 14 for both the Terman and Burt revision of the Binet-Simon scales, and then examining the reliability of the differences found. The theory behind the procedure was that if education influences intelligence, the variability of intelligence ratings obtained with the scale should either increase or, more probably, decrease with increasing chronological age.

The results of the above analysis showed that no significant differences in the coefficient's variability were revealed by either scale up to the years 10–11. From this point on however, Burt's data

TABLE I.—Distribution and Variability of Mental Ages (Terman's Revision of Binet-Simon Tests)

1 Chronological age	2 Number of cases	3 Mean mental age in (months)	4 Standard deviation	5 Coefficient of variation
5	56	60.7321	7.8478	12.92 ± .5921
6	118	74.4492	9.5718	12.86 ± .4058
7	93	86.4516	10.5346	12.18 ± .4324
8	98	98.0204	12.4260	12.67 ± .4388
9	113	107.7522	12.9475	12.02 ± .4526
10	86	124.4302	13.7465	11.05 ± .4225
11	79	134.1646	18.5182	13.80 ± .5336
12	82	142.3049	18.4481	12.96 ± .4908
13	98	150.5306	20.8702	13.86 ± .4814
14	82	163.7439	17.3373	10.59 ± .3975

showed uniformly significant differences of variability; while Terman's distributions failed to show any significant differences except for year 14. In both cases, wherever the differences did occur, they were nearly in all instances in the direction of a decrease in variability with increasing chronological age.

The writer is inclined to the view that the failure of Terman's data to show the phenomenon revealed by Burt's data is due to the insufficiencies of the Stanford Standardization of the Binet-Simon Tests.

Giving preference to Burt's data over those of Terman, the writer interprets the significant decrease in variability of mental age with increasing chronological age (from years 11 through 14 inclusive) as evidence of the influence of education on intelligence as measured by Binet-Simon mental age ratings. The absence of any significant differences below the age of 10 is interpreted to show that below this age the mental rating of the Binet-Simon tests are not influenced by education.

In general the data on MA variability show that education is less of factor in younger than in older children, as would naturally be expected, and that towards the lower end of the Binet scale (years 6 to 10) is probably negligible. If this is so, there follows the extremely interesting, though, at first thought, apparently paradoxical corollary, that the intelligence rating (mental age, or for that matter, IQ) obtained with the Binet-Simon scale of a child at an early age (8 to 10 years) more nearly represents its potential native equipment than one obtained when he is much older (14 to 16). This would probably hold true for any other scale that might be used.

TABLE II.—DISTRIBUTION AND VARIABILITY OF MENTAL AGES (BART'S REVISION OF BINET-SIMON TESTS)

Chronological age	Approximate number of cases	Mean mental age (in years)	Standard deviation	Coefficient of variation
5.5	200	5.5	0.59	10.73 ± .4008
6.5	200	6.5	0.83	12.77 ± .4376
7.5	200	7.6	1.03	13.55 ± .4653
8.5	200	8.6	1.15	13.37 ± .4589
9.5	200	9.4	1.24	13.19 ± .4525
10.5	200	10.6	1.29	12.15 ± .4161
11.5	200	11.4	1.26	11.05 ± .3772
12.5	200	12.3	1.18	9.59 ± .3264
13.5	200	13.1	1.20	9.16 ± .3115
14.5	200	13.8	1.09	7.90 ± .2797

TABLE III.—DIFFERENCES IN VARIABILITY OF INTELLIGENCE (MENTAL AGE) RATINGS AT DIFFERENT CHRONOLOGICAL AGE LEVELS (BASED ON AN ANALYSIS OF TERMAN'S DATA)

Yrs.	7	8	9	10	11	12	13	14
6	.68 ± .593[1]	.91 ± .594	.84 ± .608	1.31 ± .586	.94 ± .640	1.0 ± .637	1.0 ± .630	2.27 ± .568
7	....	.49 ± .613	.06 ± .626	1.13 ± .605	1.62 ± .687	.78 ± .654	1.63 ± .647	1.59 ± .587
8		....	.65 ± .627	1.62 ± .606	1.13 ± .688	.29 ± .655	1.19 ± .648	2.08 ± .588
9			....	.97 ± .619	1.78 ± .700	.94 ± .668	1.84 ± .683	1.43 ± .602
10				....	2.75 ± .681	1.91 ± .648	2.81 ± .641	.46 ± .580
11					....	.84 ± .653	.06 ± .719	3.21 ± .655
12						....	.90 ± .687	2.37 ± .632
13							....	3.27 ± .634

[1] Interpret as follows: The difference in variability between ages 6 and 7 years is .68 ± 593; between ages 6 and 8, .19 ± .594, etc. etc.

TABLE IV.—DIFFERENCES IN VARIABILITY OF INTELLIGENCE (MENTAL AGE) RATINGS AT DIFFERENT CHRONOLOGICAL AGE LEVELS (BASED ON AN ANALYSIS OF BART'S DATA)

Yrs.	7.5	8.5	9.5	10.5	11.5	12.5	13.5	14.5
6.5	.78 ± .639	.60 ± .634	.42 ± .629	.62 ± .604	1.72 ± .578	3.18 ± .546	3.61 ± .537	4.87 ± .519
7.5	....	.18 ± .654	.36 ± .649	1.40 ± .624	2.50 ± .599	3.96 ± .568	4.39 ± .560	5.65 ± .542
8.5		....	.18 ± .644	1.22 ± .619	2.32 ± .593	3.78 ± .563	4.21 ± .554	5.47 ± .537
9.5			....	1.06 ± .615	2.14 ± .614	3.60 ± .589	4.03 ± .549	5.29 ± .532
10.5				....	1.10 ± .561	2.56 ± .529	2.99 ± .520	4.25 ± .501
11.5					....	1.46 ± .499	1.89 ± .489	3.15 ± .469
12.5						....	.43 ± .451	1.69 ± .429
13.5							....	1.26 ± .419

EQUIVALENT TEST AND MENTAL AGES FOR THE WISC*

DAVID WECHSLER

New York University

O NE of the important features of the Wechsler Intelligence Scale for Children has been the abandonment of mental age both as a method for calculating IQ's and for defining levels of intelligence. There were several reasons [1] why this was done, the main one being the hope that it would discourage the practice of comparing individuals in terms of their mental ages, with the MA interpreted as an absolute measure of level of intelligence. This interpretation, in the author's opinion, is not valid. However, since the MA has such a firm place in clinical practice and is often a legal necessity, several methods whereby equivalent "MA's" (actually, test ages) may be derived from the WISC are presented here for those who wish to use them, in spite of the fact that these methods violate the philosophy of the Scale.

There are various ways in which an "MA" may be obtained from the weighted scores furnished by the WISC. Only three will be discussed. The first and most direct one may be termed the *Formula* method. This is obtained by treating the MA as the unknown in the formula IQ = MA/CA. Since the WISC furnishes an IQ and the child's chronological age is known, the MA is computed by multiplying the subject's obtained IQ by his CA. Thus, if a child's IQ is 115 and his chronological age 85 months, his MA would be 98 months or 8 years 2 months.

The second and third procedures are, respectively, the *Mean Test-Age* and *Median Test-Age* methods. For these, a table of equivalent test-ages for all raw scores on each of the subtests is necessary. Table 1 gives these equivalents.[1] It has been derived as follows:

For each age interval, the raw score corresponding to the scaled score of 10 has been taken to represent mean test performance for that particular age, as in point of fact it is. Table 1 records test-ages for each subtest and for each age interval. The table should be used as follows: Locate an individual's subtest raw score in the column which is headed with the name of the subtest. The corresponding test-age is the entry, in the same row, in the column headed "Test Age" at either end of the table. The raw score represents the performance level of the average child at that age.

Example: Subject S (irrespective of age) makes the following scores: Information 9, Comprehension 6, Arithmetic 8, and so on. Looking up the table, we find that an Information score of 9 is made by the average child in the age group 7 years 10 months (approximate mid-point of the interval 7 years 8 months to 7 years 11 months), a Comprehension score of 6 by a child 6 years 6 months (approximate mid-point of the interval 6 years 4 months to 6 years 7 months), and so on. The raw scores for all the other subtests are treated in the same manner.

In looking up equivalent test-ages for specific test scores, occasional lacunae will be encountered: (1) The same raw score will be found opposite several successive test ages. If the raw score applies to only two successive ages, use the lower age. If there are more than two, use a median value. (2) The obtained raw scores are beyond the limits found in the table. In such instances one arbitrarily assigns the age equivalent *4 years 10 months* (or,

---

*Reprinted from *Journal of Consulting Psychology*, 1951, 15, 381–384. Copyright 1951 by the American Psychological Association. Reprinted by permission.

[1]Test-age equivalents between ages 8 years 2 months through 12 years 2 months for raw scores on Code A and test-age equivalents from 5 years 10 months to 7 years 10 months for raw scores on Code B are extrapolated values.

TABLE 1
Test Age Equivalents for WISC Raw Scores

Test Age	Information	Comprehension	Arithmetic	Similarities	Vocabulary	Digit Span	Picture Completion	Picture Arrangement	Block Design	Object Assembly	Code A	Code B	Mazes	Test Age
5-2	5	5	3	3	15	5	6	—	4	8–9	15–16	—	5	5-2
5-6	—	5	—	3	15	5	6	4	4	8–9	17–20	—	5	5-6
5-10	6	—	4	4	16–17	6	6	5	—	10–11	21–24	10 & below	6	5-10
6-2	—	—	4	4	16–17	6	—	6	—	10–11	25–27	11–12	7	6-2
6-6	7	6	—	—	18	7	7	7–9	5	12–13	28–31	13–16	8	6-6
6-10	—	7	5	5	19–20	—	7	10–11	—	12–13	32–33	17–20	9	6-10
7-2	8	7	5	5	19–20	—	—	12–13	6	14–15	33–34	—	10	7-2
7-6	—	8	—	6	21–22	8	8	14–16	6	14–15	35–37	21–22	11	7-6
7-10	9	—	6	6	23–24	8	—	17–19	7–8	15–16	35–37	23–24	12	7-10
8-2	—	9	—	—	23–24	—	—	20–21	8–9	16–17	38–39	25–26	13	8-2
8-6	10	9	7	7	25–26	—	9	22–23	9–10	17–18	40–41	25–26	14	8-6
8-10	11	10	—	7	26–27	—	9	23–24	10–11	17–18	—	27–29	14	8-10
9-2	11	10	—	8	27–28	9	10	24–25	11–12	19–20	42–43	27–29	15	9-2
9-6	—	11	8	8	28–29	9	10	25–26	13–15	19–20	44–45	30–32	15	9-6
9-10	12	11	8	8	29–30	9	10	25–26	13–15	19–20	—	33–35	15	9-10
10-2	12	12	—	9	31–32	9	11	27–28	16–20	21–22	46	33–35	16	10-2
10-6	13	12	9	9	32–33	—	11	27–28	16–20	21–22	—	36–37	16	10-6
10-10	13	12	9	9	34–35	—	11	27–28	16–20	21–22	—	38–39	16	10-10
11-2	14	13	10	10	34–35	10	12	29	21–24	23	47	40	17	11-2
11-6	14	13	10	10	36–37	10	12	29	21–24	23	—	41	17	11-6
11-10	15	14	10	10	38	10	12	29	21–24	23	—	42–43	17	11-10
12-2	16	15	11	11–12	39	10	—	30	25–28	24	48	44	17	12-2
12-6	17	15	11	11–12	39	10	—	30	29–30	24	—	45–46	17	12-6
12-10	17	15	11	11–12	40–41	10	—	30	29–30	24	—	47	17	12-10
13-2	18	16	12	13	42	10	13	31–33	31	24	—	48–49	17	13-2
13-6	18	16	12	13	43–44	10	13	31–33	32–33	24	—	48–49	17	13-6
13-10	18	16	12	13	43–44	10	13	31–33	32–33	24	—	50–51	17	13-10
14-2	19	16	12	13	45–46	11	13	34	34–35	25	—	52–53	17	14-2
14-6	19	16	12	13	45–46	11	13	34	34–35	25	—	54–55	—	14-6
14-10	19	17	12	14	45–46	11	13	34	34–35	25	—	54–55	—	14-10
15-2	20	17	—	14	47–49	11	14	35–36	36–39	26	—	56–57	17	15-2
15-6	20	17	—	14	47–49	11	14	35–36	36–39	26	—	56–57	18	15-6
15-10	20	17	—	14	47–49	11	14	35–36	36–39	26	—	56–57	18	15-10

merely, below 5 years) for scores falling below the lower limit and *15 years 10 months* for scores beyond the upper limit.[2]

[2]In preparing the data for the correlations cited below, the method was slightly altered; see text.

To obtain a mean test (or "equivalent mental") age, sum the several test-ages and divide by the number of tests given. To obtain a median test-age, distribute the test-age scores and find the central value in the usual way. The difference in values obtained by the two methods will usually be small. If ten tests are used the Mean method is generally the easier. An example of the calculations involved in all methods is given in Table 2.

TABLE 2

COMPUTATION OF "MA" EQUIVALENTS FROM WISC SCORES

Male, Age 10 years 6 months, WISC IQ 89		
Test	Raw Score	Test Age
Information	11	8–10
Comprehension	10	8–10
Arithmetic	9	10–6
Similarities	7	8–6
Vocabulary	34	10–10
(Digit Span)	8	7–6
Picture Completion	11	10–6
Picture Arrangement	20	8–2
Block Design	14	9–6
Object Assembly	19	9–6
Coding	21	7–6
(Mazes)	16	10–6

1. *Formula Method*

$$MA = IQ \times CA = .89 \times 126 \text{ mos.} = 112.14 \text{ mos.} = 9 \text{ yrs. } 4 \text{ mos.}$$

2. *Mean Method*

$$\frac{\Sigma(\text{Test-age Sc.})}{N} = \frac{104 \text{ yrs. } 80 \text{ mos.}}{12} = 9 \text{ yrs. } 2 \text{ mos.}$$

3. *Median Method*

$$\frac{8 \text{ yrs. } 10 \text{ mos.} + 9 \text{ yrs. } 6 \text{ mos.}}{2} = 9 \text{ yrs. } 2 \text{ mos.}$$

A comparison of the correlations between the various methods is given in Table 3. These are reported separately for 100 boys at age 10-6 and 100 girls at 13-6, both taken from the standardizing population. The test-age range in both these samples was from 5 years 2 months to 15 years 10 months. Some of the obtained raw scores fell outside this range; the procedure followed in such instances was to assign a test-age of *4 years 10 months* to all cases below the lower end of the table, and *16 years 2 months* to all cases above.

Perusal of Table 3 shows high intercorrelation between the three methods used for calculating mental ages from WISC scores. The highest average correlation is furnished by the Formula method, which also tends to give somewhat higher mental age equivalents. The latter is noticeably true for the older age

TABLE 3

INTERCORRELATIONS OF THREE METHODS OF DETERMINING MENTAL AGES FROM WICS SCORES

	Mean* Method	Median† Method	Formula‡ Method
A. 100 boys, average age 10–6, from the standardization population			
Median Method	.920		
Formula Method	.969	.913	
Mean (in months)	128.4	127.5	128.9
SD	21.4	21.7	19.8
B. 100 girls, average age 13–6, from the standardization population			
Median Method	.968		
Formula Method	.971	.949	
Mean (in months)	153.0	155.9	159.6
SD	23.5	26.7	25.6

*MA = mean of test-age equivalents
†MA = median of test-age equivalents
‡MA = IQ × CA (in months)

group, as might be expected.[3] The Median Test-Age method produces somewhat lower intercorrelations with the Formula method than does the Mean method. This may be due, in part, to the fact that there are only 10 subtests; a larger number of subtests might have stabilized the median and given higher correlations. Another slight advantage of the Mean Test-Age method is that it follows closely the procedure used in derivation of IQ's in standardization.[4] The CA × IQ formula correlates very highly with both Median and Mean methods.

SUMMARY AND DISCUSSION

Three methods have been furnished for obtaining mental age equivalents from the WISC. Two of the methods require a table of equivalent test-age scores. This table also permits an examiner to obtain age norms for a given test performance. The author does not favor using MA equivalents for intelligence test scores, but he does see a legitimate use for test-age equivalents if they are employed to show how a child of a given age compares with children of his own age in performance on a given test. In such cases, however, one should remember that the test age obtained is to be

[3]This is due to the test-age ceiling or highest subtest equivalents possible (15 years 10 months) on any of the subtests.

[4]The derivation of IQ's is based on the total of standard scores for the subtests, a statistic which correlates perfectly with mean standard score.

interpreted not as a measure of intelligence but as a measure of a specific aptitude.

Received June 12, 1951.
Early Publication.

REFERENCE

1. WECHSLER, D. *The Wechsler Intelligence Scale for Children.* New York: Psychological Corp., 1949.

THE PSYCHOLOGIST IN THE PSYCHIATRIC HOSPITAL*

DAVID WECHSLER

Psychiatric Division, Bellevue Hospital

IN discussing the place of the psychologist in the psychiatric hospital it will be useful to remember that hospitals called psychiatric may differ considerably both as to setup and function. An important difference to be borne in mind is that between the observation and custodial type of hospital.[1] An observation hospital is one in which patients are referred primarily for diagnosis and are kept only for a minimal amount of time, usually less than two and seldom as much as four weeks, after which they are either discharged or committed to a state institution.[2] An example of an observation hospital is the Psychiatric Division of Bellevue Hospital in New York City. A custodial hospital, on the other hand, is one to which mental patients are committed for an indefinite period for care and treatment. All state (mental) hospitals are of this sort, but many of them also serve as observation hospitals at the same time. An example of a hospital rendering this combined service is the Psychopathic Hospital in Boston, Massachusetts. In addition, some mental hospitals, whether custodial or observation, also have outpatient departments which function in the same way as any general mental hygiene clinic.

The main differences, so far as the psychologist is concerned, between working at an observation and a custodial hospital, are that at the observation hospital he will probably have less time for extensive testing, be required to dispose of patients more expeditiously, and in most instances also have less time for research. On the other hand, he will see a much greater variety of cases, including large numbers who are not psychotic; and, in general, he will be able to acquire techniques and training which will be more useful to him in other clinical fields or in private practice. Again, in states where mental care is limited, the psychiatric hospital may be run in conjunction with an institution for mental defectives or a colony for epileptics. In such places the psychologist is frequently called upon to divide his time between psychiatric and other services. The remarks to follow, however, will be confined to the role of the psychologist in hospitals which, whatever their title, concern themselves primarily with diagnosis and care of mental cases.

DUTIES OF PSYCHOLOGISTS IN MENTAL HOSPITALS

In most psychiatric hospitals the primary function of the psychologist is to appraise the patient's intellectual functioning. The psychologist is expected (1) to define, as an expert, the patient's intellectual level and to indicate whether the I.Q. obtained represents the true or merely the present level of function-

*Reprinted from *Journal of Consulting Psychology*, 1944, 8, 281-285.

[1] In some states, hospitals for mental observation are designated as psychopathic hospitals.

[2] Under a new New York State law, effective October 1, 1944, patients may be kept for observation as long as sixty days.

ing; (2) to call attention to the presence of any special abilities or disabilities, particularly as they may be related to, or diagnostic of, the patient's clinical picture. From here on the role of the psychologist varies greatly from institution to institution. In many places he or she is called upon (3) to help in psychiatric diagnosis in terms of psychometric functioning. This may be achieved either by (4) analysis of intelligence test results, or by the use of supplementary test procedures involving special intellectual function or, more increasingly, by the use of (5) personality tests. In the latter instance, the advent of (6) projective techniques, particularly the Rorschach test, has greatly increased the diagnostic role of the psychologist.

In some institutions the psychologist is called upon to take case histories and in still others to interview patients. In such institutions the psychologist may, and generally does, participate in staff conferences on the basis of which the patients are assigned to different wards, and when up for parole and discharge, to offer suggestions as to disposition. In some institutions where vocational and special therapies are available, the psychologist will also be called upon to administer educational and vocational tests, and to make recommendations regarding them. This is true particularly of mental hospitals which have large adolescent and children's wards.

In addition to the above duties, the psychologist in a mental hospital often does a certain amount of teaching either of the institutional staff (nurses and interns) or in connection with the training program of intern psychologists and of psychology students from nearby universities. As regards the latter much can be said in favor of a more intimate tie between psychology departments in universities with mental hospitals as well as mental hygiene clinics. There are, however, a number of factors which tend to retard the association. One of these is that it has tended to be a one-way affair, namely, psychology departments like to send their students for practical work to mental hygiene clinics and hospitals but have been slow in adding members to their staff who have had practical experience in the field. In recent years, however, there has been a growing trend toward appointing psychologists working at the mental hospitals to at least part-time teaching at the university. This is a desirable trend and it is to be hoped that it will increase with time.

RESEARCH IN MENTAL HOSPITALS

Except for institutions which have special research psychologists attached, and these are few, the opportunities for research depend largely upon the initiative and zeal of the individual psychologists working in them. Most of this research has to be done on one's own "free" time, but as the free time in paid positions is relatively small, actual facilities have been correspondingly limited. Nevertheless the amount of research emanating from psychologists working in hospitals has been considerable. Most of it has dealt with psychometrics, particularly intelligence testing of various psychotic groups. Recent examples are studies by Shakow [9], Rabin [7], Jastak [5] and Whitman [12]. Another field of psychiatric research by psychologists has been the general problem of mental deterioration [1, 10, 4] and in recent years a considerable number of studies by psychologists in mental hospitals have appeared on the effects of shock treatments in therapies [6, 13, 11].

A field which has been relatively neglected, however, is that dealing with sensation and perception. Interestingly enough, the most original work done in this realm has been done by psychiatrists and neurologists [8, 2, 3]. One of the main reasons for this is the limited training which most psychologists going into work in mental hospitals have received in advanced experimental and physiological psychology. The emphasis of recent years has been on psychometrics and statistics and while both of these are important, particularly the former, original work is more likely to be produced by individuals who have had thorough grounding in the basic psychological facts and processes than in applied specialized courses.

RELATION OF THE PSYCHOLOGIST TO MEMBERS OF THE PSYCHIATRIC STAFF

As aforementioned, the role of the psychologist varies widely in different hospitals and opportunity for professional contact with other staff members likewise varies. In some places the psychiatrist prefers to look upon the psychologist as a technician. The psychiatrist wants an I.Q. report very much as he would call for a blood Wassermann or an electroencephalogram. Most clinical psychologists do not like either the restricted type of work or the status implied by this type of position. Many positions that are available in mental hospitals call for routine psychometrics and a certain percentage of psychologists wishing experience in psychiatric hospitals must expect this type of work, at least at the beginning. It is, however, equally true that psychiatrists in many places are learning that psychologists have more to offer. Any thorough psychological report makes this apparent to the psychiatrist. This is almost inevitable, as in most psychiatric cases the

subject's I.Q. is just one of the factors, and often not the most significant one, for the appraisal of the patient's problem. It is here that the supplementary and special diagnostic techniques have served to reveal the special contributions which the psychologist can make to the understanding of the total problem. It is not an uncommon experience now to hear the psychiatrist inquire, "Does the patient show mental deterioration?" or, "Does he show a schizophrenic pattern?" and so forth instead of just asking, "What is his I.Q.?"

SCOPE OF THE PSYCHOLOGICAL EXAMINATION

What should be the scope of a psychological examination in a mental hospital is a problem which is not easily solved. The difficulty resides not only in the fact that the psychologist is called upon to do a variety of jobs; but also in fact that the psychological techniques as presently developed are very time consuming. Consider, for example, what might constitute a relatively modest testing program, say for subjects aged 15-30. This would ordinarily include (1) an individual general intelligence test; (2) a personality inventory; and (3) a short battery of educational tests.

The time required for such an examination in the case of mental patients will ordinarily take about two hours, not counting write-up of the report and analysis. If to these latter, one adds as is often desirable—a projective technique such as a Rorschach or Thematic Apperception test, plus some tests attempting vocational appraisal, the time required for a complete study is easily doubled. This means that a psychologist can see at most one patient a day, a situation even if feasible is not only too costly but also contrary to the time consumed by other professions in their examinations. Psychiatrists and physicians, even if not complaining, are continually asking why a psychologist needs so long a time to do an examination. At present this problem is met in part by having an intern or graduate student do some of the routine testing and in part by cutting down the testing program to a bare minimum. A more satisfactory approach would be the development of shorter examination techniques and the increasing use of the diagnostic interview. Unfortunately neither is as yet available to any considerable degree.

TRAINING OF THE PSYCHOLOGIST

The training of the psychologist planning to work in a mental hospital setup varies in different parts of the country. Generally this variation depends not so much upon theoretical ideals as upon practical opportunities. In most cases the young psychologist is not guided but allowed to drift into this field. Very few universities offer a program preparing the student for a job as psychologist in a mental hospital.

Some part training, however, is often afforded by work at psychoeducational clinics which are now attached to a number of colleges and education departments in various parts of the country. Other areas for practical instruction are state and municipal employment and vocational services. But apart from these most of the specific training of psychologists hoping to enter the psychiatric field is being achieved through internships that have been established at various mental hospitals.[3] These in-

3 [See S. Rosenzweig, W. T. Root and G. B. Pearson, "Education for Clinical Psychology," for a discussion of an experimental intern-training program at Western State Psychiatric Hospital in Pittsburgh, Pa., to be published in a forthcoming number of the JOURNAL OF CONSULTING PSYCHOLOGY.—EDITOR.]

ternships are usually for six months to a year and carry a very small, if any, stipend beyond general maintenance. In this respect they resemble the medical internships except that the psychology students are often less prepared to begin full-time work than are medical interns. Usually the psychological intern will require considerable elementary instruction in the administration of most of the standard tests, acquaintance with which is likely to have been more theoretical than actual. Such examinations as are done by the intern on patients are usually done under supervision of the psychologist-in-charge. Cases are gone over and considerable attention is paid not only to interpretation of results but to the proper ways of writing up a psychological report. As in other fields, the intern will often have to do a bit of unlearning.

This brings us to a consideration of the desired preparatory curriculum for students going into mental hospital work while at the university. It would be easy to list the types of courses by title but obviously what is important is what the course actually consists of rather than under what title it appears in the catalogue. For example, all recommendations would include as prerequisite a course in abnormal psychology. But if the course in abnormal psychology only includes the reading of a general text and instruction by a person who has never had contact with mental patients, its value would be very limited. The point here is, of course, that the training of people preparing for psychological work in mental hospitals as well as clinical psychology in general, should be by individuals actually in the field. This holds for other applied subjects.

Apart from the introductory courses in general and an elementary course in experimental psychology, the most important preparatory courses are undoubtedly those in psychometrics. By psychometrics is meant not a theoretical discussion of tests and techniques but actual mastery of the administration and evaluation of standard clinical tests. Second, a course in the interpretation of results and instruction in report writing. Third, a course in abnormal psychology given in conjunction with a mental hospital or mental hygiene clinic. Courses in child development, and subject disabilities are desirable. So also is a course on projective techniques, especially the Rorschach. For those planning to go into research, advanced experimental, statistics and physiological psychology should be added.

In addition to his educational training the student planning to enter the field of clinical psychology should also meet a number of personality requirements. These requirements include first, emotional maturity; second, an ability to deal with and get along with people; third, an ability to utilize one's formal knowledge in practical situations. In addition, one might add a facility to express oneself clearly in writing. This is perhaps a good deal to ask for a position which generally pays less than college teaching, but the requirements are indispensable not only because they are necessary for the personal success of the individual psychologist but for the prestige of psychology itself. In more ways than one the psychologist in the field represents the practical achievements of psychology, and the individuals to whom this representation is entrusted should so far as possible be the most capable individuals available.

REFERENCES

1. Babcock, H. "An Experiment in the Measurement of Mental Deterioration," *Archives of Psychology*, 1930, 18, No. 117.
2. Bender, M. B. and Sairtsky, N. "Micropsia and Teleopsia Limited to the Temporal Fields of Vision," *Archives of Opthalolgy, Chicago*, 1943, 29: 904-8.
3. Goldstein, L. and Steinfeld, J. I. "The Conditioning of Sexual Behavior by Visual Agnosia," *Bulletin of Forest Sanitation*, 1942, 1 (2) : 137-45.
4. Hunt, W. A., Wittson, C. L. and Harris, H. L. "Temporary Mental Impairment Following a Petit Mal Attack," *Journal of Abnormal and Social Psychology*, 1942, 37: 566.
5. Jastak, J. "The Manual-Minded Child," *Delaware State Medical Journal*, 1942, 14: 126-29.
6. Piotrowski, Z. A. "The Rorschach Method as a Prognostic Aid in the Insulin Shock Treatment of Schizophrenics," *Psychiatric Quarterly*, 1941, 15: 807-22.
7. Rabin, A. I. "Test-Score Patterns in Schizophrenia and Non-Psychotic States," *Journal of Psychology*, 1941, 12: 91-100.
8. Schilder, P. *Mind: Perception and Mind in Their Constructive Aspects.* New York: Columbia University Press, 1942. Pp. 432.
9. Shakow, D. "Deterioration in Schizophrenia as Reflected in Performance on a Variety of Psychological Tasks," *Psychological Bulletin*, 1942, 39: 508.
10. Shipley, W. C. and Burlingame, C. C. "A Convenient Self-Administering Scale for Measuring Intellectual Impairment in Psychotics," *American Journal of Psychiatry*, 1941, 97: 1313-25.
11. Wechsler, D., Halpern, F. and Jaros, E. "Psychometric Study of Insulin-Treated Schizophrenics," *Psychiatric Quarterly*, 1940, 14: 466-76.
12. Wittman, P. "Psychometric Efficiency Levels for Psychotic and Age Classifications," *Journal of Abnormal and Social Psychology*, 1943, 38: 335-50.
13. Zubin, J. and Barrera, S. E. "Effect of Electric Convulsive Therapy on Memory," *Proceedings of the Society for Experimental Biology of New York*, 1941, 48: 596-97.

PART VI

INTRODUCTION

Papers reflecting interest, discussion, and research on clinical issues are included in this section. Three areas are represented: mental deficiency, effects of alcohol, and psychological disturbances.

The work of Alfred Binet, and the test developed by him, were directly oriented toward the problem of identifying children who would have difficulty succeeding in academic settings of low intellectual ability. It is not surprising that consequent tests have placed major emphasis on identifying the presence and degree of mental retardation in both children and adults. As with other psychologists, David Wechsler is concerned with mental deficiency, both in terms of its conceptual and practical natures. One of his earlier approaches to the field appeared in 1935 under the title ''The Concept of Mental Deficiency in Theory and Practice'' (1). The reader will note that even at that time, he rejects the idea of deficiency as an entity, placing emphasis instead on the fact that a definition of deficiency must reflect its practical nature. Though there may be a psychometric definition, in the long run the label must be reserved for those individuals who are unable to use the ability present to them in dealing with life situations. Certainly there are instances of individuals who may achieve scores on tests which would signify some degree of deficiency, yet they may function quite well in society. By contrast, there are individuals who score well enough on our tests to escape the psychometric label who are unable to make adequate adjustments and for intellectual reasons. These exceptions occur often enough to warrant serious consideration of Wechsler's viewpoint. He includes case studies and examples to illustrate the socially defective nature of some individuals as compared with psychometric defectives.

He concludes that there may be more than one type of mental deficiency. There is the intellectual defective who demonstrates this fate by his performance on tests. However, there is also the social defective who must be judged more on the basis of his life history and his ability to cope with the environment than test scores *per se*. Wechsler also leaves the possibility for a third type of defective, one he considers emotional or moral in nature, and one much more difficult to define and diagnose. There are sufficient instances in clinical settings, he believes, to warrant the inclusion of this possible category. In many ways his description of types of defectives and the practical meaning of the terminology could well be applied to some of the current quarrels with misclassification of individuals and the overuse of labelling on psychometric bases alone. Wechsler, throughout his career, has advocated great care in labelling with the ultimate decision being placed on the social context, not the psychometric one.

The Stanford–Binet Revision was commonly used in making judgments about mental deficiency even with adults. No appropriate scale for the purpose, standardized on an adult sample, was available prior to the publication of the Wechsler–Bellevue. Comparisons for predictive efficiency were possible by 1939, and one such study is included here (2). Wechsler's position that the Binet was an inadequate measure to be used with adults was valid; whether or not the Bellevue Scale was an improvement simply because it was designed for and standardized on adults had yet to be demonstrated. More than a comparison, however, the authors were able to make some comparisons of the precision of intellectual ability measures for diagnosis of mental deficiency.

They compared the tests in terms of "Relative Prognostic Efficiency," defined as the forecasting efficiency of the test for psychiatric diagnosis and disposition of the individual. The results substantiated the use of the Bellevue, at least in terms of its correlation with eventual decisions on a medical basis. The Stanford–Binet was much less successful in correlating with psychiatric commitment, indicating that the psychometric definition from test score with this examination was insufficient. The Bellevue did a better job, though again the forecasting efficiency was low enough to indicate that many other factors do indeed enter into the diagnosis and are not always accounted for in test scores.

The global expression contained in Full Scale I.Q.'s on the Bellevue was the basis for prediction in the study previously cited. There is also the possibility that subtest performance may be helpful in identifying deficiency. Again in conjunction with Israel and Balinsky, Wechsler conducted and published a study of this type in 1941 (3), intended as a follow-up. The subtests of the Bellevue were compared for borderline and defective individuals to determine if performance differences were great enough to clearly differentiate the two groups. Indeed, they found that the mean scores on each of the ten subtests in the Bellevue showed significant differences except for memory span for digits. Both groups performed better on Performance subtests than Verbal. This finding has been repeated in other studies, but with still other studies yielding conflicting results as well. Overall, the comparison was favorable to the Bellevue and indicated the plausible use of subtest results in making decisions about degree of mental retardation where this is an issue.

The second category included in this section deals with effects of alcohol on behavior. The first of the papers is an abbreviated form of Wechsler's masters thesis done at Columbia and published in 1917 (4). He considers deficiencies in retention which result from Korsakoff's psychosis from two viewpoints. The extensiveness of the defect in memory is the first matter of some concern here while the more specific nature or outcomes of the defect is the second question posed by the study. Wechsler used retention in this study in the restricted sense of ability to reproduce new impressions after a given interval of time. His review of the rather limited literature to that date on the problem is deleted in this quotation. Part of his rationale is also missing, and it seems worthwhile to note that he makes the assumption that the primary reason for a retention defect in Korsakoff's psychosis is the fact that the individual is unable to form new associations.

Wechsler describes his tasks and procedures. The results represented a distinct and significant contribution to the field at that time, indicating that his assumption initially was the correct one. The primary cause of retention defects with persons who have Korsakoff's psychosis is the inability to form new associations.

The second paper included, dealing with the effects of alcohol on mental activity (5), reviews the literature and the results of research done on the issue by Wechsler. As he notes, most studies have considered momentary changes in psychological functions and, important as these may be, the issue of long range effects from alcoholic consumption has been relatively unstudied. It is agreed that alcohol has a detrimental effect on immediate psychological functioning to some degree. Unfortunately, many writers tended to extrapolate from these findings to long range ones without the appropriate basis for so doing. Though longitudinal studies were not available, terminal cases offered evidence relative to brain pathology that might be primarily due to the excessive consumption of alcohol. For this purpose again, he used data from individuals who were diagnosed as Korsakoff's psychosis.

Having surveyed the matter of immediate effects from alcoholic consumption and the deteriorative effects behaviorally from brain pathology in the extreme condition of Korsakoff's syndrone, Wechsler raises an issue really untouched to that point. This is the matter of effects from prolonged use of alcohol in moderate amounts, or even where excessive consumption occurs without obvious pathological effects. He points out that theory would indicate some kind of intermediate results between the two extremes. But, more to the point, he was able to report results from a study of such a group. Performance on subtests of the Bellevue were analyzed and conclusions drawn. It is of more than passing interest that older individuals, ones who had been consuming alcohol chronically over a considerable number of years, showed a corresponding decrease in the ability to analyze and organize in a logical fashion. This effect was even greater than the loss in memory function. There is evidence, as he concludes, that prolonged use of alcohol has its effects on mental functioning even though there may not be evidence of brain pathology as such.

Ever aware to alternatives, he points out that studies have concentrated on detrimental effects: what alcohol does to the individual. He notes that it is time for someone to investigate what it is that alcohol may do for the individual, if anything, so that positive as well as negative effects can be documented.

In a contributed chapter in the book *The Psychoneuroses* by Israel S. Wechsler, his brother, David Wechsler discussed the psychoneurotic and factors bearing on intelligence. His definition of psychoneurosis is very broad, but he does relate it more specifically to disturbances in emotional and instinctive organization.

In his survey of the literature on the psychoneuroses, Wechsler points to the frequent occurrence of statements about the average or above average ability in the psychoneurotic. This is a position with which he contends, basing his opinion on personal observation and data that indicate the psychoneurotic being intellectually somewhat inferior. Thus, one must include in the diagnostic pattern not only instinctive and emotional disorganization, but also somewhat lowered intellectual ability. The picture is complicated somewhat by the fact that degree of intellectual impairment varies from one type of psychoneurosis to another. There remains the question of a cause and effect relationship.

Part of the problem lies in one's definition of intelligence. A definition determines what measures may be appropriate to use. But there is no universally accepted definition, and many generalizations may be drawn from the abundant material available from tests. General measures cannot offer evidence about specific abilities or disabilities, though the concept of "scatter" has already been recognized and employed even with some of the items in the Stanford–Binet. Wechsler concludes that psychoneurotics may differ in three ways from the normal. There is, first, the matter of general intellectual level; second, variability in performance; and, third, special disabilities affecting given mental abilities.

From research available, he states that psychoneurotics, as a group, perform significantly below the average intellectual functioning of the society. One may expect to find in the psychoneurotic special disabilities for given intellectual operations, and types of neuroses may be hierarchically ordered in a systematic fashion for mean test performance. However, this latter point is on somewhat more tenuous grounds.

As always, he considers the implications of such findings. He points out that, though there is an association between lowered ability and psychoneurosis, no correlation has been reported and certainly there is no casual relationship which may be identified. Allied with this is the fact that there is overlap between the psychoneurotic and normal in ability, making hard and fast statements impossible. Though the psychoneurotic usually will have intelligence test scores below the average for the society, the importance to attach to this fact is not so clear. Other aspects of the condition must also be considered, namely the matter of emotional imbalance and its consequences. If such factors as emotional imbalance, instinctual drive, and unconscious motivation could be measured with the same degree of reliability as is now true of intelligence, Wechsler believes that the neurotic would show even greater divergence in these traits than he does in intellectual ability. This does not alter the fact that there is indeed a lowered intellectual functioning among psychoneurotics. This fact may have value and Wechsler comments on the several values obtained from an assessment of an individual's mental capacity.

Two papers are included here which deal with psychological disturbances of various types. The first deals with the use of the mental deterioration index devised from the Bellevue Scale (6). The concept of the "hold" and "don't hold" tests is presented and applications described. Case studies are included and an appraisal of the value of the procedure and its accuracy. He suggests a number of other studies needed in order to verify the potential usefulness of the index.

A final paper is an empirical study of the ability of the WISC subtests to identify test signs which might be used with schizophrenic children (7). This study, done in conjunction with Eugenia Jaros, examined performance on the WISC to determine what signs might be usable for diagnostic purposes. Wechsler and Jaros recorded the signs and their frequency of occurrence by age levels in the sample used and applied these in turn to a cross sectional group to determine the error which might be made, particularly in terms of identifying false positives. As pointed out in the Manuals of the WAIS and the WISC, the assignment of individuals to a clinical group on the basis of test patterns or signs or scores invalidly is a matter to be avoided at all costs. Obviously, it cannot be completely avoided; it is possible however to combine enough signs, Wechsler's method of successive sieves, so that the error which may be made will be reduced to a minimum. This is illustrated in this particular study with a documented report on the accuracy of the procedure. The discussion section adds dimensionality to the data. Despite the success of the procedure followed, Wechsler and Jaros make it clear that the diagnosis should not be based on any particular test characteristics as such so much as upon the total picture of the individual child and his ability to function.

The complex of papers included in this section emphasize Wechsler's basic concern for the individual functioning in his culture. Diagnostic categories and labels may be used in the best interest of the person, but they must be accurate and appropriate. In the final analysis, the burden of proof is on the clinician, not the patient. The integrity and worth of the person remain paramount.

THE CONCEPT OF MENTAL DEFICIENCY
IN THEORY AND PRACTICE*

DAVID WECHSLER

Bellevue Psychiatric Hospital, New York City

While definitions of mental deficiency have varied both as to assumption of cause and opinions as to its nature, nearly all of them, however divergent on other points, have had this in common, namely, that they looked upon mental deficiency as a definite entity. This view, in the light of practical experience, seems to be incorrect.

Mental deficiency is not like typhoid fever or general paresis or encephalitis lethargica, a definite entity. It does not define a group along scientific but along practical lines. Mental defectives are primarily individuals who because of lack of mental ability need special care, education or institutionalization. They are individuals who, for other than special physical disabilities or brain disease or psychotic conditions, are unable to manage themselves or to cope with their ordinary environment. The older clinicians were inclined to ascribe the cause of this inadequacy to various factors, but in recent years, particularly following the introduction of psychometric tests there has been a tendency to ascribe or even identify mental deficiency with lack of intellectual ability. Accumulated experience has, however, shown that in spite of the great value of psychometric tests in detecting and measuring degrees of mental deficiency, it is not possible to define mental deficiency exclusively in terms of mental age or I. Q., for the reason that mental deficiency involves not merely a lack of intellectual ability but also an incapacity to apply that ability in concrete life situations. Practically, this is shown by the fact that individuals not defective by social and other criteria are often rated as mental defectives by test results, while, conversely, others who by their daily behavior have proved themselves defective, often attain scores which fail to designate them as such. Part of this lack of correlation is due to the inadequacy of the tests themselves, but more important is the fact that mental deficiency as actually met with is not the result or mani-

*Paper read at annual meeting of American Psychological Association, September 7, 1934.
Reprinted from *The Psychiatric Quarterly*, 1935, 9, 232-236.

festation of intellectual defect alone. The following is an illustrative case:

J. M., 26 years old, native white, was arrested on a charge of impairing the morals of a minor (a girl of 10 years). He is reported to have made similar attempts on several previous occasions and had, for some years, been a persistent problem on this account. The family states: ''We have always kept an eye on him because we felt he would get into trouble''

Physical examination: Unattractive-looking youth who appears to be younger than he is. General physical and neurological examination as well as blood Wassermann is negative.

Psychiatric examination: Appears dull and indifferent and childish. General reactions—immature. Is careless about person, but able to take care of himself. Diagnosis: mental defective—moron.

Psychological examination: Stanford-Binet, 13 years 8 months, I. Q. (15 years) 91. Scatter IX-XVI, inclusive. Except for designs (patient had bad vision), no failures below 12th year level.

Work history: Found it difficult to get a job but had a number procured for him by father through intercession. Worked for a short time as messenger in a public market; also, as laborer in Department of Public Works.

The foregoing is typical of several scores of cases that have come to my attention in a relatively brief time. Frequently, they are sex delinquents but, more often than not, individuals who have gotten in trouble with the law or otherwise proved themselves incapable of meeting the ordinary exigencies of social adjustment. On psychometric examinations they rate dull normal, average and, sometimes, higher. But, if judged by social criteria they are mentally defective.

That such a group exists has been long recognized by those dealing first hand with delinquent and socially inadequate individuals. They are patients, whom Tredgold has called ''individuals lacking both in prudence and moral sense'' though yet suffering from no scholastic or educational disability. As Tredgold well points out, an individual falling into this group ''far from being illiterate, may have quite a good range of educational requirements. He may be nimble-witted, a good conversationalist, plausible in argument and be able to give a good account of himself.'' In spite of this he is anti-social and requires supervision for his own welfare as well as for the protection of others. What he lacks essentially is an ordinary adaptiveness or, ''wisdom in the moral sense'' and it is important to realize, as Tredgold insists, that such a person ''is mentally defective in the usual and necessary sense of the term.''

In contradistinction to the above described type there is another who systematically rates as a mental defective on mental tests, but, who can in no way be judged as such, when diagnosed on the basis of concrete social standards, i. e., in terms of capacity to adjust to the normal demands of his social and economic environment. They are frequently illiterate and, commonly, individuals coming from definite social strata where opportunity for education is small, and stultifying labor the general rule; many belong to what might be termed the "peasant type", as indeed they frequently are by origin. However, the first case of this type that came to my attention was a native, white Oklahoman of 28, who had come up for individual psychological examinations because he had failed to pass the Army Alpha and Army Beta intelligence tests. On both Stanford-Binet and the Yerkes Point Scale he obtained a mental age of less than 8 years. Nevertheless, before entering the Army he had gotten along very well, was supporting a family, had been working as a skilled oil-driller for several years and, at time of draft, was earning from $60 to $75 per week. Incidentally, he was making the grade as a soldier, and would not have come to the attention of the authorities had he not failed on the psychological tests.

It would be possible to cite many cases, particularly from among adults of foreign birth, who rate systematically defective even on non-verbal tests, but whose social life history of at least an adequate adjustment contradicts this classification. Nor can we disregard at this point the question of negro intelligence-test results, which if taken at face value, would necessitate our classifying some 40 per cent of that group as mental defectives. No one, I believe, at all in contact with reality, would venture such a conclusion, however much supported by test results. In any case, actual clinical experience shows that there are certain individuals who regularly test as very inferior and frequently as mental defectives on standard psychometric tests but who, nevertheless, are able to adapt and adjust—make good housewives, adequate breadwinners, useful citizens and can and do get along not only in rural but urban environments. It is clear that these people are not mentally defective as defined by law or common sense. Nevertheless, by the tests available at present for measuring intellectual ability they are syste-

matically selected as inferior individuals on a par with those who
are recognized as needing institutional care as mental defectives.

From facts such as these I have become convinced there is not
one, but several kinds of mental deficiency—that the concept of
mental deficiency is far from a simple entity. There are at least
two and probably three types of mental deficiency. The first is the
intellectual defective, diagnosable as such by the usual psychometric tests; the second, the social, for whom the life history of
the individual is the most satisfactory criterion; and, third—the
emotional or "moral" defective whose precise definition is extremely difficult to give, but whose existence, to any one who has
had any first hand experience at a large clinic, is an observable
reality. Between all three there is frequently a certain degree of
correlation, but this correlation is not sufficiently high to make any
one an unfailing diagnostic indicator of the other.

Much of the controversy between psychologists and psychiatrists
has resulted from the fact that each assumes a different criterion
of mental deficiency and, this difference would disappear if both
realized that mental deficiency as a unitary entity does not exist in
fact. The psychologist is correct in his assertion that at present
his method is the only one that gives us a quantitative measure of
intellectual efficiency, and the psychiatrist is equally correct in
maintaining that there are types of mental deficiency which psychometric tests do not detect; but both are wrong in believing that
any single criterion will suffice.

From what has been said it is clear that the diagnosis of mental
deficiency is not merely a matter of getting the correct I. Q., but
involves a consideration of a number of factors for which clinical
and psychiatric experience is essential. There is for example, on
the one hand, the problem of differentiating between a low functioning mental level due to deterioration in conditions like general
paresis or hebephrenia and those due to true intellectual arrest.
And on the other hand, of distinguishing between inadequate social
functioning due to psychopathic personality or environment factors from persistent inadequacy due to what we have defined as
social or moral deficiency. The difficulty of making differential
diagnoses in certain cases does not, however, justify the failure to

differentiate them altogether, much less the persistence of a practice which assumes that mental deficiency can be diagnosed through any single approach.

To sum up, experience has shown that the concept of mental deficiency, based on I. Q. ratings or any other single criterion, frequently fails in actual application. The reason for this is that there is not one but several kinds of mental deficiency—actually at least two types, the social and the intellectual, and, probably a third, the emotional or the "moral" defective. Between them there is a certain degree of correlation, but this correlation is not sufficiently high to make any one a diagnostic indicator of the others, and, in any case, it is quite certain that the concept of mental deficiency as a definite entity has no reality in fact.

THE RELATIVE EFFECTIVENESS OF THE STANFORD-BINET AND THE BELLEVUE INTELLIGENCE SCALE IN DIAGNOSING MENTAL DEFICIENCY*

B. BALINSKY, H. ISRAEL, and D. WECHSLER

The Psychological Department of the Bellevue Psychiatric Hospital, New York City

O NE OF the most trying problems which confronts the clinical psychologist is what to do when his psychometric results are in disagreement either with his clinical impressions or the social history or psychiatric data. This is particularly true in the borderline case where there is an immediate practical problem of recommending or not recommending the subject for commitment to an institution. In most mental hygiene clinics and state hospitals the final onus generally falls upon the psychiatrist who, it is assumed, not only takes into consideration the results of the psychometric, but the entire social and psychiatric history of the patient. The weight given to each varies with the attitude of the psychiatrist, his training, and the relative standing of the psychologist. But even where test results are generally accepted there may occur differences of opinion as to their interpretation and discrepancies between ratings obtained on different tests as well as between estimates of the individual's actual capacity to adjust.

Various explanations have been offered to account for discrepancies between ratings obtained from psychometrics and estimates of mental deficiency based on psychiatric and social histories. In this paper we do not propose to take up the merits of these explanations, but merely to investigate one specific aspect of the problem, namely, the relative prognostic efficiency of two general intelligence scales—the Stanford-Binet and the recently standardized Bellevue Intelligence Tests. By prognostic efficiency, we shall mean the relative per cent of forecast as indicated by the degree of correlation of the respective tests with ultimate psychiatric diagnosis.

We have chosen the Stanford-Binet because it has for a long time been the basis of intelligence classification in most parts of the country and because such criticisms as have been made against the efficacy of psychometrics for detecting the upper levels of mental deficiency amounted, for most practical purposes, to strictures upon the efficiency of the Binet Tests. The Bellevue Adult† was chosen because this scale was devised to meet these strictures and, more particularly, to obtain measures of intelligence which would correlate better with practical criteria. It differs from the Binet Scale in a number of ways, but principally by the fact (1) that it is a point and not an age scale, (2) that it has been standardized on adults as well as adolescents and (3) that it consists of performance as well as verbal tests. This last item is of particular importance because of the large psychometric discrepancies frequently found between ratings obtained on the same subject when simultaneously tested with both performance and verbal

*Reprinted from *American Journal of Orthopsychiatry*, 1939, 9, 798-801. Copyright 1939, the American Orthopsychiatric Association, Inc. Reproduced by permission.

† For detailed description of the Bellevue Scales—see D. Wechsler, *The Measurement of Adult Intelligence*. Baltimore, 1939.

scales. This is especially true of the borderline and high grade defective groups. When such discrepancies are found, the common practice among most psychologists has been to accept the Binet as a "true" measure of the subject's native intellectual endowment and to look upon the performance rating as measuring rather some special ability or disability. We think that this procedure has been the source of serious error, but shall not elaborate upon its shortcomings at this time. Suffice it merely to point out that the Bellevue Scales make no such a priori assumption in regard to the inferior value of the performance tests as measures of general intelligence.

Two groups of subjects were used in this study. All of the cases of both groups were brought to Bellevue Hospital to be examined either because of simple retardation, or because of retardation with behavior disorders. The behavior disorders were of a type frequently associated with mental deficiency, such as truancy, unmanageability at home and school, petty stealing and sex offenses. None of the cases had any organic or special mental symptoms.

The first group of 63 cases were subjects who had been examined at Bellevue Hospital during 1933 and 1934. Of these cases 40 had been recommended and 23 not recommended to state institutions for mental defectives. Fifty of the cases had been given the Stanford-Binet and 13 had been diagnosed by other methods. Late in 1936 and early in 1937, 49 of the original 63 cases were re-tested with the Bellevue Intelligence Scale, with the result that ratings on both tests were now available on 36 of them. The age range of the subjects at the time of examination varied from 10 to 22 years with a median age of 16. Somewhat over 50 per cent of the cases, however, fell within the age range of 14 to 17.

The second group consisted of 134 subjects all of whom had been examined in Bellevue Hospital between December 1937 and March 1939. Of these, 70 had been recommended for institutionalization. All these cases had been tested with either the Binet, the Bellevue, or both, prior to the clinical diagnosis. One hundred and sixteen cases had been given the Binet, 81 the Bellevue Full Scale and 89 the Bellevue Performance Test. Sixty-three had been given both the Binet Test and the Bellevue Full Scale.

All recommendations were made by the psychiatrist after a study of all the facts obtained from the case history, the psychiatric interviews and the psychological examinations and observations. These recommendations were either for commitment to a state institution for mental defectives or non-commitment. Biserial correlations were computed between these recommendations in terms of commitment or non-commitment and the IQ's obtained on the various tests given the subjects.

For all the cases in the first group (the Bellevue Test having been given from 2 to 3 years after the recommendations were made) the following results were obtained:

Binet IQ × Recommendation for
commitment or non-commitment $= .664 \pm .073, N = 50$

Bellevue Full IQ × Recommendation
for commitment or non-commitment $= .753 \pm .072, N = 49$
Bellevue Verbal IQ × Recommendation
for commitment or non-commitment $= .705 \pm .079, N = 49$
Bellevue Perf. IQ × Recommendation
for commitment or non-commitment $= .577 \pm .095, N = 49$

For the cases in the first group on whom *both* Binet and Bellevue results were available, the following are the results:

Binet IQ × Recommendation for commitment or non-commitment $= .611 \pm .103, N = 36$
Bellevue Full IQ × Recommendation
for commitment or non-commitment $= .720 \pm .086, N = 36$
Bellevue Verbal IQ × Recommendation
for commitment or non-commitment $= .705 \pm .089, N = 36$
Bellevue Perf. IQ × Recommendation
for commitment or non-commitment $= .481 \pm .119, N = 36$

The correlations for the first group consisting of all the cases and those for the cases which had been given both Binet and Bellevue Tests are of similar order.

For all the cases in the second group (Binet and Bellevue Tests having been given before the recommendations were made), the following results obtained:

Binet IQ × recommendation for
commitment or non-commitment $= .325 \pm .071, N = 116$
Bellevue Full IQ × recommendation for
commitment or non-commitment $= .791 \pm .048, N = 81$
Bellevue Verbal IQ × recommendation
for commitment or non-commitment $= .409 \pm .082, N = 81$
Bellevue Perf. IQ × recommendation
for commitment or non-commitment $= .688 \pm .055, N = 89$

For the cases in the second group on whom *both* Binet and Bellevue results were available, the following are the results:

Binet IQ × recommendation for
commitment or non-commitment $= .274 \pm .100, N = 63$
Bellevue Full IQ × recommendation
for commitment or non-commitment $= .785 \pm .054, N = 63$
Bellevue Verbal IQ × recommendation
for commitment or non-commitment $= .330 \pm .097, N = 63$
Bellevue Perf. IQ × recommendation
for commitment or non-commitment $= .693 \pm .066, N = 63$

Examination of the above data reveals the following: (1) The Bellevue Full Scale IQ's give systematically the highest correlations with psychiatrists' recommendations in each investigated group, (2) The Bellevue Verbal IQ's give second highest correlations in the first group and third highest in the second group. (3) The Bellevue Performance IQ's give the lowest correlations in the first group and second highest in the second group. (4) The Binet IQ's give the third highest correlations in the first group and lowest in the second group.

These results indicate a marked superiority of the Bellevue Full Scale over the Stanford-Binet in the effectiveness of the tests as instruments in clinical diagnosis of mental deficiency. This superiority is perhaps even more effectively brought out, if instead of merely considering the numerical values of the coefficients of correlation, we translate them into their prognostic efficiencies. When this is done the forecasting efficiencies (as obtained from the bi-serial r's of the second group) of the Bellevue turns out to be about 40 per cent as against only about 5 per cent for the Stanford-Binet.

The results also suggest the importance of including performnace tests when attempting to differentiate between borderline intelligence and mental deficiency. This is indicated first by the fact that the Bellevue Full Scale (which includes the Performance Scale) always gives the highest correlations with the psychiatrists' recommendations and second by the fact that the Performance Scale correlations in the second group are significantly higher than the Stanford-Binet Test or the Bellevue Verbal alone.

The low forecasting efficiency of the Stanford-Binet in differentiating between the borderline and high grade defective groups accounts, in part at least, for the frequent complaint of psychiatrists that the Stanford-Binet cannot be used alone in the diagnosis of mental deficiency.

A STUDY OF THE SUB-TESTS OF THE BELLEVUE INTELLIGENCE SCALE IN BORDERLINE AND MENTAL DEFECTIVE CASES*

DAVID WECHSLER, HYMAN ISRAEL, and BENJAMIN BALINSKY

The Psychological Department, Bellevue Psychiatric Hospital

IN a previous paper(1) we had occasion to discuss the problem of the interpretation of differences in intelligence ratings attained by subjects when tested with different intelligence scales. Discrepancies in functioning level are, however, to be found not only when subjects are tested with different scales, but are also indicated by differences in scores or items passed on the different parts of the same scale. These differences will ordinarily not be reflected in the gross score or I.Q., but are frequently of diagnostic value.(2)

Our present day study is a further investigation of the diagnostic value of the Bellevue Intelligence Scale through an analysis of the comparative performance of borderline with high to mid-grade mental defectives on the 10 sub-tests of the scale. In terms of intelligence level, the groups compared will be subjects attaining Bellevue I.Q.'s of from 50 to 65 on the one hand, and from 66 to 79 on the other. The subjects studied have been further differentiated into three age groups, namely, ages 10 to 14; ages 15 to 19 and ages 20 to 49 respectively. To the best of our knowledge, the cases are not complicated by special psychopathies. The age distribution of our subjects and total number of cases used in the studies are given in Table I.

TABLE I
DISTRIBUTION OF CASES

Age	M. Defective	Borderline
10–14	51	63
15–19	38	53
20–49	45	82
10–49	134	198

In order to compare the test-response differences between the age groups, the respective means and standard deviation at each age level were calculated. There are shown in Table II. From these data were next calculated critical

$$\text{ratios}\left(\text{C.R.} = \frac{\text{diff.}}{\sigma \text{ diff.}} \right) \text{ between the}$$

mean scores of the groups compared. These are given in Table III. As a final point of interest, the percent of cases receiving a standard score of 9 or more on each sub-test was ascertained. A score of 9 was chosen because it is at the lower limit of the mean average adult score for each sub-test. These percents are shown in Table IV.

Examination of the data given in the various tables yields several important facts: (1) The differences between the mean scores on each of the ten sub-

*Reprinted from *American Journal of Mental Deficiency*, 1941, 45, 555-558. Reprinted by permission of the American Association on Mental Deficiency.

263

TABLE II

MEANS AND STANDARD DEVIATIONS FOR EACH SUB-TEST

Test		Mental Defective Group Ages				Borderline Group Ages			
		10–14	15–19	20–49	10–49	10–14	15–19	20–49	10–49
Inf.	(Mean)	3.05	4.32	4.26	3.81	3.91	5.56	5.66	5.13
	(S. D.)	1.14	1.71	1.45	1.55	1.78	1.96	2.16	2.24
Comp.	(Mean)	3.91	4.58	4.52	4.46	5.02	6.16	6.00	5.73
	(S. D.)	1.83	1.83	1.76	1.84	1.41	1.79	1.80	1.75
Arith.	(Mean)	1.78	2.58	2.99	2.41	3.82	4.16	4.99	4.39
	(S. D.)	1.61	1.91	2.07	1.93	2.92	2.45	2.63	2.73
Dig. Sp.	(Mean)	4.48	4.87	4.41	4.57	5.56	6.24	5.80	5.16
	(S. D.)	1.90	2.28	2.23	2.13	1.80	2.21	2.35	2.16
Sim.	(Mean)	3.50	4.28	3.45	3.62	4.27	5.50	5.47	5.17
	(S. D.)	1.81	1.23	2.21	1.95	1.83	2.05	2.34	2.20
5—Verbal	(Mean)	3.34	4.13	3.93	3.77	4.52	5.52	5.58	5.12
P. A.	(Mean)	5.01	5.42	3.31	4.57	6.99	7.99	5.05	6.47
	(S. D.)	2.14	1.94	2.04	2.24	2.65	2.24	2.16	2.66
P. C.	(Mean)	3.23	4.93	2.94	3.61	6.01	7.07	5.68	6.16
	(S. D.)	2.19	2.75	2.58	2.62	2.67	2.50	2.66	2.67
Obj.	(Mean)	4.19	4.80	3.21	4.03	7.63	7.29	6.33	7.00
	(S. D.)	2.68	2.81	2.74	2.91	2.84	2.85	3.55	3.11
Bl. Des.	(Mean)	3.95	3.82	3.43	3.74	6.20	7.22	5.26	6.08
	(S. D.)	1.88	1.98	1.55	1.82	2.41	2.44	2.02	2.40
Subs.	(Mean)	4.99	5.82	3.74	4.81	6.77	8.12	5.42	6.57
	(S. D.)	2.06	2.00	2.12	2.22	2.18	2.31	1.89	2.37
5—Perf.	(Mean)	4.27	4.96	3.33	4.15	6.72	7.54	5.56	6.46

TABLE III

RELIABILITY OF DIFFERENCES OF MEAN TEST SCORES OBTAINED BY DEFECTIVE AND BORDERLINE CASES

Test	Age 10–14 C.R.	Age 15–19 C.R.	Age 20–49 C.R.	Age 10–49 C.R.
Inf.	3.14	3.21	4.50	6.31
Comp.	3.57	4.09	4.49	6.32
Arith.	4.73	3.64	4.83	7.75
Dig. Sp.	3.10	2.86	3.38	2.46
Sim.*	....	....		3.79
P.A.	4.42	5.80	4.54	6.99
P.C.	6.11	3.76	5.79	8.62
Obj.	6.64	4.12	5.51	8.88
Bl. Design	5.59	7.33	5.86	10.10
Subs.	4.47	5.08	4.41	6.89

* Similarities test was added later. Many of the subjects given the other sub-tests were not given the Similarities. The number of cases at each age level was too few to calculate a reliable test of significance between the various means.

tests attained by the mental defective and borderline groups respectively, are all significant except in the case of Memory Span for Digits. (2) The Performance tests (Picture Arrangement, Picture Completion, Object Assembly, Block Design and Substitution) are easier than the Verbal tests (Information, Comprehension, Arithmetic, Digit Span and Similarities) for both defective and borderline groups. For the combined age groups, the mean scores for the Performance tests are 4.15 for the mental defectives and 6.46 for the borderline group. (3) Comparing absolute Performance and Verbal test scores, age by age, we find that for the age group 10–14 years and 15–19 years, the Performance is higher than the Verbal but that for the age group 20–49, the Verbal and Performance test scores are practically identical.

TABLE IV

PER CENT OF SUBJECTS RECEIVING STANDARD SCORE OF 9 OR MORE ON VARIOUS SUB-TESTS

Test	Mental Defective Groups				Borderline Groups			
	Age 10–14	15–19	20–49	(10–49)	Age 10–14	15–19	20–49	(10–49)
Inf.	0	3	0	1	5	6	11	8
Comp.	0	0	0	0	2	9	6	6
Arith	0	0	2	1	10	2	13	9
Dig. Sp.	0	3	7	3	5	17	12	11
Sim.	0	0	0	0	0	6	3	3
Average of 5 Verbal				1				7.4
P.A.	2	0	2	2	22	26	4	17
P.C.	0	8	2	3	11	17	7	11
Obj.	8	14	2	8	37	30	27	31
Bl. Des.	0	0	0	0	10	20	6	11
Subs.	0	10	0	3	13	28	2	13
Average of								

(4) Comparing the borderline and defective groups as regards the percentage of individuals receiving a standard score of 9 or more (Table IV) shows that the Verbal tests are more difficult than the Performance, for both groups. (5) Comparing the relative effectiveness of the individual sub-tests (Tables III and IV), we find that all the Verbal tests except the Memory Span for Digits discriminates between the mental defective and borderline groups. The critical ratio of the Digit Span test is less than 3 and allows 3% of the mental defectives and 11% of the borderline group to receive a standard score of 9 or more. This sub-test also has the largest standard deviation of the Verbal tests. The Similarities test was not given to all the subjects. Its critical ratio was of a lower order than most of the tests but still significant. Moreover, it showed the smallest percent of cases receiving a score of 9 or more in both mental defective and borderline groups. (6) Critical differences between the defective and borderline groups are significant for all the Performance sub-tests, but the tests differ widely in their ability to identify the two groups. Thus the Object Assembly has a critical ratio of approximately the same order as that of the Substitution test, but does not discriminate nearly so well between mental defectives and borderline cases as measured by the percent of individuals attaining a standard score of 9 or more. In this last respect, the Block Design is the best of all Performance tests. Not a single mental defective and only 11% of borderline cases received a score of 9 on this test (Table IV).

SUMMARY

This paper reports the effectiveness of the Bellevue Intelligence Scale in discriminating between borderline and mentally defective groups. The subtests scores of 82 borderline and 45 mentally defective subjects were compared as regards magnitude of differences between the mean scores, the critical ratios between same, and the percent of subjects in each group attaining a standard score equal to the average of the normal population.

(1) The results showed that by all criteria used every sub-test on the Bellevue Scale, except Digit Span and Object Assembly, discriminates very effectively between subjects of borderline and mentally defective intelligence.

(2) The Block Design and Similarities are the most discriminating sub-tests.

(3) In terms of absolute level attained, both mental defectives and subjects of borderline intelligence do less on Verbal than on Performance tests. But from ages 10 to 19, the Performance tests discriminate better between the two compared groups.

REFERENCES

(1) B. Balinsky, H. Israel and D. Wechsler, The Relative Effectiveness of the Stanford-Binet and the Bellevue Intelligence Scale in Diagnosing Mental Deficiency. Amer. Jour. of Orthopsychiatry, IX, 1939, 798–801.

(2) Cf. Wells, F. L., Mental Tests and Clinical Practice, 1927. Jastak, Jos., Psychometric Patterns of State Hospitals Patients. Delaware State Med. Jr. IX, 1937.

(Paper accepted for publication without presentation.—ED.)

A STUDY OF RETENTION IN KORSAKOFF PSYCHOSIS*

DAVID WECHSLER

Introductory.

In general, the retention defect in the Korsakoff pyschosis presents two questions. First, there is the interest in the *extent* of the retention defect, in which case we should expect from an experimental investigation a quantitative expression of what has already been observed clinically; second, there is the *nature* of the retention defect, in which case we might expect a description of it in more familiar psychological terms or, perhaps, a reduction of the defect to some simpler process than is connoted by the term retention. The term retention is rather broad, and when used loosely has been employed synonymously with memory. We shall imply by this term *the ability to reproduce new impressions after a given interval of time*. In the following experiments I have tested the failure of reproduction after short time intervals, and hence I might call the observations A Study of Immediate Retention in Korsakoff Psychosis.

Experimental Conditions and Subjects.

The experiments herein reported were done at the Psychiatric Institute on Ward's Island, New York.† They extended over a period of two and one-half months (February 1 to April 15, 1917) and consumed two hours in the morning, three times each week during that time. The experiments were done with six patients, five Korsakoffs and one general paralysis patient. According to the physicians at the Institute all the cases were "typical." Of the Korsakoff patients two were mild (Cases A and B). The remaining three were more pronounced (Cases X, Y, Z). None of them was in the acute stage. My primary interest was in the Korsakoff patients. The general paresis case was added for the additional light which, I hoped, a comparison of his performances with those of the Korsakoffs might throw upon the retention defect of the latter.

*Reprinted from *Psychiatric Bulletin,* 1917, **2**, 403-451.

† For their kind aid and many courtesies the writer wishes to express his indebtedness to Dr. Thomas Heldt, attending physician of the ward, Dr. George H. Kirby, the present Director of the Psychiatric Institute, and specially to Dr. August Hoch, its former Director, whose sympathetic interest encouraged him in his work.

Experimental Material and Procedure.

The memory experiments selected may be roughly divided into three groups. I. Experiments for reproduction of serial impressions. II. Experiments to test the formation of associations. III. Experiments to test the rate of forgetting for small intervals of time. The second group occupied the greatest part of the experimenter's time, and contributed the critical results of the investigation. In connection with the experiments on the formation of associations an intensive study was made of the errors committed by each of the subjects. IV. An analysis of the errors which, as will be seen later, threw much light on the character of the association disturbance and formed the basis for the writer's views on the nature of the retention defect in the Korsakoff patient.

Though most of the tests employed are well known, the experimenter deemed it well to describe his procedure in all of them, first because of the occasional variation in method which the type of subject used, and the circumstances of the experimentation demanded, and secondly for the sake of indicating the difficulties that were encountered in giving the tests.

Outline of Tests.

   I. Experiments for testing reproduction of serial impressions.
     A. Memory span tests.
       1. Auditory memory span for digits.
       2. Auditory memory span for unrelated words.
       3. Visual memory span for movement.
          a. Knox Cube test.
          b. Modified Cube test.
     B. Reproduction of lists of words longer than memory span.
       4. Method of Retained Members.
          a. Lists of ten unrelated words.
          b. Lists of ten related words.
  II. Experiments on the formation of associations (Method of Paired Associates).
       5. Formation of "preformed associates."
          a. Lists of ten pairs.
       6. Formation of new associations.
          a. Lists of ten pairs.
          b. Lists of five pairs.
 III. Experiments on the rate of forgetting for small intervals of time.
       7. Curve of forgetting for invervals of 15″, 30″, 60″, 1′, 3′ and 10′.
          a. Recall of series of digits after a single repetition.
          b. Recall of colors after a single presentation.
          c. Recall of single associates after one repetition.

IV. Analysis of errors.
    8.
          a. Quantitative.
          b. Qualitative.

Summary of Results and Conclusions.

All the Korsakoff subjects but one showed a normal memory span, and the memory span of that one (Y) was better than that of the general paresis patient. This for digits, unrelated concrete words and following simple movements (modified Cube Test). When the memory span was exceeded the amount of material that was reproduced was less than what could be expected of normals.

The Korsakoff cases showed a marked disturbance in the formation of new associations.

a. They were able to reproduce habitually preformed associations almost as readily as normal individuals, but as these became less of an habitual sort the associations were less readily reproduced. This was shown in the tests on preformed associates.

b. Korsakoffs were almost wholly unable to form new associations. This was shown by the tests on the formation of new associations. Whereas normal individuals could learn to associate ten pairs of unrelated words in from three to five trials (median 4, P. E. 1) none of the Korsakoffs was able to get more than two in twenty trials and four of the five Korsakoffs could not get any.

Increasing the number of repetitions had very slight or almost no effect upon increasing the number of new associations to be formed.

Reducing the amount of material (from ten to five pairs of associates) had no perceptible effect upon increasing the number of associates retained except in so far as it reduced the time interval between repetitions.

Reducing the time interval (from 30″ to no interval between successive repetitions) had only a slight effect upon increasing the number of associates retained. This was due to the fact that the time interval between rehearsing of any one pair was still too great. (In a list of five pairs it was still 20″).

New unassociated impressions produced by a single presentation of a stimulus were rapidly forgotten. A curve of forgetting produced by using digits and colored stimuli follows the curve of *Ebbinghaus,* except that it approaches abscissa very rapidly and cuts it almost after three seconds. A similar curve produced by using unrelated paired associates resulted in a curve even more steep, with one subject cutting the abscissa after one minute.

An analysis of the errors showed a preponderance of false associations over failure to recall associates, a condition which contrasted very strikingly with that found in normal subjects.

There was a marked tendency to perseverate any false associations once made. Such false associations were not diminished through correction, but rather increased, at least relatively, with the number of repetitions.

These results lead the writer to the conclusion that *the prime cause of the retention defect in Korsakoff psychosis is the patient's inability to form new associations.*

THE EFFECT OF ALCOHOL ON MENTAL ACTIVITY*†

DAVID WECHSLER

Chief Psychologist, Psychiatric Division, Bellevue Hospital; Assistant Clinical Professor of Medical Psychology, New York University College of Medicine

IN discussing the effects of alcohol on mental activity, it is important to distinguish between the transient changes in psychological functions following the ingestion of restricted amounts of alcohol and those ascribed to its continued use. The former have usually been observed under controlled experiments and, for the most part, under conditions of subclinical intoxication. The latter are largely descriptions of possible long-range effects, inferred primarily from terminal and pathological cases of chronic alcoholism. The reported observations are mutually supportive, but whether they are interchangeable is open to question.

The changes in psychological functions observed under experimental conditions have recently been summarized by Jellinek and McFarland (1) in a critical and comprehensive paper. This survey shows that while much of the work done thus far is inconclusive, and some of it contradictory, the results as a whole leave little doubt that the effect of alcohol is to lower the functioning level of nearly all mental abilities that have been tested. The immediate effect of alcohol is to constrict or impair the efficiency of the individual. The degree of impairment is dependent on the amount of alcohol absorbed, the time interval following ingestion, the specific susceptibility of the subject and, to some degree, on the complexity of the mental functions or tasks involved. Sensory discrimination in nearly all modalities is decreased, as is also liminal acuity (vision and hearing), though by no considerable amount. Perception and attention are affected. This is evidenced by such facts as the reduction in the number of letters or syllables which the individual can apprehend and the increase in the number of errors in color naming tests. Retention and recall are adversely affected, but the loss is less for rote than for logical material. Associative processes are retarded and impoverished; this is shown by a lengthening of the reaction time and the augmentation of superficial and clang associations.

*From the Psychiatric Division of Bellevue Hospital and the Department of Psychiatry, New York University College of Medicine, New York.

†Presented at the Symposium on Alcoholism of the Research Council on Problems of Alcohol, Philadelphia, December 28, 1940. Reprinted from *Quarterly Journal of Studies on Alcohol*, 1941, **2**, 479-485. Reprinted by permission of the Rutgers Center of Alcohol Studies.

271

Although data on systematic learning experiments are lacking, there is some indication that the individual's facility to acquire new impressions is reduced, and here the impairment is greater for complex than for serial impressions. Of studies on the so-called higher mental processes: judgment, reasoning and intelligence, there are little data and these are very inconclusive. As regards the affective processes and the personality as a whole, experimental studies are almost entirely lacking. One study, by Smith (2), using the psychogalvanic reflex, showed a rise in the threshold of emotional responsiveness in the subjects tested. Jellinek and McFarland (1) attach little importance to this result because of their lack of confidence in the experimenter's technique, but I believe it is rather an important finding as it confirms a general clinical observation, namely, the affective obtuseness of the alcoholic.

The general result which experimental investigation with alcohol has furnished is that all psychological functions measured thus far show a greater or lesser degree of impairment. It should be noted, however, that the changes recorded concern themselves with immediate and not long-range alterations in the individual's efficiency and hence give us no information about the probable permanence of these effects. It is necessary to re-emphasize this point because most of the quoted generalizations as regards the effects of continued use of alcohol are based on these temporarily restricted experimental investigations. The fact is that systematic studies of the long range or habitual use of alcohol are conspicuously lacking. There is, of course, a good deal of descriptive material on what habitual drinking does to the individual, but most of this is based on uncontrolled clinical observation. It is only when we come to terminal cases, the chronic alcoholics who have developed brain pathology, that we again find experimental data. And most of these data are derived from studies on a diagnostically restricted and relatively small group—those with Korsakoff's psychosis.

The clinical mental symptoms of the Korsakoff alcoholic are familiar: poor judgment, lack of insight, memory defects, confabulation, disorientation and, in many cases, retrograde amnesia. So far as experimental studies on the psychological changes in such patients are concerned, investigators seem to have been primarily interested in the memory and associative disturbances. These are easily summarized. The main memory defect is in the field of retention and in the acquisition of new associations. A person with Korsakoff's psychosis can recall material he has acquired in the past but new learning is almost impossible for him. Rote memory, like repeating digits and short sentences, is relatively unimpaired; so is memory for old events, except insofar as they involve temporal sequences. When unable to recall, he has a tendency to fill in gaps of memory with ready-made associations, a condition which seems largely responsible for his confabulation. So far as the association processes are concerned, the outstanding manifestations are a slowing-up of the speed of response, an increase of inner and superficial responses and a tendency toward preservation.

A few studies deal specifically with perceptual disturbances in chronic alcoholism. These reveal changes in the duration of sensory aftereffects and distortions in the subjects' tactile and visual fields. Extreme cases show a tendency to return to primitive *Gestalt* patterns [Bender (3)]. In general, chronic alcoholics do badly in all tests involving visual reproduction.

While memory and perceptual disturbances in the chronic alcoholic, as well as in persons suffering from Korsakoff's psychosis are often the most striking symptoms, they are far from being the most damaging. A more serious though less emphasized consequence of chronic alcoholism is its disintegrative effect on mental activity as a whole. This is reflected in the general lack of persistence and loss of goal which the chronic alcoholic manifests when confronted with any task requiring concentrated effort. Though usually coöperating on psychometric tests, he constantly complains of his inability to go through with them, must continually be prodded and needs an inordinate amount of reassurance. Some unpublished material gathered at Bellevue Hospital further shows a rough hierarchical deterioration in mental functioning, beginning with a marked loss in abilities calling for synthesis and new learning, and ending with a relatively small loss in abilities involving mere stimulus response reactions. Correspondingly the chronic alcoholic does most poorly on tests involving organization manipulation of novel situations and relatively well on tests requiring reproduction of simple ideas or involving established habits.

The deteriorative mental effects of alcohol just described pertain, as already mentioned, to cases associated with definite brain pathology. What about the effects of moderate though prolonged use of alcohol, or even immoderate use which does not lead to obvious psychopathology? In theory we might expect intermediate results. Actually we have no proof and the reason is that this larger and socially more important aspect of the problem has never been systematically investigated. I will therefore now report on a study, done in preparation for this meeting, on the chronic drinker who does not reach the state hospital. This study, it is hoped, will not only present some valid, albeit limited, data on this much neglected group, but also illustrate the value of the quantitative methods of clinical psychology.

The subjects of my study were 29 chronic, but nonpsychotic, alcoholics taken from over 100 patients admitted to the Psychiatric Division of Bellevue Hospital during the past two years, on whom psychometric examinations were available. All were English-speaking, mostly native-born adult males, with at least a 10 year history of continued drinking but showing no organic brain complications. The small number of subjects available is due in a large measure to the fact that at Bellevue, as at most other hospitals, it is the practice of psychiatrists to call for psychometric tests on alcoholics only when they suspect mental deficiency or other complicating psychological conditions.

For comparative purposes, the subjects were restricted to two age groups: one, 36 to 42 years, with a mean age of 38.7 years, and the other, 45 to 55 years, with a mean age of 48.9 years. Thus, there was a mean age difference of approximately 10 years between the two groups. Though the groups were not specifically matched, they were so chosen as to avoid any large discrepancy in intellectual level. In point of fact, when their intelligence ratings were finally calculated, the mean I.Q.'s of the two groups were within one point of each other, the actual I.Q.'s, as measured by the Wechsler-Bellevue Adult Scale, being 98.8 for the 36 to 42 age group and 98.5 for the 45 to 55 age group. The occupational range in both groups was from common laborer to newspaper editor and, while it included a number of patrolmen, did not otherwise seem to involve any particularly selective socio-economic factor. In a rough way this group of 29 may be said to differ from other comparable age groups primarily by the fact that they were chronic alcoholics.

Our data consist of I.Q. ratings and subtest scores attained by the subjects on the Bellevue Adult Intelligence Scale, supplemented in some cases by scores on a number of other tests. In this report I shall treat only the data obtained with the Bellevue Intelligence Scale. This scale consists of a battery of 10 tests with norms available, not only for the scale as a whole, but for each of the subtests. By comparing the two groups with each other, as well as with the expected norms for each age, one can discover possible evidence of deterioration.

The results are presented in Tables 1 and 2. These tables give the mean test scores of the two groups on each of the 10 subtests of the

TABLE I

Distribution of Scores on Subtests of Wechsler-Bellevue Scale.

ALCOHOLIC SUBJECTS

Age Group	No.	I.Q.	Total Score	General Information	General Comprehension	Arithmetic	Similarities	Digit Span	Picture Arrangement	Picture Completion	Block Design	Object Assembly	Digit Symbol
36 to 42	16	98.8	86.5	10.0	10.7	9.2	8.3	7.2	8.4	8.4	8.2	7.8	6.8
45 to 55	13	98.5	77.1	9.4	8.8	7.7	6.8	7.1	7.3	9.2	8.5	7.2	5.2

TABLE 2

Distribution of Scores on Subtests of Wechsler-Bellevue Scale.

*NORMAL SUBJECTS OF COMPARABLE AGES

Age Group	No.	I.Q.	Total Score	General Information	General Comprehension	Arithmetic	Similarities	Digit Span	Picture Arrangement	Picture Completion	Block Design	Object Assembly	Digit Symbol
35 to 39	100	100	88.0	9.8	9.8	9.8	9.1	8.7	8.7	9.0	8.9	8.7	9.2
45 to 49	60	100	81.3	9.6	9.5	9.2	9.3	7.8	7.7	8.1	7.8	8.8	7.2

*From standardization data by author (4).

scale. Inspection of the tables shows that the various tests contribute different amounts to the total score. Thus, while the tests of General Information and General Comprehension contribute approximately 10 points each to the total score of the 36 to 42 age group, Memory Span for digits and ability to detect Similarities contribute 7.2 and 8.3; and the Object Assembly and the Digit Symbol tests only 7.8 and 6.8 points respectively. In the 45 to 55 age group, General Information and General Comprehension each contribute approximately 9 points to the total score, Memory Span for digits, 7.1, Similarities, 6.8, Object Assembly and Digit Symbol, 7.2 and 5.2 points respectively. Some of these differences are, in part, a function of age. Thus, older persons generally do less well on the performance than on verbal tests; but the differences among our alcoholics are greater than the loss to be expected from the age factor alone.

Particularly significant in the decline of the older group of alcoholics is the falling off in the scores of the Similarities and the Digit Symbol tests; also significant is the loss in Digit Span and in the Object Assembly tests which follow closely and in that order. Examination of the abilities measured by these tests shows that they include, not only new learning and retention, but also abstract reasoning as well as perceptual organization.

The significant drop in score of the older group on the Similarities test is of particular interest because it confirms an impression, which I have had as a result of many years of psychometric testing, namely, that the capacity for logical analysis and organization in the alcoholic is often affected to a greater degree than is the familiar deterioration in memory.*

*Examination of the two tables reveals two or three apparently discrepant tendencies in some of the figures given. Thus, the Comprehension and Information test scores for normal adults, age 45 to 49, is greater than for the comparable group of alcoholics. This is due in part to the equating of the groups for mean total score for all 10 tests. Obviously, if the two groups have approximately the same mean total score and one shows higher scores on some of the tests, then the second group will have to show higher scores on certain of the remaining tests. Again, the alcoholic group, age 45 to 55, does somewhat better on the Picture Completion and the Block Design tests than the alcoholic group, age 35 to 42. This may be due to the fact that while the two groups have been equated as to intellectual level and general diagnosis, they undoubtedly differ with respect to other personality in diagnostic characteristics which also influence the test patterning. Our total number of subjects was too small to make any further dichotomies. In any case, the reader should bear in mind that the investigation just summarized was not intended as a refined statistical analysis of psychometric patterning, but only as a study illustrating the results obtainable with quantitative procedures. Thus considered, the data clearly support the reported alternations in mental functions discussed.

The results just described indicate that prolonged use of alcohol impairs the mental functioning of various abilities even before there is any evidence of brain pathology. They also indicate a positive relation between the intensity of the impairment and the chronicity of the alcoholism. There are, of course, some significant individual differences, but the general result is clear-cut.

The influence of alcohol on mental activity, which we have reviewed, is concerned almost exclusively with its effects on the intellectual and perceptual functions. The reason for this restriction is that it is only with respect to these abilities that we have any quantitative data. More important, however, than the intellectual impairment which may follow excessive use of alcohol is its deleterious effect on the individual's affective reactions and personality structure as a whole. More serious than the alcoholic's loss of memory is his loss of goal; long before he shows measurable signs of mental deterioration he gives ample evidence of being less efficient socially. As to precisely what makes him so, we are still in the dark. The satsifactory answer to this question constitutes one of the main challenges to future investigators.

There is one more thought which I wish to add in concluding this brief survey on the mental effects of alcohol: thus far nearly all psychological studies have concerned themselves with what alcohol does *to* the individual. No one, so far as I know, has made any scientific investigation as to what alcohol does *for* the individual.

It is true that psychiatrists have, from time to time, called attention to the positive role which alcohol plays in the lives of chronic drinkers; and, of course, it is not uncommon for lay individuals to testify to its stimulating effects. But, generally speaking, most of the favorable statements about alcohol have come from the pens of poets or the purveyors of tonics. Their testimony hardly constitutes scientific evidence, yet it cannot be altogether disregarded. It would seem highly desirable that future scientific investigations of the problem of alcohol include studies on its reputed positive as well as its obvious negative effects.

REFERENCES

1. JELLINEK, E. M. and McFARLAND, R. A.   Quart. J. Stud. Alc. 1: 272, 1940.
2. SMITH, W. W.   The Measurement of Emotion, p. 124. New York, Harcourt, Brace & Co., 1922.
3. BENDER, LAURETTA.   Arch. Neurol. Psychiat., Chicago 33: 300, 1935.
4. WECHSLER, D.   The Measurement of Adult Intelligence, p. 214. Baltimore, Wm. Wood & Co., 1941, 2d ed.

CLINICAL USE OF THE MENTAL DETERIORATION INDEX OF THE BELLEVUE-WECHSLER SCALE*

JOSEPH LEVI, SADI OPPENHEIM, and DAVID WECHSLER

Psychiatric Division of Bellevue Hospital, New York University College of Medicine

In the third edition of the *Measurement of Intelligence,* Wechsler suggests a quantitative method of determining loss of intellectual functioning. The measure is obtained from a comparison of the sum of the weighted scores of two groups of subtests. Subtests are differentiated into these two groups depending on whether the abilities measured are those that decline relatively little with age (known as "Hold-up-with-Age" Tests) or whether they decline considerably with age (known as "Do-Not-Hold-up-with-Age Tests"). The method is described in detail in the Third Edition. Essentially, it consists of getting the sum of the Hold Subtests (Comprehension or Vocabulary, Information, Picture Completion, Object Assembly) and the sum of the Do-Not-Hold Subtests (Arithmetic, Repetition of Digits, Digit-Symbol, Block Design). Applying the formula $\frac{\text{Hold—Don't Hold}}{\text{Hold}}$ gives the measure of intellectual loss.

In Table 6 of his book is given the "normal" amount of such loss per age group which must be allowed before obtaining actual measure of excess deterioration. Wechsler suggests a loss in excess of 10 per cent as an indicator of possible impairment, and a loss in excess of 20 per cent as definite evidence. He indicates the usefulness of this measure in detecting changes in mental functioning before patients give clearcut clinical or neurological evidence.

During the past three months we have applied this method of finding a deterioration index in specific cases where the diagnosis was in doubt, with a view to evaluating its usefulness in differential diagnosis. We have found about 15 cases where this index was a specific factor in leading to an accepted differential diagnosis.

The cases fall into the following categories:

1. Distinguishing organic memory impairment from hysterical amnesia.

2. Finding corroborative evidence of organic involvement where clinical and neurological data are not clearcut.

3. Distinguishing between mental deficiency and intellectual deterioration (not necessarily at a defective level).

4. Differentiating between psychosis with and without organic deterioration.

*Reprinted from *Journal of Abnormal and Social Psychology,* 1945, **40**, 405-407.

To illustrate the first category, "distinguishing organic memory impairment from hysterical amnesia," we have the following case:

A.B., female, 18, admitted in an unconscious alcoholic state. The subsequent psychiatric interview revealed complaints of amnesia, dizziness, uncertainty, confusion. She was considered to be mentally defective, and of unstable, delinquent makeup. A psychometric examination was requested for possible placement. The Bellevue-Wechsler composite IQ of 95 indicated average intellectual functioning, but with a deterioration index of 20 per cent.

Hold Subtests		*Don't Hold*	
Comp.	8	Digits	7
Inf.	10	Arith.	7
P. Comp.	9	Blocks	10
Obj. A.	12	D. Sym.	7
	39		31

8/39 = 20 per cent

The verbal and performance IQ's were almost identical (94 and 96, respectively). The psychometric findings, so much at variance with psychiatric evaluation, which disclosed anomalies leading to a diagnosis of psychosis with organic brain damage due to a heredito-degenerative disease, with aphasia.

In contradistinction to the case just cited is the following case of genuine hysterical amnesia.

C.F., male, 20, brought in by the police when found wandering in the streets. He was amnesic and confused. On the Bellevue-Wechsler he achieved a composite IQ of 94, made up of a verbal IQ of 107 and a performance IQ of 80. A negative deterioration index revealed that there was no loss of intellectual efficiency. Final diagnosis "psychoneurosis with amnesia."

Hold Subtests		*Don't Hold*	
Comp.	10	Digits	11
Info.	11	Arith.	10
P. Comp.	8	Blocks	10
Obj. A.	2	D. Sym.	7
	31		38

To illustrate the second category, "finding corroborative evidence of organic involvement where the clinical and neurological data are not clearcut," we offer the following example:

P.T., male, 46, admitted in a confused state. He was recommended by a private psychiatrist for possible shock treatment because of depression. Subject had crying spells, was unable to concentrate, and could not hold his job. Neurological examination indicated that this subject might be suffering from Altzheimer's disease. At a conference, diversity of opinion was expressed as to whether it was Altzheimer's or a depression, the majority favoring the former. Psychometric examination was requested, and gave the following results: Bellevue-Wechsler composite IQ of 91, indicating low-average functioning, but with a deterioration index of 32 per cent.

Hold Subjects		Don't Hold	
Comp.	6	Digits	4
Info.	11	Arith.	7
P. Comp.	9	Blocks	7
Obj. A.	11	D. Sym.	3
	37		21

16/37 = 43 per cent—11 per cent = 32 per cent

It is worth noting that the performance IQ of 100 was actually higher than the verbal IQ of 84. Final diagnosis was "Altzheimer's disease."

The following case, on the other hand, is an example of a depression uncomplicated by any organic factor:

H.F., male, 42, was brought in by his wife because he became depressed, lost interest in his job of running an elevator, quit his job, and would sit for hours staring into space. A composite score on the Bellevue-Wechsler of 108 was composed of verbal IQ of 106 and performance IQ of 110. The deterioration index was negative, indicating that no intellectual deficit had occurred. Final diagnosis: Depression.

Hold Subtests		Don't Hold	
Comp.	7	Digits	14
Info.	11	Arith.	10
P. Comp.	10	Blocks	9
Obj. A.	12	D. Sym.	8
	40		41

The following illustrates the category where the problem centers on distinguishing mental deficiency from intellectual deterioration:

W.F., male, 45, was admitted when his parents died, because a sister who tried to take care of him was unable to tolerate his temper outbursts and was afraid to trust him with her children. He had been considered defective almost all of his life, and had been taken care of by his parents. He was admitted for possible commitment, and considered mentally defective by the psychiatrist. The psychometric examination revealed dull normal functioning (IQ of 83), but with a deterioration index of 45 per cent.

Hold Subtests		Don't Hold	
Voc.	11	Digits	4
Info.	10	Arith.	4
P. Comp.	8	Blocks	3
Obj. A.	5	D. Sym.	4
	34		15

15/39 = 56 per cent—11 per cent = 45 per cent

The performance IQ of 88 was slightly higher than the verbal IQ of 83. Final diagnosis was "psychosis with mental deterioration."

The next case illustrates the use of the deterioration index as an aid in differentiating between psychosis with and without organic deterioration.

> F.R., male, 52, admitted because he was forgetful, confused, unable to keep his job. He accused his wife falsely of infidelity. There was a history of alcoholism. Psychiatric impression was of psychosis with alcoholism and Korsakoff features. He was not disoriented except when first admitted. Psychometric examination was requested for an estimate of intellectual impairment. A composite IQ of 110 indicated functioning at bright-normal level, but with a deterioration index of 14 per cent. The verbal IQ was 108, and the performance IQ was 118. Final diagnosis was "psychosis with alcoholism and Korsakoff features."

Discussion and Conclusions

1. The Bellevue-Wechsler Scale offers a method of appraising mental deterioration without the need of a supplementary test. This is of special value in a clinic setup where the testing time is limited. The scale makes available an additional clinical measure.

2. The method discussed is of specific help in differential diagnosis. Cases cited show that the index of deterioration is useful not only in confirming, but also in discovering, organic conditions.

3. The percentage-of-loss method described does not require that a subject necessarily do better on verbal than performance tests. While it is generally true that organic cases reveal impairment by a lowered performance score, a special merit of the technique is that it covers the cases that do not fall into this general class, and are therefore the more likely to be overlooked.

4. The method is sufficiently simple to suggest its routine application in all clinical cases.

It is fully realized that this is an exploratory study. Further experimentation, including the use of control groups and statistical refinement, is indicated. Experimental study is needed to answer more fully the following questions:

1. What is the critical percentage-of-loss indicating definite deterioration?

2. To what extent may purely psychogenic conditions simulate organic deterioration?

3. To what extent do we find gross test deterioration but no accompanying physical symptomatology?

SCHIZOPHRENIC PATTERNS ON THE WISC*

DAVID WECHSLER and EUGENIA JAROS

Department of Psychiatry, New York University School of Medicine

Problem

Clinical experience has shown that one can frequently detect the schizophrenic child from the overall character of his WISC performance, and a number of studies have appeared [1, 2, 4] in which the problem has been discussed. The present investigation was undertaken to see whether there were in fact any specific WISC test patterns or signs which would be systematically applied in differentiating the schizophrenic from the non-schizophrenic child. By a test 'pattern' we shall imply a typical sequence or combination of subtest scores characteristically emerging from analysis of a subject's performance. Under the term 'sign' we shall comprehend a differential level of performance on a series rather than a single test; for example, significant differences between the sum of 5 Verbal and 5 Performance tests.

Method

Subjects. The experimental group consisted of 150 white males, 7–15 years, diagnosed as childhood schizophrenics over the past 7 years at Bellevue Psychiatric Hospital. A control group of an equal number of males was selected at random from a population sample used in the original WISC standardization, matched for age and IQ. In this paper we shall report only the findings of 100 subjects falling in the age range of 8–11 with IQs from 80 to 120. A statistical analysis of the population employed in the study is given in Table 1.

Procedure. STEP 1. The first step was to distribute the WISC subtest scores of the schizophrenic population to see on which tests these children tend to do relatively well or poorly. A similar distribution was made for the control group. These distributions were not too helpful and were used only as cues, that is, as suggestions for the tests to be tried out for likely fruitful combinations.

STEP 2. Some 40 combinations of subtests were examined and tried out as potential discriminants between the Control and Experimental group, with the following criteria for selection: a) absolute and relative incidence of test patterns, b) amount of overlap, c) incidence of false-positives. Using all these criteria, only 2 significant discriminating patterns emerged consistently. These were 1) Picture

*Reprinted from *Journal of Clinical Psychology*, 1965, **21**, 288-291.

Completion greater than Picture Arrangement and Object Assembly greater than Coding, each by 3 points, and 2) Comprehension greater than Arithmetic and Similarities greater than Arithmetic by 3 points. But in the course of our analysis it became increasingly evident that, all other characteristics apart, the sign which most effectively seemed to differentiate the schizophrenic child was the greater intertest variability of the former. The main problem was to find a measure of variability which was most effective in revealing this characteristic.

STEP 3.   Several indices of individual intertest variability were tried out. Of these, the most discriminating turned out to be a measure which we have termed the "3 by 3" test sign. This is obtained by calculating the mean of a S's Full Scale score, subtracting each subtest weighted score from this mean and then counting the number of subtests which deviate by 3 or more points from the S's mean. Thus, in a record showing a mean score of 10, all scores 7 and below and 13 and over are counted as significantly deviant.

STEP 4.   The frequently observed large differences between the Verbal and the Performance parts of the Scale in schizophrenics as well as in other diagnostic groups suggested the possible use of some defined difference as a possible additional discriminant between schizophrenic and non-schizophrenic records. After some experimenting, a cut-off score of ± 16 points between the Verbal and Performance Scales (V-P) was found to be significantly and optimally discriminating, and accordingly added as another possible diagnostic sign.

STEP 5.   Our final step was to . . . see whether treating the signs in combination rather than singly would furnish a more effective discriminant. This was done by re-examining the individual subtest protocols of all Ss and scoring them

Table 1. *Age and IQ Distributions of Normal (Control) and Schizophrenic (Experimental) Groups Aged 8-11 with Incidence (in %) of Differentiating WISC Patterns*

	8.0-8.9		9.0-9.9		10.0-10.9		11.0-11.9		8.0-11.9		
	Norm.	Sch.	Norm.	Sch.	Norm.	Sch.	Norm.	Sch.	Norm.	Sch.	C. R.
N	25	25	25	25	25	25	25	25	100	100	
Mean IQ	93.6	93.0	94.3	94 4	92.8	92.8	95.2	95.0	94.0	93.8	
SD	7.4	7.8	7.5	7.2	7.6	7.7	9.4	8.2	8.0	7.7	
Sign I	4%	44%	8%	32%	4%	48%	16%	52%	8%	44%	6.4*
Sign II	8%	0%	4%	4%	0%	20%	4%	16%	4%	10%	2.9
Sign III	4%	16%	12%	16%	4%	8%	4%	28%	6%	17%	3.7
Sign IV	4%	4%	4%	4%	0%	16%	0%	36%	2%	15%	4.7
Sign V	0	36%	4%	28%	0%	44%	4%	48%	2%	39%	7.3

*All C. R.'s are significant at .01 level or better.

Sign I = 3 subtests, each deviating by 3 or more Scaled Score Points from the Mean.
Sign II = P. A. greater than P. C. *and* Object Assembly greater than Coding, each by 3 Scaled Score points.
Sign III = Comprehension greater than Arithmetic *and* Similarities greater than Arithmetic by 3 Scaled Score points.
Sign IV = Verbal IQ minus Performance IQ = $\pm$ 16 points.
Sign V = Sign I plus any one of the other 3 signs.

for the presence or absence of the pattern or sign under consideration. The proportion of each sign occurring in the respective groups was then noted (Table 1), and from the data so obtained the discriminant significance of each sign calculated. On the basis of these data a fifth sign (Table 1, sign V) was added with this dual requirement: Manifestation of the "3 by 3" test *and* in addition any of the other three.

STEP 6.   After the patterns were thus established, evaluation of their diagnostic reliability was obtained by applying criteria to two other samples of schizophrenic populations: 25 male and white cases, ages 8–11 from the Children's Unit at Creedmore State Hospital and 20 white males ages 8–12 from the League School.†

Results

Major findings will be found in Tables 1 and 2. Table 1 gives the proportion of each of the signs obtained at different age levels and of the total 8–11 age in the Control and the Experimental groups; also the critical ratios between the encountered proportions for age 8 through 11. As will be seen, all the signs are significant at the .01 level of confidence or better, though some are much more discriminating than others. There was also considerable overlap between the signs, in the sense that many of the Ss picked up by one sign are also picked up by another. This is particularly true of the "3 by 3" sign which, if taken alone, picks up as many as 90% of the schizophrenic cases detected by the three other combined.

Table 2. *Percent of Schizophrenic Cases at Creedmore Children's Unit and the League School, Correctly Picked Up by WISC Signs or Patterns*

	Mean			Signs				
	Age	IQ	N	I	II	III	IV	V
Creedmore's Unit	8–11	96.3	25	44%	4%	4%	12%	36%
League School	8–12	101.3	20	90	35	30	30	65
Combined	8–12	98.8	45	65	18	16	20	49

Sign I = 3 subtests, each deviating by 3 or more Scaled Score points from the Mean.
   II = P. A. greater than P. C. *and* Object Assembly greater than Coding, each by 3 Scaled Score points.
   III = Comprehension greater than Arithmetic *and* Similarities greater than Arithmetic by 3 Scaled Score points.
   IV = Verbal IQ minus Performance IQ = < 16 points.
   V = Sign 1 *plus* any one of other 3 signs.

† The authors wish to express their thanks to Drs. Lauretta Bender, Leonard Cobrinik and Carl Fenichel for making these data available to us.

An important consideration in the use of signs and patterns in addition to the number of cases they pick up, is the number of false positives they include, that is, the number of normals diagnosed as schizophrenics. In general, this number can be reduced by shifting cut-off points, e.g., setting the V-P cut-off point at 25, requiring a 5 rather than 3 point deviation from the mean as a critical difference, and so on; but in reducing the number of false-positives in the controls, one simultaneously cuts down the proportion of correctly diagnosed cases in the experimental groups. The final choice depends on the price one is ready to pay (in terms of false-positives) for the increased percentage of cases successfully diagnosed.

The "3 by 3" test turns out to be the best single discriminant. Taken alone, it correctly selects 44% of the schizophrenics at a cost of 8% false-positives (Table 1). By using as discriminant the "3 by 3" sign *plus* any one of the others we are able to reduce the false-positive percentage from 8% to 2% with a decrease of 5% in number of cases correctly diagnosed (Table 1). This combination of signs has accordingly been set as an optimal criterion of the differentiation between schizophrenic and non-schizophrenic children and is the one used in the cross validation study mentioned above.

The findings of the two validity studies attempted are given in Table 2. Comparison of these findings with those of the original study shows that the percent of cases correctly diagnosed in the Creedmore sample is about the same as that obtained in the original Bellevue population. The percent of children correctly diagnosed from records obtained from the League School is considerably higher. The reason for this high effectiveness can only be surmised. One is the likelihood that cases from this agency were more firmly diagnosed, and probably contained fewer mixed or borderline cases of schizophrenia, and 2) that the test scores of these children coming mostly from bright socio-economic classes were less likely influenced by such factors as lack of educational opportunity and other deprivations encountered in children referred to mental hospitals.

Discussion

Discovery of a psychometric pattern for any psychiatric entity depends not only on the discriminating potential of tests employed but on the validity of the available diagnostic criteria as well. While the diagnostic entity childhood schizophrenia is now well established, we are aware that its differentiating characteristics may vary considerably from place to place as well as with the particular orientation and competence of the individual psychiatrist. On this matter we can only add that the diagnosis of childhood schizophrenia as here used was generally akin to that developed by Lauretta Bender. As inevitable, some cases involved differences of opinion and necessarily included borderline decisions, but all carried a consensus diagnosis of schizophrenia.

One must also bear in mind that the differentiation between schizophrenia (experimental) and normal (control) subjects is a very broad dichotomy in which the term normal is equivalent to non-schizophrenic. The latter could, without further delimitation, include other subclassifications such as neurotics, mental defectives, organics, etc. In this study the choice of controls from the WISC standardized population, plus the restriction of the IQ range to 80 and over, probably eliminated all or nearly all defective and organic cases. But in the eventual use of our signs for differential diagnosis, one must consider the possibility or even likelihood of a certain amount of overlap between the latter groups and schizophrenia.

In this connection one may have to take into account the fact that test patterns may vary from age to age, as do certain of the symptoms associated with the disease process[1]. Even more clear-cut is the probable influence of IQ level on the obtained findings. This is particularly true of schizophrenic children with low IQs, and it is for this reason that the study was restricted to testable children with low IQs of 80 and over. The main effects of low IQs on test patterns is to limit the range of variability of subtest scores and thereby the number of patterns one can elicit. It is at this functioning level also where differential diagnosis between childhood schizophrenia, mental deficiency and organic brain damage is most difficult, and the problem is not solved by merely dividing the childhood schizophrenic group into organic *vs.* non-organic types of cases.

Summary

The essential finding of this study is that by analyzing the WISC subtests in terms of signs and test patterns, it is possible to differentiate between the schizophrenic and non-schizophrenic child in a considerable percentage of cases. By combining a measure of variability plus any one of 3 additional signs it is possible to pick out some 40% of schizophrenic children at a cost of only 2% false-positives. In the experience of the authors this is a higher percent than is usually achieved by psychiatric examination and interview alone. But, of course, the diagnosis of childhood schizophrenia should not be based on unique test characteristics any more than on single mental symptoms. As in other situations, it needs to be inferred from the total illness picture.

References

1. Bender, Lauretta. Childhood Schizophrenia: A Clinical Study of 100 Schizophrenic Children. *Amer. J. Orthopsychiat.*, 1947, 27, 40–56.
2. Goldfarb, William. *Childhood Schizophrenia.* Cambridge, Mass.: Harvard Univ. Press, 1961.
3. Wechsler, David. *Intelligence Scale for Children, Manual.* New York: Psychological Corp., 1949.
4. Wechsler, David. *Measurement and Appraisal of Adult Intelligence.* Baltimore: Williams and Wilkins, 1958.

PART VII

INTRODUCTION

A picture of the experimental contributions of David Wechsler is illustrated in the four papers included in this part. Although all of them were published prior to 1940, it would be a mistake to assume that this is a period of his life which has ended. Not only in terms of procedures which have contributed to influence his work, but also in terms of attitudes and methodology, the scientific training and implementation of the early years of his career continue to be an important influence on his thinking and mode of procedure.

The first paper in the series describes an apparatus, designed by him, intended to measure reaction time (1). A chronoscope was not required, which operated as a unique advantage in measurement. The machine represented a distinct contribution to experimental psychology.

Wechsler was exposed to the measurement of chronaxie while studying with Lapique in France. Two papers reflecting his training and interest are included here (2 and 3). Both studies were conducted with Freeman, a physician who joined Wechsler in the investigation and presentation of their results.

In the first of these papers, Wechsler and Freeman use the definition of chronaxie proposed by Lapique, comparing it to the historical viewpoint of neuromuscular excitability in children. They describe Lapique's contributions to the field, original and meaningful for psychology. The research, given precise measurement of the physiologist, offered evidence that the chronaxie of the muscle or nerve is directly related to its functional activity. Any alterations which may occur in physiological functioning will also alter attendant chronaxie. These facts may be related to psychomotor functions and capacities as a field unique but significant for psychology.

In the procedures section, there is an interesting consideration of difficulties and how to meet them to assure accurate measurement. The concern with scientific accuracy in order to make meaningful statements about individuals evident in this description has apparently generalized to the less precise mental and psychological measures which follow in Wechsler's distinguished career. The description of the variability in chronaxie is quite analogous to the range of physical and psychological traits reported in *The Range of Human Capacities*.

Wechsler and Freeman point out that methods used prior to their contribution allow differentiation between normal and gross pathological conditions, but little beyond this. The measurement of chronaxia greatly extended this procedure with considerable increase in precision and specificity. Diagnostic procedures and purposes implied by this precision in measurement are as applicable to the psychological and mental sphere as they are to physical functioning.

The second paper by Wechsler and Freeman presents evidence on the relationship between motor speed and chronaxia (3). The hypothesis that some degree of relationship should exist seems to be upheld by the data and they extrapolate from that relationship that movement in general may also be dependent upon the chronaxie of nerves and muscles involved in movement.

The final paper in this section is of a type which seems quite distinct from the content of any other selection in this book. Done in conjunction with Schilder, the paper deals with the illusion of the oblique intercept (4). There is a long history of the investigation of illusory materials. One might be surprised to find David Wechsler a contributor to this field until one realizes the range and scope of interests which have caught his attention.

The experimentalist attitude developed early in his career, and continues to exercise influence in his work. Though some clinicians might feel that the procedures of experimental psychology will be too constraining for the clinical setting, David Wechsler represents the alternative. To the degree that constraints may be applied for the maximum good of the patient, one might wish such training for all clinicians.

AN APPARATUS FOR MEASURING REACTION TIMES WITHOUT A CHRONOSCOPE

DAVID WECHSLER

The Psychological Corporation, New York City

This paper describes an apparatus, originally devised to measure alertness of attention and speed of reaction, which promises to be useful in the general field of experimental psychology. The apparatus consists of two units. The first enables the experimenter automatically to present several stimuli, simultaneously, successively, or both together and in sequence; the second automatically records the subject's responses as they are made. The two units may be used together or separately. When used together they furnish a means of measuring reaction-time without the use of a chronoscope.

AUTOMATIC PRESENTATION OF MULTIPLE STIMULI

Figure 1 shows the construction of the first unit. A metal cylinder (CL) is connected to an electric motor (M) which moves the cylinder at a very low speed by a series of reduction gears. The cylinder is covered with an insulating sleeve (SL). From this sleeve are cut out, at varying intervals and of different dimensions, windows which expose small portions of the metal. Over the cylinder are placed a number of metal fingers, f_1, f_2, f_3, which make contact with the cylinder whenever one of the windows passes beneath. The fingers complete one or another of several circuits, such as $f_1-S_1-Mg_1-A$ or $f_2-S_2-Mg_2-A$. S_1, S_2, S_3 are excitatory mechanisms; Mg_1, Mg_2, Mg_3 are electromagnets. Both are connected in simple series with the metal fingers. The function of each of the excitatory mechanisms is to produce a particular stimulus. The electromagnets function in connection with the second or recording unit of the apparatus.

From the arrangement of the parts and the electrical con-

*Reprinted from *Journal of Experimental Psychology*, 1926, **9**, 141-145.

nections indicated in Fig. 1, it is obvious that every time one of the fingers makes contact with the metal cylinder a par-

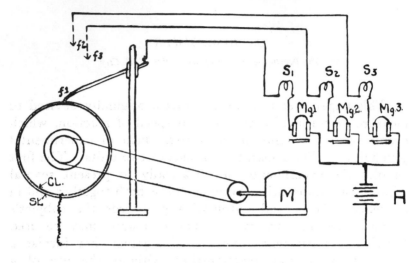

Fig. 1

ticular stimulus is set off and continued so long as the contact is maintained.   The duration of a stimulus will depend upon the speed at which the motor is revolving and the dimension of the window; the frequency with which it appears, upon the number of times a like window passes under its corresponding metal finger.   All these factors may, of course, be determined in advance by the experimenter, who can thus control the frequency and the order of his stimuli as well as their duration. Moreover, the number of different *kinds* of stimulus that can be employed simultaneously is only limited by the width of the cylinder.

Recording the Responses

The mechanism of the second unit of the apparatus (Fig. 2) enables the experimenter to obtain an automatic record of the reactions to a series of stimuli.   Connected in series with the source of current (25 volts) are several make-and-break mechanisms (R_1, R_2, R_3), *e.g.*, push buttons or telegraphers keys, certain of which the subject uses in response to the various stimuli, and likewise a number of electric counters

(C_1, C_2, C_3) which will register these responses when the individual circuits of which they form part are entirely closed or completed. But each of these circuits can be completed only if already partially closed at the points p_1, p_2, p_3, which are controlled by the electromagnets Mg_1, Mg_2, Mg_3 in series with the stimulus-provoking mechanisms shown in Fig. 1. Thus, when the stimulus S_1 is presented, the current flowing through the circuit f_1–S_1–Mg_1–A (Fig. 1) causes the armature, a_1, to be attracted to the metal block, b_1, thereby closing the circuit a_1–b_1–p_1–R_2–B (Fig. 2) at point p_1. But the circuit is still

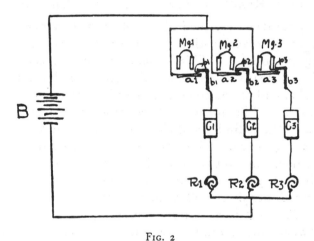

FIG. 2

open at point R_1 and can be completed only when the subject makes contact at this point by reacting with the appropriate response. Hence, if R_1 is the correct response to S_1, the circuit can be completed only when the subject reacts with R_1. If he accomplishes this within the time that the stimulus is being maintained, the response will be recorded by the counter. C_1; if he responds too late, or with any other reaction, such as R_2 or R_3, the circuit cannot be completed and the counter C_1 will fail to register. Nor will any of the other counters (*e.g.*, C_2 or C_3) register, since the circuits of which they form part are open at the points p_2 and p_3 respectively.

The automatical record of responses to various forms of stimulus is made possible, as indicated above, by the use of electric counters which both record and total the subject's reactions as they are made.   The only task left to the experimenter is to note the counter-readings at the beginning and at the end of the experiment.   The difference between the two figures is the number of correct reactions made within the permitted time. Errors or wrong reactions could also be recorded by the use of additional counters and by certain modifications in the electric circuits.   For the sake of simplicity these have not been considered.

Measuring Reaction Time without a Chronoscope

The apparatus described above offers a very easy method of calculating reaction-times without the use of a time-recording instrument.   This is made possible by the fact that it supplies a means of automatical control of the duration of the stimulus and of the time within which the correct reaction may be made.   The duration of the stimulus is determined by the speed of the cylinder and the size of the windows cut from the insulating sleeve.   Given the speed the windows are made of such dimension that the duration of the stimulus will be of any desired length.   A sufficiently large number of windows of varying dimensions will then furnish a graded [1] series of stimuli.   The rest is a matter of making the proper connections between Unit 1 and Unit 2 of the apparatus.   All stimuli of a given duration are connected with a particular electric counter which then registers the total number of correct reactions for this time; that is to say, the total number of successes for a particular reaction-time interval.   From the figures thus obtained it is then easy to calculate a subject's mean reaction-time in a manner similar to that employed in calculating a limen by the method of right-and-wrong cases.[2]

An illustration will make the method clear.   Suppose that we desire to calculate the motor reaction-time to a visual stimulus.   We decide first on the limits of our durations.

---

[1] The durations of the stimuli, should, when possible, vary by some constant interval.   This simplifies the calculations.

[2] In our experiment a successful reaction would correspond to a correct (right) judgment, a failure to react within the time interval to an incorrect (wrong) judgment. No distinction is made between a failure to react and an incorrect reaction.

For practical purposes 100 to 300 sigma are convenient limits. We next select the constant interval by which our reaction times are to differ. Suppose that it is 25 sigma. Then we cut windows in the insulating sleeve of such dimensions that the metal fingers will form contact with the cylinder for periods of 100, 125 . . . 300 sigma.[3] A sufficiently large number of windows are cut out to present each stimulus at least 10 times during the course of the experiment. This furnishes us with a graded series of stimuli of durations differing by a constant interval. Our apparatus enables us to record separately the successful reactions to each of these stimuli. This is done by the electric counters. All that we require at the end of the experiment is, then, to read off the totals from each of the counters and to tabulate them in an ascending or descending series thus:

Duration of Stimulus	Per cent. of Correct Reactions [4]
100 Sigma	0
125 "	10
150 "	25
175 "	45
200 "	70
225 "	85
250 "	95
275 "	98
300 "	100

It is then a matter of simple arithmetic to calculate the mean reaction-time or other desired value by means of available psychophysical formulas.

[3] Allowance must be made for the 'lags' in the various parts of the apparatus, and the dimensions of the windows corrected accordingly.

[4] The figures are hypothetical.

STUDIES IN CHRONAXIA
Methodology and Normal Variations, with a Report on Thirty Cases in Children*

DAVID WECHSLER and ROWLAND GODFREY FREEMAN, JR.

*The Child Development Institute, Teachers College, Columbia University,
and the Seaside Hospital, St. John's Guild*

This study is the first of a series of investigations which we have undertaken on the possible correlation between fundamental neuro-muscular responsiveness and the more complex psychomotor capacities in normal persons. Investigations on the separate aspects of the problem have absorbed the interests of both physiologist and psychologist, but correlations between the two thus far are wanting. The main reason, curiously, does not seem to be the absence of a technic for measuring the more complex processes (reaction time, motor speed, etc.) but the difficulty in obtaining reliable measures of neuromuscular responsiveness. This difficulty has seemingly now been removed by the researches of Lapicque and his pupils which furnish physiology with a constant and characteristic measure of neuromuscular excitability, chronaxia. We accordingly attempted to make use of this method in studying its possible availability in the investigation of our problem, and the present paper purports to give a résumé of our experience with it, together with the results obtained by its use on about thirty children.

Chronaxia, as defined by Lapicque, is an experimental constant of excitability which characterizes muscle-nerve responsiveness to electrical stimulation. It is a time threshold—the time required by a current to produce a liminal muscular contraction, with an intensity twice that necessary for it to produce the same contraction when permitted to continue for an indefinitely long duration. More generally, the chronaxia of a muscle or nerve is its electrical time coefficient of excitability or the minimal duration of electrical (galvanic) stimulation that will suffice to evoke from it a liminal response.

This definition differs from the historical view as regards neuro-muscular excitability in two important respects: It asserts (1) that the duration of a current as well as its intensity determines its effectiveness as an exciting stimulus, and (2) that the minimal time required for the

*Reprinted from *Archives of Neurology and Psychiatry*, 1929, **22**, 558-567. Copyright 1929, American Medical Association.

excitation of a particular muscle or nerve (under certain conditions) is a characteristic of its excitability. Both of these generalizations have proved of tremendous significance.

A detailed discussion of the researches which led to these generalizations is beyond the scope of this paper. But it may be pertinent to recall those which are of special interest.

The historical view as to the effectiveness of the galvanic current as a source of stimulation which continued unchallenged from the time when it was first put forth by DuBois-Reymond (1848-1850) until displaced by the modern researches, was that the excitability of a muscle or nerve was exclusively a function of the variation of intensity of the stimulating current and independent of its duration. This view was based on the fact that investigation had shown that the galvanic current acted as an exciting stimulus only on the make or break of the current, whereas no change was perceived during its continued passage. Hence, argued DuBois-Reymond, it must be the change in the intensity of the current and not its actual duration which produced the excitation. Furthermore, in his own attempts to study the influence of curtailing the time of passage of the current on the excitability of muscle and nerve, he had never succeeded in noting any difference in the effectiveness of the current, however short the duration which he employed. He was, however, not aware of the fact that two factors accounted for his failure to observe this: the first, that he was working with a rapid muscle and nerve (the gastrocnemius muscle and the sciatic nerve of the frog), and the second, that his instrumentation did not permit him to obtain a current of sufficiently short duration. The shortest time which DuBois-Reymond employed was about 0.005 second; it happens that the chronaxia of the frog is in the vicinity of 0.0003 second, so that the duration of his shortest current was still more than ten times too large to begin to play any rôle.

During the years following the enunciation of DuBois-Reymond's generalizations, several investigators reported experiments that clearly contradicted the dicta of DuBois-Reymond, but the "laws," as his generalizations came to be known, continued to be accepted until definitely shown to be false by the Dutch physiologist, Hoorweg. In 1892, Hoorweg published the results of a series of experiments on the electrical excitation of motor points in human subjects in which, by the use of condenser discharges, he was able to show that the voltage and, since he was using an approximately constant resistance, the intensity required for effective stimulation varied inversely as the capacity of the condenser employed. Since the time of discharge of a condenser is a function of its capacity, Hoorweg had thus demonstrated that the duration of the passage of a current is not without significance in the excitation of a muscle, and that, on the contrary, there existed a definite relation between this time of passage and the voltage employed.

Weiss (1901), taking up these experiments and substituting directly measured durations instead of condenser discharges, verified the work of Hoorweg and established what has since become known as the laws of Weiss; namely, that the liminal intensity required for the excitation of a muscle or nerve diminished as the time of passage of a current increased up to a certain minimal point beyond which the increase in its duration had no further perceptible effect. The relation was expressed by him as i.t = a+ b.t, in which t is the time of passage of the liminal current, i the intensity of the current, and a and b two experimental constants which depend on the particular tissue excited and the conditions of the experiment, a being a quantity (Q) and b an intensity (I).

Lapicque's contributions were essentially threefold: (1) he showed that the generalization of Weiss held (approximately) for all muscle and nerve; (2) that the relation of a to b suggested by Weiss as a possible characteristic of irritability was in effect the only constant which characterized neuromuscular excitability, and (3) he furnished a method by which this characteristic, or chronaxia ("chronaxie"), as he named it, could be reliably determined. These contributions[1] have proved of momentous importance and have opened up a new vista of psychologic research and discovery. We mention here only two of them. The first and the more general one is that the chronaxia of a muscle or nerve is closely related to its functional activity. There is a direct relation between the speed of contraction of a muscle and its chronaxia, as is illustrated by the following examples (given by Lapicque):

TABLE 1.—*The Relation Between the Duration of a Muscular Contraction and Chronaxia*

Muscle	Chronaxia, Seconds	Duration of Contraction
Gastrocnemius (frog)	0.0003	0.15–0.20
Claw of crab	0.0030	5
Stomach of frog	0.0100	15–20

The general rule seems to be: with a short chronaxia, a quick response, and with a long chronaxia, a slow response.

The second contribution is that those factors which alter the physiologic function of a muscle or nerve also alter its chronaxia; for instance, temperature, fatigue, degeneration and the action of drugs. Thus, cooling or fatigue lengthen a muscle's chronaxia; increase of

---

1. Lapicque, L.: L'excitabilité in fonction du temps, Presses Universitaires de France, 1926.

temperature and veratrine shorten it. When a nerve degenerates, its chronaxia is lengthened; as it regenerates, it tends to return to its normal value, etc.

One thus sees that the chronaxia of muscle and nerve is a significant indicator of their functional activity and is influenced by the same factors which affect the organism as a whole. It is these facts which suggested to us the possibility of correlating the differences of psychomotor capacities in general with variations of chronaxia. There was, however, first the problem of methods to be considered. It is therefore the question of the availability of the technic and its practical application with which, as already mentioned, this paper is concerned.

PROCEDURE

The measurement of chronaxia in human subjects, as indicated by Lapicque and perfected by Bourguignon, is effected by the use of condensers. The procedure involves two essential steps:

1. The first is to obtain a liminal response (contraction) of the muscle examined. This is done in a way similar to the method employed in monopolar exploration. One determines the minimal voltage required with a make of a galvanic current, using the negative pole as a stimulating electrode. This is the rheobase of Lapicque.

2. With a current twice this voltage, the experimenter successively charges and discharges a series of condensers, using the same points of stimulation. The capacity just sufficient to produce a contraction equal to that obtained with a rheobasic voltage gives the chronaxia sought.

We shall now discuss each of the required operations.

(1). *Finding the Motor Point and the Rheobasic Voltage.*—The charts for locating motor and sensory points, as given in the textbooks on anatomy and neurology, are of little assistance because at best they are only approximate. In practice, it is necessary to find them for every subject anew. Their precise localization is often both a difficult and a tedious task. The same difficulty is present when one merely seeks a sensory or motor threshold, but for ordinary electro-diagnosis exact localization is not so essential. To obtain accurate measures of chronaxia it is absolutely necessary. When the passage of a current is of short duration, it has not the same opportunity to diffuse as when the duration is indefinite. It is sufficient to displace the stimulating electrodes only a few millimeters to "lose" the point; then one has to start over again. This is particularly true in the case of young children whose nerve trunks are naturally thinner and hence offer smaller "points" at the surface of the skin. Another difficulty is the elasticity of the skin. If one is not careful one risks having the motor point slip from under. It is absolutely essential that the electrode be applied with uniform pressure and without change of direction. Movements, however small, whether of the examiner or of the subject, are likely to throw the electrode off the motor point.

It sometimes happens, after a rheobase with a particular voltage has been obtained, that repetition of the experiment gives a considerably higher or lower value. Such variations almost invariably turn out to be due to inaccurate localization of the motor point. Even with a small area (from 5 to 15 sq. mm.) which constitutes the motor point region, there is often an optimal or central point. With children we found that displacement of the electrodes for as little as 1 or 2 mm., or even merely changing the angle at which the electrode was applied, made a difference between a normal and a heightened chronaxia.

This last problem brings us to a final important consideration. In searching for the rheobase it is essential to employ unpolarizable electrodes and, what is more important, to avoid polarization of the tissues by the use of continued unidirectional stimulation. This is achieved by changing the direction of the current, through the use of a commutator, with each alternate excitation.

(2) *The Measurement of Chronaxia by the Use of Condensers.*—The measurement of chronaxia, which is a time dimension, by the use of condensers depends on the fact that the rate of discharge of a condenser is a function of its capacity, and the resistance of the circuit across which it is discharged, being proportional to the product RC. If then the capacity is the variable to be measured, the resistance must be kept constant. It happens, however, that the resistance of a tissue, and particularly that of the body, varies from subject to subject and with the conditions of the experiment (temperature, size of electrodes and other factors). Hence, a method must first be found to eliminate or to compensate for these causes of variability. This is achieved by introducing in series and in parallel, a large fixed resistance, such that the subject's individual variation becomes negligible with regard to the total resistance of the circuit. The resistance (R) of the circuit being approximately constant, the chronaxia-time (t) may be calculated as follows: $t = RC \times K$, when C is the capacity used to give the liminal contraction with a rheobasic voltage, and K is the experimental constant, obtained by comparing the condenser discharge with direct rheotomic measurements. This can be done once for all, and was found by Professor Lapicque to be 0.37. The formula then becomes $t = RC \times 0.37$. R being known, t may be calculated by multiplying C by a constant ratio. Thus in Bourguignon's circuit for the measurement of chronaxia in man (which we employed in our investigation), R, the mean reduced resistance, is 11,000 ohms; whence, $t = Ct \times 11,000 \times 0.37$, and, expressing Ct in microfarads, $t = 11,000 \times 0.000001$ (mf) $\times 0.37 = 0.004$. That is to say, when the resistance of the circuit is 11,000 ohms, $t = Ct \times 0.004$, when $t =$ chronaxia in seconds and Ct, capacities in microfarads.[2]

(3) *Normal Variations in Chronaxia.*—The fundamental contribution of Lapicque to the problem of neuromuscular excitability of a muscle or nerve[3] was a constant which characterized its excitability and was correlated with its functional activity. Different muscles in the same organism and the same muscles in different organisms have their characteristic chronaxias. Bourguignon verified this for the human body and has been able to show by extensive investigation of almost the entire skeletal system that the chronaxias of these muscles classify them into various groups according to their synergetic function. Table 1 gives the figures for the chronaxia of the arm, forearm and hand, given by Bourguignon.

Two facts thus stand out: 1. It is not the anatomic distribution of a muscle or nerve that determines its chronaxia but its synergistic function. 2. There is

2. Bourguignon, G.: La chronaxie chez l'homme, Paris, Masson & Cie, 1923, p. 79. When R is a different value, Ct will have to be multiplied, of course, by another number. The term Ct, designating the minimal capacity needed to obtain a threshold contraction, when seeking a chronaxia, was introduced by Bourguignon.

3. A muscle and its nerve have the same chronaxia.

a definite line of demarcation between the chronaxias of different groups of muscles.

There is yet a third fact, the one which inspired our researches. If one examines the values for chronaxia in each of the groups, one notices that they are not single (mean) figures but represent a range. Thus the chronaxia of the biceps and deltoid muscles is not 0.10 or 0.12 sigma, but from 0.08 to 0.16 sigma; that of the extensor communis digitorum is not 0.40 sigma or 0.60 sigma, etc., but from 0.44 to 0.72 sigma, and so on. The question is whether this range is due to experimental sources of error or whether it represents individual differences. Unfortunately, Bourguignon does not take up this last point. There is some external evidence, however, that the variation is due to individual differences. The range of variability is the same as one finds in the measurement of most biologic and psychologic traits, namely, as 1 : 2.[4] Thus, omitting the extreme

TABLE 2.—*Chronaxias of the Muscles of the Arm, Forearm and Hand,*
According to Bourguignon

Group	Muscle	Chronaxia Sigmas
I	Biceps Deltoid Brachialis anticus Supinator longus Internal head of triceps	0.08–0.16
II	External head of triceps Intermediate portion of triceps	0.16–0.32
III	Pronators Superficial and deep flexors Palmaris brevis and longus All muscles of hand Muscles innervated by the median nerve	0.20–0.36
IV	Supinator brevis Extensor carpi ulnaris All the extensors Abductor longus pollicis	0.44–0.77

measures, the weights of white adults fall approximately within the range of from 100 to 180 pounds, their intelligence quotients roughly between 60 and 130, and so on. Indeed, the ratio seems to hold for such different data as the variation in the size of green peas and the weekly salaries of American stenographers.

Now if one examines the chronaxias in figures reported by Bourguignon, one finds that they fall roughly within this range of variation and one might accordingly assume, on *a priori* grounds, that they represent individual differences.

The question, of course, is whether they do represent such differences. Bourguignon, in presenting his figures, speaks merely of averages (moyens), but it is not clear whether they stand for mean values or average or extreme variations, since no measure of dispersing is given, and the answer necessarily awaits further statistical analysis.

---

4. The figure is approximate, of course. Often it is more nearly as 2 : 3 and sometimes as high as 2 : 5, depending largely on the true or assumed zero. The generalization is based on unpublished researches by one of us (D. W.) which will appear shortly in a separate article.

In any case, further data and verification seem desirable, and the researches that we have to report are an attempt in this direction.

PERSONAL INVESTIGATIONS

Our efforts consisted in obtaining measures of chronaxia on a series of thirty children between the ages of 7 and 12 years. As a determination of chronaxia takes a considerable time (from ten to fifteen minutes) we limited our preliminary study to three muscles, that is, the biceps, the superficial flexors of the fingers (stimulating over the median nerve) and the extensor communis digitorum. These were chosen because they have distinctly different chronaxias, that is, chronaxias of different orders of magnitude, and because the location of their motor points and the detection of the liminal contraction are much easier than in the case of most other muscles.

Apparatus and Technic.—As regards both method and instrumentation, we followed as closely as possible the technic described and employed by Bourguignon.[5] A description of these has already appeared several times in the literature, but the following outline of our present set-up is given to indicate both its correspondence with that of Bourguignon and any deviations that we may have introduced:

Circuit employed......................	Same as that used by Bourguignon
Source of current......................	180 volt storage batteries
Condensers *...........................	0.01 to 1.0 mf. (paper, accuracy 2 per cent)
Resistance of potentiometer..........	650 ohms
Reduced resistance of circuit.........	11,000 ohms
Electrodes.............................	Silver and silver chloride, covered with asbestos soaked in normal physiologic solution of sodium chloride
Size...................................	Stimulating (negative) electrode, 1 sq. cm.; indifferent (positive) electrode, 5 × 10 cm.
Area of application †.................	Stimulating electrode over motor point; indifferent electrode, thigh of right leg

* For the determination of normal chronaxia, condensers of greater capacity are not required.

† Bourguignon attached the indifferent electrode to the subject's chest. In the case of children we found it more convenient to attach it to the place indicated. The reduced size of the indifferent electrode is made necessary by the fact that our subjects were children. Both these deviations from the indicated technic do not, however, influence results in any way.

RESULTS

The following readings were taken: (1) rheobasic voltage, (2) the intensity of the current (milliamperes passing through the subject at rheobasic voltage) and (3) the capacity (Ct) to obtain minimum contraction with the double rheobasic voltage.

Three readings were taken during the course of each examination, making nine chronaxia determinations per subject, or three for each muscle examined. In making our calculations, the median of the three measures taken in each case was used.

---

5. Bourguignon (footnote 2, chap. 3).

The analyses of our observations are summarized in the following four tables:

TABLE 3.—*Current Intensity of Rheobasis*

Muscle *	Average, Milliamperes	Standard Deviation, Milliamperes	Total Range, Milliamperes
Biceps ...	1.03	0.37	0.6–1.8
Superficial flexor of fingers...	1.07	0.38	0.3–1.4
Extensor communis digitorum...	1.56	0.42	0.8–1.3

* The region of stimulation was the motor point of the muscle; in the case of the flexors of the fingers, the median nerve.

TABLE 4.—*Chronaxia in MF (Ct)*

Muscle	Average, Microfarads	Standard Deviation, Microfarads	Total Range, Microfarads
Biceps	3.28	0.69	2–5
Superficial flexor of fingers...	6.27	1.30	4–9
Extensor communis digitorum...	14.40	2.70	12–21.5

TABLE 5.—*Chronaxia (t) in Thousandths of Seconds (Sigma)*

Muscle	Average, Sigma	Standard Deviation, Sigma	Total Range, Sigma
Biceps	0.131	0.038	0.08–0.20
Superficial flexor of fingers...	0.251	0.052	0.16–0.36
Extensor communis digitorum ...	0.576	0.108	0.48–0.85

TABLE 6.—*The Comparative Range of Chronaxia*

Muscle	Bourgignon's Range, Sigma	Total Range in Our Experiment, Sigma	Per Cent of Our Measures Falling within Bourgignon's Range
Biceps	0.08–0.16	0.08–0.20	90
Superficial flexor of fingers...	0.20–0.36	0.16–0.36	93
Extensor communis digitorum..	0.44–0.76	0.40–0.85	89.3

Table 3 gives the variation in intensity of current needed to evoke a liminal contraction at the rheobasic voltage. This corresponds to the familiar cathodal closure contraction used in electrodiagnosis. The intensity required varied roughly from 0.5 to 2 milliamperes, being practically identical for the superficial flexors and the biceps muscles, and somewhat larger for the stimulation of the extensor communis digitorum. The identity in figures for the biceps and the median again illustrates well how mere intensity of current fails to reveal any fundamental difference in muscular excitability. The higher milliamperage required for stimulating the extensor muscle is not due to the greater intensity of current needed for effective stimulation per se, but to the fact that in the case of the extensor muscle there is a greater diffusion of the current before it reaches the motor point, owing to the somewhat hidden position of the nerve. In any case, it should be noted that there is much over-lapping in the total ranges of amperage for the three muscles.

Tables 4 and 5 give the values for the chronaxia of the three muscles tested in terms of microfarads and sigmas, respectively. Table 5 is derived from table 4 by multiplying the values for chronaxia in micro-farads by 0.004 second. The figures show: 1. There is a close cor-respondence with the values given by Bourguignon. The chronaxias of muscles and nerves in children, within the ages specified, are thus the same as those in adults. 2. The total range of variance in normal chronaxia which we found is somewhat larger than that indicated by Bourguignon (see table 6) even for our median values. But here two facts must be considered: In the first place, we do not know whether Bourguignon's extreme figures represent total range or not. In the second place, it is possible, and indeed probable, that owing to our limited experi-ence with the method, our figures are not so accurate as they might be. While the chronaxia technic as such is simple, considerable practice is required for making reliable determinations. Nevertheless, comparison of our total range with the extreme figures given by Bourguignon shows that for the biceps 90 per cent of our (median) measures, 93 per cent in the case of the superficial flexors, and 90 per cent in the case of the extensor communis digitorum, fall within the range given by Bourguignon.

In addition to these observations we noted, as did Bourguignon and Strohl, that in the case of the extensor muscle one sometimes finds chronaxias of an entirely different order from those expected. Among the twenty-eight cases, in addition to the chronaxias given in table 5, we encountered chronaxias of from 0.24 to 0.40 sigma, or, roughly, approximately one-half that ordinarily characteristic of the extensor communis digitorum. The explanation for the discrepancy, according to Bourguignon, is that the extensors have in reality two different chronaxias corresponding to two different motor points, each cor-related with a distinct function of the muscle. Bourguignon observes that whether one hits on the motor point having the higher or lower chronaxia depends largely on whether, when searching for it, one pro-ceeds from below upward or vice versa. In our procedure we were not aware of any systematic method of experimentation, and it would thus seem that the motor point of the higher chronaxia is the more easily located. Like Bourguignon, however, we found that it is always possible to obtain the other by further search.

SUMMARY AND CONCLUSIONS

The normal chronaxia of various muscles in children, aged from 7 to 12 years, is the same as that in the adult.

The extreme range of variation in normal chronaxia for the muscles tested (the biceps, superficial flexors and extensor communis digitorum) is somewhat greater than that given by Bourguignon for adults. It is probable, however, that the discrepancies are due to errors of measurement.

The range of normal chronaxia (the ratio of its extreme limits) is, roughly, as 1 : 2.

The method for measuring chronaxia in men, as perfected by Bourguignon, is simple in both principle and technic, but because of the time, care and practice required for accurate measurements, it appears as yet to be a method for the special technician and research investigator rather than for the general clinician.

While the older clinical determinations of minimum intensity of current required to produce the muscular contraction may suffice for differentiation between normal and gross pathologic conditions, it does not permit the measurement of individual differences in normal neuromuscular excitability. This can be done only through the measurement of chronaxia.

The study of chronaxia opens up a new vista of psychophysiologic research. In view of the fact that the chronaxia of a muscle or nerve is affected by the same factors which influence the functional activity of the organism as a whole (fatigue, etc.), it seems probable that there is a positive correlation between the two. Subsequent studies by us will be devoted to the investigation of possible correlations between chronaxia and psychomotor and neuromuscular tendencies, particularly as manifested in the variability of childhood development.

ABSTRACT OF DISCUSSION

DR. A. B. HIRSH: Ten years ago, while stationed at the Walter Reed Hospital, I read a short paper at an annual meeting of the American Electrotherapeutic Association on some recent advances in muscle-nerve testing; this covered the old formula plus the use of the Lewis Jones condenser and, incidentally, having met at the time Dr. T. A. Williams, just back from Europe, I included material and illustrations which he furnished me on the chronaxia mode of testing. He had intended at that time to include it in a textbook on the treatment of nerve wounds during warfare. At the Walter Reed Hospital we had ample clinical material serving this purpose, but not having the apparatus, we lacked the opportunity of testing chronaxia in our cases. I lost touch with that side of practice for some years, but last summer, while in Europe, I went to the Salpêtrière hoping to meet Bourguignon and have him explain more to me about the technic of chronaxia. He was away on his vacation, however, and his assistants were seen using the method. What interested me particularly was the clinical side of chronaxia. One of the gentlemen present, a New York physician who was studying the method, and who used the French language fluently, acted as interpreter. This brought out the fact that, instead of requiring but three hours for the practical conclusion of one examination, the best part of a day was sometimes devoted to testing one case, and that is what interested me more than any other phase of the subject. I am not familiar with the physiologists' more recent studies of the method, but the fact that this method, scientific and thorough as it may be, requires so much time, of course, almost precludes its use, viewing it from the clinical point of view.

DR. WECHSLER: I suppose it is because Bourguignon examines so many muscles and nerves that his examination takes so long. During the last few years he has spent a great deal of time gathering material. Actually it takes about fifteen minutes to secure a reliable measurement of chronaxia in a muscle, and much of that time is spent, as in the ordinary clinical test, in finding the motor point. What reduces the time of examination in ordinary electrodiagnosis is that the physician does not have to find it accurately. In the case of chronaxia one does. After a little experience, it took us about thirty minutes per subject to do three complete chronaxias. The values on the chart we made are the medians of nine readings. We took three readings for each muscle, using the middle figure in each case to avoid extreme errors.

DR. JOHN LEVY: I am sure Dr. Wechsler will be good enough to straighten out for me a few points that arose in my mind while listening to his interesting discussion of chronaxia. As I have heretofore understood chronaxia, from my limited reading on the subject, it has seemed to mean a time relationship of nerve tissue. Muscle has acted only as an indicator of this time relationship. Dr. Wechsler sometimes refers to the chronaxia of nerves, sometimes of muscles. Is he not a little vague in that respect?

The next point is the physiologic constant that the speaker sets up for chronaxia. By chopping off both ends of his distribution curve, he is able to establish a 2:1 relationship between the extremes of his chronaxia range. This process seems to me to be artificial. Moreover, it disguises the possibility of a truer relationship. This relationship, or distribution, would more likely follow a normal distribution curve; in other words, it is a continuous series, such as is found in the distribution of intelligence. The fact that the extremes in Dr. Wechsler's range do not peter off to a much higher and lower level, when this 2:1 relationship no longer holds, is probably due to the selectivity of his subjects or the relative grossness of his measuring apparatus.

Has the lecturer any idea as to the possible relationship between chronaxia and intelligence? Some suggestive work has already been done on the relationship between reaction time and intelligence, and chronaxia seems to me to be related to the former. With reference to the possibility of making practical application of chronaxia time, one would be interested in knowing just how constant this time is for the same subject from day to day, and even for the same day. It would surely have to be constant before such application could be made.

I trust Dr. Wechsler will continue to work out these practical points. When this is done, Dr. Pierce Clark may then be able to say that, by means of psychoanalysis, the chronaxia time of the mentally defective patient has been raised eight sigma.

DR. WECHSLER: I am aware of the confusion which indiscriminate and indefinite use of the terms makes, but I have been constrained to repeat the bad usage, because I have never been able to conclude from my reading, whether of textbooks or articles on neurology, what the terms precisely were intended to include. The interchangeable use of muscle, muscle-nerve and nerve, however, does not affect our discussion, because as far as chronaxia is concerned, they are all the same. A muscle and its nerve, as demonstrated by Lapicque, have the same chronaxia.

As to the 2 : 1 ratio, we used this observation as a source of inspiration only. The thing about it which inspired us was the similarity in the total range of chronaxia with that met with in other biologic and psychologic measurements. This fact indicated that we were dealing with normal variations and not experimental errors. As to dropping 0.5 per cent of the cases, the amount is rather small. We cut off only the extreme portions of the curve, which I think is negligible, when one considers that the remainder includes over 99 per cent of the cases. The importance of the generalization derives not from the fact that the range includes a definite number of cases, but from the fact that it is true in its general aspect.

As regards the correlation between chronaxia and intelligence, I do not know that there are any figures for it. Because of the fertile fields of speculation and investigation which chronaxia has suggested, numerous hypotheses have already been advanced on the basis of it. A book which appeared about two or three years ago attempted to explain all the associative processes on the basis of similarity or identity of neural chronaxia. Association takes place not because of the hypothetic closing up of the dendritic processes, but because a nerve impulse finds its way most readily along paths of nerve processes with the same chronaxias. Irrespective of any theories, however, my personal opinion is that chronaxia will probably not correlate to any degree, if at all, with intelligence, because motor speed enters but little into the intellectual processes.

Dr. Louis S. Aronson: I should like to ask whether, in stating that there is a general constancy for chronaxia, it is relatively or really true in this respect, first, physiologically, and second, pathologically. Physiologically, does it make any difference whether we test out a certain muscle, say the biceps, whether it is a muscle used by brainworkers, or used a great deal for hard work, and second, as regards the age of the subject, would there be a marked difference in the reading of an adult and a child? To come to the second point: Pathologically, have any differences been found in muscles which showed subsequently atrophy or dystrophy, and has there been any experience with muscular atrophies or dystrophies in clinical subjects?

Dr. Wechsler: The first point brought up is one in which we are particularly interested, because it involves the question of individual differences and the factors which may determine them. A variation of several tenths of a sigma may appear negligible when one compares it with the large differences that are met with in the chronaxias of widely different types of musculature (for instance, the gastrocnemius and the muscles of the walls of the stomach in the frog, which have chronaxias of $3/10.000$ second and $1/100$ second, respectively), but may be significant in the case of any particular muscle. Thus the chronaxia of the biceps varies normally only within the range of 0.08 and 0.16 sigma, and it may be that a difference of from 0.04 to 0.06 sigma is sufficient to indicate a fundamental difference in neuromuscular responsiveness. It is differences of this kind, within the normal range, that we hope to study.

As regards the second point, we have no data ourselves, but various French authors, and particularly Bourguignon, give figures on the differences between normal and pathologic chronaxias. The differences are marked in certain myopathies and in the different types of degeneration, the chronaxia of pathologic or degenerated muscles and nerves ranging anywhere from two to one hundred times and more that of the normal.

NOTE ON THE CORRELATION BETWEEN CHRONAXIE
AND REACTION TIME*

R. G. FREEMAN, JR., and D. WECHSLER

*The Department of Biological Chemistry, College of
Physicians and Surgeons, Columbia University*

The researches of Lapicque and Bourguignon have shown that
the excitability of muscles as measured by their chronaxie is closely
associated with the form and duration of their contraction, the general rule being that the slower the contraction the longer the chronaxie and vice versa. This has been attested, on the one hand, by
the comparatively long chronaxies of smooth as compared with
striated musculature (animals) and on the other hand, by the chronaxie changes following nerve degeneration and those met with in
the various muscular dystrophies.

In view of this association it seemed to us that there might be
some correlation between motor speed and neuromuscular excitability, which might account for differences in speed of movement,
on the basis of a constitutional (organic) factor. The present note
is a report on the results obtained by simultaneous measurement of
the chronaxie and reaction time in 20 normal human subjects.

In obtaining the chronaxie we followed Bourguignon's technique,
employing a method described by us in a previous paper,[1] with the
apparatus assembled into a simple portable form devised by one of
us. The chronaxie was taken over the motor point of the biceps
muscle. The average of five readings was taken as the chronaxie.

The speed of bicepital contraction against which we correlated
the muscle chronaxie was obtained as follows: Each subject after
placing his forearm, fist clenched, upon a table in front of him was
instructed, upon a given signal, to move his fist horizontally to the

---

*Reprinted from *Proceedings of the Society for Experimental Biology and Medicine*, 1932,
29, 957-958.

[1] Wechsler, D., and Freeman, R. G., Jr., *Arch. Neur. and Psych.*, 1929, **22**, 558.

right (a distance of six inches), strike a key and then flex his arm as quickly as possible in a vertical direction. The height and distance through which the subject could flex his arm was limited by an extended board fastened 12 inches above the surface of the table and parallel to it, on the under surface of which was attached a legless telegraph key against which the subject's fist inevitably struck. The interval between the striking of the first and second keys was measured by a 1/100 split second chronometer started by the first blow and stopped by the second, and the interval taken as the reaction time. By breaking up the response into two steps the perceptual component was eliminated.

The table shows the individual data obtained in respect to the 2 variables measured.

TABLE I.

Case	Chronaxie (Σ)	Reaction Time (0.01 sec.)	Case	Chronaxie (Σ)	Reaction Time (0.01 sec.)
1	0.10	1.23	11	0.10	1.15
2	0.10	1.23	12	0.06	1.00
3	0.10	1.47	13	0.10	1.00
4	0.12	1.37	14	0.06	1.10
5	0.06	1.28	15	0.12	1.30
6	0.06	1.01	16	0.06	1.05
7	0.10	1.05	17	0.08	1.10
8	0.10	1.32	18	0.06	1.10
9	0.10	1.20	19	0.06	1.14
10	0.10	1.29	20	0.04	1.00

A correlation, by Sheppard's coefficient method of unlike signs, of 0.84 was found between the two measures. We interpret the results as showing that the speed of muscular contraction, and probably of movement in general is in some way dependent upon the chronaxie of the nerves and muscles involved.

THE ILLUSION OF THE OBLIQUE INTERCEPT*

PAUL SCHILDER and DAVID WECHSLER

The Psychological Department of the Psychiatric Division of Bellevue
Hospital, New York University Medical College

The literature of optic illusions is so enormous and the
interpretations given them are so numerous that one hesitates
to add to them. Our justification for doing so now is, first,
that the illusion to be presented has, so far as we know, not
been described before, at least not in its present form; second,
that the experiments to be detailed seem to throw some
additional light on the laws of form perception.

The optic illusion to which we wish to call attention and
which we shall call the *illusion of the oblique intercept*, consists
of a number of peculiar optical phenomena which are produced
in any system of narrowly spaced parallel lines when cut by a
transversal. The effects produced are in both parallel lines
(pr.l.) [1] and intervening spaces (i.sp.) [1] between them and are
to be observed at the edges of intersection. The phenomena
are illustrated in Fig. 1. Here a series of lines of approxi-

FIG. 1.

mately 1 mm in width are drawn on a white background at a
constant distance of about 1½ mm with a strip of white paper
placed across the lines so as to cut them at an angle of about
45° from the vertical. Fixating on the edges of intersection

[1] In subsequent references to the figures, pr.l. stands for parallel lines; i.sp. for the
intervening spaces; and trs. for the cut transversal or intercept.

*Reprinted from *Journal of Experimental Psychology*, 1936, **19**, 747-757.

one will observe (1) that the horizontal lines at the point where they are cut by the transversal are slightly clubbed; (2) that the spaces between them seemingly diverge; (3) that where the transversal meets the lines they appear to curve; (4) that the curvature or bending is downward—that is, obliquely towards the horizontal; (5) that in the case of any given line the curvature of its upper edge is always less than that of the lower edge, so that its cut thickness viewed singly appears to be arched; (6) the intervening spaces (i.sp.) show the same phenomena as the parallel lines (pr.l.). It is immaterial whether the i.sp. or pr.l. are seen as figure or background; nor does it matter whether the trs. is a white or black line (see Fig. 2).

Fig. 2.

A pair of lines showing the phenomena just described in a grossly exaggerated fashion is shown in Figs. 4a and b, in order to illustrate the features which may escape the unpracticed observer.

Figs. 4a and 4b.

There are a number of factors which influence the intensity of the illusion. The most obvious of these is the angle at which the oblique transversal crosses the parallel lines. If the transversal is placed perpendicular to the lines, that is at an

angle of 90°, the illusion is entirely absent. The clubbing of
the horizontal lines, for example, does not become noticeable
until the transversal is rotated some 15° from the vertical
(that is, forms an angle of about 105° with the intersected
horizontal). From that point down it increases progressively
until an angle of about 140° to 150° is reached, after which
the phenomena remain fairly constant for another 15° of
clockwise rotation. As an angle of about 165°, however, is
reached, some rather peculiar phenomena take place. The
clubbing of the lines persists, but there is a change in the direction of their curvature; instead of both edges of the intersected
pr.l. curving downwards, the upper edge now seems to be
turned upwards; whereas the lower edge continues to curve
in its original direction (Figs. 6a and 6b).

If the transversal instead of being rotated from the perpendicular towards the horizontal, is placed parallel to the
horizontal and then rotated from 0 to 90° (counter clockwise),
similar phenomena will be observed except that the effects
described at the critical angles will be reversed.

In addition to the foregoing there are a number of other
details regarding the phenomena which are well worth noting.
Among the most important are the following:

It does not matter whether the parallel lines are horizontal
or vertical. Of importance is only the angle at which the
transversal cuts them.

The illusion is less striking if the parallel lines are very
thin or very thick. (Under ordinary conditions, a maximal
effect is obtained with parallel lines having a cross-section of
about 1 mm; spaced at a distance of about 1½ mm from each
other.) If the lines are too thick, the curvature appears to
be only slight, and the clubbing of the lines tends to disappear. The latter, probably, because the illusory effect is
relatively negligible when the diameter of the lines is already
considerable.

Darkening of the visual field has no measurable effect on
the phenomena.

When the parallel lines are short, the phenomenon de-
creases considerably. Some extension of the pr.l. is seemingly

necessary in order to give the impression of a difference between the oblique and perpendicular cut of the transversal. This difference is particularly outstanding when one has a number of pr.l., and covers them obliquely with a black paper so that the lowest line has about a length of 20 mm, the subsequent line about 25 mm, etc. (See two lowest lines in Fig. 2.)

The phenomenon of bending and clubbing can be seen even when only one parallel line is used, but it is much more marked when we deal with a series of lines. This is true even when the distance (i.sp.) between the parallel lines is increased to about 1 cm; but it is more outstanding when the distance between the horizontal lines is only about $1\frac{1}{2}$ or 2 mm.

The illusion persists under tachistoscopic exposure down to 1/25 of a second, though under short exposures it is greatly attenuated; generally speaking, the shorter the exposure, the less striking is the perceived illusion.

Fatigue and fixation of long duration accentuates the illusion.

We were not able to produce the illusion stereoscopically. It was not possible to combine corresponding figures owing to visual rivalry.

The illusion is particularly marked if the lines are observed at a distance sufficient to give one a total impression of the system. Under this condition the area about the parallel lines in the region of their interception seems to be extended, and both the lines and the intervening spaces seem to diverge like the strings at the base of a harp.

There is also a marked alteration in the appearance of the cutting transversal (trs.). In the region where the clubbing occurs, whether on the black lines (pr.l.) or on the white spaces between (i.sp.), the intersected portion of the transversal seems to be definitely curved inwards. The intercept (trs.) as a whole is also slightly curved, and the entire transversal takes on convex appearance, encroaching as it were on the spaces between the parallel lines (pr.l.). This effect is particularly striking if one attends to the figure as a whole. (It is as if the whole trs. system has undergone changes similar to those of the intercepted parts of the single pr.l. and the spaces between them.)   (Figs. 1–4.)

If one concentrates on the appearance of the cutting line (trs.), one finds that it does not appear as a straight line but looks like a staircase, the parallel lines representing the succeeding levels or 'steps' of the staircase. The transversal is broken into small pieces each succeeding one of which is pushed inwards as it approaches the next higher 'step' of the pr.l. system.   This staircase phenomenon (Fig. 3)

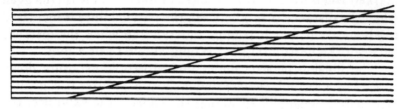

FIG. 3.

augments as the cutting trs. is rotated from the vertical towards the horizontal.   It is particularly clear as it approximates an angle of 10 degrees from the horizontal, where the illusion of a staircase is almost complete (Figs. 6a and b).

As may be supposed, the explanation of the illusion is more difficult than its description. The interpretation of geometrical illusions generally call upon three principles: There is, first, the illusion of perspective, or the tendency of lines to take on three dimensional aspects, as in the pseudoscopic prisms or the Oppel figures. Second, there is the illusion of variable space, where different portions of space are attracted to the figure, depending upon the orientation of the limiting lines, as in the case of the Müller-Lyer illusion. Third, there is the illusion resulting from the tendency to overestimate small angles and underestimate large angles, as in the case of the Poggendorf phenomenon.[2]

---

[2] To these are often added some subsidiary principles, like the tendency to see obtuse angles as right angles, the attraction of the horizontal for the oblique at its intersection, the influence of eye movement in traversing a figure, etc.   But none of these taken alone seem sufficient as ultimate explanations.   We agree with Koffka that these principles take on significance only when considered in connection with more fundamental *Gestalt* principles.

Of these three, it is clear almost at once that the first two, namely the principles of perspective and of variable space, can be of little assistance to us.   On the other hand, the principle of over and under estimation of angles seems, at first, quite pertinent.   This particularly, in view of the fact that the illusion of the oblique intercept has a rather close resemblance to the Poggendorf phenomenon, which is commonly accounted for in terms of the overrating of sharp angles.   The resemblance between the illusion of the oblique intercept, or at least certain aspects of it, to that of the Poggendorf phenomenon is perhaps best seen from the simultaneous inspection of the modified Poggendorf figure as illustrated by Wundt (Fig. 5) in his *'Physiologische Psychologie.'* [3]   Wundt describes

Fɪɢ. 5.

it as follows: "A vertical black stripe is crossed at a sharp angle by an oblique line. The ends of the oblique line bordering the stripe seem to be bent towards the stripe." [4] The oblique intercept (trs.) in our illusion corresponds to the crossing line in the Poggendorf phenomenon.   The Poggendorf phenomenon, however, never has been sufficiently studied with any considerable number of the striped lines arranged into a system, and the phenomena described by us have,

[3] 6th edition, Vol. 2, page 588:
[4] Werner has further noted that the vertical stripe is also curved.

therefore, escaped the attention of previous investigators. Although one observes in our figures the continuity of the pr.l. system as one does in the crossing line of the Poggendorf phenomenon, we nevertheless feel justified in attempting an interpretation of them based upon the phenomena primarily observed in our illusion.

Of fundamental importance in the interpretation of the illusion of the oblique intercept is the fact that the horizontal lines are curved in the region where they are intersected by the transversal. One cannot speak, therefore, merely of the overrating of small angles, since we are here confronted with a new phenomenon, namely a curving effect. This curving may be observed in Figs. 1 and 2 and is particularly noticeable on the lower part of the parallel lines. No interpretation can neglect this curving [5] which cannot be referred back to any other phenomenon. It is not dependent on the luminosity of the crossing system (trs.) nor is it due to irradiation. The tendency to curving on the other hand is closely bound up with the characteristic of the crossing line (trs.). Thus, it increases with the diminution of the angle between the parallel system (pr.l.) and the intercept (trs.). Our view is that the mass of the parallel lines attracts the mass of the crossing system as a whole, and also the single portions of the crossing system. The curving of the parallel lines is therefore less noticeable when the crossing line (Fig. 3) is thin and accordingly exerts less mass attraction. If such a mass attraction takes place one would expect it to be stronger on the lower edges of the pr.l. which are more exposed to the attraction of the crossing system, owing to the reduced inner pull of the pr.l., *per se*.

It is very probable that the tendency to see angles as curves is to a great extent due to the mutual attraction between their two sides. Any two intersecting lines seemingly exert a mutual pull on each other, and the phenomenon with its consequent effects (curving) is not restricted to lines cutting each other at sharp angles. Thus F. B. Hoffman

[5] In describing the modified Poggendorf phenomenon, Wundt refers to the bending of the cutting line. This is quite different from a curving, and is an incorrect description of what actually occurs.

has shown that even very obtuse angles appear curved when the wides of the angle are made very small.

When the angle between trs. and pr.l. becomes 165 degrees, the upper edge of pr.l. is curved upwards as mentioned above (Fig. 6). At this angle the mass attraction of the trs. be-

FIGS. 6a and 6b.

comes paramount, also for the upper edge of pr.l., whereas the inner pull of the pr.l. is reduced. It thus seems that the tendency to see lines curved in virtue of their mutual mass attraction is a widely recurring phenomenon. The attraction between lines is dependent on the mass of the figure and on the relation of the different parts to one another. Many details of our findings point into this direction. The mass distribution in figures plays the most important part. Our view is that the overrating of small angles in our figures is due to the curving of the enclosing lines at the point where they meet. Contrary to Wundt's opinion, there is no suggestion that either perspective or overrating of such angles is the cause of the curving.

The clubbing of the lines may be interpreted as being due to different attractions exerted on the upper and lower borders of the pr.l. stripes by the trs., though it is very probable that this explanation is insufficient. Another factor to be considered is that when a transversal cuts a stripe (pr.l. or i.sp.) at an angle, the diameter of the section is actually much greater than it is when cut perpendicularly. We tend to orient ourselves towards the vertical; this, seemingly because we are accustomed to see lines cut at approximately right angles. The tendency is very general and was already noted by Fechner and used by him in explaining "Why sausages are cut on the slant." The answer is that the slice looks much bigger. The sausage is more imposing, since the obliqueness of the cut has not been taken into full consideration. That this effect plays really a part in the phenomenon, is reinforced by the illusion experienced from the rotation of the transversal through an angle of 90°. During such rotation each segment of the cut transversal changes from the vertical to the horizontal. In doing so it broadens out, and this change is closely related to the clubbing effect. The effect produced by the gradual rotation of the transversal suggests that the mutual mass attraction is particularly strong when there is movement in the optic field, and also that intrafigural movement may be an important factor in what we have called mass attraction. There is no evidence that eye movements, *per se*, play an important part in this phenomenon.

We are inclined to underrate the deviations from the fundamental directions of orientation, namely the horizontal and the vertical. When the horizontal line is intercepted obliquely the deviation of the crossing line from the perpendicular will be reconstituted, that is, will tend to appear nearer to the vertical than it really is. When we see the intercept nearer to the vertical, the effect of the apparent rotation is to make the intersected bit of the intercept appear to be thicker.

It is especially difficult to explain the changes in the crossing system (trs.). They seem to be closely related, however, to the curving-in phenomenon which is present both in the parallel lines and the intervening spaces. In any case, there is a seemingly stronger attraction between the trs. and the lower border of the intercepted lines, than between the trs. and its upper border. This difference is especially marked when the transversal cuts the parallel lines at a very small angle to produce the staircase phenomenon already mentioned (Figs. 3 and 6).

The curving-in phenomenon is the expression of the effect of the counter mass attraction of the parallel lines on the transversal. As might be expected, the smaller the internal angle between the two intersecting lines the greater will this effect be. Under such conditions, particularly when the angle is very small, if we focus our attention on the transversal segment between any two parallels, it will be observed that the lower edge of the upper parallel exerts a marked attraction for the upper third of the transversal segment, and the upper edge of the lower parallel a similar attraction for the lower third of the transversal segment. The middle third appears to be brought to a vertical position so that the total illusion is as shown in Fig. 7. Here again then, the observed phe-

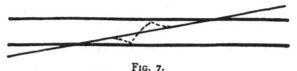

FIG. 7.

nomenon seems to be mainly due to two factors, (1) mass attraction, (2) the tendency to orient towards the vertical or the horizontal.

In the final interpretation of the illusion, therefore, we are left chiefly with the problem of mass attraction between the different parts. This mass attraction might be referred to as a sort of 'gravitational pull.' This principle is bound up with the principles of intrafigural movements. Our view is that mass attraction is the basic principle which explains the phenomena we have described. Supplementing it are the principles of intrafigural movements and the tendency of the human eye to orient all intersecting parts towards its preferred directions, namely the horizontal or vertical. All the other principles such as the overrating of angles, the tendency to see curves instead of straight lines, are seemingly subordinated to these two. The principle of mass attraction has to do with the organization of the total visual field, and thus explains the enormous influence which the repetition of the motive has on the illusion. We think that the principles here presented will also furnish a better explanation of the Poggendorf phenomenon, and the Herring and the Oppel figures for which Sanford ventured a similar interpretation.

SUMMARY

The authors describe an hitherto unreported optical illusion, with the factors which seemingly determine it. The illusion, termed *the illusion of oblique-intercept*, is observed whenever a system of parallel lines is crossed by a line cutting them obliquely. The main characteristics of the illusion are a clubbing of the parallel lines at the edge of interception, an apparent spreading or 'fanning' of the intermediate spaces, a curving of these as well as of the intercepted line, and finally a staircase effect along the intercepting transversal.

The phenomena described are accounted for in terms of a number of psycho-physiological tendencies of which the two principal ones are: 1. The phenomenon of mutual mass attraction of the sides of intersecting lines upon each other. This mutual attraction accounts for the rounding up of sharp angles and the overrating of small angles. The mutual mass attraction is closely related to the total organization of the visual field and its intrafigural movements, and increases, therefore, with reduplication. 2. The human eye has a preference for the vertical and horizontal, and accordingly shows a tendency to orient points of the compass to one or another of these principle directions. In virtue of this preference there is a further tendency to neglect directional deviations from the principal visual coördinates. In consequence of this neglect, the sides of the angles depending upon characteristics of the visual field, are attracted nearer to the one or the other of the main visual coördinates.

This last phenomenon is particularly clear in the case of the staircase illusion in which the deviations of an oblique line are in part attracted to the horizontal and in part to the vertical directions of the crossing system.

(Manuscript received November 11, 1935)

REFERENCES

1. HOFFMAN, F. B., Die Lehre vom Raumsinn, 1st and 2nd edit.   *Hand. der Gesamten Augenheilkunde* by Axenfeld and Elschnig, 2nd edit. Vol. 3, Chapter 13, Berlin, Springer, 1925.
2. KOFFKA, K., *Psychologie der optischen Wahrnehmung. Ibid.*, pp. 1215–1271. *Handb. d. norm. und path. Physiol.*, 12, 2.
3. SANFORD, E. C., *Course in Experimental Psychology.* 1898.
4. WERNER, H., Uber Structur Gezetze in der sogenanten Geometrich optichen Tauschungen, *Zeit. f. Psych.*, 1929, 14, 248.
5. WUNDT, W., *Gundzüge der Physiologischen Psychologie.* Vol. 2.   6th edition, 1910.

PART VIII

INTRODUCTION

As might be expected of the clinician, David Wechsler early established and has maintained an interest in emotional states and their measurement. This section includes nine papers, the first published in 1922 and the last in 1945. The earlier papers reflect a strong experimentalist viewpoint, dealing as they do with definition and measurement problems. In the latter papers, the influence of the experimental method is still evident, but there is a movement toward clinical assessment and interpretation as well.

The first of the papers in this series represents something of a special case. After World War I, David Wechsler had been awarded a scholarship to study in France, and had used the opportunity for the training with Lapique which eventually led to the doctoral dissertation conducted at Columbia. At one point, however, it was necessary to make a decision as returning to this country or furthering a stay in France. Having made the decision, Wechsler speculated about the state of indecision in which he had found himself, and this paper is a result of that insightful speculation. The content of the paper is largely definitional, but proposes ideas which allow psychological interpretation of the term as well.

The succeeding four papers are related to each other and form a cohesive reflection of measurement and interpretation of matters dealing with emotions. "The Measurement of Emotional Reactions" (2) is abstracted here to reflect some conclusions about the nature of emotion using physical measures. Measurement was based upon a psychogalvanic reflex which Wechsler defines in a physical sense, but relates as well to a psychological meaning. It is the latter which becomes of some importance in judging the validity of the research. The position taken, not only by him, but by others to the present day, is that the psychogalvanic reflex does reflect the status of an affective reaction when some stimulus is applied which is excitatory in nature. Indeed, Wechsler takes the position in this paper that the psychogalvanic reflex is a direct response to some specific excitation which is affective in nature.

The importance of this position, if viable, is that measurement of the reflex can be useful to the clinician in matters of differential diagnosis for given mental and nervous conditions. In its entirety, the publication abstracted dealt primarily with methodology and technique, an essential first issue before application and interpretation. Wechsler assumes that the preliminaries reflected in the article

323

indeed allow for some consideration of the use of the psychogalvanic reflex to measure the emotional state, in a specific fashion, of the individual.

There follows a lucid discussion of the term "emotion" and its meaning. In the writings to the day there was considerable ambiguity. Wechsler avoids the ambiguity, in part, by using the term emotion only in a very general sense and trying to describe specific aspects of this general state for scientific communication.

The following article (3) explores more fully the position that emotional reactions are specific in nature. Based upon available data and theory, he concludes that an individual will tend to react in a specific rather than a general way to emotional excitation. For this reason, whether or not the emotional state will reoccur for the same conditions, and if it does the degree to which it will reoccur, depends upon other conditions. He does not close the door to the possibility of a general emotional state, but he does point out that the evidence is lacking and that it would be much more defensible to define and study specific emotional states and actions than to try and take a generalist position.

Two studies done with Harold E. Jones and based upon the procedures and conclusions elaborated in the two preceding papers then follow. The first (4) reports the results of a study with a sample of 35 undergraduate and graduate students exposed to a series of 40 stimuli, and with the use of the psychogalvanometer as a means of determining the response to the various stimuli employed. From the results, some 112 rank order correlations were computed. Results seemed congruent with prior research, including that by Wechsler.

The second study done with Jones (5) uses the same procedures, but with more restricted task content. Stimulus words were chosen from work by Smith, rank-ordered on the basis of psychogalvanic response in an experiment which he had conducted. Jones and Wechsler find that position of a word of high potential emotional state in the total series is important, a finding of some significance. Individuals are able to adapt to words of high emotional content despite efforts to arrange situations to reduce this possibility. This finding has importance for the clinical situation, as Jones and Wechsler point out. "Hence, in clinical studies or in the detection of guilty knowledge, the emotional values of stimulus words cannot be compared without taking into account the factor of position in series. . . ." Such results are a significant contribution to both the literature and the practical field of clinical and criminal work.

A study[1] employing the psychogalvanic reflex was done with preschool children to determine the utility of the procedure with the very young child. The children ranged in age from 26 to 44 months, and were reported to be above average in ability though the particular test used for this measurement is not reported. Of the 30 children in the initial sample, Wechsler, Crabbs, and Freeman were

[1]"Galvanic Resources of Preschool Children." *The Pedagogical Seminary and Journal of Genetic Psychology*, 1930, 38, 203–222.

able to gather complete data on 28 of them, a most impressive result. The reader will note that some 21 different stimuli were used, cutting across visual, auditory, and kinesthetic modes.

Considering that the children were between the ages of 2 and 4 years, the procedure followed may be interpreted as a good opportunity to arouse emotional reactions in children.

> . . . The child was next placed in a high chair, electrodes were attached to his feet, and the experiment was at once begun. There were generally three or four persons present: one experimenter (behind a screen) who manipulated the apparatus and obtained a graphic record of the child's psychogalvanic reactions; another investigator (seated next to the child) who manipulated the tippings and was the only one who spoke to the child during the course of the experiment; and an assistant who kept a record of the time, order of sequence and moments of excitation, and in certain instances, a verbatim record of the child's spontaneous speech and a detailed description of his overt behavior.

Correlation coefficients were computed and reported under the several headings. As might be expected, the method using the psychogalvanometer was successful in eliciting affective responses of the young children in a fashion which might be interpreted scientifically. The meaning of the measures obtained for a given child is not clear and as a result the authors must propose other research. The problem may be resolved either as a difficulty in defining what constitutes an "emotional child" or in terms of the lack of relationship between psychogalvanic reflexes and what is generally accepted as emotion.

The coefficients were closer to zero than expected, but rejection of possible relationships was not reasonable because of the relative unreliability of some of the subjective ratings. There was something of a U-shaped function in the results, with children who recorded the smallest responses to the psychogalvanometer either being rated unemotional or highly emotional. There is an attempt to interpret this result based upon observations and data in the setting, but it is essentially left unresolved.

In combination, the papers on emotional measurement and meaning offer a cohesive and clear picture of Wechsler as scientist and psychologist on a specific topic. The picture is typical of other areas with which he has dealt.

Wechsler explored the occurrence and meaning of fingernail biting in children at various age levels using a Freudian interpretation in "The Incidence and Significance of Fingernail Biting in Children" (6). The data were drawn from observations of over 300 children ranging in age from 1 to 17 and therefore, probably representing a stable set of values. The incidence issue was fairly easily resolved by a comparison of the condition of the nails for each age group. There is the initial finding, of some interest, that nail biting does not occur with any degree of frequency before the age of 5 years or so. There is a steady increase to the age of about 15 and then a decrease as one approaches maturity. Wechsler also reports some sex difference, apparently related to the age at which puberty begins.

Given these facts, he attempts interpretation and uses Freud's three stages of psychosexual development for the purpose. Each stage is described and compared to the obtained observations.

Of perhaps even more importance, Wechsler discusses the meanings and implications of the findings and the explanation on a Freudian basis. Incidence of nail biting is so large for children between the ages of 6 and 16 that some persons would consider it a habit, and a habit not of a pathological nature. Wechsler believes it is not so much a habit as it may be a symptom, and a symptom representing an unresolved Oedipus state. This suggests that there could not be a reduction in the habit through the usual procedures of control, though current-day behavior modification techniques might be more effective than would have appeared possible at the time of the writing of this article. At least the negative procedures, the application of bitter materials or taping of the finger, he felt would be virtually useless under the circumstances. We must look at the cause and determine it and treat it.

The final paper included in this part (7) deals with the measurement of anxiety and its application in the clinical setting. Wechsler and Hartogs, his co-author in this study, used an operational definition called a "disintegration concept of anxiety." The phenomenological position of each individual acting in a fashion to maintain himself in an integrated fashion and to defend whatever level of integration he may have achieved is the basis upon which the study is done.

Within this framework, maladjusted persons are compared with adjusted ones, adding validity to results and conclusions about the hypotheses.

SOME REMARKS ON THE PSYCHOPATHOLOGY
OF INDECISION*

DAVID WECHSLER

The term "ambivalence," which was introduced by Bleuler, now widely used in psychoanalytic literature to designate a mental state in which the sentiments of love and hate are experienced simultaneously by the same person.

More generally, this term can also be used to designate two, mutually exclusive, and opposing ideas of whatever nature that continue to exist simultaneously in the mind. Thus defined, ambivalence is a mechanism that one often encounters in functional mental disorders, and also, although in a somewhat different form, in normal people during various states of indecision, persistent doubt, prolonged hesitation, etc.

The difference between the two types of ambivalence, that appearing in individuals with functional disorders, and that appearing in normal individuals, are not well defined. Nor are the lines of demarcation between the two clearly drawn. But I believe that the following two differences serve to distinguish them from a practical point of view:

1. Ambivalence in individuals with functional mental disorders is more pervasive than in normal individuals, and the emotions accompanying it are much more intense.
2. Indecision in normal individuals results only in temporary abandonment of voluntary action, whereas in disturbed individuals it produces a complete paralysis of action.

The remarks that follow are principally devoted to a description of this ambivalence and to a more precise analysis of the phenomenon.

The state of ambivalence can be characterized by five principal traits:

1. The continual reappearance of two (or several) conflicting ideas before the mind, which sometimes results in
2. An alternation of the ideas in which one or the other is dominant, or else
3. A reciprocal inhibition of the ideas,
4. An emotive perturbation in the form of general agitation during elaboration of an idea followed by a depression reaching its peak at the moment the subject must make a decision;

*Translated and reprinted from *Journal de Psychologie,* 1922, 47-54.

5. A breakdown of voluntary action

These symptoms can be taken as characteristic features, so to speak, of ambivalence; but on the other hand, one must remember that, from a psychological point of view all types of indecision are in the final analysis, nothing but a difficulty, an incapacity to judge. Now, for subjects in the state of ambivalence, this incapacitation can be provoked by any decision at all; from the most simple, the choice of a tie, to the most grave, suicide; and what is most curious is that it seems to bear no relation to the difficulty of the choice or the gravity of the decision that must be made.

What tortures the subject is the necessity of having to make a decision, and one cannot say that the choice of a tie will not provoke, in a psychasthenic, a more severe emotional crisis then an irresolute intention to put an end to his life. Yet, this powerlessness does not devolve from an inability to distinguish between acts and their consequences, or a lack of preference between things that must be chosen, and as a result, an incapacity to arrive at the decision to be imposed.

Moreover, not that this powerlessness is connected at least in the beginning, only to personal judgments. For example, the subject who hesitates over the choice of a green tie or a blue tie may not hesitate to resolve a world financial crisis or the question of Irish independence.

Another fact, even more striking, is the time spent by the subject on innumerable reflections, to all appearances outside the subject matter, and thoughts that seem altogether foreign to the problem which he is considering. A most insignificant event may be the source of very agonizing moral suffering. The sending of a letter, the buying of a gift, the simple response to an invitation provokes a crisis that may last for hours, days or even weeks.

It is of moment to note this lack of rapport between the effort devoted and the importance of the problem to be resolved, as well as the irrationally, complicated, detailed, but useless reasoning engaged in the detriment of consideration of the important points at issue. That is, in effect, a very characteristic trait of the state of ambivalence and will serve as the basis of one of the explicative theories of this state.

Let us return now to the second characteristic of ambivalence noted above, namely, that of the alternating dominance of two opposing ideas. It is difficult to separate objective facts from those that are tied on the whole to the hypothesis, and I will not attempt to distinguish them clearly. In general, this alternation of ideas seems to be the result either of an inhibition or of a near total loss of the power of comparison, which, as we know, is the psychological process *sine qua non* of judgment. What happens is that the subject elaborates separately each one of the possible ideas.

During elaboration of one or another of these ideas, all that may be connected to what is envisaged is esteemed to be very important, and minor facts, however unrelated to the subject, seem to bring new reasons for the execution of this idea. The subject sees nothing but desirable characteristics, and after some time, becomes convinced enough to believe himself ready to make the decision. But he does not do it right away, he wants to envisage, one last time the result that will follow if the decision is made, and this last consideration is his misfortune because it suddenly brings to light, all the objections to the decision that appeared imminent. After this moment, all that seemed very important loses value, and in return, all the reasons that were discarded as insignificant gain in importance. The dominant idea begins to fade, and the adverse idea which, until now did not exist in the mind, appears and opposes the first. For some time, there is a conflict between the ideas in which neither one nor the other can be vanquished. It is during this time lapse that the subject experiences his greatest mental suffering. It is the period of reciprocal inhibition of conflicting ideas. This period has no set duration; it can last from several minutes to several days. However, that may be, at a given moment, when the subject is very tired, one of the ideas gains the upper hand, or rather one of the two dies away, leaving the other as free champion. That one does not wait long to be elaborated in its turn. In its elaboration it follows a route similar to that given above. This second idea, during its turn, becomes dominated; and after some time, the subject begins to believe anew that he can reach a decision; and the same events repeat themselves. At once, the subject finds himself again obsessed by hesitations, and the question returns to the point of departure. In his despair he tries several times to make new attempts to resolve the problem. Sometimes he abandons it, sometimes he leaves it for a while, but the same cycle always repeats itself and with the same negative result.

We now examine in detail the period during which there is complete opposition between the ideas, that which we have called the period of reciprocal inhibition. This inhibition which can either continue or be discontinued has two phases:

1. *The active phase.* During this phase, the subject experiences a great deal of agitation, and becomes increasingly distressed as he tries to examine the one or other of the ideas that pass him. This restless agitation is, at the same time, both mental and physical; but it is the mental suffering, above all, that characterizes this period. The physical wavering (the subject wrings his hands, bites his nails, walks back and forth, etc.) is also encountered although in a less obvious form, in the second phase:

2. *The passive phase.* This phase is characterized principally by the fact that the inhibition has resulted in a total suppression of all conflicting ideas. In short, it no longer seems to exist in the mind, which has become a vacuum. It is the kind of emptiness that characterizes inattention or distraction

when the mind moves suddenly from one subject to another. After this time displaced activity will engage the attention of the subject. He will begin to read a letter that he has by chance found within his reach, and will suddenly remember that he must write; he will begin to say poetry, to sing or dance, in short, to do anything that can prevent him from applying himself to resolve the problem that has begun to occupy him.

The fourth characteristic that I have noted is the phenomenon of emotional perturbation. The principal facts that are tied in to this trait have already been given during discussions of other traits. Let us simply recall that the greatest emotional distress always comes at the moment when the subject must make a decision. I emphasize this point because I conclude from it that the cause of the emotional distress is the very act of decision. There remains the question of the subject's lapse of capacity for voluntary action. Here again it is useful to distinguish two different types. In the first we comprehend the case of what one can properly call inaction; in the second type, the case where because of the intrinsic nature of the situation a decision is necessarily effected but does not actually represent a voluntary action on the part of the subject. Instances of the first type are sufficiently clear to require special study. From the point of view of our interior analysis, they represent the state of mind where the opposing ideas are completely inhibited by each other. As a simple example, we can again take the case of the individual who does without a tie because he cannot choose between blue and green; as a more extreme example, that of a psychasthenic whose obsessions of suicide are never realized.

The second type includes a great number of different cases. One can distinguish three principal categories.

First, the case where the decision, no matter how made, is never effected. Examples of it are numerous. Here is one of a part: After much hard work a workman finally decides to ask for a raise. Despite this decision, he never actually asks for it. One day, he puts it off for finding his boss too occupied. The next day, he gets as far as the office, but learning that his boss is not in a very good mood, says to himself that it would be better to wait for a more opportune moment, that it would be bad psychology to broach the subject at such a time. Thus, he continually finds reasons to postpone his demand until a more favorable time, but this next day, so much desired, as one can well imagine, never arrives.

In other cases, contrarywise circumstances themselves achieve a decision, independent of the will of the subject. Example: A subject is beset by the question as to whether to be present at a competition or not; the subject hesitates for some time; he fails to enroll himself before enrollments close; the problem resolves itself independently of him: He will not be present at this competition.

Finally, there is the case where the subject, after having firmly decided to act in a determined manner, ends by acting in an altogether unexpected manner, often absolutely opposed to what he had just decided. For example, Miss X goes out to make a purchase. She wishes to buy a new dress and hat. Unfortunately her funds allowed her only to buy one of the articles. She hesitates a great deal, but finally decides to buy the latter. She goes into a store. In looking for the hat department, she happens to pass the jewelry counter. The attraction of this new display makes her stop for a moment. And so our young lady finally spends her money on a bracelet.

In addition to the cases already cited, there is another very important and frequent category that I shall treat separately, for lack of knowing where to place it. It covers the case where a choice is made fairly rapidly and a decision is arrived at without difficulty, but where the subject, after having accomplished the act, soon experiences the feeling of having made a poor choice or of being able to do better. On the whole he always lacks the feeling of relief that one usually has after resolving a difficulty. I have not studied this type of case very closely but it seems to me, nevertheless, that one is dealing here with the phenomenon of indecision; no judgment is made: the problem that posed itself to the subject was not truly resolved by him.

The analysis of the phenomena is now sufficiently complete to allow us to consider some theories to explain them. To be noted first is the fact that although this behavior manifests itself in normal people as well as in sick ones, it differs in its respective manifestation not so much by the traits that characterize it, as by the renewal, the intensity, and the duration of the phenomena. In a sane subject, the crises of indecision are less frequent, usually not so intense, and, even if the importance of the question pondered makes them intense, they are of short duration. Completely contrary, in an ill person strongly overcome with ambivalence, any judgment, no matter how insignificant, can provoke a new crisis.

The simplest explanation of ambivalence, but one which requires no new hypotheses, is that this state arises from habit. According to this concept, pathological indecision is nothing but a bad habit acquired by frequent past failures to act promptly. As a first reaction, one may perhaps say that this theory does not explain the phenomena at all, because it tells us nothing of the initial cause of the indecision, that is, it tells only that there were past cases. Evidently it remains to explain them, but I do not believe this to be absolutely necessary in many cases of indecision. In a large number of cases, there is no need to search for reasons beyond those implied by the meaning of the word habit, for whatever were the initial factors that gave rise to the habit, they show no causal relationship to the actual manifestation of the habit as it now appears; likewise, there are no reasons to explain morphine addiction in individuals, as a response to a need to ease insomnia because originally someone gave them morphine for this reason. In any case if one admits this first conception, then it follows that a part of the psychotherapy of indecision could consist uniquely in the substitution of good habits for bad ones. Yet this first theory, taken alone, seems to me insufficient because it is limited. It is necessary to supplement it, and this brings us to a second hypothesis which in one form or another, has often been expressed, and which I believe is still the most current. According to this theory, indecision must be considered as a type of fear, a fear of the consequences that can be provoked by our actions, that is, a fear of responsibility. This theory is clearly based on experience. We know that, when there are great interests at play, when our actions can have grave consequences, we proceed slowly, we hesitate a long while. In these circumstances, we generally consider those who act promptly, if not always as the wisest at least as the most courageous. In short, the courageous man is the man, who in the face of danger, acts without hesitation; it is clear that those who jump into the water to save a drowning person, or those who go into a burning building to save a child, do not have very much time to think about it. On the other hand, we know that cowards are, in general, persons of vacillating character, although the converse is not necessarily always true. In short, according to this theory, indecision in general has its origin in the fear of responsibility or, what amounts to the same, in the apprehension of chastisement or moral and social sanctions that our actions can provoke. That certainly very often corresponds to the facts themselves and in practice one can understand it.

Indecision defined as a fear of responsibility is necessarily considered, in principle as a moral act. That is very useful to the sociologist, but insufficient for the psychologist. Pierre Janet, who shares this point of view, in treating the same subject gave us a wider and more psychological way to look at this "feeling of incompleteness of action" of which indecision is only one type. For Janet all resolutions of problems supposes not only a sense of responsibility, but a promise by a subject to himself to execute the action involved. In order that this pledge be treated not merely as an imaginary fact, it is necessary that the action, in order that it leave the "domain of sure possibility," be considered as already adopted and even achieved. It must be conceived, according to Janet as "a feeling of unity, as if a single tendency had persisted, a feeling that the development of this tendency was becoming stronger than before, and so a reflection of the whole personality, because the action was adopted and seemed to depend on ourselves, a certain feeling of pleasure like that which accompanies the end of a struggle and the exaltation of power." These feelings in their entirety constitute a larger overall sentiment to which Janet has recently given the name "sense of action." According to this definition indecision must be considered as a lack of this sense of action.

That decision results from a fear of responsibility or that it is the consequence of a lack of "sense of action," it is evident that it concerns, as indicated by way the use of the terms "fear" and "feeling," some troubles of emotional life. Yet, on this point neither of these two theories gives us precise details. It is a question of knowing which parts of the affective mechanism have been reached by the subject's trouble. I believe that a satisfactory answer is furnished us by some of the facts previously noted in our analysis and description of the state of ambivalence.

The fundamental fact is the state of continual alternation of dominant ideas. This state presents us with a very paradoxical phenomenon, which is the simultaneous existence in the mind of two ideas, neither of which influences the other, which is equivalent to saying there must be a dissociation between them. The first conclusion that one must infer from this hypothesis is that ambivalence is a particular type of dissociation. Still to be learned is what the mechanism of this dissociation may be. For that, let us recall the series of facts bearing on the lack of relation between the effort devoted to a problem and the importance of the circumstances that engendered it. I have already indicated above, it is the displacement of a number of useless reflections on details having no relation to the object of the action, to the detriment of the central points involved that most strikes the observer. We can admit only two possibilities: 1. These reflections, which seem to be out of place and outside the subject matter, are not in reality so; 2. These reflections are out of place but they signal more important difficulties the true natures of which are concealed. The second alternative appears more probable. It is also, it seems, akin to the points of view of Freud and his school, but although we begin with the same premises I do not believe we arrive at altogether the same conclusion. Yet in order for me to explain as briefly as possible I shall make use of some of the terms already used and defined in psychoanalytic literature.

Accordingly, here is how I conceive the mechanism of those cases of ambivalence that cannot be explained either by fear or by bad habits.

When an idea or a feeling has become for any reason distressing for an individual, it is repressed in the unconscious, or it constitutes, according to Freudian terminology, a psychological complex. To the extent that the difficulties that gave rise to this feeling persist, the conscious psyche makes an all out effort to drive back this repressed complex. On their part, these distressing ideas are always looking for ways to emerge and thus re-appear in the conscious, but they cannot cross the threshold so long as they are recognized. What do they do then? According to Freudian theory, they dissimulate themselves, take on another appearance and thus cross the threshold by deceiving the conscious psyche. How can this be? It is from here that I would like to bring some ideas that, moreover, do not depend on the Freudian mechanism just outlined. When a distressing idea is repressed, it is by the very act of repression removed from its emotional component. Now, that which seeks to express itself is not the cognitive part, but the effective part, and for that any vehicle available will suffice to transport it. The affective component attaches itself thus to any element that will permit it to express itself. It is there precisely that which happens when the state of ambivalence occurs. The affective elements are temporarily attached to fortuitous ideas. This accidental union is often very strange, and that explains, for example, the reason why there seems to be no relation between the objective cause of the indecision and the intensity of the crisis that produces it.

The state of ambivalence is thus the result of an affective dissociation.

GENERAL CONCLUSIONS WITH SOME REMARKS
ON THE NATURE OF EMOTION*

DAVID WECHSLER

In the preceding chapters we have examined more or less in detail the main problems, both theoretical and practical, connected with the measurement and interpretation of the galvanic response, together with those salient facts and general principles upon which the phenomenon seems to depend. We shall conclude our discussion of the psychogalvanic reflex by first summarizing these facts and principles and then calling attention to some important general interpretations to which the results of our experimental investigations seem to point.

The psycholgalvanic reflex is a brusque variation in the electrical conductivity of the skin as a response to an affectively toned excitatory stimulus during the passage of a galvanic current. The traversing current may be of endosomatic or exsomatic origin. The variation in the electrical conductivity of the skin is due to a diminution of the counter electromotive force of polarization at the points of entrance and exit of the current, as a result of an increasing secretion of sweat at these points. (There is no difference between psychogalvanic response obtained with the two sources of current except as regards the magnitude of the response.)

On the physical side, the magnitude of the reflex would seem to be some function of the intensity of the current traversing the skin. For this reason it is necessary to work with identical intensities of current whenever comparative data are to be gathered. Physiologically, the magnitude of the response depends upon the general activity of the skin. Among the factors which determine this, the state of fatigue of the individual tested is very important. The effect of fatigue is to reduce the responsiveness of the skin and so cause a corresponding falling off in the magnitude of reflex.

There appears to be a diurnal variation in the electrical conductivity of the skin such that it is highest in the early hours of the morning and late hours in the evening, and lowest

*Excerpt from the Ph.D. thesis of David Wechsler. Reprinted from "The Measurement of Emotional Reactions: Researches on the Psychogalvanic Reflex," *Archives of Psychology*, 1925, No. 76, 165-175.

towards the middle of the day. It is therefore important that in comparing galvanic responses of subjects that they be tested at approximately identical hours. In general the early morning and evening hours are to be avoided. Largest responses are usually obtained between the hours of 10 a. m. and 4 p. m.

Psychologically, the psychogalvanic reflex is to be taken as an index of the occurrence of an affective reaction in response to an exciting stimulus. Neither the affective response nor the exciting stimulus need be consciously perceived by the subject experiencing them. Nevertheless introspective ratings correlate rather highly (.66) with objective evaluations of the response.

The psychologalvanic response appears to vary roughly as the intensity of the affective tone elicited. It does not vary as the intensity of the stimulus, except in so far as increasing the intensity of the stimulus tends to evoke a proportionally greater affective reaction.

The psychologalvanic reflex is a direct response to a specific affective excitation. It is, therefore, best elicited by stimuli that evoke such affective responses in a direct way, notably such as pain, surprise and the like.

Results from a number of intercorrelations between various types of stimuli would indicate that individuals tend to be *specifically emotional*, that is, react emotionally to specific types of situations rather than uniformly to all types of situations.

Attempts at the practical application of the psychologalvanic reflex have shown that the method can be of valuable clinical aid in the differential diagnosis in a certain number of mental and nervous disorders. Among these the most important is the differentiation of hysterical anesthesias and analgesias from similar conditions due to true organic lesions. Another is the differentiation between apparent and real affective deterioration, as for instance between stuporous manic depressive insanity and catatonic dementia precox.

With certain modification in the technique of its measurement, the galvanic response has also shown itself useful in the study of certain types of exopthalmic goitre where different phases of the disease (indicating the degree of the subject's state of agitation) as well as its progress may be determined from the qualitative character of the galvanic curve.

Still another application of psychologalvanic reflex has been shown to be possible in connection with the study of the effects of drugs on the nervous system. Experiments of this nature have already been made with alcohol, atropine and a few other drugs. Finally the psychogalvanic reflex can be used as a complex-indicator in connection with the association test. Compared with the reaction time it is both a more reliable and more sensitive indicator.

Summarizing the attempts at practical investigation of the psychologalvanic reflex, we may conclude on the basis of the studies reported that such application has been shown to be possible in a number of special fields. The results, though more positive* than the data themselves would indicate, however, do not enable us to answer in a conclusive way the question as to whether the galvanic response is available as a general method for the investigation of the emotions. Attempts to attack this greater problem have in fact hitherto proved abortive. They have failed owing to the limitations of technique and the incomplete knowledge of the fundamental physiological and psychological factors influencing an individual's galvanic responsiveness, which prevented quantitative studies of the reflex.

This thesis has been devoted largely to the investigation of these fundamental factors and methods of technique. The results obtained, I think, have now sufficiently solved these preliminary problems to enable us to attack the main problem of the psychogalvanic reflex as a measure of the individual's emotional responsiveness, his specific emotivity. To this much larger task I hope to devote my next study.

Certain of the experimental results herein reported, particularly those obtained with subjects asleep and those obtained from others in abnormal states, indicate that the current description of the affective processes is in need of revision, and calls for a more detailed analysis of mental facts which have been described under the term emotion.

What, in fact, are we to understand by the term emotion? What is an emotion? It is now forty years since James posed this question in his now famous article that appeared in *Mind*.

---

* More positive, because the errors resulting from the limitations of technique and lack of standard conditions under which the hitherto attempted studies were made naturally tended to attenuate all the correlations found.

Much has been written on this topic since then, but it is still a fact that psychologists are today not much nearer agreement on the definition of emotion than they were when James' article first appeared. This disagreement is not limited to theories as to the nature and mechanism of emotion but to the very meaning of the term. There is no universally accepted meaning which would make the reader feel sure that the phenomena intended to be included under the term by one author are precisely those assumed by another.

Confusion arises chiefly for three reasons: The first is the indiscriminate use of the term to include sometimes all and at other times only a number of the physiological and mental facts that are assumed to constitute the phenomenon. For example, some authors have applied the term "emotion" to cover only the subjective, affective state; others the physiological, bodily changes; and so forth. The second reason is the indiscriminate mixing of fact and theory in the description of the phenomenon. The last and most important reason, to my mind, is that the description of the psycho-physical processes that constitute an emotion have been over simplified.

The phenomena which have usually been distinguished as constituting the various aspects of emotion are first: the perception of some unusual or threatening fact; second: some bodily changes, and, finally: a subjective state, or affect; and depending upon the theory adopted, the bodily changes are said to precede, follow, or accompany the subjective state. Now, this description of the various aspects of emotion, while correct in a general way, simplifies the facts altogether too much and constitutes the greatest source of confusion. We can see this best by examining any of the more important theories of emotion based on this simplified analysis, for instance the James-Lange theory. Let us confine ourselves to James, for whatever fault one may find with this author it is certainly not lack of clarity of expression.

James' theory of emotion is embodied in the following oft-quoted sentence "Bodily changes follow directly upon the perception of the exciting fact and—our feeling of the changes as they occur is the emotion."[45] The novel point in the theory as thus expressed is that the common sense account of the order in which the phenomena constituting an emotion follow each other is inverted. The sequence is not, "we see a bear, are frightened and run; we are insulted by a rival and strike";

but, "we see a bear and run and are frightened; we are angry because we strike," afraid because we tremble, etc. This statement of the case appears on first approach clear enough. Let us see if it really is.

Consider the phrase "exciting fact." What does James precisely mean by it? Does he mean the mere sensory perception of the exciting object? Is it the visual image of the bear that immediately provokes the bodily changes, or is it the fact that the bear is interpreted as a dangerous animal? Those who have accepted the former meaning have refuted James by pointing out that we see a bear (as for instance in the zoo) and do not run. To the experienced hunter the sight of bear may not only not provoke the action of running away, but, on the contrary, the impulse to run towards the animal. He will not be frightened, he may in fact be overjoyed that his prey is in sight. If, on the other hand, perception of fact means also its interpretation as an object of danger, "being afraid" forms part of the "perception of the fact" and the theory loses much of its novelty.

We are not concerned at the moment as to which of the two interpretations is correct. We merely call attention to the ambiguity of the phrase and to the fact that it includes two separate entities. There is first the perception of the object as a mental representation and second the interpretation of the perceived object as a menacing or threatening fact.

Consider now the phrase, "feeling of bodily changes." When one runs at the sight of a bear, does James mean that it is kinesthetic sensations from the legs, resulting from their flexion and extension, that give rise to the feeling of fear; or the sensations produced by the filling of the tear ducts, that give rise to the feeling of sadness? Or is it the palpitation of the heart or the flushing of the cheeks or the increased peristalsis of the intestines that are the source of the feellings? From the emphasis James lays on the vasomotor and respiratory changes one might suppose that is primarily these that contribute to the sum total of the feelings experienced. Since James' first enunciation of his theory other kinds of organic sensations have been described and those sponsoring the modified theory include under bodily changes these added organic sensations. I, for one, see no reason why sensations derived from the stimulation of the smooth musculature should enjoy this privileged position in the scheme of bodily changes supposed to be the cause of the psychic state known as feeling. We are however not interested whether the above view is correct. We are merely calling attention to the fact that the term bodily changes as used by James may include a variety of psychologic responses which need to be considered apart. Much of the discussion of the James-Lange theory has been more or less futile because this has not been done.

The above discussion is sufficient, I think, to demonstrate the ambiguity which now exists in the current description of what constitutes an emotion and to indicate the pressing need of revising it. Attempts to do this have been made from time to time, but with apparently no significant results. It is therefore with some temerity that I approach the task. I appreciate, of course, that the term emotion, having an accepted meaning in common language, and in addition historical connotations both in philosophy and psychology, one has not at this late date the right to appropriate and give it a new signification. But while one may not appropriate the term, might not one suggest its elimination from rigorous scientific discussion or at least demand that it be used in only its very general sense? I have attempted to do this in the description below, and proceeding upon the theory that one ought to adopt some specific label, however arbitrary, to distinguish clearly the various aspects of the phenemon described, have further ventured to introduce a number of new terms.

The first obvious fact about every emotion is that it is initiated by some stimulus. The nature of the stimulus does not itself determine whether an emotion will be evoked. This will depend upon the particular significance the stimulus may have for the person experiencing it, and upon the conditions under which it occurs. Thus, the discharge of a gun is an upsetting stimulus for the man on the street but one that passes unnoticed by the soldier in the trenches. The stimulus may be subjective or objective, moral or physical; it may be a sensation, an image, an idea, etc. A burn, the sight of a beautiful picture, the thwarting of a plan, may all be the source of an emotion. The effect of such a stimulus under certain conditions is to produce what I shall call a "*choc*," that is, a hyper-excitation of the centers habitually involved in the mediation of the particular stimulus and a general excitation of some non-habitual but related nervous centers, and, finally, through them, the organs which they control. Any sensation, percept, image or association pattern, capable of producing such a *choc* is an *emotive*. An *emotive* is thus any stimulus which, because of its intensity, or because of the particular significance which it may have for the individual experiencing it, produces a *choc*. The distinction is important because the same stimulus may not be an emotive for the same individual on different occasions, or for different individuals on identical occasions.

In addition to giving rise to variations of physiological activity in individual organs of the body, in consequence of the *choc* reaction elicited, the effect of an *emotive* is further to provoke a general orientation of the body as a whole with respect to the exciting stimulus. At the sight of a bear, for instance, not only is there a likelihood of the heart beating faster, the knees to begin to tremble, etc., but there is a definite impulse to move away from the bear, that is, to run. The reaction of running away, however, as a response to the unexpected discovery by a bear seems to differ from that of the palpitation of the heart in that it appears a less invariable reaction to the situation. For instance, a seasoned hunter may have learned through experience that it is more advisable when being discovered by a bear to remain absolutely quiet, and so he will not run away but try to remain as motionless as possible, although his heart will continue to palpitate in spite of him. In general, it appears that the physiologic reactions of the organs are invariable, whereas the bodily orientations are often modified through training, or experience or custom. The rule is not without exceptions in either direction. Nevertheless, I believe it is extremely useful to distinguish the two types of response, and I suggest the term *physio-affective response* to designate the organic physiological reaction evoked by an *emotive* and *affective behaviour reaction* to designate the bodily orientation to the exciting agent. Thus, in case of fear, variations of blood-pressure or secretion of sweat are *physio-affective responses*, whereas flight from the source of danger that may have provoked the fear is an *affective behaviour reaction*. The increase in the rate of the heart-beat and modification of respiration in anger, are physio-affective responses, whereas the pugnacious attitude, the threatening voice, and the like, are behavior reactions. Again, trembling upon hearing bad news would be a physio-affective response, while crying, I should term a behavior reaction. All of them together would be included under the term expression of emotion.

Continuing our analysis, the effect of *choc* through its direct or indirect action on the brain is to give rise to a peculiar psychic state, or affect. The quality or qualities which characterize this psychic state is what I should call affective tone.

All affective tone is not identical but seems to be qualitatively different in different emotions. It is the perception of these differences in affective tone which enables us to distinguish subjectively the several "emotions" from one another; as fear from anger, etc. What factors enter to determine the value of the affective tone evoked, I am as yet unready to assert. Probably among them are the intensity of the choc, the immediately preceding psychic state upon which it was superimposed, the mental make-up of the individual experiencing it. And if we assume that its physiologic basis is the perception of certain bodily changes, it will also depend on the particular organs or organ whose functioning has been modified. The last factor mentioned is to my mind, and contrary to the view implied in current theory, only of incidental importance.

In this analysis, there are several novel aspects which deserve special attention. The first is the differentiation of the so-called perception of fact into stimulus and *emotive;* second, is the introduction and elaboration of the term *choc,* third, is the differention of expression of emotion into *physio-affective response* and *behavior reaction.* These distinctions are simply matters of objective analysis. In themselves, they do not imply any particular theory. Their virtue, I believe, lies in the fact that they eliminate that baneful ambiguity which has been the source of so much fruitless discussion and perhaps also investigation.

Using the terms in the sense defined above, our researches on the psychologalvanic reflex have shown that affective tone may be conscious or unconscious. The conclusion that it may be unconscious rests upon the fact that the galvanic response may be elicited from subjects while asleep, and also upon the fact that subjects have been found to respond to subliminal (that is, nonconsciously) perceived stimuli. These considerations also recall the possible role of the cerebral cortex in the mediation of the psychologalvanic reflex, and indirectly of the affective reactions as a whole. The fact that the psychologalvanic reflex is obtainable without concomitant awareness on part of the subject either of the exciting stimulus or the affective tone to which it gives rise, does not in itself answer the question one way or another. For, while it has been shown that the cortex is the seat of consciousness, it has not been shown that non-conscious states are necessarily subcortical. Nevertheless, the fact that the reflex has been obtained from a decerebrated frog (experiments Schubert and Schiltf) and that mimetic responses that at least simulated affective reactions, from the decerebrated dogs (experiments of Goltz) would indicate that the cortex is not essential in the mediation of affective reactions. In opposition to these findings, however, is the fact that the galvanic response is suppressed in the cat under anesthesia (experiments of Veraguth and the writer). It is also to be questioned, as already pointed out, whether conclusions regarding the psychologalvanic reflex in the frog may be carried over to the interpretation of the phenomenon in higher animals and particularly in man.

Prideaux's view on the subject is that the psychogalvanic reflex in man is conditioned by the state of cerebral cortex for the reason that, "in those cases where we have definite evidence of cortical degeneration or maldevelopment there is only a small or no reflex at all; (and) in those cases where cortical degeneration is probable and also in conversion hysteria there is a comparatively small reflex."* This may be true, but it is not certain whether the patient showing the cortical degeneration mentioned does not also suffer simultaneously degeneration of subcortical regions of the brain. Further, admitting that the degeneration is limited to the cortex, might not the diminished affective response be due to a degeneration of the perceptive rather than the affective centers or mechanisms? It is for instance, on this basis that the heightening of the sensory thresholds in idiots and imbeciles, particularly for pain stimuli, is generally explained.

Prideaux is further of the opinion that the reflex will not occur unless the inhibitory centers are stimulated, and gives as evidence "the fact that when a central excitement is aroused and much muscular movement reflexly results there

* Prideaux[70] p. **43**.

is very little galvanic response, while on the other hand the suppression by reflex inhibition of the muscular reflex is accompanied by large galvanic "response"* My own observations do not confirm this "evidence." I have found that, generally, subjects who showed muscular reactions (as indicated by frequent occurrence of the *Vorausschlugphänomen* were among those who gave the largest galvanic response.

My own view on the subject is that while the galvanic response is undoubtedly influenced by the state and condition of the cortex and also by the efficacy of its inhibitory action, the reflex itself is primarily a subcortical phenomenon. This view becomes more convincing if, instead of speaking of the phychologalvanic reflex as an indicator of emotion, we think of it, as it has been insisted throughout this thesis as an index of affective tone. The production of affective tone is a direct response to an affectively significant excitation. As a direct response it is an unconscious phenomenon and the cortex will condition the response only to the extent that it determines the affective significance of the excitation. In a large number of instances, of course, affective tone will also be perceived as a conscious experience, and in those instances the inhibitory functions will play an important role.†

---

* Prideaux[70] p. 45.

† Abramowski[2] reports the case of a subject who during a series of experiments consistently failed to give any galvanic response. After the experiment the subject informed the author that she had made deliberate effort not to react to any of the stimuli presented. This seemed to indicate to the author that the reflex might possibly be suppressed through the action of the will.

In the course of my own investigations I became acquainted with a Polish lady (about 45 years of age) who said that she had always been able to suppress her emotions and as proof asked to be tested with a galvanometer. I very willing agreed to do this and accordingly performed an experiment using repeated pin-pricks, the sound of a bell and pinching the cheek as means of testing her affective responsiveness. In no case did she fail to react to an excitation, although in all, excepting the pinch on the cheek, the reflex was very very small. To the last named excitation however, the response was quite large, and I observed that at the moment the subject showed much irritation. When informed that she had responded to these excitations the lady explained that not being well disposed she had not really been able to master herself on this occasion as she was wont, and expressed a desire to repeat the experiment. This however was never done. From the manner of the subject's behavior during the course of the experiment, I gathered that her method of putting herself in the resistant state consisted very much of going through the same acts which mediums are observed to go through before entering into their trance. Thus she demanded absolute quiet, shut her eyes, breathed heavily, etc., and asked that the experimenter do not begin the experiment until she gave a signal. It appeared to me that what she was trying to do was to get into a state

It is perhaps of some interest to evaluate the biologic signi-cance of the reaction of the skin under the circumstances we have been studying it. The physiologic changes that occurred under emotion have been interpreted biologically as adap-tations on the part of the organism to meet extraordinary situations. These situations generally involve a rapid and intensified expenditure of energy, and therefore call for in-creased rate of metabolism, and it has been found that the physiologic changes that do take place are precisely such as will favor this. Thus the increased blood sugar content (emotional glycosuria), redistribution of the blood to those organs which are called upon to make the adaptations (notably the brain and voluntary muscles), and the augmented intake of oxygen (through more rapid breathing).* As a result of the increased rate of metabolism there is, of course, a rapid accumulation of waste products and one might naturally look for some adaptation on the part of the organism to meet this consequence. The increased activity of the sweat glands under emotion probably serves just such a purpose.

---

where she could be oblivious of any excitation to which she might be subjected. It seems that Abramowski's subject was able to do this. Her suppression of the reflex through an effort of the "will" accordingly consisted merely of getting herself into a state where the stimuli made no impression upon her. It was not the reflex but the stimulus that was suppressed.

In this connection it should be noted, however, that when the average subject tries to inhibit his reaction the effect of this attempt is to cause a greater rather than a smaller galvanic response. (I am indebted for the last observation to the late Prof. Waller).

* For fuller discussion see Cannon[12] particularly chapter XI, dealing with utility of bodily changes in pain and great emotion.

ON THE SPECIFICITY OF EMOTIONAL REACTIONS*

DAVID WECHSLER

In the last decade much discussion has been devoted to the question whether what is called 'general intelligence' is something dependent upon a single general factor or is merely a convenient expression for the central tendency of a number of more or less independent factors or specific abilities. I wish to call attention to the fact that a similar problem exists in explaining the nature of emotion, and that the assumption of one or the other point of view in the case of emotion is of considerable theoretical and practical importance.

The question as it relates to the problem of emotivity may be stated as follows: Does an individual termed "emotional" react in an emotional way to all affective stimuli, or does he tend to react specifically to only certain types of affective stimuli or situations? In the first case we might infer that his uniform responsiveness is due to a single central factor which might be called 'general emotivity'; in the second, we could conclude that the selective responsiveness is due to some specific factors which might be termed specific emotivities, comparable to special abilities or types of intelligence in the intellectual domain.

No experimental data are at hand to enable us to argue for either alternative with absolute conviction. Nevertheless, some results which I have obtained in connection with certain experiments with the psychogalvanic reflex[1] as well as a number of empirical observations seem to show some evidence in favor of the view that individuals tend to be "specifically" rather than "generally" emotional.

In the case of the experiments referred to, the specificity of emotional responsiveness is indicated by the nature of the correlations between the magnitudes of galvanic responses obtained with each of a number of different types of affective stimuli for some 20 Ss. The experiment consisted of subjecting 20 individuals to the same series of emotional stimuli, ranking them in order of magnitude of response to each of the stimuli employed, and finally calculating the correlations and intercorrelations between the galvanic responses on the various types of stimuli. If there existed such a thing as general emotivity in the sense of a single common factor, we should

*Reprinted from *American Journal of Psychology*, 1925, 36, 424-426.

[1]D. Wechsler, The Measurement of Emotional Reactions, *Archives of Psych.*, 1925, No. 76.

346

expect that the average intercorrelations between different stimulus-series would tend to be high, since the type of stimulus employed, providing it had been previously established as being effective in provoking emotional responses, ought not to alter significantly the relative position of the S among the individuals with whom he is being compared. A highly emotional individual, for instance, should react with comparatively large galvanic deflections, whether the excitation is that of pain, surprise, or what not. If individuals, however, tended to be specifically emotional, the S might react very markedly to sudden noises (surprise or fear) but only moderately or insignificantly to pain. In this case, of course, an individual's relative emotional standing as measured by the galvanometer would change with the type of stimulus employed, and the correlations obtained would be likely to be very low.

Examination of the actual figures obtained shows that, while many of the correlations were fairly high (as much as .81), some were quite low (around .20) or even negative (—.16). In general correlations were high between responses to types of stimuli evoking psychologically similar affective states, but small or insignificant between responses to stimuli evoking different affective states. Thus, the correlation between the responses to the sound of a Klaxon horn and those to a flash of magnesium (both, probably, evoking surprise) was .77; that between the reactions to the same Klaxon and the responses provoked by a pin-prick (pain), .47; but the correlation between the reactions to the Klaxon and the responses elicited by the situational stimulus of being asked to solve an arithmetical problem (giving rise in most Ss to a feeling of apprehension or expectancy) was only .20.

The above results I take to indicate, for reasons already given, that individuals tend to react in a specific rather than in a general way to emotional excitation; but the results are not offered as unqualifiedly demonstrative of the conclusion indicated. The interpretation of the results is necessarily restricted by the limitations of the experimental method employed. Among these are, first, the relatively small number of Ss studied and, secondly, the limited range of the stimuli employed. Further experiments are obviously needed to make the general conclusion more cogent. In the meantime, I would call attention to the fact that the conclusion is not unsupported by many instances that might be recalled from general observation. We find, *e. g.*, people who tremble at the sound of thunder but are quite unafraid of most other things. A nurse who will assist calmly at a bloody operation may shriek at the sight of a harmless mouse. The same man who applauds vociferously at a baseball game may fall asleep at the opera. Unless these instances are exceptions rather than the rule, it would seem erroneous to use the term 'emotional' as implying a characteristic type of reaction. To be correct, we should in each case have to specifiy 'emotional with respect to such and such stimuli' or 'in such and such situations.' This limitation of connotation in the term 'emotional' is in fact assumed when the term is used in a practical way. If a railroad company, for instance, is selecting motormen and inquires whether the applicant is or is not emotional, it is not interested in finding out whether he is much stirred by music, gets quickly excited in an argument, or is readily provoked by his wife; what it wants to know is whether he is readily frightened by sudden noises, tends to lose his head under danger, and the like. And in using the term 'emotional' it restricts it to precisely these specific types of situations which it has in mind.

In summary of the above observations, it would seem that there is much against the assumption of a theory of general emotivity dependent upon a single central factor. On the other hand, there appears to be some good evidence for the view that individuals tend to be 'specifically' rather than 'generally' emotional. But the two conditions are not mutually exclusive. It is altogether possible that what is termed general emotivity may be determined by both a single central factor, analogous to Spearman's "g" in the case of general intelligence, and a number of less important but contributory independent factors which give emotivity its 'specific' character. Evidence for this point of view is, however, not yet at hand. Until it is available, I think that we are more justified and shall find it more useful to speak of specific emotivities than of general emotivity.

A STUDY OF EMOTIONAL SPECIFICITY*

DAVID WECHSLER and HAROLD E. JONES

University of California

The concepts of 'temperament' and 'emotionality' have appeared to assume a common factor or group of factors occurring in a great variety of emotional situations. This common or constitutional element is believed to produce a positive correlation between emotional responses, however stimulated and however measured. Clinical evidence has tended to support this view; such conditions as subthyroid lethargy, vagotonia, sympathicotonia, the manic and schizophrenic reaction types, and the abnormal irritability occurring in various forms of metabolic disturbance, are presented as illustrative of emotionality systems or levels.

Within a normal range, however, we have little certainty as to the extent to which general factors can be demonstrated. What is the relation between a person's 'anger' threshold and his 'fear' threshold? How specific are his anxieties and excitements? Unless an individual shows a certain consistency in his emotional reactions, we are obviously not justified in classifying him as emotional or unemotional; rather we would be constrained to denote his emotional tendencies separately with respect to specific contexts or situations.

PROBLEM

The problem as here defined[1] was first presented by Wechsler in connection with his studies on the psychogalvanic reflex.[2] His method of approach was through an analysis of the intercorrelations obtained from a comparison of the galvanic responses of a variable number of Ss to a series of different emotion-provoking stimuli. The theory of this procedure was that, if emotionality was due to a single or general factor, an individual ought to show a consistency in his galvanic responsiveness irrespective of the type of stimulus used, whereas if it were due to a number of different factors specifically conditioned, individuals would show a corresponding degree of variable or specific reaction. The initial experiments supported the latter hypothesis. The correlations depended almost entirely upon the kind of stimuli used; they were high between galvanic reactions to stimuli evoking identical or similar affective states, and low or insignificant between psychogalvanic reflexes to stimuli evoking dissimilar affective states. Wechsler's conclusion, accordingly, was: "Individuals tend to react in a specific rather than in a general way to emotional situations." Due to limitations in the experimental data, this conclusion was advanced with some reserve.

---

*Reprinted from *American Journal of Psychology*, 1928, **40**, 600-606.

[1]This experiment was conducted in the Psychological Laboratory of Columbia University.

[2]D. Wechsler, Researches on the psychogalvanic reflex, *Arch. Psychol.*, 1925, no. 76; On the specificity of emotional reactions, this JOURNAL, 36, 1925, 424-26.

PLATE I

350

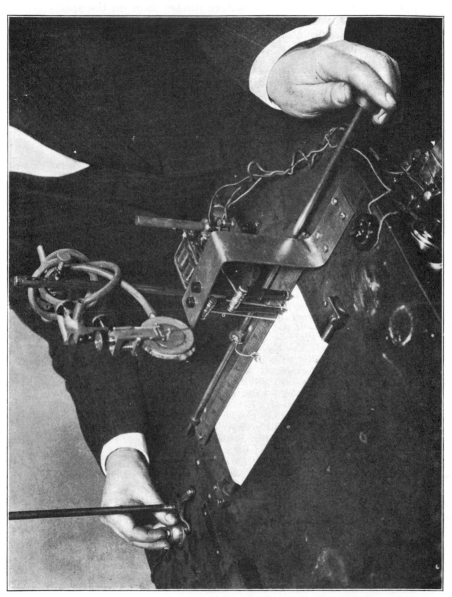

PLATE II

351

The object of our present investigation was to test out the position taken above and to obtain further data on the specificity problem. As in the cited experiments, our method of approach was through a study of self- and inter-correlations of the psychogalvanic response to emotionally stimulating situations.

METHOD AND PROCEDURE

Records were taken with 35 *S*s (a random selection of college undergraduates, with a few graduate students) employing a standard series of 40 stimuli. The galvanic reactions were obtained by means of a D'Arsonval moving-coil type of galvanometer and exsomatic current, with the subject inserted as unknown resistance in the fourth arm of a Wheatstone bridge. A standard current of approximately 0.0001 M.A. was employed with every subject, variations of body resistance being compensated for through the use of a potentiometer. The electrodes were applied to the fingers of the hand, and consisted of small clay cups filled with normal saline, resting in somewhat larger cups of saturated $ZnSO_4$. Into the saline solutions the *S* was required to place the index and second finger of his right hand. The fingers were immersed the full length of the third phalanx, the surface exposed to the liquid being kept constant by the use of fitted rubber finger cots.

The galvanometric excursions were recorded by a mechanical device designed to give continuous graphic records of each subject's reactions. The essential features of the apparatus are apparent in the accompanying photograph, Plate I. The beam of light coming from the galvanometer is intercepted by a plane mirror which is so inclined as to reflect the beam perpendicularly down upon a moving surface of white paper. The paper is being displaced at a very slow speed over a narrow plate from a large roll of paper below. Above the paper a small ink-syphon is mounted on a horizontal bar (see Plate II) which moves laterally across and at right angles to the paper. The *E* observes the beam of light and, as it moves, follows it with the ink-syphon in the direction of the beam's displacement. In this way excellent graphs of the galvanometric excursions may be obtained, which compare favorably with direct photographic records. An advantage of this technique consists in the immediate visibility of the records, and in the opportunity to make accompanying notes on the same sheet. Further, the deflections can be magnified to a greater extent than in ordinary work with sensitive paper or film, since it is possible to use kymograph paper 9 in. in width. Errors, due to lag or slight deviations of the *E* in following the course of the light, are negligible save where very precise measurements of latent period are desired. Various electric markers can be readily attached, and two such are shown in the photograph, one connected with a metronome to mark seconds, and another to indicate moments of excitation.

The experimental situation was simplified as far as possible. The *S* was asked to seat himself in a chair equipped with an arm rest and electrodes. While he was making himself comfortable, he was shown how to keep his fingers in the saline-filled cups and given brief instructions as to what was to follow. The *S* had a general idea as to the nature of the experiment but knew nothing of its actual content. There were two *E*s, one who controlled the apparatus and another who gave instructions and presented the stimuli. The apparatus and the first *E* were at all times screened from the *S*.

TABLE I

CHARACTER AND ORDER OF STIMULI USED

Stimulus No.	Nature of Stimulus
I	Unexpected noise (turning on of motor).
2	Verbal Instructions: "I am going to read you some numbers. When I am through I want you to repeat them backwards."
3–6	Four series of digits to be repeated backwards.
7	Verbal Instructions: "I am going to show you some pictures on a screen. As soon as you see each picture say out loud the first word that comes to your mind."
8–11	Four colored pictures thrown on a Trans-Lux screen by means of an opaque projector. The pictures were advertisements from the *Saturday Evening Post*. Although chosen for a supposed provocativeness, their content proved to have little emotional value.
12	Verbal instructions: "Now I am going to say some words. You are to respond to each word by telling me the first word that comes into your mind."
13–29	Seventeen association words (one buffer and sixteen taken from Whateley Smith's series).[3] Eight of the words were chosen for minimal emotional value, and eight because of their position at the head of Smith's list. The former we termed "non-critical," the latter "critical." The two classes of words were given in alternate groups of 4 each.
30–32	Physical aggression: *E* approached *S* unexpectedly and grasped his nose between thumb and forefinger. Repeated once, and the third time merely simulated.
33–35	Loud auditory stimulus (klaxon sounded).
36	Adjustment of inductorium electrodes to *S*'s leg.
37	Verbal instructions: "Now I am going to give you an electric shock. At first it will be mild, but later it will be very severe. When you begin to feel the current say 'feel' and when you can't stand it any longer say 'stop.'"
38	Auditory stimulus (buzz of make-break on inductorium).
39	Inductorium shock. *S* reports 'feel.'
40	Inductorium shock. *S* reports 'stop.'

The above stimuli were given without undue interruption, and so far as possible in the same manner, to all *S*s. Where the standard conditions could not be adhered to, the records were thrown out; this occurred in the

---

[3] W. Whateley Smith, *The Measurement of Emotion*, 1922, 76.

case of 6 Ss (due to failure to follow instructions, interruptions from outside, or apparatus defects). The duration of an experiment varied from 20–30 min.; this variation was largely due to the extra time that had to be allowed to certain Ss between successive stimulations, owing to the character of their galvanic reactions. Thus, although we planned to allow only 20 sec. between the first and second digits tests, it was sometimes necessary to wait 20 or 30 sec. additional, owing to the occurrence of spontaneous or multiple reactions to the initial stimulus. In a sense, however, it might be said that the interval between stimuli was physiologically standardized, since it was determined by the time required for the achievement of stability in each individual's resistance.

The reactions of the *S* were thus recorded as a continuous graph 6 or 7 feet in length, presenting a large number of undulations, the successive 'waves' of which represented the responses to the various stimuli in order of presentation (together with secondary responses.) The deflections were measured to the nearest millimeter and recorded in their proper place on a 40-fold table covering the total number of stimuli employed. Owing, however, to the fact that stimuli 36–40 (electric shock) were hard to control and in sensitive Ss often produced deflections beyond the edge of the paper, the results for these last 4 stimuli were not used in our calculations. The final data available from our experiments thus consisted of the psychogalvanic reactions of 29 adult male Ss, to a series of 36 distinct stimuli standardized for the given conditions of the experiment, and quantitatively comparable.

RESULTS

Our first step in the analysis of the data was to calculate individual correlations between galvanic reactions to any given stimulus with any other series in the series. We calculated 112 such correlations using the rank-order method (ρ converted into r).[4] The correlations were then grouped into 3 classes: (1) self-correlations, those between repeated or identical stimuli, *e.g.* between the first and second startle evoked by a klaxon; (2) intercorrelations between responses to similar stimuli, *e.g.* association words by pictures, or the sound of starting motor by sound of klaxon; (3) intercorrelations between responses to dissimilar stimuli, *e.g.* word association by aggression stimuli. The values for each group of coefficients were then averaged and compared, both as to magnitude and reliability.

TABLE II
SELF-CORRELATIONS

Stimuli	r	P.E.
Mental effort (Digit repetition stimuli 3,5 x 4,6)	0.81	0.05
Aggression (Stimuli 30 x 31)	0.80	0.05
Startle (First by second klaxon)	0.67	0.07
Average	0.76	

[4]The writers are indebted to Mr. Herbert S. Conrad for this statistical work.

The reliability of the single items, or pairs of items, in tests of motor skill, memory or intellectual ability is seldom as high as the average found above. Yet such traits or abilities are commonly considered more stable and more subject to precise measurement than the emotional reactions with which we are concerned. Applying the Spearman-Brown formula, $r_{nn} = n \cdot r_{xy}/[1+(n-1)r_{xy}]$, the reliability of our psychogalvanic reflex measures for the total of 4 mental effort stimuli becomes 0.90; the reliability of the 3 responses to aggression is 0.92, and of the 3 startle responses, 0.83. This is almost certainly an exaggeration, however, for (1) the rapid 'exhaustion' of the psychogalvanic reflex when the same stimuli are repeated, cuts down the variability of the later measures, and hence reduces self-correlation; and (2) the first and second responses, given at any one time, may be supported by a temporary mood condition, yielding a higher correlation than if they were separated by a day or more. With due regard to these considerations, however, the consistency of the results remains higher than had been expected.

TABLE III

SELF-CORRELATION IN THE ASSOCIATION TESTS[5]

Stimuli	r	P.E.
Critical words (1st four x 2nd four)	0.55	0.08
Non-critical words (1st four x 2nd four)	0.53	0.09
Pictures (1st and 3rd x 2nd and 4th)	0.44	0.10
Average	0.53	

The absolute deflections and variability of the deflections to these stimuli are considerably less than are the responses to the mental effort, aggression and startle stimuli just discussed. Not a few *S*s gave zero deflections to the uncritical words and pictures coming at or near the end of the series. As might be expected, the degree of self-correlation appears to vary with the emotional intensity of the stimulus.

The series of digits, the pictures, and the association words are similar in that they present to the *S* a situation, more or less simple, requiring the formulation of a verbal response. The emotional involvement is most marked when conflicts interfere with a prompt formulation. The sound of the electric motor and the klaxon warning, are also similar to each other in that they are loud and unexpected.

---

[5]The association test data will be reported in more detail in a separate paper.

TABLE IV

INTERCORRELATIONS OF DEFLECTIONS TO SIMILAR STIMULI

Stimuli	r	P.E.
Word by picture association (Stimuli 8-11 x 13-29)	0.56	0.08
Word association by mental effort (3-6 x 13-29)	0.46	0.09
Picture association by mental effort (3-6 x 8-11)	0.55	0.08
Verbal directions (2 x 7)	0.25	0.11
(2 x 12)	0.43	0.09
(7 x 12)	0.68	0.08
Startle (motor by klaxon) (1 x 33-35)	0.46	0.09
Average	0.48	

TABLE V

INTERCORRELATIONS FOR DISSIMILAR STIMULI

Stimuli	r	P.E.
Startle (motor) by mental effort .(1 x 3-6)	0.21	0.12
by picture association (1 x 8-11)	0.24	0.12
by word association (1 x 13-29)	0.03	0.12
by aggression (1 x 30-32)	0.15	0.12
Mental effort by aggression (3-6 x 30-32)	0.04	0.12
by startle (klaxon) (3-6 x 33-35)	0.13	0.12
Picture association by aggression (8-11 x 30-32)	0.21	0.12
by startle (klaxon) (8-11 x 33-35)	0.35	0.11
Word association by aggression (13-29 x 30-32)	0.11	0.12
by startle (klaxon) (13-29 x 33-35)	0.47	0.10
Aggression by startle (klaxon) (30-32 x 33-35)	0.44	0.10
Average	0.22	

The coefficients run considerably lower than in the previous groups, and the P.E.s are of course higher. Only two coefficients are more than four times their P.E.s. The higher correlation between aggression and startle, if due to other than chance features, might be considered as the outcome of a certain similarity of the stimuli; both are of a primitive and provocative character. The correlation between klaxon and word association cannot be attributed to this, but perhaps rather to the fact that in these two classes of stimuli the decrement due to exhaustion of the psychogalvanic reflex is more conspicuous than elsewhere: with the klaxon because of its intensity, and with the word association because of the extended number of stimuli used. Hence the correlation would be expected to be reënforced by individual differences in the rate of negative adaptation.

The predictive value of each class of stimuli for other classes is indicated by the average of the intercorrelations with each of the other classes. For the 5 principal groups under discussion these are as follows:

TABLE VI
THE PREDICTIVE VALUE OF STIMULI

Stimuli	r	k
Startle (klaxon) (33–35)	0.37	0.93
Word association (13–29)	0.33	0.94
Picture association (8–11)	0.32	0.95
Mental effort (3–6)	0.29	0.96
Startle (motor) (1)	0.22	0.97

The predictive value of dissimilar stimuli for each other is thus seen to be extremely low. Of the classes considered, the three sounds of the klaxon have the highest predictive value, but the differences possess slight reliability and in any case the coefficient of alienation is so great that the interpredictive functions can have no value.

SUMMARY

Correlations between psychogalvanic reflex deflections can be classified into three groups, the coefficients constituting a hierarchy with but little overlapping.

Self-correlations between repeated stimuli (*e.g.* two identical sounds) give an average of 0.76 (Table II).

Inter-correlations between stimuli imposing similar tasks (*e.g.* associations to two words, or to a word and a picture) average 0.50 (Tables III and IV).

Dissimilar stimuli (*e.g.* a loud sound *vs.* an association word) yield very low coefficients, averaging 0.22 (Table V). Correction for attenuation, if proper data were available, would raise cross correlations from 0.05–0.15 points. But under the conditions of the experiment, even the corrected intercorrelations would leave the coefficients of alienation from 0.80 upwards, indicating a high degree of specificity in the galvanic response.

Our data agree very closely with previous results obtained by Wechsler. The question that still remains is whether a similar specificity would be shown by other physiological indicators of emotion.

GALVANOMETRIC TECHNIQUE IN STUDIES OF ASSOCIATION*

DAVID WECHSLER and HAROLD E. JONES

University of California

During the past two decades recurrent use has been made of the psychogalvanic response in attempts to measure the affective values of words, in the detection of 'guilt,' and in clinical studies of emotional complexes.[1] The major portion of this work has been of a tentative and exploratory nature, with estimates of the method ranging from the very confident claims of Whately Smith[2] to opinions less wholly enthusiastic.[3] It would appear that progress has been slow, and that technical difficulties have discouraged many psychologists from continuing in this field.

It is of course true that the psychogalvanic response involves a delicate and complex procedure, with many variable factors having to do with the electrodes, the E.M.F., the area and location of the skin contacts, the coil suspension, and the processes of recording the deflections. Irregularities or lack of standardization at any one of these points may result in grave disturbance of the data. In the present report, the writers are concerned not with matters of apparatus technique which have been held as constant as possible,[4] but with the effect of alterations in the schedule of stimuli, and the influence of sequence and temporal position in series.

The stimuli employed were the following association words, given in the order shown with one half of our *S*s,[5] and in the reverse order with the remaining half: table, work, carrot, white, money, afraid, dance, woman, glass, flower, swim, pencil, insult, marry, love, kiss.

The stimuli were derived from Whately Smith's list of 100 words, arranged by him in a rank order according to a weighted mean psychogalvanic response obtained in an association experiment with 50 *S*s. Eight of the words (kiss, love, marry, insult, woman, dance, afraid, money) were taken from the 12 standing at the head of his list, and showing average deflections ranging—in terms of his recording system—from 72.8 to 35.6.

---

*Reprinted from *American Journal of Psychology*, 1928, 40, 607-612.

[1]This paper includes results reported in part at the 1926 meeting of the American Psychological Association, and abstracted in the *Psychol. Bull.*, 24, 1927, 173-174.

[2]"I believe it will be be clear to any reader ... that this phenomenon [the psychogalvanic response] is by far the most delicate, reliable, and quantitatively accurate method at present known for detecting and measuring emotional changes." Whately Smith, *The Measurement of Emotion*, 1922, 25.

[3]Cf., for example, J. A. Larson, The cardio-pneumo-psychogram and its use in the study of the emotions, with practical application, *J. Exper. Psychol.*, 5, 1922, 324.

[4]The writers' apparatus has been described in the preceding article *supra*, 601.

[5]The *S*s were a random selection of male undergraduate and graduate students of Columbia University. Thirty-five *S*s were tested, the reversed order of stimuli being used with every other *S*. Due to interruptions, or errors of technique, the total number of cases was reduced to 29 for the later statistical treatment.

The remaining 8 (pencil, swim, flower, glass, white, carrot, work, table) were chosen from the 12 at the bottom of the list, with deflections from 18.5–14.2. In subsequent discussion, words from the top of the list, having conspicuous emotional values, will be called 'critical,' while the others will be called 'indifferent' or 'non-critical.' The order of stimuli indicated in the above list, beginning with table, will be called A; the reverse order, given to alternate Ss, will be called B. In all cases the association words were preceded by a buffer word, 'salt;' the total series occurred in the middle of a stimulus schedule, the first part of which consisted of a picture association test and a test of repeating digits backward. When the association words were reached in this schedule, instructions were given: "Now I am going to say some words. You are to respond to each word by telling me the first word that comes into your mind." The stimulus words were given orally, separated by an interval (from 10–30 sec.) sufficient to permit the resistance of the S to return to its previous level after the psychogalvanic response. As each word was sounded, the E pressed a key which gave a stimulus signal on the continuous kymograph record. A second E (concealed from the S) tended the apparatus and made observations on qualitative aspects of the reactions. A reproduction of two representative responses by the same S, is given in Fig. 1.[6]

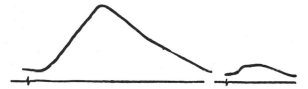

FIG. 1. REPRODUCTION OF TWO REPRESENTATIVE RESPONSES FROM THE SAME S

S: "afraid"   S: "flower"
R: "not"   R: "beautiful"

The deflections to each stimulus word were measured to the nearest mm. and measures of central tendency were computed. In Table I the stimulus words are arranged in the order of magnitude of the Whately Smith means for the same words, and the comparative data of the two investigations are listed.

The gross magnitudes obtained are of course relative to the arbitrary standard conditions of the experiment.[7] The two lists agree in the demarcation of critical and non-critical words, and in placing the sex words conspicuously at the top of the list. A correlation of 0.90 was obtained between the two rankings on the basis of the means, and of 0.95 when the second list is ranked on the basis of the medians. Another important comparison is in what Smith terms the resolvability or range of variability of the psychogalvanic response. The mean value of the word eliciting the largest deflection in Smith's list is 72.8, while the mean value at the other end is only one fifth as great. In the writers' data this ratio becomes about 3.5 to 1, but remains greater than the resolvability of reaction time (2.5 to 1) for the same words. This may be considered to be one of the advantages which the psychogalvanic response shows over reaction time, or for that matter over most of the laboratory indicators of emotion. Its wider relative variability allows for greater precision of measurement, and tends to increase the reliability of the results.

[6]Owing to its length, an entire record cannot conveniently be reproduced here.
[7]The scale on which the deflections occur depends upon the reflecting system used, the E.M.F., the original sensitivity of the galvanometer, and the shunt.

Table I gives the average deflection for each word, combining the two orders A and B. If, however, we compute averages separately for the two orders of presentation, a striking difference appears.

TABLE I
SHOWING THE MEAN DEFLECTION FOR EVERY STIMULUS WORD OBTAINED BY SMITH, AND THE MEAN AND MEDIAN DEFLECTION OBTAINED IN THIS EXPERIMENT

Stimulus-word	Smith: Mean deflection	This Experiment: Mean deflection	Median deflection
kiss	72.8	11.46±1.04	9.50±1.30
love	59.5	10.69±0.96	8.33±1.19
marry	58.5	10.39±0.97	8.67±1.22
woman	40.3	7.96±0.92	7.67±1.15
dance	37.4	7.31±0.60	6.67±0.77
afraid	36.8	9.12±1.23	7.00±1.55
money	35.6	7.58±0.69	5.00±0.86
insult	32.5	8.65±0.75	7.50±0.94
table	18.5	4.23±0.54	4.00±0.68
work	18.3	6.85±1.10	4.50±1.37
carrot	18.2	6.70±1.20	3.33±1.50
white	17.8	4.69±0.60	3.00±0.77
glass	17.6	5.31±0.70	4.60±0.88
flower	16.5	6.12±0.72	5.00±0.90
pencil	15.4	4.65±0.60	3.25±0.77
swim	14.2	3.38±0.33	2.60±0.41

TABLE II
SHOWING THE MEDIAN DEFLECTION FOR THE TWO ORDERS IN WHICH THE STIMULUS-WORDS WERE PRESENTED

Stimulus-word	Order of presentation	A Median	Order of presentation	B Median
table	1	5.25±1.06	16	0.72±0.81
work	2	7.75±1.25	15	0.93±2.24
carrot	3	6.50±2.12	14	3.17±2.11
white	4	5.25±1.06	13	0.81±1.17
money	5	4.75±1.03	12	5.50±1.31
afraid	6	7.75±2.18	11	6.50±1.15
dance	7	7.25±1.11	10	6.25±1.05
woman	8	7.75±0.42	9	7.50±1.73
glass	9	4.88±1.41	8	2.50±0.99
flower	10	4.50±0.84	7	5.25±1.55
swim	11	1.50±0.39	6	2.88±0.87
pencil	12	1.50±0.93	5	3.83±1.25
insult	13	6.50±1.01	4	8.50±1.63
marry	14	8.25±1.32	3	10.50±2.00
love	15	8.75±1.90	2	7.50±1.37
kiss	16	8.75±1.32	1	10.50±2.14

Inspection of Table II immediately suggests the importance of position in series. The effect of adaptation is obvious, in spite of the fact that an attempt was made to minimize this by employing a buffer word, and by giving the association test in the middle of a much larger schedule of stimuli. The median[8] deflection for 'table' is 5.25 when it appears first in the list, and 0.72 when it appears last. The median deflection for 'work' is 7.75 when it appears second in the list, and only 0.93 when it is given next to the last. It will be observed, however, that in the case of the most 'critical' words the emotional value is not greatly negatived by a late position in the series. The words 'kiss,' 'love' and 'marry' give the highest median deflections whether they appear first or last in the list. In the A order the 'non-critical' words are given positions 1-4 and 9-12 in the list; the mean of the 8 medians is 4.64. The less favorably situated 'critical' words (positions 5-9 and 13-16) yield a mean of 7.47. If now we change to order B, the mean for the 'non-critical' medians drops nearly one half to 2.51, while the mean of the 'critical' words increases slightly (and unreliably) to 7.82. It is, then, established that the factor of position in series exerts a greater influence upon the words of slight emotional tone than upon those which already have a significant affective value. This relation is further emphasized in Table III.

Several of the above differences, particularly for the 'critical' words, have a very low reliability; nevertheless, of 16 differences, 13 are in favor of the earlier position in series, and the exceptions, in two of the cases at any rate, appear to be reversals due to the influence of emotional carry-over from contiguous words. Thus, the word 'glass' when it occurs 8th in series has a smaller deflection than when it occurs 9th, but in the latter case it occupies a post-critical position, following the word 'woman.'

The influence of position in series may be brought out in another manner. In the group of *S*s taking the A order of words, each individual's average deflection was computed for the 8 'critical' and for the 8 'non-critical' words; the correlation between these two variables was 0.61 (rho corrected to r). For the *S*s given the B order of words a practically identical correlation (0.64) was obtained. If now we consider the total group and correlate the critical by the non-critical averages, a similar r should be found, unless some disturbing influence has affected the comparability of the two groups. The obtained r, 0.23, may be considered as evidence for such a disturbing influence. But the sole difference in technique with the groups was in the order

---

[8]In these and in further comparisons, we have made use of the median deflection for each word rather than the mean; the median more genuinely represents the distribution, and is freer from the influence of aberrant individual responses.

of presentation of the words; the effect of which was to give large deflections of the 'non-critical' words when they occurred first, and small or insignificant deflections when they were given in the middle or at the end of the series.

TABLE III

SHOWING THE IMPORTANCE OF THE POSITION OF THE STIMULUS-WORDS IN THE STIMULUS-SERIES

Stimulus-word		Change in position	Deflection difference in favor of earlier position	% of increase, per unit of change in position
Non-critical	table	16 to 1	4.53	41.9
	work	15 to 2	6.82	56.4
	carrot	14 to 3	3.33	9.5
	white	13 to 4	4.44	61.7
	pencil	12 to 5	2.33	22.2
	swim	11 to 6	1.38	18.4
	flower	10 to 7	.75	5.5
	glass	9 to 8	−2.38	−48.7
	Mean		2.65	20.8
Critical	kiss	16 to 1	1.75	1.3
	love	15 to 2	−1.25	− 1.1
	marry	14 to 3	2.25	2.4
	insult	13 to 4	2.00	3.4
	money	12 to 5	− .75	− 1.9
	afraid	11 to 6	1.25	3.9
	dance	10 to 7	1.00	5.3
	woman	9 to 8	.25	.33
	Mean		.81	2.1

Table III should be read: The word 'table' shows a median deflection 4.53 mm. greater when it is presented first in series than when it is presented sixteenth. Taking as a base the median value when it is presented last, this value is increased 41.9% for each unit of change in forward position, or a total of 628% for a change from sixteenth to first.

A question may arise as to the equivalence of groups A and B in the functions measured. The mean of the 16 medians is 6.09 for group A, and 5.18 for group B. From Table II it is obvious that this difference is due to the fact that in group A the 'non-critical' words have priority. A fairer basis of comparison would be with the middle 8 words rather than with the total series; here the means are respectively 4.99 and 5.03, and we may accept this as an indication that the two groups were comparable, for the purposes of this experiment.

CONCLUSIONS

(1) In a serial association experiment, the magnitude of the psychogalvanic response varies with the temporal position of the stimulus. Hence, in clinical studies or in the detection

of guilty knowledge, the emotional values of stimulus words cannot be compared without taking into account the factor of position in series. This of course might be inferred from the general experience with the rapid 'exhaustion' of the psychogalvanic response in repetitions of the same stimulus, but the application of the principle to association experiments has frequently been neglected. Such an error may account, in part, for the inconsistent results occasionally reported in the use of the psychogalvanic response.

(2) 'Critical' and 'non-critical' words cannot readily be distinguished unless a preceding series of at least five buffer words has been used.

(3) The importance of position is greater with 'non-critical' than with 'critical' words; stimuli connected with complexes yield reactions of considerable uniformity, regardless of where they occur.

(4) If different Ss are to be compared as to emotivity, the schedule of presentation can be varied only within very narrow limits.

(5) When reduced to a comparable scale, the median deflection values for each of the 16 words are closely similar to the results obtained by a previous experimenter. In terms of averages, this indicates a high degree of dependability of the psychogalvanic response.

THE INCIDENCE AND SIGNIFICANCE OF FINGERNAIL BITING IN CHILDREN*

DAVID WECHSLER

I have to report the results of a study which is of interest because of the further confirmation it gives to Freud's original three-stage division of the individual's psychosexual development, and because of its value in showing the possibilities of the statistical method in the investigation of psychoanalytic problems.

The study consisted of the simple procedure of observing and then recording the frequency of fingernail biting among children, at different ages. For this purpose I made observations on some 3,000 children of both sexes, ranging from one to seventeen years in age. The subjects were for the most part children attending the New York public schools or in the case of the very young ones, of infants at public nurseries. The children of school age were asked to place both hands, palms downward, on their desks, and as the examiner passed he noted on a slip of paper previously prepared, and having on it the name, age and sex of the subject, the fact whether there was or was not any evidence of fingernail biting. A plus sign indicated that the child did, and the minus sign that it did not bite its nails. These slips were then sorted as to age and sex and tabulated in a manner presently to be indicated. In the case of the nursery children the examiner recorded the presence or absence of nail biting directly as the children filed by him. Owing to the smallness of the number of cases the children were not separated as to sex in recording the cases up to four years of age.

The children examined represented quite a random and diverse sample of the normal school population, being derived from schools in all parts of Manhattan, and representing nearly all racial groups and social levels. No distinction was attempted as regards degree of biting and those marked plus ranged .from cases where there was evidence of only occasional biting, say of a single finger, to those of inveterate biting of practically every finger of the hand. The disregard for this quantitative difference does not, of course, imply that it is not of practical importance, but in this preliminary study in which the primary interest was in the incidence of the habit, I thought

*Reprinted from *The Psychoanalytic Review*, Vol. 18, 1931, through the courtesy of the Editors and the Publisher, National Psychological Association for Psychoanalysis, New York, N. Y.

it best not to complicate the method whose great merit was that it could be applied to a great number of cases in a comparatively short period. Besides, as need hardly be pointed out, any classification as to degree of fingernail biting would of necessity be a highly subjective procedure. Indeed, it might even be interposed that even a simple classification as to the mere presence or absence of fingernail biting would present some difficulty. However, this difficulty was considerably less in practice than might be suspected. The general rule

TABLE I

(Boys)

Age	Total Number	Number Biting	Per Cent Biting
Under 3 years	31	0	0.0
*3–4	31	1	3.3
*4–5	40	10	20.0
5–6	70	19	27.1
6–7	177	52	29.4
7–8	153	55	35.9
8–9	112	40	35.7
9–10	122	47	38.5
10–11	127	43	33.9
11–12	104	35	33.7
12–13	103	36	35.0
13–14	110	48	43.6
14–15	150	63	42.0
15–16	114	37	32.4
16–17	68	19	27.9
17–18	21	4	19.0

* Boys and girls.

which I followed when in doubt was to give the child the benefit, that is, to classify it as a non-fingernail biter. I do not think that the errors introduced by this method could have been very large, and in any case, as the ratings were all made by a single person, were necessarily of constant character, so that while they may influence the absolute numbers, they do not influence the age ratios.

With these preliminary remarks we now turn to examination of the data themselves. These are summarized in Tables I and II and their appended graphs. Table I is for boys and Table II for girls. The first column of each table gives the age interval, the second, the total number of cases examined at that particular age, and third, the per cent of children biting their nails. Obviously, the per cent that do not is equal to the difference between 100 and the per cent given. As indicated above, children under four years of age were not separated as to sex; the percentages for the mixed group are given in the table marked "Boys." There are as yet no sex differences at this level, and as will be obvious from an examination of the graphs no significant sex differences, indeed, occur until the age of puberty.

Examination of the figures shows: (1) That fingernail biting under the age of three does not occur. Only one case was met with below the age of three, and that was doubtful. The tendency first begins to manifest itself during the fourth year, rises slightly in the

TABLE II

(Girls)

Age	Total Number	Number Biting	Per Cent Biting
Under 3 years	..	..	....
3–4	..	..	....
4–5	34	7	20.6
5–6	58	18	31.0
6–7	184	57	30.9
7–8	158	63	39.9
8–9	91	23	25.6
9–10	98	33	33.7
10–11	76	25	32.9
11–12	87	38	43.7
12–13	81	36	44.4
13–14	163	56	34.3
14–15	196	61	31.1
15–16	184	44	23.9
16–17	82	13	15.9

next, and then suddenly jumps at age six, from which year it maintains a fairly constant level until puberty. That is, at age twelve for girls and age fourteen for boys the percentage once more rises and continues at a high peak for two years. It then quickly recedes to a very low level, thus dropping from 44.4 per cent in age fourteen (girls) to 15.9 per cent in age sixteen, which is probably the per cent at which it continues for the entire adult period. The most remarkable thing about this last rise is that it occurs at different ages for boys and girls, the two years' difference corresponding roughly to the age difference in the onset of puberty in the two sexes. This rise in the incidence curve is not unlike the "humps" met with in the growth curves of various anthropometric measures, but is here very much more marked and as we shall have occasion to see, of special signifi-

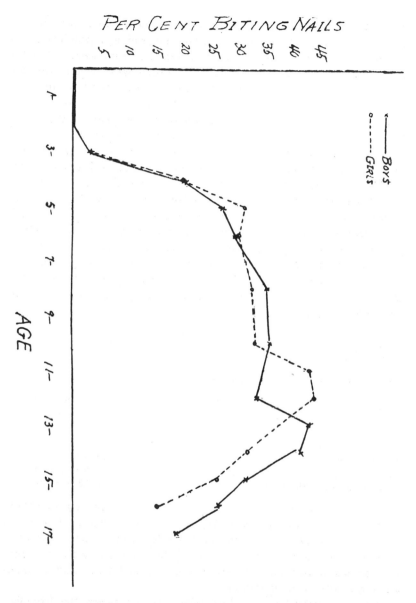

PER CENT BITING NAILS

AGE

——— Boys
o- - - - - Girls

cance. Its meaning, as indeed the entire incidence curve just described, becomes obvious only in the light of psychoanalytic contributions to the theory of sexual development.

In his three contributions to the theory of sex, Freud distinguished three main stages in the psychosexual development of the individual:

(1) The period of infantile sexuality covering the first five years of the child's life; (2) the latency period, beginning approximately at the age of six and continuing until the onset of adolescence; (3) the period of adult sexual development, beginning with puberty through the completion of the adolescent period. The period of infantile sexuality, furthermore, divides itself into two clearcut phases. The first, or autoerotic phase, occupying the first three years of the child's life; the second, the genital phase, covering the next two years. The characteristics of these periods together with their further subdivisions, as for instance, the autoerotic into the oral and anal, the genital into the urethral and phallic, etc., are sufficiently familiar to psychoanalysts to need no further elaboration. We wish here to examine only the association if any which may exist between the variations in the incidence of fingernail biting with the various periods of psychosexual development. For this purpose I have tabulated the delimiting years of the various periods of the psychosexual development of the individual as adduced by psychoanalysis and the ages at which critical variations in the incidence of fingernail biting occur, as furnished by the analysis of our data.

Fingernail Biting

No biting .... Age 1 to 3
Beginning of fingernail biting with gradual rise....... Age 3 to 5
Increased fingernail biting at approximately same level $\begin{cases} \text{(Boys) Age 6 to 14} \\ \text{(Girls) Age 6 to 12} \end{cases}$
Sudden rise in biting frequency...................... $\begin{cases} \text{(Girls) Age 12 to 14} \\ \text{(Boys) Age 14 to 16} \end{cases}$

Psychosexual Development

Autoerotic period .... Age 1 to 3
Genital period .... Age 3 to 5
Latency period .... Age 6 to puberty
Achievement of adult sexuality..................... Age 12 to adolescence

From the above comparison it becomes at once apparent that there is some close relation between the incidence of fingernail biting and the various periods of psychosexual development. The correspondence is indeed nothing short of remarkable considering the fact that the various phases have generally been defined with only a rough attempt at precise delimitation.

Having established the close relationship between the Freudian defined periods of the individual's psychosexual development with the age variations in the intensity of the nail biting habit, it remains to explain why these changes occur at the epochs indicated. The explanation can be found from an analysis of the psychic determinants of the habit itself.

From the point of view of psychoanalysis, fingernail biting is a manifestation or a symptom of one of two regressive proclivities. In the first place it may serve as a means of oral erotic gratification, and thus may be looked upon as a continuation of the infantile thumb sucking habit. This libidinal significance of the act is perhaps most clearly indicated by the type of situation which calls forth the activity in the adult who is not an habitual nail biter. These situations are almost invariably instances of stress, as when the individual is under mental strain, worried, absorbed in deep thought, etc. Taking the finger in the mouth, like thumbsucking, serves as a pacifier, being a reversion to that archaic activity which was the supreme assuager of all distress, the mother's nipple. But the more common significance of the habit, and the one that explains the biting of the nail as well as the introduction of the finger into the mouth, is that it serves as an onanistic equivalent. Fingernail biting, as psychoanalysis has shown to be the case of most tics, is nothing but a particular form of unconscious masturbatory activity. Its indulgence becomes possible, as in the case of all neurotic symptomatology, by carrying with it the punishment which the tabooed act calls for. The punishment for playing with (using) the penis is of course castration. The symbolism involved is obvious to psychoanalysts: I defy the prohibition to manipulate my penis (taking finger in mouth) and accordingly must suffer the penalty of having it cut off (biting the nail off). Continued fingernail biting is thus a symptom of an incompletely resolved Œdipus situation.

With the above in mind, the correspondences between the psychosexual phases and the ages at which the different intensities of the fingernail biting occur, becomes almost self-explanatory. Before the age of three there is no nail biting. That is inevitably so, for the child is still in the prephallic stage of its psychosexual development. The nipple or its equivalent has continued as its source of oral gratification, and the Œdipus situation has not as yet come to trouble its libidinal strivings. There is as yet no occasion for substitute formations. Age three to five. Beginning of nail biting activity with gradual increase. This is again as we should expect. For this age period at which the child is confronted by the Œdipus situation on the one hand and the beginnings of directed prohibitions on the part of the parents against manifestations of genital activity, an activity which is precisely at this time at its height. The genital activity is of course a reaction to the Œdipus conflict, but the onanism which it represents no less than the incest strivings are taboo. It must be similarly given up. The beginning of the fingernail biting represents a beginning at vicarious attempts at genital and onanistic activity. It is as yet slight because in the first place, a certain amount of overt activity is still tolerated, and secondly because the process of psychic repression (of the Œdipus conflict) is still under way. But by the age of six such tolerance more or less ceases, and what is more the Œdipus situation with its accompanying genital activity has come to a close. It is supposed to have been more or less successfully resolved or at least effectively suppressed. Now it is at precisely this age (six) which according to psychoanalytic observation marks the beginning of the latency period, that we find a substantial rise in the incidence of fingernail biting. This rise can be readily accounted for if we accept fingernail biting as a vicarious onanistic activity. The rise here is an indication of the fact that the transition from genital activity to latency is in a large percentage of cases unsuccessful. A considerable number of children have as yet failed to resolve the Œdipus situation, and as the incest strivings must nevertheless be repressed, the continuance of the conflict has quickly to be transferred to a different level. Fingernail biting in that it affords an outlet for the libidinal gratification is accordingly seized upon, and its presence here as at later periods is an indication of the persistence of an unresolved Œdipus situation.

Between the ages of six and twelve (girls) to fourteen (boys) the incidence of nail biting maintains itself at a fairly constant level or " plateau." The incidence of fingernail biting is fairly high but no significant changes are observed. Like the psychosexual period of latency to which it corresponds it is essentially uneventful. And this uneventful period continues until the age of puberty, when again there is a sudden rise in the incidence curve. And this rise occurs once more precisely when we should expect it according to psycho-analytic theory. For, with the onset of puberty the Œdipus situation is revived, and the guilt feelings of the infantile sexual period reacti-vated. The increase in fingernail biting during puberty is an index of the reactivation of these feelings and the recurrence of the Œdipus problem prior to its final disposition with the acquisition of adult sexuality. With its disposition we should accordingly expect a rapid fall in the incidence of fingernail biting and that is what is actually observed. The frequency at the height of the pubertal period (girls, twelve to fourteen years, boys, fourteen to sixteen years) is over 40 per cent; two years later it is less than 20 per cent. This percentage is probably still significantly higher than what is to be found in exclusively adult population, but from casual observation, I should venture, greater than what is generally supposed. My own guess would be that for adults it is somewhere in the vicinity of 10 per cent. However, where facts could be so readily obtained, guesses are distinctly unwarranted, and in a subsequent study I hope to answer the question more precisely.

Our remarks thus far have been concerned principally with a discussion of the incidence and significance of fingernail biting, and the light which psychoanalysis throws upon the problem. Over and above the possible value of the study in elucidating the immediate problem at hand, I esteem it important because of the evidence it presents as to the possibilities of the statistical method in substantiating if not testing at least certain of the hypotheses which psychoanalysis is as yet constrained to make.

Psychoanalysis has never entertained great expectations from the applications of the statistical method to the science. Its own method being so primarily concerned with an intensive study of the individual, it has rejected almost *à priori* all suggestions as to its possible usefulness or even feasibility. The objections made at first were that the statistical method was not applicable to psychoanalytic investigations, and more recently that, in any case, it was quite impracticable. Thus at the recent International Congress of Mental Hygiene, Dr. Franz Alexander, replying to a plea of Dr. Wm. Healy for some statistical studies by psychoanalysts, discouraged any hope of such efforts by pleading in turn that it would take an analyst ten years working ten hours a day to achieve results on so small a number as even 100 cases. To which the reply is, of course, that if one analyst working alone can't do it, twenty working together can. Moreover, the long time it takes to accumulate data is not a very substantial excuse for any science. After all, comets come even less frequently than psychoanalytic patients, and still astronomy has not shunned at accumulating data about them. But over and above that, and this is the thing to which I wish to call attention, there are certain types of problems in psychoanalysis, whose solution in no way calls for intensive technique required for individual therapy. They are for the most part questions requiring verification rather than elaboration, of which the study here reported is an example. And there are many others which one could readily mention. Mrs. Chadwick, for instance, also at the First International Congress of Mental Hygiene, reported some observations as regards the preponderance of the assumed fetal position during sleep in patients who subsequently died, as compared with others suffering from the same disease, but who " pulled through," giving, however, no figures. It would have been not a very difficult matter, instead of reporting some striking observations, to have made a systematic study of the problem and through actual record keeping and proper numerical analysis, to have determined whether the association noted was other than one of chance or bias. Or, again, take the problem of the significance of the absence of a father for the development of the child's ego and superego. According to psychoanalytic theory, we should expect to find certain character traits or behavior tendencies more marked in children deprived of a father or a strong father imago, than in those where this was not the case. For example, they should show a greater tendency towards delinquency. The fact that they do has of course frequently been asserted, but the matter could be definitely settled by a reliable statistical study of the problem. And so also with the determination of a great many other points of fact necessary to the solution of psychoanalytic problems, determinations which, because they are gross effects produced by the interaction of innumerable small causes, as in the case of other science, can in no way be made without application of statistical methods.

In conclusion it will perhaps be useful to call attention to some practical implications which the results of this study seem to suggest. In the first place, in view of the large percentage of children who bite their nails (between ages of six and sixteen, in the vicinity of 30 per cent), the "habit," certainly in its milder form, cannot be looked upon as pathological. In the second place, nail biting is not a habit, in the ordinary sense of the term, but a symptom, a symptom as we have seen of the persistence of the unresolved Œdipus situation. Hence, all efforts at reducing it, based on the psychology of habit formation must be doomed to failure, and anybody who has had any experience in the application of such habit breaking procedures as applications of aloes and taping of fingers knows how useless they are. They are not only useless but injurious because they merely serve to fix or at best displace the symptom. So also is probably the effect of calling attention to or constant harping on the " habit " and the infliction of punishment on the child for failure to desist, in any form. For an understanding of the significance of the " habit " shows us at once that by the former method we merely serve to increase the child's feelings of guilt, and by the latter serve to gratify its need for punishment. Such gratification, really absolution, merely enables the individual to continue more stubbornly the activity from which we are trying to wean him. The only way to treat nail biting, as in the case of any other condition, is to attack the cause and not the symptom itself.

THE CLINICAL MEASUREMENT OF ANXIETY:
AN EXPERIMENTAL APPROACH*

DAVID WECHSLER and RENATUS HARTOGS

THE PROBLEM OF ANXIETY

The aim of this study is to present an objective method of appraising and diagnosing anxiety. So far as the present writers know, no such technique is at present available. The need for one is, however, obvious, since anxiety is admittedly not only the central problem in most of the neuroses and psychoses, but a manifestation of maladjustment or temporary difficulty in many situations of everyday life.

Before presenting the method and the material from which the results reported here have been obtained, a brief review will be given of some of the more commonly cited concepts of anxiety. The aim here is not to enter into a theoretical discussion of anxiety so much as to find a conceptual basis for its objective evaluation and measurement.

The most commonly referred to theory of anxiety—at least in psychiatric circles—is that of Freud. According to Freud,[1] anxiety is the individual's response to threats to the ego, caused by the repression of sexual impulses. This neurotic anxiety, he distinguishes from the normal reaction of fear, which is a defensive response to external danger.

Two other theories derived from psychoanalysis deal with the problem of anxiety. According to Rank,[2] anxiety is the continued "abreaction" of affective tension originally occasioned by the "birth trauma." Adler[3] considers anxiety primarily an affective state resulting from inferiority feelings and secondarily a pattern which the individual uses to satisfy his needs and to escape frustration. Horney[4] combines the Freudian and Adlerian concepts with sociological ideas to give a socio-psychological interpretation of anxiety.

The nonpsychoanalytical concepts are represented by Cannon,[5] whose idea of anxiety is primarily psychophysical, and by McDougall,[6] who sees in anxiety a complex emotion caused by a conflict between hope and despondency. Allied to them, are theories

*Reprinted from *The Psychiatric Quarterly*, 1945, 19, 618-635.

developed by military psychiatrists[7] who explain acute anxiety in syndromes like "combat fatigue" and "flyer's fatigue" as due to the failure of the individual's ability to repress or suppress normal fear reactions.

All these theories attempt an analysis of anxiety by starting from a description of certain psychological situations in which, or as the result of which, an individual may be expected to develop anxiety. They do not fully explain why equally threatening dangers generate anxiety in one individual and not in another and why there are among normal as well as among neurotic individuals great varieties of reaction to the same situational danger. Such an insufficiency is due in part to the fact that the foregoing theories are concerned with anxiety as a phenomenon rather than with the personality structure of the individual which gives rise to it and more specifically with his level of personality integration.

The present writers accordingly propose as an operational concept what they should like to call the "disintegration concept of anxiety." Under this concept it is assumed: (1) that every individual tends to reach a level of integration maximal for himself; and (2) that he seeks to defend the particular level he has attained against any threat or danger, because any lowering of this level constitutes a vital injury to his ego. Accordingly, anxiety may be expected to arise whenever the individual feels threatened not only by actual danger, but by any situation which threatens his personality as a whole. In both instances, the individual reacts with a state of general alertness and mobilizes whatever defenses he has to avert any and all disintegrative forces.

Since psychological disorganization and motor incoordination are easily observable and objective manifestations of anxiety, it seemed reasonable to assume that one could obtain a projection of the integration level of an individual by placing him in a non-habitual or surprise situation and by investigating his integrative behavior and his motor productions in such a situation.

On this assumption, one might expect that the poorly integrated personality, always prepared and ready for a defense of the self against any threat, would also be greatly disturbed on the motor level and project his helplessness and anxiety in the form of specific graphomotor disturbances. Such disturbances do in fact occur; and their psychological analysis permits, as the writers will show presently, an evaluation of the specific conditions which gave rise to them.

TEST PROCEDURE AND APPARATUS

In order to measure anxiety along the lines indicated, the writers made use of a simplified mirror drawing test and devised an apparatus (the "Katoptograph") which permits one to obtain an objective record in less than six minutes.

While the technique of mirror tracing is familiar, it is perhaps important to point out an essential difference between mirror drawing and mirror tracing, which is often referred to under the former term. Mirror tracing is the form of the experiment that has generally been used in experimental psychology (Starch, Snoddy, Weidensall, Louttit)[8] and usually consists of making the subject follow the outline of a geometric figure, generally a six-pointed star, while looking at it in the mirror. The writers' test is actually not a tracing, but a drawing test and it was their aim *not* to provide for the subject any cues or continuous points of reference for his performance.

The present test consists of two parts. Part I requires the drawing of the diagonal of a square of which only the lower right and the upper left vertices are indicated on the test blank (See Figure 2). Part II requires the successive joining of five points distributed irregularly over the space of the blank, followed up by the connecting of two additional points which are screened from the field of vision (See Figure 3). The drawing is done with an ordinary, but well sharpened, pencil about four inches long.

Although there are a number of mirror tracing apparatus available, it seemed desirable to have an instrument which would combine simplicity of construction with special suitability for the test procedure. The apparatus to which the writers have given the name "Katoptograph" (Figure 1) consists of two plywood boards (10 x 12 inches), articulated by means of hinges so that when not in use they can be folded together and carried in a briefcase. The mirror (7 x 7 inches) is mounted centrally on the inner face of one of the boards and the adjustable screen is attached to the other board.

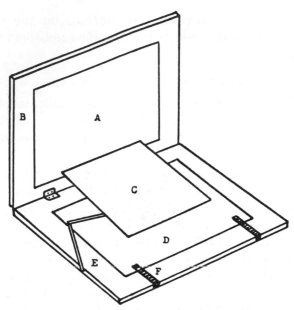

Figure 1. The Katoptograph. A, mirror; B, mirror-board; C, screen; D, test blank; E, drawing board; F, metal clamp.

ADMINISTRATION AND DIRECTIONS

The test is administered in the following way: After the subject has been seated comfortably in front of the Katoptograph, he is informed that he will be asked to do some mirror drawing. He is shown a sample of Part I of the test blank and told that he will be required to draw a straight line from point 1 to point 2 and to do this while looking in the mirror. He receives the short pencil, and his hand is guided by the examiner to point 1. After the subject has found point 1, he receives the following instruction: "When I say 'Go,' draw a straight line from where the pencil is now to point 2, as quickly as you can and without at any time lifting the pencil from the paper." The subject then receives the signal "Go" and is permitted to continue his effort to draw the line until he either has reached his goal or has worked at the problem for three minutes.

After completion of Part I, Part II of the test blank is exposed in the mirror, and the subject is instructed as follows: "When I say 'Go,' draw as quickly as you can a straight line from point 1 to point 2, then from point 2 to point 3, etc., until you reach point 5. Remember that at no time may you lift the pencil from the paper." When the subject has reached point 5, the examiner asks: "Do you see point 6?" After having received an affirmative answer, he places a screen between the subject's eyes and the mirror and says: "Now go to point 6 from memory." As soon as the subject indicates that he thinks he has reached point 6, the examiner lifts the pencil in the subject's hand from the paper and places it on point 6. Then the examiner removes the second screen, permitting the subject to locate point 7 in the mirror, replaces the screen and says: "Now go to point 7." After the subject has completed Katoptogram I and II (K I and K II), the entire test is repeated immediately.

The experiment as outlined has been administered to some 300 subjects, roughly 150 normals and 150 nonnormals (ranging from mild personality disturbances to severe anxiety neurosis and forthright psychosis). In this preliminary paper, the writers wish merely to present and discuss the general results, the fundamentals of interpretation and the characteristics of the individual performance which enable one not only to detect the existence of anxiety, its level, intensity and control, but also to appraise a variety of basic personality traits which either enter into, or modify, or are modified by, the subject's anxiety.

The Criteria and Fundamentals of Interpretation

While detailed information about the katoptographic criteria and the technique of their interpretation will have to be reserved for a more extensive publication, the writers wish to outline in this paper some of the quantitative and qualitative scoring categories founded on the linear and motor aspects of the obtained responses.

The graphomotor categories which are objectively measurable and which are used here as quantitative indicators are time (T), distance (D) and the time-distance-ratio (D/T). Generally, subjects with strong anxiety tension present long time scores. Sometimes the anxiety tension is so great that some individuals become "paralyzed;" that is to say they are completely unable to proceed with the task within the time limits.

Subjects may connect one point with the other by straight or nearly straight lines or proceed in circuitous and deviating paths. The distance required by the subject, measured to the nearest half-centimeter by a precision distance recorder, indicates to what degree the individual is able to control his anxiety.

Finally the relation between the time and distance scores is important. On the basis of a single dichotomy in each, one obtains four possible combinations:

Short Distance/Short Time   = SD/ST
Long Distance/Long Time   = LD/LT
Short Distance/Long Time   = SD/LT
Long Distance/Short Time   = LD/ST

The significance of these relationships varies with the magnitude of the ratios and may be associated with different types of personality structure under special consideration at the attained integration level. Provisional norms have been established.

In addition to the foregoing, the writers have found no less than 14 other basic categories that may be used in describing a subject's katoptogram. The following are the most general and are perhaps sufficient to indicate the graphomotor principles they employ.

Graphomotor Block (See Figure 6). This describes a paralysis-like inhibition of the subject and appears on the blank as an accumulation of abortive pencil strokes within a relatively small area. A block always presents considerable density, but the direction of radiation of the strokes is variable. Block expresses, if it occurs right at the start, basic or endogenous anxiety—of considerable intensity and accompanied by a neurotic form of helplessness.

Graphomotor Complex (See Figure 7). This is a variant of the block, indicating a lower degree of anxiety tension. It is less dense, and is usually met with in the middle rather than at the beginning of a subject's drawing.

Segmentation (See Figure 4). This is indicated by the number of linear interruptions, stops, cuts and breaks occurring during a performance.

Spread (See Figure 5). This designates amplitude of the graphomotor response; it may be extensive or retensive, unilateral or bilateral.

Field-Distribution. This is indicated by the specific regions of the available space, which are covered by the performance.

Pencil Pressure. This may be appraised qualitatively by inspection or evaluated quantitatively by means of a self-recording pressure-scale.

Atactic disturbances. These include tremor, jerkings, incoordination, discontinuity, etc., which can be observed in the performances of even neurologically normal subjects, and are related to specific types of personality disintegration.

Blind-drawing. This involves the subject's performance on K II without visual guide and takes into consideration the direction and distance of the line so drawn, as well as the delay between signal and response.

Comparison of test with retest. This involves the comparison of the subject's performances on trial I and trial II with quantitative and qualitative evaluation of an improvement or deterioration. The second performance, which is particularly disturbed and deteriorated in organic cases, is especially important because it seems to give indications as to the severity and probable continuance of the anxiety state (prognosis).

Traits other than anxiety. Although the test was originally designed to give a measure of the subject's anxiety, a number of other characterological traits are projected by the individual into his performance. This is due to the fact that anxiety is not an isolated function of personality, but is related and interconnected with other behavior determinants.

Thus aggression, frequently a result of converted anxiety, is manifested by the tendency to use the distal half of the test blank, combined with constant heavy pressure and with alternating convexity and angularity of the katoptogram.

Similarly, it is generally easy to detect the impulsive individual by the extreme rapidity and headlong quality of his response.

On the other hand, feelings of insufficiency are always indicated by proximal field-distribution, high segmentation, restartings and recrossings.

The writers are now in the process of tabulating and validating as many of these linear and spatial characteristics* as lend them-

*This material will eventually be worked up in a monograph which the writers hope to complete in the near future.

selves to analysis and interpretation. Some of the data will be appraised statistically; others will remain qualitative in nature; and the interpretation of a katoptogram will, like that of a Rorschach record, depend a great deal on the investigator's experience.

Appraisal of all the writers' data is not yet complete, but analysis of individual records is sufficiently encouraging to justify confidence in both the method and results. The following cases are presented to illustrate the clinical possibilities of the test as well as the technique of interpretation.

REPORT OF CASES

Case 1. *Z. T.*

This subject is an unmarried woman of 27. She draws Katoptogram I (K I) in four seconds (See Figure 2) and Katoptogram II (K II) in 19 seconds (See Figure 3). Her type of speed is SD/ST. Her responses have no lateral spread, the pressure is medium and constant, but little segmentation is observable, field distribution is

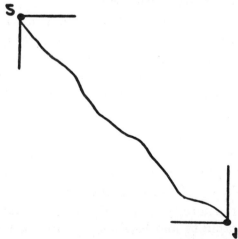

Figure 2. Normal Katoptogram, first part (K I), presenting short distance, minimal lateral spread, constant medium pressure, absence of segmentation and atactic disturbances.
(Note numerals, reversed for mirror-reading.)

medial, graphomotor difficulties do not occur. Her response in the blind-drawing part of K II shows correct choice of direction and good observance of the required distances. The performance on a second trial improves in time and distance.

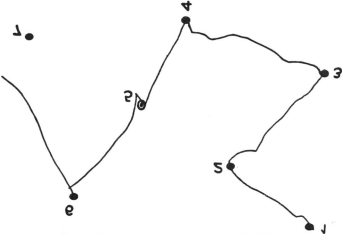

Figure 3. Normal Katoptogram, second part (K II), presenting in addition to the characteristics of performance in K I absence of disturbance due to directional changes and good, but not perfect blind-drawing responses (5-6, 6-7).

Interpretation. Absence of any disturbing anxiety tension, complete and secure self-control, mental-emotional integration and balance, integrative ability.

Comment. This young woman, although born and educated in England, left the home of her parents with their consent at the age of 18 in order to make her own way in the United States. She had no friends or relatives here, but nevertheless was able to become successful as actress and writer in a surprisingly short time. The Rorschach Test and the Minnesota Multiphasic Personality Inventory (MMPI) were administered as control tests and the records obtained show spontaneous and secure self-control, good social adjustment and self-adjustment and absence of anxiety in any form.

The performance of this subject may be considered the typical response of an emotionally stable and well-integrated individual. No disturbing basic, secondary, or situational, anxiety is likely to interfere with the self-organization, social adjustment and mental-emotional development of this personality.

Case 2.   *M. F.*

This subject is a man of 32, married.   M. F. needs 150 seconds to draw K I (See Figure 4) and 212 seconds to draw K II.   A graphomotor complex at point 1 in K I indicates that the subject was apprehensive at the start and had some difficulties in getting away

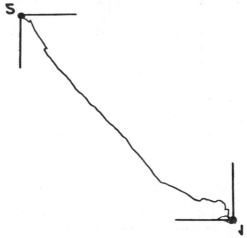

Figure 4.   K I of a subject with intense basic and secondary, but well-controlled anxiety.   Initial complex, SD/LT type of speed, retensive spread, heavy pressure, heavy segmentation.

from the starting point.   Risking only little steps or segments, he tries to catch the right direction and once he has found it, proceeds slowly and carefully toward the goal.   In K II (not shown), he goes quickly from 1 to 2, but the required change of direction at point 2 causes him so much difficulty that he develops a graphomotor block from which he can free himself only after 120 seconds. The outstanding criteria which characterize this performance are lack of spread, high time score, low distance score, high segmentation.

Interpretation.   The interpretation is basic and secondary anxiety which is carefully controlled under the cover of inhibited and rigid behavior.

Comment.   This subject, a Belgian, is described by five judges as "reserved, withdrawing, rigid, deliberate, suspicious, suffering from strong inferiority feelings."   It may be interesting to note that this young man is only five feet tall, though of a family in

which nobody else is shorter than five feet nine, and that he has
been bald-headed since the age of 19. He is extremely apprehensive, constricted, shy and evasive, and is able to keep his mental-
emotional balance only by a most detailed planning of nearly every
step he makes. He is rigid and overdeliberate and these and other
of his traits mentioned were reaffirmed and supported by his Rorschach and TAT records, as well as by a self-description.

This case illustrates a form of anxiety in which basic and reac-
tive elements are combined, but in which the individual is able to
maintain his control, as long as only minor situational difficulties
arise. The subject will therefore appear ''normal'' when things
run smoothly, but is likely to exhibit severe anxiety in situations
with which he is unable to cope.

Case 3. R. F.

R. F. is a woman of 26, married, born in the United States. R. F.
needs 50 seconds for K I (See Figure 5) and 28 seconds for K II.
She has difficulties in freeing herself from the starting point in
K I, but instead of getting involved in a graphomotor block she
tries to orient herself by a few impulsive and angular strokes.
Unable to find her direction, she is finally forced to break up the

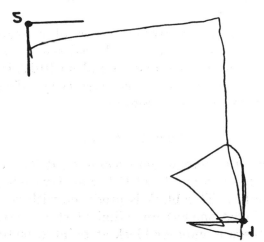

Figure 5. K I of a subject with intense anxiety, converted into aggression. Initial extensive complex, considerable segmentation, extensive
unilateral spread, distal field-distribution, medium pressure,
angular breaks of direction.

required diagonal into component vertical and horizontal movements. In doing so, she makes sharp angles and exercises heavy pressure. On her second trial, she follows exactly the same pattern, although requiring less time.

Interpretation. Intense basic anxiety is covered up by, and partly converted into, aggressive behavior. The predominant use of the distal field indicates that the subject feels strongly threatened by external dangers and is forced into a defensive position. Her aggression has therefore to be seen as a self-defensive measure.

Comment. This subject, like the subject in Case 2, suffers from strong organic inferiority feelings, due to an unilateral congenital dislocation of the hip. Early frustration, occasioned or aggravated by a narrow-minded, highly-egocentric mother provided the basis for feelings of inadequacy and anxiety. Her frustration has been translated into strong aggression, which causes her to fight against all sources of actual or suspected threats. Rorschach and TAT records confirm the statements of five judges personally acquainted with the subject who describe her as "extremely aggressive, self-centered and basically insecure." In an analytical self-description, R. F. sees herself as "asocial, aggressive and insecure."

This young woman illustrates a case of conversion anxiety. While the exclusive use of the distal field seems to indicate that anxiety is converted into aggression and hostility, it appears that other types of conversion anxiety can also be specifically diagnosed by the katoptographic test procedure.

Case 4. *K. K.*

Case 4 is that of an unmarried woman, aged 34. K. K. produces a graphomotor block in point 1 of K I (See Figure 6), lasting more than three minutes. This block is produced with very heavy pressure. In K II (not shown) an initial block appears, lasting 125 seconds; and there is another block at point 2, lasting more than 180 seconds. These two K II blocks are also produced with very heavy pressure; but on a second trial considerable improvement is shown.

Figure 6.   KI of a subject with anxiety neurosis.   Noncompletion of
test within time limits, initial graphomotor block, very heavy
pressure, innumerable restartings.   During performance
choreiform movements are observed.

Interpretation.   Here is severe basic anxiety in the form of an
anxiety neurosis.   The heavy pressure projects the intensity with
which the subject attempts a control of her anxiety.

Comment.   K. K. has suffered for over a year from anxiety attacks and typically neurotic feelings of inadequacy and helplessness. Her MMPI test reveals depressive, psychoneurotic and paranoid tendencies, her Rorschach severe anxiety and depression. The
subject writes in an analytical self-description: "My inferiority
complex accounts for my unsuccessful, frustrated life.   This is my
subconscious reluctancy to get into a situation which might involve
a risk, the tendency to give up even before the fight started.   I am
afraid that I will not be able to live up to the expectations of the
people with whom I live."

This is a case of anxiety neurosis, showing as the basic symptom intense free-floating anxiety and presenting in addition obses-
sional elements.   The threat of personality disintegration, resulting from a chronic conflict between deep-seated insufficiency feelings and environmentally stimulated ambition arouses anxiety of
such an intensity that K. K. breaks down when confronted with a
relatively simple, but nonhabitual task like drawing in a mirror.

The result is initial graphomotor block. At the time of her examination, the subject had started on a psychoanalysis. The marked improvement of her performance on a second trial permitted a favorable prognosis which was substantiated by the result of the subsequent treatment.

Case 5.   *W. K.*

W. K. is an unmarried man of 36. He needs 140 seconds for K I (See Figure 7) and 425 seconds for K II (See Figure 8). His speed type is LD/LT; the spread is unilateral and extensive; the pressure is extremely variable; the segmentation is intense; the field-distribution in K I on the first and the second trial is distal; the linear quality is characterized by tremor and filiformity. Sev-

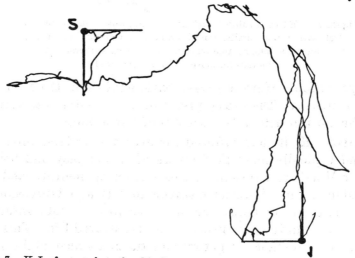

Figure 7. K I of a psychopath with Ganser syndrome. Absence of initial block or complex; unilateral extensive spread; heavy segmentation; distal field-distribution; tremor and filiformity of line retracings.

eral complexes are produced, but no blocks; several retracings are observable. On K II, the subject fails, on both trials, to follow the sequence of the numbers. His blind-drawing responses are curved, instead of the normally straight lines. Some improvement of the time and distance scores on a second trial is noticeable.

Interpretation. Here is a poorly integrated personality, with lack of self-organizing ability, psychopathic instability, basic in-

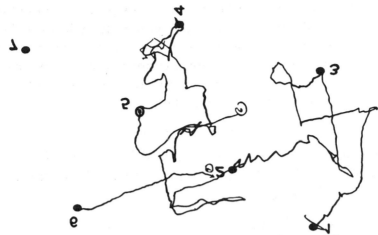

Figure 8. K II of the same subject as in Figure 7. Failure to follow sequence of numbers, curved and fragmented blind-drawing responses with wrong choice of directions, extremely variable pressure, extensive bilateral spread, heavy segmentation, disorganized progression, atactic disturbances, complexes in absence of blocks, frequent retracings.

security and anxiety with attempts at conversion into aggression. The patient manifests awareness of environmental threats. Lack of forthrightness and evasiveness are indicated.

Comment. This man was born in Austria and came to the United States at an early age. He was graduated from high school. W. K. was referred for examination by the federal court after a charge of forgery which included the use of a false name and the making of false statements. He had spent one year at a federal penitentiary for representing himself as a lieutenant in the naval reserve. His occupation prior to arrest was that of seaman. On admission to the ward, W. K. presented a classical Ganser syndrome, which continued unaltered until his return to court with a clinical diagnosis of psychopathic personality. His psychometric examination revealed average intelligence. W. K.'s Rorschach record was characterized by a large percentage of W and S responses, an unusually high percentage of Chiaroscura responses (26 per cent) and a low straight F percentage, thus showing marked anxiety combined with evasiveness.

The katoptogram of this subject is of interest because it reveals the extreme anxiety met with in certain types of psychopaths. The manifested anxiety is neither neurotic nor psychotic in nature (as shown by the absence of initial and intermediary blocks); but consequent to intense feelings of helplessness, the subject reveals an inability to profit from experience in spite of a certain amount of insight. He is at once evasive and aggressive, and both qualities are pretty much at the conscious level*

Case 6. F. R.

This subject is a married man, aged 53. On the first trial, he needs 160 seconds for K I (See Figure 9) and 200 seconds for K II.

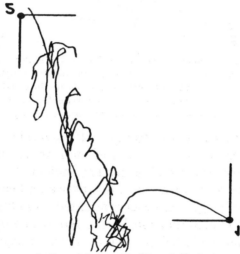

Figure 9. K I of a psychotic subject, with Korsakoff features. Absence of initial block, presence of intermediate block, LD/LT speed type, unilateral and retensive spread, recrossings and retracings, heavy segmentation, variable medium pressure, distal field-distribution, disorganized progression, atactic disturbances.

On the second trial, he takes 25 seconds for K I and 98 seconds for K II. Blind-drawing on both trials shows identically wrong choices of direction. In K I, which is primarily used for the katoptographic diagnosis, one observes an LD/LT ratio, unilateral and retensive spread, recrossings and retracings, intense segmentation, variable medium pressure, exclusive use of the proximal field,

*After being sentenced by the court, the patient's Ganser symptoms disappeared. His final psychiatric diagnosis was: psychopathic personality with pathological emotionality, hysterical features and evidence of malingering.

disorganized linear quality, intermediate block and atactic disturbances. In addition, one notices, in K II in point 4 on both trials, an intermediate block.

Interpretation. F. R. shows a progressing personality disintegration, a psychotic type of anxiety, paranoid tendencies, strong feelings of insufficiency and helplessness, unpredictable violent reactions, intense awareness of the ego as main danger zone.

Comment. This patient presents a clinical picture of progressing mental deterioration. He appears rather confused, his memory is bad. He has been unable to keep a job. There is a long standing history of alcoholism. The clinical diagnosis is: psychosis with alcoholism, Korsakoff features. The patient underwent a Wechsler-Bellevue Intelligence Test and a Rorschach Test. On the intelligence test, he made a composite I. Q. of 110 which places him at a bright normal level. There was considerable intratest and intertest variability of such a nature as to indicate organic impairment. The Rorschach record supports this picture: automatic phrases, tendency for repetitions, card description, long time needed for responses, white space interpretations, tension m's, poor form responses indicating feelings of insufficiency and anxiety.

The katoptogram of this subject is interesting because it presents manifestations of psychotic rather than neurotic anxiety. To be especially noted, is the combination of considerable graphomotor disturbances without initial block, while intermediate blocks occur repeatedly.

SUMMARY

1. A simple and objective method and apparatus are described for the detection and the measurement of anxiety.

2. This method consists in a simplified form of mirror drawing and the consequent interpretation of the subject's motor performances.

3. The interpretation of the data is based on the disintegration concept of anxiety.

4. A number of cases are presented to illustrate the practical application of the method and its possibilities in diagnostic work. Department of Psychiatry

New York University College of Medicine, and
Psychological Department, Psychiatric Division
Bellevue Hospital
New York, N. Y.

REFERENCES

1. Freud, S.: Hemmung, Symptom und Angst. Wien. 1923. Translated under the title, ''The Problem of Anxiety.'' New York. 1936.
2. Rank, O.: Das Trauma der Geburt. Wien. 1923. Translated under the title, ''The Trauma of Birth.'' New York. 1929.
3. Adler, A.: Understanding Human Nature. New York. 1927.
4. Horney, K.: New Ways in Psychoanalysis. New York. 1939.
5. Cannon, W. B.: Bodily Changes in Pain, Hunger, Fear and Rage. New York. 1929.
6. McDougall, W.: Outline of Psychology. New York. 1923.
7. One Hundred Years of American Psychiatry. Chapter on ''Military Psychiatry; World War II,'' by Albert Deutsch. New York. 1944.
8. Louttit, C. M.: The mirror tracing test as a diagnostic aid for emotional instability. Psychol. Rec., V:9.

PART IX

INTRODUCTION

The difficulties of some children in learning to read successfully is a significant educational problem. Reasons for reading disability cases are diverse and almost as numerous as there are experts in the field. In many instances, however, there has not been a systematic nor scientific approach to the problem to determine areas needing treatment. Procedures and techniques to use have not been specified. Defining aspects of the problem and designating the consequent correctives are reported in two papers included in this section.

Many children, particularly in the early phases of reading, have difficulty in distinguishing words where reversals are possible. In the first paper dealing with this issue, Wechsler and Pignatelli surveyed the literature to determine what is considered a reversal by reading experts and how inclusive the term may be. They found, as might be expected, the term could be used to cover a variety of circumstances. It is of some interest to note that the literature created classifications in a descriptive sense and avoided the issues of the nature of the errors. Such an approach Wechsler and Pignatelli concluded to be much too vague for any scientific attack on the problem. They define a reversal in terms of the axial rotation which occurs in the error. An interesting finding is that up and down reversals are more common than left to right reversals, at least in their sample. This is not unexpected statistically since the possibility for reversals of an up and down nature is much greater than left to right.

Other explanations for reversals than axial rotation are plausible. Such matters as figure-background relationships, attention to a portion of the letter which may be misperceived, and the like, are specifically described by Wechsler and Pignatelli. This leads to the obvious conclusion that reversals may be a more complex problem than merely one of orientation. Consequently, much further work is needed.

A portion of this further work is reflected in the article by Wechsler and Hagin published in 1964 (2). Though other authors, had not pursued the possibilities inherent in the earlier article, Wechsler felt some continuation of that matter would be worthwhile. A test was designed to help appraise the tendency of a child toward axial rotation. Because of the shape of the design used in the test items the test was called the Lamb Chop Test.

It is to be noted that teacher ratings of progress were used for the first-grade group and standardized test scores for the third-grade group. Results on these were compared to performance on the Lamb Chop Test for several comparisons. Apparently the Lamb Chop Test is a valid measure from the standpoint that children who performed best, i.e., made the fewest incorrect rotations, showed a higher degree of reading readiness in the first grade and greater progress in reading as estimated by their teachers. These findings were not duplicated with the sample of third-grade youngsters in comparison with the standardized achievement test.

As might be expected, in the first grade left to right reversals were quite common. The authors concluded that perhaps that is "normal" in such a group. Such vertical rotations are less commonly found as the child matures and progresses in school. They conclude that problems of depth and horizontal rotation occurring before age 6 may represent greater problems in terms of reading progress for the child.

Two book reviews are included in this section. Each of these gives a little more insight into the humane qualities of Wechsler and his attitude toward others. In both instances, there is the objectivity necessary to an appraisal of the work. Beyond the role of the critic, there is the depth of a knowledgeable person in communication with the intent and purpose of the work being reviewed.

Of all the tests devised by Wechsler over the years, one of the most unusual is that done for the Yellow Cab Company in Pittsburgh. The test was devised to meet a purpose: the selection of those individuals who would be the safest drivers and consequently most trustworthy. Wechsler designed and built the apparatus himself. Perhaps the significant feature of the study is that he found the most significant factor to be carefulness. The current concept of defensive driving, advocated by the National Safety Council, reflects the same idea. Some things have not changed over the course of approximately 50 years, then. Wechsler did anticipate a change which has certainly occurred: the increasing congestion on public highways by automobiles and the consequent increase in the number of accidents. He anticipates a need for tests which will better discriminate the careless and careful driver for licensing.

REVERSAL ERRORS IN READING:
PHENOMENA OF AXIAL ROTATION*

DAVID WECHSLER and MYRTLE L. PIGNATELLI

Bellevue Psychiatric Hospital and New York University College of Medicine

In recent years investigators have laid increasing emphasis on the importance of the type and character of errors committed by individuals suffering from reading disabilities. Already, there is quite a substantial literature on the subject,[1] a large part of which is devoted to an attempted classification of errors either from a theoretical or practical point of view. These classifications often differ considerably from one another, but all of them contain a category termed "reversals." It is this category, in many ways the most important, which we propose to discuss in the present paper.

It is necessary to begin with a definition of terms. Taken literally, the word "reversal" means "a turning over," and in the case of reading errors is expected to mean a turning over or reorientation of a letter or group of letters (word) about a particular axis. As actually used, however, it has come to include much more as may be seen even from a cursory examination of illustrative examples. The partial list of "reversal" errors culled from various authors[2] as well as our own material is shown on page 216.

The foregoing far from exhaust the "errors" that have been listed as "reversals," but even from this relatively small list it is apparent that the term "reversal" is used to designate a variety of different phenomena. A number of investigators, among them Monroe,[3] have attempted to bring some order into their appraisal by classifying into

---

*Reprinted from *Journal of Educational Psychology*, 1937, 28, 215-221.

[1] A good review of this literature will be found in the recent article by J. Jastak, "Interferences in Reading." *Psych. Bull.*, Vol. XXXI, No. 4, April, 1934, pp. 245–272.

[2] Orton, S. T.: "A Physiological Theory of Reading Disability and Stuttering in Children." *New England Jour. Med.*, 1928, pp. 199, 1047.

"An Impediment to Learning to Read." *School and Society*, Vol. XXVIII. 1928, pp. 286–290.

Monroe, Marion: "Methods for Diagnosing and Treatment of Cases of Reading Disability." *Genetic Psychology Monographs*, Vol. IV, 1928, p. 375.

Monroe, Marion: *Children Who Cannot Read.* Pp. 34–38.

Gates, Arthur I.: *Improvement of Reading.* New York, 1935, Appendix I, Test VIII, p. 521.

[3] Monroe, M.: *Children Who Cannot Read*, Chicago, 1932.

various groups. Monroe, for example, divides them into three main groups:

1. Reversed orientation of letters, as when $b = d: p = q: n = w:$ are interchanged.

2. Reversed sequence of letters, as when *no* is read as *on*, and *saw* is read as *was*.

3. Reversed sequence of words, as when child reads *There once was* instead of *Once there was.*

p read *b*	*k* read *f*	*T* read *I*	*Q* read *D*
b read *d*	*g* read *y*	*G* read *O*	*F* read *E*
p read *g*	*y* read *u*	*W* read *M*	*J* read *L*
h read *y*		*Z* read *N*	*Y* read *U*
m read *w*		*H* read *N*	
am read *ma*		*was*	read *saw*
on read *no*		*ton*	read *not*
of read *fo*		*hen*	read *and*
at read *to*		*how*	read *who*
is read *in*		*arms* read *rams*	
su read *use*		*squirt* read *spring*	
ip read *pit*		*left*	read *felt*
net read *ten*		*dig*	read *pit*
yo read *boy*		*ever*	read *never*
There once was	read	*Once there was*	
He come again	read	*He again came*	
"Mother," he said	read	*"Mother," said he*	

If we examine classifications like that above critically, two things are, perhaps, immediately obvious. The first is, that the classifications are descriptive, and accordingly, though useful for practical purposes, tend to throw little light upon the inner nature of the errors. As a matter of fact, some of the categories include subspecies which are neither subordinate or capable of being logically subsumed. We will show later, for example, that the interchange of $b = p$, or $d = q$, is in no way similar, to the misreading of *n* for *u*. Again when a child reads, "There once was" for "Once there was" we are not dealing with reversals in the true sense, but merely with the displacement of words.

Perhaps the fullest elaboration of the significance of reversals will be found in the studies of Orton in whose theories of reading the factor of left-right sequences play a dominant role. Orton distinguishes two kinds of reversals—those involving "vertical disorientations" . . . as when *u* is mistaken for *n*, and *p* for *b*; and those involving right and left disorientations as when *d* is mistaken for *b*, and *p* for *q*. Of these findings the latter appear to be the most common, and while he also mentions other "cross disorientations," it is the sinistral dextral reversals which play the basic rôle in his theory of strephosymbolia.

It is not our purpose to enter at this time into any discussion of reading theories or the relation of reversal errors to reading disabilities; the aim of this paper, rather, is to call attention to a variety of spatial disorientations in the configuration of letters. In this connection, the first point to be emphasized is the one made at the outset of this paper, namely, that the term "reversal" as used at present, is too vague to be of scientific value. As now used in the classification of reading errors, it is a supposed change in spatial orientation of a letter or group of letters which cause them to be confused with another letter or word because of an acquired identity or similarity in appearance with it. When, as a result of such disorientation, a letter or word is read for another, the misreading in question is called a reversal. The general stricture which may be made to such a definition is, that it tells us very little of what has really happened.

An examination of even the brief list of "reversal errors" given on page 216, shows that the term "orientation" covers a variety of facts. For example, when b is read as d the visual phenomena involved is quite different from that taking place when n is read as u, and considerably less complicated than what occurs when N is read as Z. The process common to all three is that the confused letter in each case has been rotated about some imaginary axis: b to be changed to d has been rotated about its vertical axis: n when changed to u has been rotated about its horizontal axis: and N to produce Z has been rotated about its depth axis. Furthermore, while b and n required a rotation of 180°, N needed only a rotation of 90°; in fact, had it been rotated 180° it would have resumed its original form, or become N again.

It thus appears that in the analysis of reversals one has not only to deal with the fact of rotation, but one must also consider the plane in which this rotation takes place, and at times, also, the angular distance involved. In the studies up to the present most authors have assumed that the rotation occurs primarily around one of the axes, namely, the vertical axis. At least, that is the implication of their predominant preoccupation with mirror writing and the so-called sinistro-dextral inversions. Actually the rotation may take place in any one of the three spatial planes, giving rise to inversions about the horizontal and depth axes as well as about the vertical axis. In any case, the analysis of different "reversal" errors show that in order to explain them intelligibly we must have recourse to a rotation not only about one or two but all of the three axes, and sometimes to a combination of two of them.   Thus, to use some of the familiar examples again: $b = d$ when rotated about its vertical axis: $u = n$ when u is rotated about its horizontal axis; $N = Z$ when rotated about its depth axis.

But sometimes an identical reversal may be achieved through different axial rotations.   Thus one may account for the common $b = q$ "error," either as a clockwise 180° rotation about the depth axis or by a double rotation, thus; first about its horizontal axis which gives $b = p$, then again about its vertical which gives the required q. Similarly for $y = h$, either rotate the letter 180° counter clockwise, or rotate it first along its vertical axis (which gives $h = $ ꭄ), and then again about its horizontal axis which gives the desired y.   Furthermore, it must be remembered that rotation along different axes with the same letter will cause different types of errors.   Thus d becomes b when rotated vertically, but q when it is rotated on its horizontal axis. On the other hand the same final "error" will occur by the rotation of different letters in different axes; thus $p = d$ when rotated on its horizontal axis and so does b when rotated on its vertical axis.

This last fact may account for the view that most reversals are sinistro-dextral, a legitimate confusion.   On the other hand, to call "was" a sinsitro-dextral reversal as is frequently done, is incorrect, because "was" reversed does not become "saw" but W ꟗƧ which is entirely different.   The new configurations resulting from different axial rotations is not immediately apparent.   Some facility at visualization is necessary, and as an aid to this we give in Tables I and II, a record of the transformations effected in the appearance of the letters of the alphabet when rotated around their different axes.

On the basis of a rotational analysis one may venture the following classification of reversal errors:

1. The rotation about vertical axis (right and left reversals), *e.g.*, $d = b$: $p = q: Z = S$:

2. Rotation about horizontal axis (up and down reversals), *e.g.*, $b = p$: $d = q: M = W: f = t$:

3. Rotation about depth axis (clock and counter-clock reversals), $w = m$ (script): $d = p: Z = N: M = E$:

4. Rotation of letters about two axes (double reversals), *e.g.*, $h = y: b = q$: (although these may also be gotten by 3).

The occurrences of various types of rotations are, of course, not equally frequent, but our own experience shows that the up and down reversals, contrary to general assumption, are much more frequent than left-right reversals. This would be expected from the examination of our tables because the number of letters which are transformed by

TABLE I.—TRANSFORMATION OF ALPHABET RESULTING FROM AXIAL ROTATION OF LETTERS (CAPITALS)

A	B	C	D	E	F	G	H	I	J	K	L	M	N	O	P	Q	R	S	T	U	V	W	X	Y	Z

rotation into others which may be easily confused with them, is very much greater when they are rotated about the horizontal than about any other axis.

It is, of course, not implied that axial rotation is the only factor which enters into the explanation of reversals of errors. A number of others, undoubtedly, play a rôle, among them the most important, perhaps, being those of perspective and the relation of figure to background. Altogether, we must remember that while the printed page involves only two dimensions, the reading of it, like all vision, is a tri-dimensional process. From the study of illusions we know what an important part angular relationships play. It is almost impossible

TABLE II.—TRANSFORMATION OF ALPHABET RESULTING FROM AXIAL ROTATION OF LETTERS (SMALL)

to juxtapose any two lines without producing some perspective effects, especially when the abutting lines make certain angles.

Again, there is the matter of fixation. A letter may be easily "transformed" into another letter by the simple fact of fixating on a particular part of it as, for example, when *h* is read as *n*. This may easily be achieved by fixating strongly on the lower half and thereby suppressing the upper part.

In other cases, several factors may enter into the combination to effect the perceived error. Thus when p is called d one may account for it on the basis of a clockwise rotation about the central axis, but one gets the same effect more directly by focusing on the central part of the letter and fixating strongly on the figure rather than on the background. When this is done the orientation of the letter on the paper is disregarded and the letters p and d are perceived as identical, which in fact, they are, when the background is disregarded.

The above conclusion will, perhaps, be sufficient to show how much more complicated is the problem of "reversals" than is implied by the statement that it consists of a change in orientation. We have in this paper confined ourselves first, to pointing out the importance of rotation as a factor in tri-dimensional vision, and, secondly, to a part analysis of reversals in terms of formations in letters of the alphabet when rotated along different visual axes. The problem is even more complicated when instead of considering letters alone we take up groups of letters (words). At best, it only explains a minor part of the errors that occur. The transformations that occur as a result of rotation of different axes help to account for some, but much more work will be necessary to explain all so-called reversal errors completely.

THE PROBLEM OF AXIAL ROTATION IN
READING DISABILITY*

DAVID WECHSLER and ROSA HAGIN[1]

New York University School of Medicine and Bellevue Psychiatric Hospital, New York

Summary.—The problem of axial rotations in reading was investigated by the use of the Lamb Chop Test. Comparisons of reading readiness scores, levels of reading achievement, and scores on the Lamb Chop Test for first and third grade Ss indicate significant association between these factors and incidence of rotational errors. Frequency of rotational errors was not found to be greater among left-handed than among right-handed Ss. Analysis of types of rotational errors showed a decrease in both vertical and depth rotations when data for first and third grade samples were compared. The persistence of horizontal rotations among poorer readers in the third grade suggests that (1) the hitherto predominant emphasis upon vertical (Left-Right) rotations may have been misplaced and (2) consideration of all types of axial rotations, rather than any single one, is necessary in the diagnosis of reading disability.

In the investigation of perceptual errors made by young children, beginning readers, and Ss with reading disabilities, much study has been devoted to the description and analysis of reversals (Orton, 1937; Monroe, 1932; Krise, 1949, 1952; Potter, 1949; Park, 1953). The present paper is a further study of the subject with special emphasis on the problem of axial rotation, and a description of a test for evaluating it.

The general problem of axial rotation was investigated by one of the authors in an earlier paper (Wechsler & Pignatelli, 1937). In this paper it was shown that in order to account for the various types of rotational errors in reading, it is necessary to relate such errors to all *three* spatial axes and not merely to the one (left-right reversals) usually made use of by most authors. Briefly, Wechsler and Pignatelli showed that rotations may take place in any of three spatial planes, vertical, horizontal, or depth. For example, the letter *b* rotated on the vertical axis becomes *d*, on the horizontal axis *p*, and on the depth axis (180°) *q*; Z rotated vertically becomes S, horizontally S, and only when rotated 90°, clockwise or counterclockwise, N. A table showing the transformations which all the letters of the alphabet undergo (both capital and lower case) when rotated in the different planes is given in the paper cited. Inspection of these transformations impresses one with the ease with which our alphabet lends itself

*Reprinted with permission of publisher:
Wechsler, D., and Hagin, R. A. The problem of axial rotation in reading disability. *PERCEPTUAL AND MOTOR SKILLS,* 1964, **19,** 319-326.
[1]The cooperation of G. Bert Carlson and James M. Callam in authorizing the study in schools in which they serve as principals and of Ruth Engelmann in the collection of data is gratefully acknowledged.

to axial rotations, and with the fine perceptual discriminations that may be required in reading.

In the ensuing study we shall examine the relation between the incidence of rotation errors made by samples of first and third grade children and progress in learning to read. Reading readiness and achievement was appraised in terms of standardized test scores and teachers' ratings; the incidence of axial rotations was assessed by means of a test specially devised for this purpose and provisionally designated as the *Lamb Chop Test*.

THE LAMB CHOP TEST

The test consists of an asymmetric figure, roughly shaped like a lamb chop, imprinted in eight different positions which S is required to match or recall. The test is presented in two series. In the first series (Matching), S is asked to match a stimulus card (a single lamb chop on a 2-in. × 2-in. card), by selecting one of six figures imprinted on one of the two response cards (see Fig. 1), while

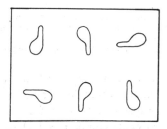

FIG. 1. Lamb Chop Test: stimulus cards and response card for matching series

the stimulus card remains in view. These response card figures represent the lamb chop in the various axial rotations. In the second series (Recall) the stimulus card is exposed for 3 sec. and then removed from sight. S is then asked to select from among the six figures on one of the response cards that one like the figure just presented. Each presentation offers the opportunity for rotation of the figure on horizontal, vertical, and depth axes. Scoring is possible not only by the counting of correct and incorrect responses, but also through the analysis of the kind of axial rotations made by S^2 (see Table 1).

METHOD

One hundred children served as Ss for the study. The first grade sample comprised 50 pupils, the entire first grade of an elementary school in Irvington,

---

[2]The reliability of the test, based upon Froelich's approximation of the Kuder-Richardson formula, is estimated to be .80.

TABLE 1

ORDER OF PRESENTATION AND ERROR ANALYSIS OF "LAMB CHOP TEST"

Stimulus Card	Correct Response	V	H	180°d	90°c	90°cc	90°c+H / 90°cc+V	90°c+V / 90°cc+H
		— Rotational Error Made in Responses						

Stimulus Card	Correct Response	V	H	180°d	90°c	90°cc	90°c+H 90°cc+V	90°c+V 90°cc+H
				Matching Series				
A	5	2	6	1	4			3
B	1	6	2	5		4	3	
C	6	1	5	2		3	4	
D	2	5	1	6	3		4	
E	5	3	6	1		4		2
F	1	6	3	5	4			2
G	6	1	5	3	2			4
H	3	5	1	6		2		
				Recall Series				
A	1	6	2	5		4		3
B	5	2	6	1	4		3	
C	2	5	1	6	3		4	
D	6	1	5	2	3		4	
E	1	6	3	5	4			2
F	5	3	6	1		4		2
G	3	5	1	6		2		4
H	6	1	5	3	2	4		

Note.—Letters identify and give order of presentation of Stimulus Cards. Numbers refer to positions on the Response Cards. For example, when Card A of the Matching Series was presented, Position 5 on the Response Card was the correct response. If *S* responded by pointing to position 6, he had made a horizontal rotation. In the last two columns separate frequencies for double rotations are reported, e.g., 90°c+H.
Code.—V=vertical, H=horizonal, c=clockwise, cc=counter clockwise, d=depth.

New Jersey. The third grade sample also contained 50 pupils selected by lot from the third grade population of an elementary school in Westfield, New Jersey. The age range for the first grade sample was 5-11 to 6-11, with a median age of 6-5. The age range for the third grade sample was 7-11 to 9-11, with a median age of 8-5.

Data were collected during the first week in December, and so it was possible to obtain teachers' ratings of progress in beginning reading for the first grade sample. Scores on the Metropolitan Readiness Test (Hildreth & Griffiths, 1959), which had been administered at the beginning of the school year, were available for first grade sample. Scores on the California Reading Test (Tiegs & Clark, 1959), administered at the beginning of the school year, were available for the third grade sample. These data were utilized with the results of the Lamb Chop Test for our *S*s to determine: (1) the frequency of rotational errors, (2) the relationships between axial rotations and progress in learning to read, (3) the nature of rotational errors made by good and poor readers, and the (4) association between rotational errors and handedness.

RESULTS

Frequency of Errors

Table 2 reports the numbers of correct responses for the groups as a whole. These data show that, although there is increased accuracy in the perception of the Lamb Chop figure when scores for first and third graders are compared, errors appear with some frequency in both samples. Only three of the first graders and five of the third graders attained perfect scores.

TABLE 2
CORRECT RESPONSES ON LAMB CHOP TEST

Group	N	Total Items		Matching Series		Recall Series	
		M	SD	M	SD	M	SD
Total	100	11.77	3.59	6.61	1.59	5.37	1.99
First Grade	50	10.34	4.11	5.88	2.28	4.54	2.15
Third Grade	50	13.62	2.07	7.42	.92	6.20	1.24

Relationship to Progress in Reading

Table 3 reports product-moment coefficients of correlation between the scores on the Lamb Chop Test and standardized tests of reading readiness for Grade 1 and of reading achievement for Grade 3. The obtained rs ranged from .25 to .46, being generally higher and significantly different from zero for Grade 1.

TABLE 3
PRODUCT-MOMENT CORRELATIONS BETWEEN LAMB CHOP AND STANDARDIZED TESTS

Lamb Chop Test	Grade 1 Metropolitan Reading Readiness Test		Grade 3 California Reading Test (Upper Prim. Level)	
	r	p	r	p
Matching Series	.39	.01	.25	NS*
Recall Series	.46	.01	.26	NS
Total Score	.43	.01	.29	.05

*NS = not significant.

In order to determine differences between the performance of good and poor readers on the Lamb Chop Test, samples were drawn on the basis of teachers' judgments of progress in both word recognition and reading comprehension in the first grade group and on the basis of scores on the California Reading Test, in the third grade group. The results of comparison of the mean correct responses for these subgroups are reported in Table 4.

Standard deviations for the good and poor readers within a grade group

TABLE 4

DIFFERENCES BETWEEN MEAN CORRECT RESPONSES FOR GROUPS OF GOOD
AND POOR READERS

Grade and Series	Good Readers	Poor Readers	SD	t	p
Grade 1 (Ns = 13)					
Matching Series	7.23	5.07	±1.91	2.86	.01
Recall Series	6.08	3.53	±1.89	3.43	.01
Total Score	13.31	8.60	±3.28	3.65	.01
Grade 3 (Ns = 13)					
Matching Series	8.00	7.00	±1.09	2.32	.05
Recall Series	6.67	5.46	±1.29	2.42	.05
Total Score	14.67	12.46	±1.88	3.02	.01

were computed by pooling the sums of the squares of the deviations on the assumption that the real difference between the two subgroups was zero (Garrett, 1948, p. 205). Significant differences were found between the means on both the Matching and the Recall Series of the Lamb Chop Test for good and poor readers within both first and third grade groups. Note also that mean numbers of correct responses on the Matching Series are higher for all subgroups than for Recall Series.

Nature of Rotational Errors Made

Kinds of errors for each of the groups are analyzed in Table 5. Error frequencies are reported in terms of per cents based upon the total possible rotations on a given axis in a series. It can be seen from Table 5 that both

TABLE 5

ANALYSIS OF ERRORS (%) FOR GRADES 1 AND 3 (Ns = 50)

Rotations	Possible Rotations per Group	% Errors		p*
		Grade 1	Grade 3	
Vertical Rotations				
Matching Series	400	13	3	.01
Recall Series	400	19	9	.01
Horizontal Rotations				
Matching Series	400	10	3	.01
Recall Series	400	12	10	NS
180° Rotations				
Matching Series	400	4	0.8	.01
Recall Series	400	8·	2	.01
90° Rotations				
Matching Series	400	1	0.5	NS
Recall Series	450	4	0.4	.01

*t tests for the significance of differences between percentages. NS = not significant.

vertical and horizontal rotations appear frequently in the first grade group, while depth rotations appear less frequently. When proportions of errors made by first and third grade groups are compared (standard error of the difference between two per cents), we find statistically significant differences in all error types but two: 90° rotations on the Matching Series and horizontal rotations on the Recall Series. The former may be accidental since very few pupils made this error. The latter error, the horizontal rotation, was found to occur with about the same frequency among the third as among the first graders (12% vs 10%). The importance of this type of error can be seen when the performance of the groups of good and poor readers is considered in Table 6. These data indicate

TABLE 6

ANALYSIS OF ERRORS (%) FOR GOOD AND POOR READERS ($Ns = 13$)

	Possible Errors Per Group	First Sample			Third Sample		
		Good Readers	Poor Readers	p^*	Good Readers	Poor Readers	p^*
Vertical Rotations							
Matching Series	104	5	18	.01	1	3	NS
Recall Series	104	11	23	.05	9	12	IS
Horizontal Rotations							
Matching Series	104	3	12	.01	0	9	.01
Recall Series	104	7	18	.02	4	16	.01
180° Rotations							
Matching Series	104	1	6	.01	0	1	NS
Recall Series	104	4	13	.01	1	3	NS
90° Rotations							
Matching Series	104	0	1	NS	0	0	NS
Recall Series	117	3	3	NS	0	0.9	NS

*t tests for the significance of differences between percentages. NS = not significant.

that the poor readers in Grade 1 showed a variety of axial rotations, but that with the third grade group the horizontal rotations are the only type to reach statistical significance when the standard error of the difference between per cents of good and poor readers is computed. It is interesting that errors are fewer on the Matching Series than on the Recall Series in all cases except of 90° rotations for good third grade readers.

Rotations and Left-handedness

Data for the first grade group were analyzed to determine whether there was an association between type of rotational error and hand used in writing. Although it might be expected that left-handed children might make more rotational errors, our data do not support this expectation. Proportions of errors were approximately the same for both left ($N = 9$) and right-handed ($N =$

first graders with one exception: 63% of the right-handed group and only 22% of the left-handed group responded with vertical rotations on the Matching Series. The difference between these per cents is the only one of the six which reached statistical significance when the standard error of the difference between per cents was computed ($p = .02$).

DISCUSSION

Analysis of data from the Lamb Chop Test from samples of first and third grade pupils shows the kinds of errors in their perception of asymmetric symbols. These errors can be defined as rotations on vertical, horizontal, and depth axes. Our data indicate that children who most frequently perceive the figure in its correct orientation also show a higher degree of reading readiness, as assessed by conventional standardized tests and make more rapid progress in classroom instruction in beginning reading as estimated by their teachers' judgment. However, the relationship between accuracy of perception of the figure and progress in reading is less marked when data for the third grade group are considered. This finding may be a function of the reading test used or of the fact that teachers' judgments differ from test scores as measures of progress in reading. Another explanation might be that, while beginning reading draws heavily upon perceptual accuracy, reading achievement involves considerable cognitive ability as well as perceptual abilities. However, validation of this hypothesis requires additional study.

Frequency of axial rotations was not found to be associated with left-handed preferences in writing. Scores on the Lamb Chop Test did not show that left-handed children were more prone to make any type of rotational error more frequently than right-handed children. Indeed, our data, like those of Woody and Phillips (1934), suggest that left-handed children, when well taught, avoid some rotational errors to an even greater extent than do right-handed children.

Vertical rotations, the common left-right reversals, appeared frequently in our study. Apparently through age 6, such rotations can almost be regarded as "normal." Other investigations (Kennedy, 1954; Furness, 1956), as well as unpublished data on the Lamb Chop Test which we have accumulated in a study of older age groups, suggest that vertical rotations become increasingly infrequent among older children. On the other hand, depth and horizontal rotations represent a more serious problem in spatial orientation. Where horizontal and depth rotations persist to age 6 we can conclude that reading progress will not be rapid.

REFERENCES

FURNESS, E. L. Perspectives on reversal tendencies. *Elemen. Eng.*, 1956, 33, 38-41.

GARRETT, H. E. *Statistics in psychology and education.* New York: Longmans, Green, 1948.

HILDRETH, G., & GRIFFITHS, N. L. *Metropolitan Readiness Tests.* New York: Harcourt-Brace, 1959.

KENNEDY, H. Reversals, reversals, reversals! *J. exp. Educ.,* 1954, 23, 161-170.

KRISE, E. M. Reversals in reading: a problem in space perception. *Elemen. Sch. J.,* 1949, 49, 278-284.

KRISE, E. M. An experimental investigation of theories of reversals in reading. *J. educ. Psychol.,* 1952, 43, 408-422.

MONROE, M. *Children who cannot read.* Chicago: Univer. of Chicago Press, 1932.

ORTON, S. T. *Reading, writing and speech problems in children.* New York: Norton, 1937.

PARK, G. E. Mirror and reversed reading. *J. Ped.,* 1953, 42, 120-128.

POTTER, M. D. *Perception of symbol orientation and early reading success.* New York: Bur. of Publ., Teachers' College, Columbia Univer., 1949. (No. 939)

TIEGS, E. W., & CLARK, W. W. *California Reading Tests.* Los Angeles: California Test Bureau, 1959.

WECHSLER, D., & PIGNATELLI, M. Reversal errors in reading: phenomena of axial rotation. *J. educ. Psychol.,* 1937, 28, 215-222.

WOODY, C., & PHILLIPS, A. J. The effects of handedness on reversals in reading. *J. educ. Res.,* 1934, 29, 651-652.

Accepted June 11, 1964.

YOUR PERSONALITY IS IN YOUR HANDS*

A Review of "M. K. P.: Myokinetic Psychodiagnosis" by Emilio Mira y Lopez

Reviewed by *DAVID WECHSLER*

Procedures for evaluating human traits in terms of body characteristics or idiosyncrasies of physiological response have always had a strong appeal to the behavioral psychologist. Professor Mira, once Spain's distinguished psychologist at Barcelona and now Director of the Institute for Professional Selection and Guidance at Rio de Janeiro, has long been interested in the development of expressive techniques for the study of the personality. His Myokinetic test (M.K.P.) is a new effort in this direction, and one of the most promising. Like other quantitative measures of expressive movement, the M.K.P. has an initial appeal of being "objective," that is to say, of requiring minimal interaction between investigator and subject. It furnishes a motor approach to the appraisal of personality and, because of its simplicity, offers the beleaguered clinician a less tortuous road to psychodiagnosis. For any or all of these reasons, one would have expected Professor Mira's ingenious test to have attracted American psychologists. Actually it has not.

Professor Gordon Allport, in his foreword to the present volume, expresses the view that the lack of American interest in the M.K.P. may be due in part "to the aura of charlatanry" with which graphological methods have been viewed in this country and, in part, "because studies in this area are difficult to execute." These factors, however, are at most but a small part of the story. A more immediate reason for the scant attention which the M.K.P. has received in America arises from the competition it has had to meet from already espoused projective techniques, particularly the TAT and the Rorschach. American clinicians have not only been thoroughly 'sold' on the latter, but, in this reviewer's opinion, have been unduly impressed by the role which perception plays in the structuring of personality. They have seemingly lost sight of the fact that the *personna* is determined not only by how one takes in the world but also by what one does to it. Professor Mira's researches do a great deal to reinstate the motor components of behavior as correlates of human personality.

The volume under review is Mira's third presentation in English of the theory and technique of his Myokinetic Test for Psychodiagnosis. His first paper, and in some ways the most provocative because it was accompanied by experimental

*Reprinted from *Contemporary Psychology*, 1959, 4, 362-364. Copyright 1959 by the American Psychological Association. Reprinted by permission.

data, appeared in 1940 under the title, *A New Device for Detecting Conative Trends in Personality* (Proc. Roy. Med. Soc., London, Feb. 1940). The second was in a chapter which formed part of the author's Salmon Lecture for 1942, published under the title, *Psychiatry and War*. This chapter summarized Mira's previous study and discussed some of the more general and clinical applications of the test. The current volume is a definitive exposition of the present status of the M.K.P. as a systematic technique for appraising various aspects of personality. It is also organized to serve as a manual for the administration and interpretation of the test. Along with detailed directions for administering and interpreting the test, including some measures of reliability, the book contains a number of normative tables for different age populations. The last are of subjects examined in various South American countries.

As to the test itself, the M.K.P. consists essentially of a number of simple motor tasks in which the subject is required to make a series of movements "in the fundamental directions of space." The requirement is met by having the subject first trace lines of set length in different spatial planes (later, also some supplementary figures) and then requiring him to continue drawing the same lines with his vision occluded. He does this alternately with the right and the left hand, and in the case of several of the figures, with both hands simultaneously. The general assumption of the test procedure is that the movement of each hand "has a particular significance according to the way it is executed" and that "disturbances of psychic tension should be transferred into the domain of muscular tension provided we can eliminate the voluntary correction of the subject."

Evaluation of the subject's production is made in terms of the differences in the length of his drawn lines in comparison with the standard. Displacements in direction of the movement are termed primary deviations; displacements to the right or left of the standard are termed secondary deviations; and degrees of angular displacement are axial deviations. The deviations are measured separately for the subject's right and left hand, the movements of which are considered to represent the dominant and nondominant side of his body. According to Mira, movements of the dominant and nondominant hands are related to the different levels of conscious and unconscious control respectively. The right is the educated, the left the uneducated hand. The former represents the acquired, the controlled; the latter, the primitive and instinctive trends. Concomitantly, deviations in the different planes (vertical, horizontal, sagittal) are associated with temperament and characterological traits. Thus, positive primary deviations in the vertical plane signify elation, negative deviation signifies depression. A positive deviation in the horizontal plane shows extratension, a negative deviation reveals intratension. Positive deviation in the sagittal plane is indicative of heteroaggression, negative deviation of autoaggression. Interpretation of these indicated traits depends, in addition, upon whether the deviations are manifested more intensively by the left or right hand. In general, traits inferred from the movements of the left hand are interpreted as constitutional and deep-rooted; those of the right hand as temporary and culturally determined.

The foregoing trait assessments are derived primarily from the execution of the initial portion of the test, namely, from the drawings of the lines in the different planes, and are referred to as the *lineograms*. The other parts of the test involving reproduction of various figures such as the *zigzag, chains, staircase,* etc., are used primarily to confirm the information already obtained from the lineograms, although in some instances they also furnish additional diagnostic material. In the reviewer's experience, execution of the added figures consumes much more time than the basic lineograms, and his feeling is that most of the supplementary figures could be omitted without seriously impairing the value of the test. The time factor is of moment not only in the matter of administration but also in the scoring of the test. Mira mentions some 79 recommended measurements, many of which are difficult to make and for the most part are unsupported by available norms. Some of the recommended measures may be of value for research purposes, but in the practical application of the test the reviewer has not found most of them utilizable. The test would gain much as a clinical instrument if substantially shortened.

One regrettable weakness of the book is the author's somewhat cavalier presentation of his theoretical formulations, which are often cryptic and not infrequently hard to follow. Some of the difficulty in comprehending parts of the text may be due to strict linguistic fidelity to which the editors seemingly committed themselves in translating from the original Spanish or French versions. They note that "translation difficulties arose in which the balance might depend upon a single word that meant nothing to us." As one who has had similar experience in reading Mira on the M.K.P., I can sympathize with them, but I think they would have done much better by the author, as well as the reader, if they had felt free to paraphrase rather than strictly to translate Mira's expositions. One also has the impression that the author and the editors could have made out a better case for the predictive potential of the test by presenting in some detail the findings of other investigators.

The book has a bibliography of some 127 titles, but very few of them are effectively utilized or referred to in the text. It is to be hoped that the promised forthcoming volume by H. Michael Finn will contain a fuller and more systematic review of the literature.

Altogether, the M.K.P. constitutes a basic contribution to the evergrowing field of projective tests. It is rooted more firmly on the objective performance of the examinee and less subject to arbitrary interpretations by the examiner than are most other projective techniques. Moreover it deals with and brings to light aspects of the personality which sensory-perceptual approaches often fail to reveal. M.K.P. has the important virtue of being independent of content and relatively unfettered by interjacent symbolism. While Mira states that the test is influenced by cultural factors, that can be true only in a small degree. Many of his claims for M.K.P. need to be confirmed and, while some of the findings reported, like the high correlations (.75 of the M.K.P. and intelligence), seem spurious, the over-all validity of the test as a clinical tool is amply supported.

ODYSSEY OF A FERTILE MIND*

A Review of "A Psychologist of Sorts" by Stanley D. Porteus

Reviewed by *DAVID WECHSLER*

Stanley D. Porteus, the author, is Emeritus Professor, University of Hawaii. Further biographical material about the creator of the Porteus Mazes is contained in the review.

David Wechsler, who reviews the book, is a familiar figure. The Wechsler Intelligence Scales are among the most widely used individual intelligence tests in the country. In 1967 he marked his retirement from Bellevue Psychiatric Hospital, after 35 years, with the publication of a new scale of intelligence, the WPPSI. *The Range of Human Capacities, which he personally calls his "favorite" brain child, was republished in 1969. Under way is his book on* The Role of Intelligence in the Modern World. *His other works include* The Measurement and Appraisal of Adult Intelligence.

Applied psychology has been lucky in the pioneers it has attracted to its folds, and never more so than in the case of Stanley Porteus. Son of a Methodist parson in far-off Australia, he began his career as a teacher at a one-room schoolhouse at the edge of a virgin forest. From there he 'cycled' his way into psychology. *A Psychologist of Sorts* is the story of how it all started and what he accomplished in the next sixty years.

It is an absorbing autobiography of an adventurous and creative life, told by a man endowed with a sense of the important as well as a gift for writing. He is the author of several novels and a number of literary pieces, including an unforgettable eyewitness account (described in the book) of "what was nearly the most decisive military defeat in human history," Pearl Harbor. It also gives us a synoptic history of clinical psychology in its early years, of the role of the author in directing its course, and, inevitably, of the inspired labyrinth with which his name has become identified.

The Porteus Mazes hardly require new comment. Their extensive and varied applications have been detailed by the author in a separate book *(CP,* November, 1966, 11, 517–18.) But the summary in the present volume justifiably rehearses their contributions to the problems of intelligence testing. They not only have made possible the testing groups otherwise inaccessible but also have served to define the concept of intelligence itself. Insight, planning ability, and social

*Reprinted from *Contemporary Psychology,* 1970, **15**, 347. Copyright 1970 by the American Psychological Association. Reprinted by permission.

competence are basic aspects of intelligence, and there is no test which appraises these aspects nearly as well as the Porteus Maze.

A Psychologist of Sorts details many of the personal as well as scientific events in the author's exciting career. The former are best read firsthand, and space permits reference to only a few of the latter. One of the earliest deals with his experience as a teacher in the already mentioned one-room schoolhouse. Instruction of the heterogeneous pupils often called for novel pedagogical approaches, among which was the invention of a mechanical device to help slow readers, and a method of teaching arithmetic with the aid of colors, and the use of a gold-buyer's scale. Later, while director of Special Schools in Melbourne, Porteus demonstrated the limited utility to mental defectives of manual training, much advocated at the time because of the then current belief that the "retarded were better with their hands than their heads." In this connection Porteus was also among the first to caution against the uncritical use of the Montessori method in teaching the normal young as well as the retarded. "The only thing," he states, "that is wrong with her method is that she was training the wrong senses, and directing the training to the wrong objects." We are now in a similar situation, but it is hardly likely that we shall get beyond it so long as toy manufacturers exert the strong influence they do on educational theorists.

Timely for today's confrontations are the sections dealing with race differences, revealed by the data which the author obtained from his expeditions into the primitive countries of North Australia and Central Africa. Some of these were undertaken to study the influence of a harsh vs a friendly environment on primitive people. Contrary to expectations the findings showed that "the greater the struggle for existence the greater the demand for alertness." The reader may or may not agree, but on the general problem of heredity vs environment the author makes a good case for his generalization, "Heredity deals the cards to the player but experience teaches him how to play them."

Of particular interest to many readers will be the author's role in establishing clinical psychology as a viable profession. Porteus was among the first to coordinate university and community involvement in staff training, and along with William Healy, to make available the clinic's services to courts. Like Healy, Porteus emphasized diagnosis and evaluation of the subject's personality and abilities as the psychologist's primary function. In this connection he recalls, "Since I had no brass plate, kept strictly to my field, and charged no fees, doctors began to accept me as a psychological colleague." But this was in the 1920's and 1930's. Times have since changed.

At the age of 86, or at least until the publication of this book (April, 1969), Stanley Porteus continues in his scientific proclivities. It is hard to surmise which subjects he favors—the Psychology of Primitive People, Intercultural Testing, the Mazes, of course; but one would hardly have guessed, Correlates of Brain Structure. "In spite of all appearances to the contrary, [he informs us] my main interests have centered about the story of the building of the brain." *On retourne toujours a ses premiers amours.*

TESTS FOR TAXICAB DRIVERS*

DAVID WECHSLER

The Psychological Corporation, New York

The day is coming when tests for carefulness in operating an automobile will be widely used as part of the examination required of all professional chauffeurs. Dr. Wechsler here reports an experiment with tests of carefulness, of reaction time and of mental alertness, which he correlates with accident records, earnings and supervisors' ratings. The carefulness test proved to be the most effective.

THIS paper represents some results showing the value of certain psychological tests in eliminating the unsafe and incompetent taxicab driver. The results are based upon an investigation made at a large cab company in Pittsburgh, where the psychological tests to be described were installed. The investigation was made over the period April 22 to June 15, 1925, and omitting the first week which was devoted to the installation of the apparatus, covered a period of six weeks of intensive testing. Over 250 men were examined and their scores compared with their records, as shown in the files of the company. On the basis of the results obtained, norms and standards were devised to serve the company as a basis for the selection of more efficient and safer drivers and also to reduce the cost of operation. The psychological tests proposed to do this by:

1. Selection of men who would have fewer accidents.

2. Selection of men who would earn more money for the company.

3. Reduction of labor turnover.

DESCRIPTION OF TESTS

In order to accomplish this a series of tests was drawn up. They were designed to measure those traits and abilities apparently necessary for a safe and efficient driver, and to be administered in the most economical way consistent with scientific demands. Two tests were selected: a written or paper test which could be given to as large a group as desired, and a practical test to be given individually.

Written or group test It. This part of the examination consists of a series of psychological tests measuring mental alertness and general intelligence. It is a compilation of material taken from standard tests in this field. The tests[1] were selected on the basis of their high correlation with the traits intended to be measured and their suitability for the type of subjects on whom they were to be used. Thirty minutes is required for this part of the examination.

*Reprinted from *The Journal of Personnel Research*, 1926, 5(1-2), 24-30.

[1] The tests include a learning test (digit-symbol), an arithmetical reasoning test and a picture completion test.

417

Reaction time and carefulness test, or individual test D and De. This test is intended to measure the driver's alertness of attention, quickness of reaction under distracting stimuli and above all, his carefulness. The fol- colors are flashed at irregular intervals. When seated in the car he is told to take the position for ordinary driving, that is, his left foot to the left of the clutch, his right foot on the accelerator, and his hands on the

Fig. 1. Dummy Car and Flash Board for Testing Drivers' Carefulness and Speed of Reaction

lowing is a description of the test as given: The subject is seated in a dummy car which resembles an ordinary cab. He is instructed to look straight in front of him at a gray board ten feet from where he is seated, upon which intermittent lights of different steering wheel. He is told to imagine that he is driving along at ordinary speed, and that in no case is he to press down upon the gas which is already being fed at the proper rate. However, upon the flash of certain lights, which serve as signals, he must react in certain ways by an appropriate movement of the hands or feet, or both. For instance—at the flashing of a yellow light (meaning to slow up) he must come down upon the clutch and foot brake. After each movement or response he is told always to come back to his original position, but in doing so he must not come down hard upon the accelerator. If he does this a mistake is registered.

The apparatus is so devised that the signal lights are flashed automatically and remain lighted for a definite short interval of time. In order to be credited with a correct response the subject must react with the appro-

is necessary at the end of a test is to read off the figures from the several electric counters. The duration of this test is fifteen minutes.

RESULTS

In order to determine the value of the tests it was necessary to correlate

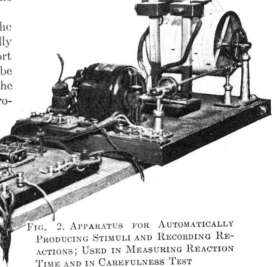

FIG. 2. APPARATUS FOR AUTOMATICALLY PRODUCING STIMULI AND RECORDING REACTIONS; USED IN MEASURING REACTION TIME AND IN CAREFULNESS TEST

priate movements within that given interval of time. If he makes incorrect movements or reacts too slowly this response is not registered. On the other hand, if he is not careful and in his excitement strikes the accelerator, his mistake is registered automatically on an electric counter. The number of correct responses gives an index of his alertness and speed of reaction; the number of errors, a measure of his carelessness. Throughout the test the subject's responses and reactions are automatically recorded on electric counters which total each type of response separately. All that

the results with established criteria. The standards used were the records the men had established for themselves as shown by the files of the company. The facts taken into consideration were such items as the number of merits received over the given period, the number of accidents during the same period, average daily revenue, revenue per cab-mile, etc. In the analysis of our results we made use only of the scores of the "old" men or such samples of them for which we had sufficiently complete records, in order to make valid comparisons.

The following principal results revealed by the analysis of our data are arranged in such a manner as to show how and to what extent the tests are effective in accomplishing their purpose.

1. Test results and accident records

The *De* test is most effective in picking out the men having the fewest number of accidents from those having the greatest number of accidents. It forms part of the individual examination in which the subject is required to react as quickly as possible to stimuli without making mistakes. The careful men are those who make few or no errors, the careless men are those who make a considerable number of errors, the degree being measured by the number of wrong reactions. Setting the failing score at 5 errors we calculated the average number of accidents per man of those failing as against those passing and found the following results:

Test De

Accidents per man for those *passing*
on test...........................1.3
Accidents per man for those *failing*
on test...........................3.0

These figures show that those who failed on the test averaged more than two accidents to every one that was reported against those making the passing score.

The relation between frequency of accidents and scores on the test is further brought out by figure 3. Here men have been classified into three groups: those making 0 errors, those making 1 to 3 errors and those making 4 or more errors, and the percentage of men having no accidents re-

corded against them over the period considered.

Similar results are revealed by comparing the men's scores with their superintendents' ratings. Several superintendents were asked to rate their men on carefulness and safety in driving, by giving the rating 1 to those whom they considered to be the safest and most careful drivers, 2 to those who were not so careful but were still considered reliable, 3 to those of barely average safety or inclined toward

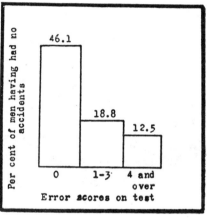

Fig. 3. Frequency of Accidents in Relation to Scores on Test *De* (35 Cases Considered)

recklessness. The relation between the superintendents' ratings of the men and their performance on the test is shown by figure 4. This figure shows also that there is a good correlation between the superintendents' ratings of the drivers as to safety in driving and their performance on the test. The men who were rated high generally made the best scores, while those who were rated low made, on the whole, the poorest scores.

The figures on the relation between

speed in reaction to distracting stimuli and frequency of accidents are interesting because they show some unexpected results. Our expectation was that the men with the greatest number of accidents would have the slowest reaction times. In this the results of the test bear us out. But in addition they also reveal the interesting fact that those who had the fastest

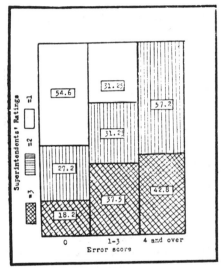

FIG. 4. RELATION BETWEEN SUPERINTENDENTS' RATINGS AND DISTRIBUTION OF SCORES, TEST *De* (35 CASES CONSIDERED)

reaction times also had a great number of accidents, as shown in figure 5. This result, however, is not to be interpreted to mean that a very quick reaction is a handicap to driving, but that men who are very quick are liable to take chances because of over-confidence, and thus risk accidents.

2. How tests indicate degrees of efficiency

One of the most important measures of a chauffeur's efficiency, so far as the

company is concerned, is his earning capacity. How much revenue does a man bring in? The company was therefore, particularly interested to know how the men's performances on the tests compared or correlated with their earning records. We first compared the men's records as to average daily revenue with their scores on the general intelligence or group test, *It*. In general we found that men having higher scores on this test also tended to have greater daily revenue, but this

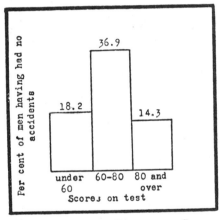

FIG. 5. ACCIDENTS IN RELATION TO SCORES ON TEST *D* (35 CASES CONSIDERED)

was true only up to a certain point. When we came to the men making the highest scores, their revenues, instead of continuing to rise, began to fall off. The poorest earners were relatively most frequent among those making the highest scores, as well as among those making the lowest scores. This can be seen from the following table where we have calculated the percentage of men for each group turning in less than a certain amount of daily revenue. The amount taken is $12.00 which is approximately one dollar below the average daily revenue of the group examined as a whole. The groups labelled "under 35" and "70 and over" represent, respectively, the men making approximately the lowest and highest 10 per cent of the scores on the intelligence test.

Relation between low average daily revenue and scores on Test It

SCORES ON TEST	UNDER 35	35 TO 60	70 AND OVER
	per cent	*per cent*	*per cent*
Per cent of men averaging less than $12.00 per day.....	50	35	45

These figures show that there is such a thing as being too bright as well as too dull for the job of chauffeur. This is not because intelligence is a handicap to driving a taxi but because a man of superior intelligence who takes to cabbing as a profession is likely to have some special limitations.

More important than a man's daily revenue average, as a measure of efficiency, is what the company terms "average revenue per cab-mile." This item not only takes into consideration the average revenue a man has been able to earn, but also the mileage he has had to drive or cruise in order to make that amount, and indirectly, his gas consumption as well as wear and tear on the car. The average daily revenue of the average driver among the men examined is approximately 20.5 cents per cab-mile. Eighteen cents per cab-mile thus represents a significantly low figure and a correspondingly inefficient driver. Figure 6 shows the percentage of such inefficient drivers among the tested men, in relation to their test scores.

For easy comparison the men have been divided into three equal groups, each representing one-third of the total (135). The lowest third is included by the scores labeled "under 50," the middle third by the scores "50–60," and the highest third by the scores "60 and over." Results show that there were more than two inefficient drivers among the men making the low scores, to every one among those making the high scores. (See fig. 6.)

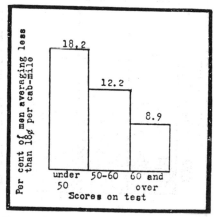

FIG. 6. AVERAGE EARNING PER CAB-MILE IN RELATION TO SCORES ON TEST *It* (135 CASES CONSIDERED)

3. How tests will reduce labor turnover

The third object of the tests, and one of the most important to the company, is the reduction of labor turnover. In order to demonstrate that the tests can effect this, a sufficient length of time must be allowed so as to enable us to compare the labor turnover of the company after the introduction of the tests with what it was before. This time has not yet elapsed, but on the basis of results obtained by other companies with similar intelligence tests we may confidently expect that labor turnover will be greatly reduced.

It is probable that the test will do this by weeding out at the start those too dull to make good on the job who would soon leave or be fired, and by singling out those too bright for the job who would probably leave either because of lack of incentive or because they take the position merely as a temporary stopgap.

SUMMARY AND CONCLUSIONS

Summarizing our work up to the point to which it has been carried, the analysis of the results obtained shows that the tests have proved themselves capable of accomplishing the things they proposed to do in a very satisfactory manner. They are capable of picking out to a considerable degree the safe from the unsafe and the efficient from the inefficient drivers, and promise to be effective in reducing labor turnover.

The most important results are those obtained with the carefulness tests. It is generally agreed by those who have investigated the problem of accidents in a first-hand way that the greatest single causative factor is carelessness. The carefulness test described seems to be capable of picking out very specifically the careless individual. As far as we know, this is the first time that such a test has been effectively employed.

In this paper we have made no reference to previous studies in the same field, as it was our purpose to limit our report to the presentation of the results obtained from our own investigation. Encouraging results from previous studies, however, have been reported, notably by Snow[2] at Chicago and Moss[3] at Washington. From the point of view of numbers the studies on the effectiveness of tests in the selection of automobile drivers have been fewer, so far, than those made on motormen.[4] This will probably not long continue to be the case for the ever increasing number of accidents and the congestion of the public highways by the automobile is beginning to receive much attention both here and abroad. In our own country the National Research Council has been investigating the problem for the past year. Reports of results of some of the sub-committees will probably be available in the near future.

[2] Snow, A. J.: Psychology in Business Relations. Chicago: A. W. Shaw Co., 1925. Chap. 30.

Snow, A. J.: Tests for Chauffeurs. Industrial Psychology, Vol. 1, No. 1, January, 1926, pp. 30–45.

[3] Moss, F. A.: Standardized Tests for Automobile Drivers. Public Personnel Studies, Vol. 3, No. 5, May, 1925, pp. 147–165.

[4] Viteles, M. S.: Selection of Motormen. Jour. of Personnel Research, Vol. 4, Nos. 4–5, 1925, pp. 100–115; 173–199.

Shellow, Sadie Myers: Selection of Motormen in Milwaukee. Jour. of Personnel Research, Vol. 4, No. 6, October, 1925, pp. 222–237.

(Manuscript received November 30, 1925.)

PART X

INTRODUCTION

There have been numerous awards made to David Wechsler over his lifetime. Perhaps the three included here are representative of the attitudes and awareness of many groups and persons of the contributions of the man to psychology.

In 1972 the American Association on Mental Deficiency presented to him a special award for distinguished contributions to the field of mental deficiency. The citation speaks well for his lifetime.

The acknowledgement in 1960 by the Clinical Division of the American Psychological Association of his distinguished contribution to clinical psychology may be generalized to all aspects of his career. One must agree that "David Wechsler as a person will be remembered as long as his works."

At the 81st annual convention of the American Psychological Association, held in Montreal in 1973, he received two further honors. The Division of School Psychology honored him with a Special Tribute, testimony of his contributions to a growing and important aspect of psychology. An even greater distinction was accorded by the APA with the announcement of his selection to receive the American Psychological Association Distinguished Professional Contribution Award.

To DAVID WECHSLER
for his
DISTINGUISHED CONTRIBUTION to CLINICAL PSYCHOLOGY
from the
CLINICAL DIVISION
of the
AMERICAN PSYCHOLOGICAL ASSOCIATION
1960

One of the senior, best known, and most widely respected of clinical psychologists, David Wechsler has had a major role in the establishment of the profession and the strengthening of the science. He was responsible for the development of one of the earliest training programs in the field, a program designed to meet the particular needs of a vastly populated, highly cosmopolitan urban center.

One of the early presidents of the Clinical Division and member of the board of ABEPP, he has had an important voice in the councils of psychology throughout its formative years.

His writings have been numerous and extensively read and quoted, his primary contributions in recent years being theoretical.

Most of all, of course, he is recognized for developing the Bellevue scales and testing procedures, and for supervising the Herculean task of standardization which created the most popular objective test in our field, unquestionably the primary instrument for the measurement of adult intelligence. Over the years it has been administered to millions of patients by clinicians around the world, in many languages, and in many countries on both sides of the Iron Curtain. In all probability only a minute percentage of the membership of our division have not repeatedly administered this test, and for many it was the first diagnostic procedure they learned to use.

Kindly, thoughtful, patient, and wise, David Wechsler as a person will be remembered as long as his works. In honoring him for what he has done, our profession honors itself as well.

AAMD
AMERICAN ASSOCIATION ON
MENTAL DEFICIENCY

Banquet
and Awards
Program

96th ANNUAL MEETING PRESIDENTIAL BANQUET

The Leamington Hotel • Minneapolis, Minnesota

May 19, 1972

Special Award

DAVID WECHSLER

Our guest of honor is truly a man of distinction in psychology. David Wechsler has been active as clinician, teacher, researcher, writer, theory builder and test-maker, and should anyone ask how he does so many things, one might give the answer attributed to Noel Coward in response to a similar question: "Superbly."

The name of Wechsler is virtually synonymous with the measurement of intelligence. Wechsler intelligence tests now exist for people from age 4 to past age 75. In dozens of foreign countries individuals may be tested with adaptations of one or more of Dr. Wechsler's impressive scales known to every psychologist in this country by their acronyms: WISC, WAIS, and WPPSI.

Along with Edgar Doll, David Wechsler was among the emergent group of post World War I practitioner-scientists who emphasized the view that mental deficiency was as much a social as a medical and psychological construct, and in practice should be assessed primarily from that point of view.

The titles, and even more than the titles, the careful reading of some of our Awardee's publications reveal the extraordinary depth of his thinking and the debt that those who are interested in the field of mental deficiency owe him. In 1935, Dr. Wechsler wrote on "The Concept of Mental Deficiency in Theory and Practice." In 1938, he published "Mental Deterioration; Its Measurement and Significance." With co-authors, Dr. Wechsler published "The Relative Effectiveness of the Stanford-Binet and Bellevue Intelligence Scale in Diagnosing Mental Deficiency" in 1939, and "A Study of the Subtests of the Bellevue Intelligence Scale in Borderline and Mental Defective Cases" in 1941. An impressive and important book, "The Range of Human Capacities," was first published in 1935 and revised in 1955.

There is, of course, the famous book "The Measurement of Adult Intelligence," first published in 1939. This went through three editions and became in its fourth edition in 1958, "The Measurement and Appraisal of Adult Intelligence."

Among the more abiding of Wechsler's contributions is the view that intelligence is not a single or signal ability, but a global capacity, a term first introduced by him (1939) and incorporated into his since oft-quoted definition. Equally important is his insistence that "intelligence, however defined, is an aspect of the total personality. I look upon intelligence," he wrote "as an effect rather than a cause, that is, as a resultant of inter-acting abilities, non-intellective included."

In the book "Individual Mental Testings (1971)," Allen J. Edwards states: "Perhaps the most distinguished name in intelligence testing today is that of David Wechsler," with these words:

> *The scales constructed by Wechsler have received wide acceptance and use, both clinically and educationally. Though other contributions by him have been relatively overlooked in the dedication to the testing devices, there is the possibility that the scales may be less significant than theoretical matters. . . . Wechsler's influence on the testing movement has barely begun, and may offer alternatives and directions much superior to any test yet available, including the scales authored by him.*

Dr. Wechsler retired as Chief Psychologist of Bellevue Psychiatric Hospital and Professor at the New York University College of Medicine in 1968. Since then he has been busy with travel, lectures, writing; and for the past two years, working on the revision of the WISC.

Dr. Wechsler, it honors AAMD to present you with this "Special Award" for distinguished contributions to the field of mental deficiency.

—HAROLD MICHAL-SMITH

Special Tribute

presented to

David Wechsler

In recognition of his pioneering contributions in the assessment of human capacities, the Division of School Psychology of the American Psychological Association pays special tribute to David Wechsler. His scales have opened new horizons for the clinician and the researcher. His influence has reached far beyond his own discipline and his own country.

His ideas on the nature of intelligence, the use of point scales and deviation quotients, and the influence of nonintellective factors upon psychometric indices continue to challenge and inspire psychologists of two generations.

As a professor of psychology, a department chairman, and a founder of the American Board of Professional Psychology, he set high standards for his profession. Scholar, teacher, scientist, his influence upon the practice of psychology is profound and lasting.

September 1973

PART XI

BIBLIOGRAPHY OF DAVID WECHSLER
FROM 1917 THROUGH 1974

1. A study of retention in Korsakoff Psychosis. *Psychiatric Bulletin*, 1917, **2**, 403–451.
2. Quelques remarques sur la psychopathologie de l'indécision. *Journal de Psychologie*, 1922, 47–54.
3. What constitutes an emotion. *Psychological Review*, 1925, **32**, 235–240.
4. The measurement of emotional reactions. *Archives of Psychology*, 1925, No. 76, 1–181. [Ph.D. thesis]
5. On the specificity of emotional reactions. *American Journal of Psychology*, 1925, **36**, 424–426.
6. An apparatus for measuring reaction time without a chronoscope. *Journal of Experimental Psychology*, 1926, **9**, 141–145.
7. Tests for taxicab drivers. *Journal of Personnel Research*, 1926, **5**, 24–30.
8. On the influence of education on intelligence as measured by the Binet–Simon tests. *Journal of Educational Psychology*, 1926, **17**, 248–257.
9. A study of emotional specificity [with H. E. Jones]. *American Journal of Psychology*, 1928, **40**, 600–606.
10. Galvanometric technique in studies of association [with H. E. Jones]. *American Journal of Psychology*, 1928, **40**, 607–612.
11. General intelligence, mental level, and the psychoneuroses. In I. S. Wechsler (Ed.), *The neuroses*. Philadelphia: W. B. Saunders, 1929. Pp. 289–306.
12. Studies in chronaxia [with R. G. Freeman, Jr.]. *Archives of Neurology and Psychiatry*, 1929, **22**, 558–567.
13. Galvanic responses of preschool children. *The Pedagogical Seminary and Journal of Genetic Psychology*, 1930, **38**, 203–222.
14. The range of human capacities. *The Scientific Monthly*, 1930, **31**, 35–39.
15. The incidence and significance of fingernail biting in children. *Psychoanalytic Review*, 1931, **18**, 201–209.
16. On the limits of human variability. *Psychological Review*, 1932, **39**, 87–90.
17. Analytic use of the Army Alpha Examination. *Journal of Applied Psychology*, 1932, **15**, 254–256.
18. Attitudes of children towards death [with P. Schilder]. *Journal of Genetic Psychology*, 1934, **45**, 406–451.
19. *The range of human capacities*. Baltimore: Williams & Wilkins, 1935.
20. The concept of mental deficiency in theory and practice. *Psychiatric Quarterly*, 1935, **9**, 232–236.
21. The illusion of the oblique intercept [with P. Schilder]. *Journal of Experimental Psychology*, 1936, **19**, 747–757.
22. Reversal errors in reading: phenomena of axial rotation [with M. I. Pignatelli]. *Journal of Educational Psychology*, 1937, 215–221.
23. *The measurement of adult intelligence*. Baltimore: Williams & Wilkins, 1939.
24. The relative effectiveness of the Stanford–Binet and the Bellevue intelligence scale in diagnosing mental deficiency. *American Journal of Orthopsychiatry*, 1939, **9**, 798–801.
25. Psychometric study of insulin-treated schizophrenics. *Psychiatric Quarterly*, 1940, **14**, 466–476.
26. *The measurement of adult intelligence*. (2nd ed.) Baltimore: Williams & Wilkins, 1941.
27. The effect of alcohol on mental activity. *Quarterly Journal of Studies on Alcohol*, 1941, **2**, 479–485.
28. A study of the sub-tests of the Bellevue Intelligence Scale in borderline and mental defective cases [with H. Israel and B. Balinsky]. *American Journal of Mental Deficiency*, 1941, **45**, 555–558.
29. Intellectual changes with age. In *Mental health in later maturity*. Public Health Reports, 1941, Supplement No. 168. Washington, D.C.: U. S. Department of Health, Education, and Welfare.

30. Non-intellective factors in general intelligence. *Journal of Abnormal and Social Psychology*, 1943, 38, 101–103.
31. The psychologist in the psychiatric hospital. *Journal of Consulting Psychology*, 1944, 8, 281–285.
32. The Cornell Selectee Index: A method for quick testing of the selectees for the armed forces. [with A. Weider, B. Mittleman, and H. Wolfe]. *Journal of the American Medical Association*, 1944, 124–224.
33. *The measurement of Adult intelligence*. (3rd ed.) Baltimore: Williams and Wilkins, 1944.
34. The clinical measurement of anxiety: An experimental approach [with R. Hartogs]. *Psychiatric Quarterly*, 1945, 19, 618–635.
35. A standardized memory for clinical use. *Journal of Psychology*, 1945, 19,87–95.
36. The Cornell Indices and Cornell Word form [with A. Weider]. *Annals of the New York Academy of Sciences*, 1946, 46, 579–587.
37. La relation entre les aptitudes et l'intelligence. *L'Annee Psychologique*, 1949, 51, 26–34.
38. *Wechsler Intelligence Scale for Children*. New York: The Psychological Corporation 1949
39. Cognitive, conative, and non-intellective intelligence. *Americal Psychologist*, 1950, 5, 78–83.
40. Equivalent test and mental ages for the WISC. *Journal of Consulting Psychology*, 1951, 15, 381–384
41. *The range of human capacities*. (2nd ed.) Baltimore: Williams & Wilkins, 1952.
42. *Wechsler Adult Intelligence Scale–Restandardized (WAIS)*. New York: The Psychological Corporation, 1955.
43. Your personality is in your hands: A review of "M. K. P.: Myokinetic Psychodiagnosis," by E. Mira y Lopez. *Contemporary Psychology*, 1959, 4, 362–364.
44. *The measurement and appraisal of adult intelligence*. (4th ed.) Baltimore: Williams & Wilkins, 1958.
45. Intelligence, quantum resonance, and thinking machines. *Transactions of the New York Academy of Science*, 1960, 22, 259–266.
46. Conformity and the idea of being well born. In I. A. Berg and B. M. Bass (Eds.), *Conformity and deviation*. New York: Harper, 1961. Pp. 412–423.
47. Intelligence, memory, and the aging process. In P. Hoch and J. Zubin (Eds.), *Psychopathology of aging*. New York: Grune and Stratton, 1961. Pp. 152–159.
48. Engrams, memory storage, and mnemonic coding. *American Psychologist*, 1963, 18, 149–153.
49. The problem of axial rotation [with R. Hagin]. *Perceptual and Motor Skills*, 1964, 19, 319–326.
50. Intelligence et fonction cérébrale. *Revue de Psychologie Appliquee*, 1958, 8, 143–147.
51. Schizophrenic patterns on the WISC [with E. Jaros]. *Journal of Clinical Psychology*, 1965, 21, 288–291.
52. The I.Q. is an intelligent test. *New York Sunday Times Magazine*, 26 June 1966, 12–13.
53. *Wechsler Preschool and Primary Scale of Intelligence*. New York: The Psychological Corporation, 1967.
54. Intelligence: Definition, theory, and the I.Q. In R. Cancro (Ed.), *Influence of heredity and environment*. New York: Grune and Stratton, 1971. Pp. 50–55.
55. The concept of collective intelligence. *American Psychologist*, 1971, 26, 904–907.
56. *Wechsler Intelligence Scale for Children–Revised*. New York: The Psychological Corporation, 1974.
57. Intelligence in a changing world. In D. Wechsler, *Selected papers of David Wechsler*. New York: Academic Press, 1974. Pp. 81–89.
58. Machine and human thinking. In D. Wechsler, *Selected papers of David Wechsler*. New York: Academic Press, 1974. Pp. 174–178.
59. *Selected papers of David Wechsler*. New York: Academic Press, 1974.